STUDENT ACCESSIBILITY SERVICES

OCLC#
631748583

M-F 8a.m.-4:30p.m.
262.524.7335 | sas@carrollu.edu

THE MEN
WHO KILLED
THE LUFTWAFFE

0 11557 00659 9

THE MEN WHO KILLED THE LUFTWAFFE

The U.S. Army Air Forces against Germany
in World War II

Jay A. Stout

STACKPOLE
BOOKS

For the mothers—all the mothers of every time and place—
who lost their baby boys in battle.

ISBN 978-0-8117-0659-9

CONTENTS

PREFACE

Spring 1934. Fourteen-year-old William Heller settled himself into the "cockpit" of his homemade glider and took one last look at the lath-and-wire contraption. It seemed sufficiently airworthy. Its wings, sheathed in linoleum tablecloths, looked large and sturdy enough to lift him airborne.

He squinted up at his friend "Squee" Miller who sat at the wheel of the pickup he had taken from his parents' nursery. A sturdy rope ran from the truck back to where Heller sat. He gave Squee the prearranged signal, and the pickup whined and bucked and lurched forward. The rope snapped tight and snatched Heller and his makeshift craft across the grass at a quickly accelerating rate.

Heller's heart beat fast as the glider scraped and bumped and careened along the ground. Finally, the nose pointed skyward for just a brief instant before one of the wings dipped, caught the ground, and cartwheeled the little plane into a disintegrating ball of wire and wood and linoleum sheeting.

It was not too long before Mr. Heller arrived with a pair of dikes and set about cutting the bloody boy out of his ill-considered dream. Finished, he stood his son up, looked him in the eyes, and declared: "Next time you fly, you better have an engine!"

Heller would eventually fly with four engines, and rather than bump along a Pennsylvania cow pasture, he would deliver bombs deep inside Hitler's Germany. Although none of them knew it that spring of 1934, tens of thousands of his peers from around the nation would be flying with him.

INTRODUCTION

No period in the history of air warfare is a more fertile field for writers and scholars than the fighting that raged over Europe during World War II. It was remarkable not only because of its its magnitude, but because the stakes were so high. The air war against Nazi Germany had to be won before Europe could be liberated. Beating the Germans in the air was a gargantuan effort made up of hundreds of major elements, any one of which deserves book-length treatment. In fact, hundreds of books *have* been written about the fight against the Luftwaffe, the German air force.

Capturing every component of that air war in a single work is impossible; there is simply too much material. Likewise, there are too many key personages. What I aim to highlight here are the experiences of individual airmen, mostly unknown, who were representative of the enormous numbers of young Americans who made up the U.S. Army Air Forces (USAAF) during the air war over Europe. Accordingly, in order to maintain a sharp focus on these airmen, I have purposely refrained from mentioning the literally hundreds of outstanding leaders without whom the fight might have been lost.

By the time of my childhood in the 1960s, most of these unheralded airmen had long before hung up their uniforms and made civilian lives for themselves. They piqued my schoolboy interest with an occasional story or offhand reference. I was struck that these men who seemed so unremarkable were the ones that had fought the war over Europe. But now, older and with a military flying career of my own fading into memory, I understand and appreciate these men in a way that I could not when I was a child. And I want to honor them. Accordingly, I have crafted a framework of strategy and doctrine, of tactics and equipment, of time and place, of well-known leaders to showcase how they beat the Luftwaffe—since it was mostly the USAAF that defeated the Luftwaffe.

But what about Great Britain's Royal Air Force, the RAF? How can I justify crediting the killing of the Luftwaffe to the United States? First, there is no doubt that Great Britain, America's dearest ally, played a major role in the defeat of the Luftwaffe. I will declare up front that I am a great admirer of the RAF's airmen, and I will further offer that had the men of Fighter Command not turned back the Luftwaffe in the skies over England during 1940, the Nazis might have taken the British Isles and subsequently won the war. But instead, Great Britain's airmen saved not only their nation, but also the base from which the United States later launched its crippling air campaigns. Those raids ensured the destruction of the Luftwaffe, guaranteeing that Hitler's armies never had a prayer of surviving the war, much less winning it.

Furthermore, the quality and professionalism of the RAF's aircrews was superb; throughout the entire war, Great Britain fielded perhaps the best trained airmen of all the belligerents. Moreover, its equipment was good, technically sound and of high quality. Its night-bombing campaigns burned German cities to ashes and forced the Luftwaffe to commit significant resources, especially night fighters, that could have been useful elsewhere. Its tactical operations, just like many of the USAAF's tactical operations described in this book, had a chronic, if not fatal, effect on the Luftwaffe.

On the other hand, the RAF's leadership did not have a plan for destroying the Luftwaffe. Terror bombing aside, the most the RAF could hope to achieve beyond its own shores—certainly before the United States arrived in strength—was to establish local air superiority above a given battlefield. But even that never happened with certitude when it was really important. The RAF only barely covered the evacuation of Dunkirk, was badly handled during the Dieppe raid, and was never able to push the Germans out of North Africa by itself.

Bomber Command did take the war to Germany, but it did not put together an effective or coherent campaign to target the industries that supported the Luftwaffe. Rather, following a dreadful savaging by the Luftwaffe during a brief and utterly ineffective attempt at daylight bombing, it turned to night raids. Those operations early in the war were simply too inaccurate to deliver the sorts of effects that were required. Consequently, the decision was taken to simply strike Germany's cities in order to terrorize, kill, and "dehouse" the population. Even after Great Britain pioneered night-bombing devices—radar among them—that enabled it to strike with more accuracy, it generally chose to continue flying area-bombing raids rather than hitting specific war-related targets.

Accordingly, after the Battle of Britain, the RAF and the Luftwaffe never really engaged in anything more than a tit-for-tat series of engagements that did neither of them great harm. The RAF's day fighters and light bombers poked around the edges of the continent and fought small World War I–type duels against a few Luftwaffe fighter squadrons while Bomber Command droned into Germany under the cover of darkness and dropped bombs on cities. The air war could have gone on forever.

The Soviet Union's Red Air Force was even less effective. After the Luftwaffe nearly destroyed it in the first few months, the Soviets rebuilt it into a massive tactical air force that it used with little cleverness or skill. That being said, the Eastern Front was immense and did tie down a substantial portion of the Luftwaffe. Still, air operations between the Germans and the Soviets were tactical in nature as the Red Air Force possessed no strategic equipment.

On the other hand, the USAAF showed up to the fight intent on killing the Luftwaffe, which had to be accomplished before Europe could be retaken. The Americans had the strategy, will, equipment, and, most importantly, the people to do the job. It took them fewer than three years. On July 2, 1942, the Eighth Air Force had three combat aircraft in England. When Germany surrendered on May 8, 1945, the USAAF was operating more than 17,000 aircraft in Europe and the Mediterranean. That figure alone is impressive, but more extraordinary is the fact that the men, materiel, and infrastructure to operate those aircraft were mobilized and sent across the Atlantic in such a remarkably short period. Never before had such an air force been formed, trained, and fielded. It was made up of men who stepped into uniform when their nation called and just as quickly stepped out when the need passed. Virtually none of them were military professionals.

I have had the honor of talking with a few of them, the unsung eagles who made up the vast majority of the USAAF. Their efforts constituted the implementation of the grand plans created by the Allied leadership. President Franklin Roosevelt, together with Prime Minister Winston Churchill and Generals Hap Arnold and Carl Spaatz and Ira Eaker and their RAF counterparts, drafted plans to destroy the Luftwaffe. But they did not execute those plans themselves. Rather, they were carried out by hundreds of thousands of young men who flew, crewed, and serviced the planes.

These accounts are not extraordinary because the men were special, but instead, they are remarkable precisely because the men were *not* special. They were everyday people like you and me; this point was driven home every time I spoke with them. They made up a group of Americans that I might find anywhere regardless of age or origin. The vast majority of these men were considerate, intelligent, and helpful, but I also encountered—just as I might anywhere—a couple of horse's asses and one or two liars.

What was extraordinary was that the nation, the United States, was made up of people who not only had the resources and energy to create a military unlike any ever seen, but it was also a nation that offered young men who were willing to travel across the world to meet and defeat tyranny, just as their fathers had before them and just as their sons and grandsons would do after them. This character, this willingness to commit to a great cause knowing full well its fearful cost, is what has always been extraordinary.

CHAPTER 1

Building an Air Force

I t started with the president.

When President Franklin Delano Roosevelt chaired the meeting of November 14, 1938, the United States was the greatest industrial nation on earth, yet possessed a military air arm that was little more than a hobby set. Certainly, America had made great contributions to aviation, not least of which was the invention of powered flight. Americans had performed remarkable feats, including Charles Lindbergh's crossing of the Atlantic, and men like Billy Mitchell and Jimmy Doolittle had done much to advance the doctrine and technology of military air operations. But its own air arm, the U.S. Army Air Corps, badly lagged those of other great nations.

Perhaps "lagged" is too kind a word. Compared to those being fielded by Germany, virtually all of the 1,600 aircraft operated by the Air Corps were a laughingstock. Even Gen. Henry "Hap" Arnold, the chief of the Air Corps at the time, recalled the service's dismal state: "Well, to be realistic, we were practically nonexistent."[1] On the other hand, Germany's air force, the Luftwaffe, numbered almost 3,000 increasingly modern types and was undergoing a considerable expansion. In fact, only a couple of months earlier, Lindbergh had warned that Hitler's air force was "the strongest in the world in both quality and quantity, more powerful than the combined air forces of Britain, France

1

and the United States."[2] In fact, the Luftwaffe was not quite so large, but it was big, modern, and growing.

The U.S. Army Air Corps was not in such an abysmal state because its leaders wanted it that way or because they were incompetent or ignorant. Rather, the United States was still in the bowels of the Great Depression, and its citizens did not want to pay for a world-class air force. It was not that the country could not afford one; Germany, Great Britain, and Japan had certainly built up substantial air arms while enduring the same decade of debilitating economic hardships. Instead, protected on both sides by vast oceans, most Americans did not see a large, expensive air force as an immediate imperative for their well-being. They felt no threat, and a substantial portion of the population—perhaps a majority—subscribed to the tenets of isolationism.

On the other hand, the leadership of the Air Corps, oftentimes at odds with the greater institutional Army, had long championed carefully studied concepts for the development and fielding of a grand strategic air force capable of precisely targeting and destroying an enemy's military and industrial infrastructure. Indeed, Arnold had already published themes that advocated just such an air force. And he was hardly alone. The American air force that ultimately emasculated the Luftwaffe, then bludgeoned it to death, was built on concepts that were conceived and evolved by a number of airmen during the 1920s and 1930s.

It must also be acknowledged that there had been interservice issues at play since at least 1921. During that year, the dynamic and mercurial Billy Mitchell stirred up public interest in the potential of airpower. He used that enthusiasm to whipsaw Army and Navy leaders into allowing him to stage a demonstration during which he used aircraft to sink a handful of captured World War I German warships. Since that time, there had been a barely concealed animosity between the two services where airpower was concerned. The Navy, jealous of its traditional mandate to protect the nation from foreign invaders, forced an agreement whereby the Air Corps could operate out to a range of only 100 miles from the coast. So constrained, the Air Corps had difficulty justifying the requirements for a long-range strategic air force.

All these factors together—economic destitution, public indifference, and interservice discord—produced an ugly, ineffectual, and small air force that offered scant promise of being able to influence events abroad.

This was of considerable concern to Roosevelt on November 14, 1938. German nationalism was, for the second time in as many generations, pushing Europe toward another war. Just two years earlier, in March 1936, Nazi Germany broke terms established at Versailles and reoccupied the demilitarized zone in the Rhineland. Austria was annexed two years later in March 1938. And less than two months before Roosevelt called the meeting, on September 30, 1938, France and Britain had capitulated at Munich, sanctioning Hitler's annexation of the Czech Sudetenland. Following that shamefulness, Roosevelt can perhaps be forgiven for not believing Britain's prime minister, Neville Chamberlain, when he declared that "peace in our time" had been secured.

Through it all, Hitler's persecution of his nation's Jews became more overt. That fact was underscored with terrible clarity just shortly before Roosevelt called the meeting. On the night of November 9–10, state-sponsored mobs killed nearly a hundred German Jews and burned thousands of businesses and synagogues in what came to be known as *Kristallnacht*, the "Night of Broken Glass."

When Roosevelt called his top advisors to him in mid-November, there was a real fear that Europe was tilting toward another catastrophic conflict. He certainly did not know at the time that the United States would be sucked into the fight, but he did know that its air force, the U.S. Army Air Corps, was ill-prepared for such an eventuality. He further knew that even before Hitler's *blitzkrieg* showcased the terrible potential of the warplane, the United States could never hope to prevail in a war with its pitifully inadequate Air Corps.

Roosevelt meant to correct that inadequacy as soon as possible. In fact, during the weeks immediately following Munich, Roosevelt energized his staff to create an expanded air force. This included a meeting on October 14 and a press conference that justified growing the Air Corps based on changing world dynamics.

The meeting on November 14 included Hap Arnold; as chief of the Air Corps, his presence was a prerequisite. But he was *only* the chief of the Air Corps. What Roosevelt wanted done would take far more horsepower, far more expertise, far more experience than Arnold alone possessed. Harry Hopkins, who headed the Works Progress Administration and was one of the president's staunchest and most stalwart lieutenants, also attended, as did Secretary of the Treasury Henry Morgenthau. Also present, among others of Roosevelt's most powerful men, were Louis Johnson, the assistant secretary of war; Malin Craig, chief of staff of the Army; and Craig's eventual successor, George Marshall.

What the president wanted was an unprecedented expansion of the U.S. Army Air Corps. Although he envisioned and desired a much larger organization, he was realistic about what Congress would fund. Still, what he actually proposed was much grander than what any air advocate at that time believed realistic. Specifically, Roosevelt called for 10,000 new aircraft to be built and delivered within two years. He directed that 8,000 of those machines be produced in existing factories and that seven new government aircraft plants be built. Five of those factories were to be mothballed for future use while the other two were to be put to work immediately to produce the remaining 2,000 aircraft. (Recall that the Air Corps possessed only 1,600 aircraft at that time.)

The president's men left the gate at full tilt. Roosevelt's direction was bold, but it was not detailed and appeared to be almost naïve. The air force that he outlined would be useless without the infrastructure and personnel to support and man it, yet he had said little on the subject. Consequently, Arnold and his staff went for broke. They took it upon themselves not only to do the planning required to produce the aircraft the president called for, but also to lay the groundwork needed to assemble all the pieces—personnel, airfields, training facilities, logistics pipelines, and other elements—to make the expanded Air Corps a viable force.

Roosevelt was irate when the scheme for producing the 10,000 aircraft, together with all the components required to operate them, was presented. It was too expensive and included provisions for much more than the aircraft he had asked for. It was then that the planners realized that the president was not necessarily interested in a massively increased air arm, but rather was gambling that a well-publicized warplane-building effort would cause German expansionists to curb their aggression. He wanted to cow them with numbers rather than build a large air force that would not only be costly to build and staff, but would also require substantial budget outlays for maintenance and operations in the future. In fact, it became apparent that Roosevelt intended to mothball a good number of the aircraft he had requested and sell a considerable portion to Great Britain and France.

To Roosevelt's way of thinking, it was better to have the British and French forestall the Germans with American equipment than it was to have the United States fight another European war. That notion was no doubt reinforced by British and French interest in American aircraft. Foreign money for large orders of aircraft would help finance the construction of American aircraft plants while at the same time producing economies of scale that the U.S. government could later leverage in its favor.

Arnold and many of Roosevelt's staffers did not agree with his line of thought. In the event that the United States was drawn into the war, the U.S. Army Air Corps would need every aircraft the nation could produce. In fact, they argued that the United States needed not just a strong air force, but a rejuvenated, dramatically enlarged, and modernized military across the board. This, the president's advisers insisted, was a prerequisite if the United States was to prevail in any military conflict.

Roosevelt did not necessarily disagree with any of the arguments that were presented to him, but he had political factors to consider. Aside from isolationist sentiment, there was the matter of money: there simply was not any. Still, there was a line of thought suggesting that government expenditures on manufacturing would create jobs and spread money across the economy, which would help pull the nation out of the stubborn Depression that still plagued it after nearly a decade. In effect, Roosevelt could kill two birds with one stone by sponsoring massive defense bills, creating the military he needed for the coming war while simultaneously lifting the economy.

Ultimately, Roosevelt's energy and charisma, together with the rapidly deteriorating global situation, permitted him to push through a series of defense appropriations that gave American industry a running start before World War II erupted. Although the $500 million request the president submitted to Congress for material, aircraft acquisitions, and supporting infrastructure in January 1939 did not come anywhere close to meeting the needs of the envisioned air force, it made a good down payment when it was approved a few months later in April. It was enough to pay for 3,000 new aircraft and enough infrastructure so that when world events compelled Congress to open the money spigot a short time later, there were already factories where the money could be spent.

This effort—getting the American defense industry on its feet—was no mean challenge. Rather, it took enormous energy and imagination. First, there was not much of an aviation industry to rally. There were scores of small firms, many of which were little more than garage shops, but only about a dozen larger-scale concerns. Nearly all of them were on slippery financial footing, and as a whole, they had traditionally measured their combined deliveries to the Air Corps in hundreds of aircraft per year. What Roosevelt ultimately wanted would require deliveries of *thousands* of aircraft per *month*.

Up to that time, aircraft were not mass-produced in the same way as automobiles. They were manufactured in small batches by experienced craftsmen rather than assembly-line workers. Those craftsmen counted themselves among the fortunate since many of their peers, representing an enormous pool of talent, had been scattered by lack of work. Getting the right people back on the payrolls and getting them trained in the latest manufacturing techniques would take time and money. So, too, would expanding the production lines.

Moreover, aircraft manufacturers existed to make money in what was a very uncertain business. For instance, Lockheed spent $761,000 to win the 1937 contract that ultimately produced the famous P-38 Lightning. However, the government award for the first prototype was only $163,000. Ultimately, of course, the company recouped its investment and much, much more, but this example illustrates the business risks involved. So when representatives from the government and military traveled the nation to urge companies to spend money on equipment, plants, and workers, they were met with skepticism. Talk of expansion was fine, but without contracts in hand, the manufacturers were loathe to commit their own resources.

Further, the months-long lead time between the placement of aircraft orders and the actual deliveries created uncertainty. A great deal could change in a short time. The ambiguity was seriously magnified in the context of overseas transactions. Certainly, large orders from foreign governments might come, but what if those governments reversed their policies or were changed or overthrown? Would the contracts still stand? What if the rising tensions were negotiated away and there was no need for thousands of warplanes? And what about the nation's Neutrality Act? Ironically, this act demanded an embargo against the sale of weapons to nations at war—that is, if the foreign customers went to war, the manufacturers would not be allowed to deliver the aircraft that had been ordered.

Nevertheless, the aircraft manufacturers were willing to listen; the government was the primary customer for many of them and had the deepest pockets. For its part, the government worked to salve many of their concerns. One welcome change was an assurance that they would not be forced into expensive competition with each other, but instead would be rewarded with profit margins of approximately 10 percent as long as they met their contractual obligations.[3] In fact, two orders totaling more than 1,100 B-26s were made right off the design table even before the first example had flown.

Ultimately, when the war started in Europe, the Neutrality Act was repealed and the manufacturers were allowed to continue to sell their aircraft. Moreover, when foreign governments fell, the United States took delivery of the aircraft they had ordered or brokered other deals that protected the manufacturers.

All the activity that Roosevelt put into motion was undertaken to support the U.S. Army Air Corps, which Maj. Gen. Henry Harley Arnold headed. Arnold had been born to an old American family in Gladwyne, Pennsylvania, in 1886, the son of a physician father and a dutiful and attentive mother. One of five children, his family called him by his middle name, Harley. Mostly at his father's insistence, he sought admission to West Point but was successful only in being designated as an alternate. When the primary appointee opted for marriage rather than the rigors of West Point, Arnold got the nod and joined the class of 1907 in July 1903, a month after the start of classes. Known by his classmates as "Pewt" or "Benny," Arnold was evidently likeable and sociable but spent the next four years doing little to distinguish himself, graduating sixtieth in a class of 111.

Arnold, like many of the cadets at that time, was eager for the prestige, romance, and excitement of a cavalry assignment, but instead found himself posted to the infantry. He exploded in indignation and disbelief and threatened to decline his commission. Nevertheless, common sense prevailed, and he accepted both his commission and orders to the Philippines, where he arrived at the end of 1907. Army life at that time and place offered little excitement, and Arnold attached himself to a signal corps detachment that was charting Luzon and Corregidor. He remembered in later years that Japanese "botanists" dogged their trail as they similarly mapped the islands.

In 1909, he was assigned to Governor's Island in New York City. There he witnessed early aviation activities, including a flight by the Wright brothers. Arnold was uninterested in an infantry career, and after passing an examination for aviation training as part of the Signal Corps, he was sent with one other lieutenant, Thomas Milling, to flight training at Dayton, Ohio, under the tutelage of the Wrights. Arnold started flying almost immediately, taking his first lesson on May 3, 1911, and completing his training ten days later. His instruction during that brief period included twenty-eight sorties averaging just minutes each, for a total of less than four hours. He was designated as the army's second aviator.

Right away, Arnold set to work advancing the discipline of aviation. In fact, goggles came about after Arnold took a bug in the eye and was barely able to recover his aircraft. Perhaps more important was the series of altitude records he established in the flimsy aircraft characteristic of that period. The highest of those marks was 6,450 feet. This figure, more than a mile above the ground, was astounding to the layperson of the day. In 1912, in recognition of a successful roundtrip reconnaissance flight of forty-one minutes, the Aero Club of America made Arnold the inaugural recipient of the now-famous Mackay Trophy.

During this time, Arnold was given the nickname that followed him through the rest of his life. He and other flyers were allowed to work part time with the movie industry to highlight and publicize the service's work in aviation. The film crews noted Arnold's gracious and cheerful attitude and began calling him "Happy," a sobriquet which his peers picked up and eventually shortened to "Hap."

Nevertheless, early aviation was a dangerous and terrifying business. Accidents and deaths were commonplace, and although figures vary, more than half of the army's aviators were killed between 1909 and 1913. Arnold also had a least one close brush with death. One of them in 1912—the same year he won the Mackay Trophy—affected him so negatively that he declined to fly further and had himself removed from flying duty. Arnold was far from the only U.S. Army flyer to do so; in 1913, the service had fifteen aircraft and only six active pilots.

There followed a period of staff work in Washington, D.C., his marriage to longtime love interest Eleanor "Bee" Pool, and a return to the infantry, including another tour in the Philippines, where Arnold's superiors lauded his talent and energy. On his return to the States in 1916, he was offered the opportunity to return to flying by Maj. William L. Mitchell, with an immediate promotion to the rank of captain. Arnold took the assignment and overcame his fear of flying later that year. America's entry into World War I found him assigned to stateside staff work despite his desire to get into the fight. While en route to France during the last few weeks of the war, he was laid low by the same influenza that killed millions across the globe. The war ended while he was still recovering.

As early as 1913 and throughout the rest of his life, Arnold's early association and experience with aviation, his native intelligence, and his connections and notoriety all combined to make him a credible witness in various congressional and military hearings. Perhaps the most important of the appearances in the early part of his career was his testimony on behalf of the iconic Brig. Gen. William "Billy" Mitchell during the latter's court-martial in 1925. Mitchell's continuous attacks on Army and Navy leadership for what he considered criminal ineptitude in the development of the nation's airpower came to a head during that year. Although Arnold was warned against supporting Mitchell, he not only did so, but also shared information—against orders—with the press that enhanced Mitchell's standing. Consequently, when Mitchell was convicted of insubordination, Arnold endured a period of unofficial exile intended to kill his career.

Still, this was hardly Arnold's first clash with his superiors. It was not unusual for him to rub his commanding officers and others the wrong way. One of his seniors described him as a "troublemaker" and declared that he was unsuited for "independent command."[4] On the other hand, others commented positively on his staff work and his ability to get things done. Taken together, Arnold's characteristics made him an asset or an irritant, depending on the perspectives of those his work affected.

Despite the fact that he created enemies in the Army's leadership, Arnold continued to perform well and was soon back with army aviation. A series of assignments during the 1920s, including schools and operational commands, gave him opportunities to gain experience in planning, procurement, logistics, safety, training, public relations, and, perhaps most important of all, Washington politics. All of this would prove to be invaluable later in his career and would greatly inform the decisions he would make when the nation most depended on him.

Arnold was a colonel by 1934. During that year, he won his second Mackay Trophy for leading a flight of the Army's new B-10 bombers from Washington, D.C., to Fairbanks, Alaska, and back. The return leg included a 1,000-mile segment from Juneau to Seattle. Its overwater nature, especially the length, irked the Navy although there was little that the Army's sister service could do about it. Despite the fact that he tried to pass the accolades for the accomplishment to his staff and crews, Arnold received the lion's share of the credit, which subsequently created jealousy and contempt among his peers.

It did not matter. The following year, the U.S. Army's chief of staff, Malin Craig, called Arnold to Washington as assistant chief of staff of the Air Corps under Oscar Wendover. When Wendover was killed in a crash in September 1938, Arnold was promoted to major general and made chief of the Air Corps on September 22.

As 1938 became 1939 and Roosevelt's advisors went to work to lobby for a great air force, the responsibility for putting it all together belonged to one person, Maj. Gen. Henry H. Arnold. After all, neither the president nor his cabinet knew anything about the care and feeding of such an organization, but they were hardly ready to let Arnold have free rein. On the contrary, getting the U.S. Army Air Corps organized in the manner Arnold wanted proved almost immediately to be a maddening and terrible challenge, one that almost cost him his career.

While the government got organized, the aircraft manufacturers worked as quickly as they could to get their designs ready for the impending war. The twin-engine, twin-boomed Lockheed XP-38 had been a secret project until shortly before Arnold unveiled it to the press at

March Field, California, on February 11, 1939. It had made its first flight only the previous month, on January 27. In a press release, Arnold declared that the aircraft "opens up new horizons of performance probably unattainable by nations banking solely on the single engine arrangement." He was wrong, but it was not readily apparent; the aircraft was radical beyond anything ever seen to that point.

The following day, the Army sent the XP-38 out to break the transcontinental record set by Howard Hughes in his H-1 racer two years earlier in January 1937. At that point, the XP-38 had less than eight hours of total flight time, and the record-breaking attempt, so early in the aircraft's development, was a careless publicity stunt. Lt. Ben Kelsey, an Army pilot, was at the controls of the polished silver ship when it roared out of March Field and across the southwest before setting down in Amarillo, Texas, for a quick refueling. Just more than twenty minutes later, Kelsey was airborne again en route to Dayton, Ohio. After another short stop, he took off on the final leg, bound for Mitchel Field on Long Island.

The next week, *Time* magazine recorded what happened as Kelsey brought the ship down toward its final destination:

> Swinging swiftly in a wide arc he squared away for a landing, let down his landing gear. Then came some more of the sort of bad luck that has dogged new Army ships of late. As Pilot Kelsey suddenly realized that he was falling short, he opened his throttles to drag into the field. Without so much as a cough his left engine died. Plowing her wheels through a tree, the XP-38, with right engine throttled, slammed into the sand bunker of a golf course, came to a stop with her right wing torn off, her props hopelessly snaggled, her fuselage twisted. A passing motorist helped dazed Ben Kelsey from the wreck. He had been only slightly cut.[5]

An investigation showed that the engine had quit because of carburetor icing. The Army did not care. It was so enamored with the performance of the new fighter—including its top speed of more than 400 miles per hour—that it placed an order for thirteen preproduction YP-38s. Vastly larger orders would follow for much-improved models.

In fact, within a year, the U.S. Army Air Corps was ordering as many aircraft of as many types as it reasonably could. The German invasion of Poland in September 1939 was finally enough to goad France and Great Britain into declaring war on Germany, and it began to appear more and more likely to some observers that the United States would enter the fight. Still, by the end of 1940, its air force was far from ready despite near-heroic efforts by all the principal players.

Even at that time, the complexity of new aircraft was such that several years were required to field a new design. In fact, every major type the Air Corps would use during the war was already designed, if not far along in development. Among the fighters, the P-40 was already in service, and the Air Corps had accepted its first P-39s. These two types would prove themselves to be adequate during the early years of the war but were eclipsed by better designs later on. Of those later types, the P-38 was being extensively tested by the Air Corps; the P-47, already informed by the earlier P-43, was in an advanced state of development; and even the P-51, arguably the best fighter of the war, had made its first flight.

Where bomber and attack aircraft were concerned, the same situation existed. The B-17, destined for greatness, had languished for several years because of political dithering but was finally in continuous production in 1939. A longer-range heavy bomber, the B-24, had already flown, as had the three main medium and light-attack bombers, the B-25, B-26, and A-20. Even the initial design for the B-29, the aircraft that would burn Japan to ashes before blasting it into surrender with two atomic bombs, had been submitted in 1939.

So with relevant aircraft available and production ramping up to support both foreign and domestic orders, the expansion of the U.S. Army Air Corps was well underway by the end of 1940. Nevertheless, technical and production issues aside, policy issues dogged Arnold and his plans. One of his chief challenges was the fact that even though France had fallen, too much of his equipment—in his mind, at least— was being sent overseas, primarily to Great Britain.

This was a problem that had frustrated Arnold since the end of 1939 when Roosevelt put Harry Morgenthau, the secretary of the treasury, in charge of aircraft procurement and allocation. Arnold's very firm ideas on how to build the Air Corps did not necessarily coincide with Roosevelt's notions. Increasingly, Roosevelt and some members of his cabinet came to view Arnold as an annoyance, and there was even discussion that Arnold might be removed from his post.

This was extremely vexing for the chief of the Army Air Corps. Arnold noted that Morgenthau was not responsible for building the nation's air force, yet he had the power to "give away" every aircraft produced. And still, it was Arnold, not Morgenthau, who was accountable for expanding the Air Corps. It was a dark time for Arnold during which his presence at the White House was taboo and when he was not always involved in high-level decision making that affected the Air Corps.

Although Arnold was incensed that Morgenthau was selling approximately half of the nation's aircraft production to Great Britain, he still knew that the Air Corps was realizing some benefits. For instance, as Great Britain's Royal Air Force (RAF) gained experience in combat operations—often at the cost of lives—it paid for improvements to the American designs it purchased. Some examples included self-sealing fuel tanks, armor plating, bulletproof glass, and structural changes. These improvements were subsequently available to the Air Corps at little or no cost. Furthermore, as more aircraft were produced, they became less expensive to buy. Additionally, the earliest models of any given aircraft design were typically prone to teething problems. Since these aircraft were often delivered to foreign purchasers, the manufacturers had time to mitigate design and production issues before delivering later, more refined models to American units.

At any rate, some of the sting must have dissipated when Roosevelt asked Congress in May 1940 to fund the nation's aircraft industry to a capacity of 50,000 aircraft per year, nearly 75 percent of which were intended for the U.S. Army Air Corps.[6] At that point, Arnold could not even use that many aircraft; he did not have enough pilots to man them. This was the case despite the fact that the pilot production goal had been raised to 7,000 per year.[7] In reality, as frustrated as Arnold was, a great deal of energy was being spent to build his air force.

All the same, it took time to convert intent and funding into real aircraft flown by trained pilots, maintained by competent mechanics, and supplied by capable logisticians at modern airbases. Even as late as May 1941, the state of the Air Corps was such that Arnold declared that its ability to strike was at "zero strength."[8] Still, he did not waste time while he waited for equipment and personnel to flesh out his units. He knew that, equipment aside, knowledge and experience would increase the effectiveness of the Air Corps many times over. He also knew that knowledge and experience gained secondhand from a dedicated ally was a much better bargain than knowledge and experience bought first-hand with blood and ignorantly used equipment. Consequently, he arranged for liaison missions to be sent overseas to Great Britain.

One of the experts Arnold sent overseas was Carl "Tooey" Spaatz. Spaatz (pronounced "spots") was born in Boyertown, Pennsylvania, in 1891, the son of a printer. Spaatz attended West Point seven years later than Arnold. Like Arnold, Spaatz was an utterly unremarkable student bored by military routine, and he regularly collected demerits for a variety of infractions. In fact, he narrowly missed being expelled for having liquor in his room. It was at West Point that he picked up his nickname thanks to his marked resemblance to another cadet, Francis Toohey, an upperclassman.

Unlike Arnold, Spaatz had his eye on an aviation career before he ever left West Point. After completing the year of service as an infantry officer that the army required, Spaatz reported to San Diego for flight training in November 1915 and was subsequently assigned in May 1916 to the 1st Aero Squadron for service with Gen. John Pershing's expedition in Mexico. Spaatz was still with the squadron when the United States entered World War I in April 1917.

At that time, there were fewer than seventy aviators in the army, and incredibly, only three years after leaving West Point, Spaatz was promoted to major and sent to Fort Sam Houston in San Antonio, Texas. After a quick marriage to Ruth Harrison, the daughter of another officer, Spaatz was on his way to France. Arriving in September 1917, he completed a series of short assignments before being made the commander of the Aviation Instruction Center at Issoudon.

Issoudon was an under-construction mess of mud, apathy, and frustrated student mechanics and pilots when Spaatz arrived. He went to work immediately. When he left Issoudon the following September, it was the world's largest pilot training center with finished facilities, more than a dozen practice airfields, and an outstanding record for producing pilots and support personnel. The experience Spaatz gained in leadership, organization, and contracting—not to mention flying—would serve him well throughout his entire career.

Brig. Gen. William Mitchell was keen to send Spaatz back to the States so that he could work the same sort of magic with the struggling training establishment there. Spaatz was not ready to go. He had spent his entire time in France getting young pilots ready for combat, yet he had not done any fighting himself. He prevailed on Mitchell to give him two weeks with a flying unit on the front.

Spaatz attached himself to the 13th Aero Squadron, which was operating in the Toul sector, and on September 15, 1918, flying a French-made SPAD XIII biplane, he shot down his first German aircraft.[9] He took it upon himself to extend his own orders, and on September 26, in a single engagement, he won the Distinguished Service Cross when he downed two more German aircraft before running out of fuel and crash-landing on the French side of the lines.

Spaatz left France on excellent terms with Mitchell and arrived back in the States on October 13, 1918. His time at Issoudon, along with his short period in combat, made him the perfect choice for his next assignment: the inspector of pursuit training. No one in the U.S. Army Air Service was more qualified for the posting. While he was receiving his new orders in Washington, D.C., he had a brief encounter with Arnold before the latter left for Europe. It was the start of an association during which their careers would intersect over and over again.

Spaatz's postwar tours were similar to Arnold's. He labored through a continuous cycle of staff, school, and operational jobs of increasing responsibility and importance. Like Arnold, with whom he was serving at the time, he also testified at Mitchell's court-martial proceedings during 1925. He was loyal to Mitchell, and his testimony reflected his personality—blunt bordering on taciturn. This was characteristic of Spaatz, who was never considered overly articulate although his instinct and actions were, more often than not, right on the mark.

As an early aviator, Spaatz was part of the dramatic technological leaps that aviation underwent during the 1920s and 1930s. He led a team during January 1929 that used a Fokker tri-motor, nicknamed *Question Mark*, to set an aerial-refueled endurance record of just more than 150 hours. The four-man crew included Ira Eaker, a younger associate who would become a professional colleague of the closest order.

Spaatz was a pursuit aviator during much of his early career and had a hand in writing tactical and operating manuals as well as in fitting aircraft with early expendable fuel tanks. Later, he commanded bombardment units during the early 1930s when bomber growth began to greatly outpace pursuit (fighter) development. This was also the time when the Army Air Corps struggled to reorganize itself and define its roles not only within the Army, but also in national defense in general. Spaatz was one of those who advocated greater autonomy for the Air Corps.

Spaatz maintained a close relationship with Arnold throughout the 1930s, when he commanded a bombardment group in California; served in Washington, D.C., on the Army's air staff; attended the Command and General Staff College; and was a staff officer at Langley Field in Virginia. Almost immediately after the momentous meeting of November 14, 1938, Arnold called on the younger Spaatz, who by this time had been a close associate for more than twenty years. During his nearly three decades of service, Spaatz had developed tremendous depth and breadth in operations, training, planning, and organization. This experience, combined with his common sense and moral certitude, made him just the man whom Arnold needed to help guide the U.S. Army Air Corps.

Consequently, Arnold made Spaatz head of the Plans Section of the Office of the Chief of the Air Corps and entrusted him with the administrative work for planning the expansion of the Air Corps. From that point through the middle of 1941, whenever Arnold submitted a plan, it was one that had been put together by Spaatz. It was a perfect teaming as Spaatz and Arnold usually shared the same opinions. Their minds were particularly aligned when it came to what both of them viewed as the Roosevelt administration's over-generous aircraft allocation to Great Britain. A few months after his appointment, Spaatz wrote a memo to Arnold warning that "it might be difficult to explain in the case of the collapse of England . . . how we can agree that any airplanes can be diverted at a time when we have only sufficient modern airplanes to equip a paltry few squadrons."[10]

On Arnold's orders, Spaatz left for England via Italy and France during May 1940. The journey must have seemed somewhat surreal considering Italy's alignment with Germany and the fact that British and French soldiers were losing their battle with the Germans in Belgium and northern France. Spaatz described himself during this time as a "high-class spy," although his official orders directed him to observe the RAF's training and operations. His unofficial mandate was to collect as much information as he possibly could about all aspects of the air war.

Spaatz arrived in England on June 1, 1940, at the height of the British evacuation from Dunkirk. The British were initially reluctant to share information with their American visitors. For one, the defense of France was a hopelessly executed disaster on which Great Britain had already spent too many men and too much valuable equipment. Accordingly, with France's defeat a certainty, England was quite literally preparing to fight for its existence as there was a not entirely unwarranted fear that the Germans would attempt a cross-Channel *blitzkrieg* within the next several months. It made sense that the British might have been too preoccupied to be overwhelmingly gracious and open with their American guests.

Further, the officers with whom Spaatz was visiting likely had not received unambiguous direction from the highest offices on what information they could share; certainly, they must have felt compelled to err on the side of caution rather than give up too much information that might be leaked to great disadvantage. However, France's capitulation on June 17 drove home the reality that Great Britain was increasingly alone against Hitler's Germany. In the end, the British became much more forthcoming, and Prime Minister Winston Churchill went so far as to authorize the release of the most sensitive secrets, contingent on his personal approval.

Too, human nature began to work to the advantage of both nations. It did not take long before Spaatz gained the trust of his counterparts. The observation of Air Cmdre. John Slessor is informative. He recorded that Spaatz's sparing use of words and his understated sense of humor could "reduce me to a state of schoolboy giggles quicker than anything I know." On a more serious note, he observed that Spaatz was "a man of action rather than of speech, rather inarticulate with an uncommon flair for the really important issue and a passionate faith in the mission of air power."[11]

In the end, Spaatz's visit yielded real and tangible results. His stay coincided with a considerable portion of the Battle of Britain, and therefore, the time he spent observing RAF's Fighter Command was especially informative. As the British evolved their operations and tactics, he was able to develop an understanding of how they used their latest technologies, such as radar and IFF (identification friend or foe) equipment. He also spent considerable time with Bomber Command and was particularly unimpressed with the accuracy of the RAF's night-bombing operations. This exposure reinforced his confidence in the U.S. Army Air Corps' dearly held daylight precision-bombing concepts.

One of the most important results of Spaatz's trip was his affirmation to the American leadership in Washington that the RAF—and England—could hold out against Germany. He was not especially impressed with what he learned of the German air force and declared that its bombing was "particularly lousy" and that it did not appear to be well organized.[12] When the Luftwaffe changed its tactics and ceased hitting the RAF in favor of indiscriminate night bombing of English population centers, Spaatz immediately recognized that it was a sign of German frustration and failure: "By God, that's good, that's fine. The British are winning. . . . Nope, the British have got them now. They've forced them to bomb at night. The Krauts must be losing more than we know."[13]

Spaatz returned to the States in September 1940, having extended his mission much longer than originally planned. It was inarguably a success that not only exposed him to early air operations, but also gave him an opportunity to form relationships with RAF counterparts who would prove to be exceedingly important following the U.S. entry into the war. Liaison visits like his continued to grow in frequency and size and helped the United States prepare for its own imminent combat operations.

While Spaatz was in England, Arnold and his staff kept adjusting to meet the moving target that was the expansion of the U.S. Army Air Corps. Whereas a new goal for pilot training of 7,000 pilots per year to man forty-one aircraft groups had been established in May 1940, that target was raised to 12,000 pilots per year to operate fifty-four air groups only a few months later in August. By the end of the year, the pilot-training goal was changed to 30,000 per year. It is worth remembering that the existing pilot strength of the entire Air Corps in July that same year was only 3,650. In that context, the pilot-training goals seemed not just ambitious, but almost ridiculous.

Although the American aircraft industry had not yet come close to hitting its stride, the aircraft it was producing were still in great demand overseas, particularly in Great Britain. Indeed, the RAF was still being allocated a good deal of America's aircraft production, a situation that continued to irk Arnold. Nevertheless, Roosevelt outranked him and made it clear in his famous "arsenal of democracy" speech on December 29, 1940, that he had very strong ideas on how he would distribute aircraft: "As planes . . . are produced, your Government, with its defense experts, can then determine how best to use them to defend this hemisphere. The decision as to how much shall be sent abroad and how much shall remain at home must be made on the basis of our over-all military necessities."

It is a common misconception that the quality of the early equipment America sent to its allies was not especially good and that it matched up poorly with what the Axis powers were fielding. The Bell P-39 and Curtiss P-40 are often singled out. This was not particularly fair—or even true. Although, as already noted, the United States generally sent early unproven models to its friends, they were models that the Air Corps would have gladly accepted if given the opportunity.

In reality, the types sent overseas acquitted themselves reasonably well. Of particular note was the performance of the Curtiss P-36 Hawk—as the Hawk 75 variant—in the hands of French pilots against the Luftwaffe. On paper, this predecessor to the P-40 was a dated and less powerful machine than the German Me-109, yet it was more maneuverable and did more than hold its own against the premier German fighter during the Battle of France. Although the French air force was bereft of decent leadership, many of its individual pilots were quite skilled and used the little Curtiss fighter to great effect.

In fact, in the first encounter to draw blood between fighters of the Armée de l'Air and the Luftwaffe, the French came out on top when Hawk 75s downed two Me-109s on September 8, 1939. The successes continued, and although the figures are no doubt inflated, the French flyers claimed approximately 230 German aircraft for a loss of only about 30 Hawk 75s.

The first aerial combat encounter of Günther Rall was against French Hawk 75s. It was during this first combat while flying an Me-109E that the famous German fighter pilot scored the first of his 275 credited aerial victories. Nevertheless, it came at a price:

When we approached this area I saw already ten spots in the air. And this was ten P-36s [Hawk 75s]. [The] French Air Force in those days was not well equipped and didn't have masses of airplanes. They had to buy American airplanes and they bought the P-36 as a fighter. So, we got engaged. You know, the first contact, it is a very exciting thing. You are concentrated [*sic*], but you are excited, also. . . . And we started turning very roughly and dogfighting. . . . And in this dogfight I got my first hit. This French plane caught fire, American plane from a French wing, caught fire. And right when I was behind him, and the . . . big flame, I got hit. And you hear that, you know, the bullets, "bang, bang." So it was a confusing thing, the first dogfight. And, due to fuel shortage we both broke up. They lost three and we lost one.[14]

The Finns enjoyed similar successes using Hawk 75s provided by the Germans from captured French and Norwegian inventories. Against the Soviets, they claimed 190 aerial victories while sustaining only 15 losses. These Curtiss fighters were aircraft—supposedly obsolete—that Arnold had wanted for the Air Corps.

The British rejected the P-39 because of performance deficiencies at high altitude, but the Soviets embraced it. Indeed, there were Soviet pilots who scored more victories while flying P-39s than American pilots achieved at the controls of much more advanced aircraft. For example, Soviet ace Aleksandr Pokryshkin scored forty-eight of his fifty-nine credited victories while flying the P-39. Francis Gabreski, the highest-scoring American pilot in Europe, tallied only twenty-eight aerial kills flying the P-47. Admittedly, there are several qualifiers, but there is no denying the Soviet successes against the Germans with an aircraft that the British refused.

The RAF put the P-40 on the front lines in North Africa in early 1941, where it replaced the Hurricane in many instances, and the Soviets also used it extensively and successfully. In fact, the U.S. used the P-40 operationally through the entire war. In particular, the type acquitted itself reasonably well against the Germans in North Africa and the Mediterranean. When compared to both the Me-109 and the FW-190, particularly the earlier marks, its performance was never so deficient, even later in the war, that it could not give a good account of itself, especially at lower altitudes. The 99th Fighter Squadron had flown only one mission when African-American pilot Charles Bailey, flying a P-40, downed an FW-190 over Italy on January 27, 1944. His victory would not be the last by a P-40 pilot.

The British appetite for American aircraft had been insatiable since long before June 1940, when they offered to take every aircraft the United States could produce, up to 3,000 per month. That number of aircraft was not delivered, but a tremendous fraction of the aircraft produced was. The transfer of American aircraft to Great Britain was further codified on March 11, 1941, when the United States Congress passed "An Act to Promote the Defense of the United States." It was more commonly known as Lend-Lease and was aimed at assisting Great Britain.

Arnold felt the sting almost as if he were paying for the aircraft personally. However, he recognized the president's perspective and appreciated the fact that if Great Britain fell, the United States would be standing alone. There would be no realistic springboard from which to liberate Europe, and the world would be grotesquely changed forever.

Variations of this rationale were used later that year when China was included in the Lend-Lease arrangement, although the 1,225 aircraft allocated to the Chinese were much fewer than the 38,811 sent to the British. When the Soviet Union was invaded by Hitler in 1941,

Lend-Lease was extended to Stalin later that year. The United States subsequently sent 14,717 aircraft to the Soviets, together with many billions of dollars worth of other war materiel.[15]

Lend-Lease had a decisive impact on the final outcome of the war. The dollar quantities were staggering and amounted to more than $50 billion ($750 billion in current values). Great Britain received the greatest amount of aid, and that it was well worth it is not debatable. It was from Great Britain that the greatest part of the battle to destroy the Luftwaffe was waged.

CHAPTER 2

The Nazis and Eaker

Great Britain gained some relief during 1941 as Germany focused on invading the Soviet Union. At the same time, the United States continued to race toward a war footing, and the U.S. Army Air Corps, as with every branch of every U.S. service, underwent a tremendous transformation in size and organization. Indeed, on June 20, the War Department stood down the U.S. Army Air Corps and formed the U.S. Army Air Forces (USAAF) in its place, still headed by Arnold. The reorganization not only ensured that Arnold was in charge of every aspect of army aviation, but also gave it distinct and equal status with the other branches of the Army. It also included an air staff, which Arnold insisted be headed by Spaatz.

Cooperation between the United States and Great Britain continued, with emphasis on the division of roles and responsibilities, together with strategies, in the increasingly likely event that the United States entered the war. These meetings, the American-British Staff Conversations, produced two reports that were especially relevant to the U.S. Army Air Forces. Published on March 27, 1941, ABC-1 declared that the preservation of the British Commonwealth was a primary objective and that if Japan entered the war, the main effort would still be in Europe, with an emphasis on the early elimination of Italy. ABC-1 outlined deployment plans and established basic precepts for unity of effort and command. Importantly for the USAAF, the plan highlighted the importance of a sustained bombing offensive against Germany and Italy, as well as the establishment and seizure of bases from which to mount both land and air operations.

A second report, ABC-2, followed only a couple of days later on March 29. It was wholly focused on aviation and stated that approximately half of America's aircraft production would go to the RAF until the United States entered the war. At the same time, the United States would train enough personnel to man the planned fifty-four air groups, assigning aircraft as they became available. Predictably, both Spaatz and Arnold objected vigorously to the notion that the American air force would not be the chief beneficiary of American aircraft production. Their objections were not without merit: although the British were doing the fighting at that moment, the USAAF needed to be equipped and ready if the United States joined the fight. As it stood, the country still was not ready by the spring of 1941.

Virtually concurrent with ABC-1 and ABC-2, the U.S. Army and U.S. Navy jointly wrote a plan outlining force dispositions and actions in the event of war. This plan, *Joint Army and Navy Basic War Plan Rainbow No. 5*, was approved by the secretary of war and subsequently by the president in June 1941. It presumed operations with the British.

In July, Roosevelt asked the Army and Navy to prepare a plan outlining their production requirements in the event of war. After some dickering, the task for writing the section applicable to Army aviation was passed around the War Department's overloaded organization until it landed right where it should have: Spaatz's air staff, specifically the Air War Plans Division.

Maj. Haywood S. Hansell Jr. was one of the four officers on the team. There was no doubt among them about the importance of their task. Hansell recalled: "The Air War Plans Division had a very brief period in which to complete and brief its plan. But if the task was staggering, so was the opportunity. In a very real way, we sensed that the future of American air power depended, in large part, on what we accomplished in the next few weeks."[1]

What emerged in August 1941, informed greatly by the ABC agreements and Rainbow, was not just a shopping list of equipment and munitions. Rather, AWPD-1 was the document from which the USAAF's subsequent strategies and planning requirements were derived. It outlined three major assignments for the service in the event of war. Those assignments were the execution of a strategic aerial offensive against Germany, air operations to support a defensive strategy in the Pacific, and air operations in defense of the Western Hemisphere.

In the case of the bombing offensive against Germany, AWPD-1 called for a specific focus against Axis air and naval capabilities as well as manufacturing. These operations were intended to prepare the way for an Allied invasion of Europe. Importantly, because its authors did not include any ranking ground officers, the plan's focus was on strategic operations and was not muddied by the sorts of distracting requirements necessary for tactical air operations in support of ground combat. Perhaps the most clever aspect of the plan was that it was written along a tightrope that was bold enough to advance the doctrine of strategic air operations, but not so aggressive as to be dismissed out of hand.

In succinctly describing the material requirements for winning the coming war, the accompanying tally of men and equipment did not appear outrageous. AWPD-1 called for an air force in excess of two million men, 60,000 aircraft, and the infrastructure and material to support them. However, at the time the document was completed in August 1941, the USAAF numbered only 195,000 men and 8,200 aircraft. Although the service had more than tripled in size since the previous year, it still had a tremendous amount of growing to do.

With an urgency fueled by world events, AWPD-1 was quickly approved up the chain and reached Roosevelt in September. It was published as part of the "Victory Plan" on September 25, 1941. Considering the nation's previous reluctance to prepare for the war, it is remarkable that this document, which called for expanding the already greatly enlarged USAAF tenfold, was so readily embraced. Indeed, AWPD-1 was so compelling, so "on the mark," that it was recognizable at the core of every USAAF strategy from the time it was accepted until the end of the war.

So, as 1941 drew toward a close and events around the world made America's entry into the war almost a foregone conclusion, the USAAF was still woefully undersized and underequipped. On the other hand, its expansion was gaining momentum, and perhaps more importantly, its leadership had a vision, as well as plans and strategies, to fight the war.

Following the surprise attack on Pearl Harbor, the United States declared war on Japan on December 8, 1941. Hitler, vexed at America's moral and material support of Great Britain and the Soviet Union and citing several minor naval clashes between Germany and the U.S. Navy, declared war on the United States on December 11. Italy's Mussolini followed Hitler's lead that same day. If Germany had previously cradled any hope of surviving the war it had started, it vanished then. Whereas stomping France and a grab-bag of small and ill-prepared European countries was a calculated risk that Germany had won, taking on Great Britain and the Soviet Union was a gamble with much longer odds. But to declare war against the world's greatest industrial power, regardless of the fact that it was an ocean away, was a grave error.

He admittedly did not realize it at the time, but it eventually dawned on the great Luftwaffe combat leader and 176-victory ace Johannes Steinhoff that the entry of the United States into the fighting marked the beginning of the end for Hitler's Germany:

> When this happened, we were in the middle of the first Russian winter, and we were too busy to think about it. I was just south of Moscow when I heard the news. However, it later penetrated my mind that this was a decisive step. The Americans had tremendous willpower and an unmatched industrial capacity for building big bombers, fighters, ships, and so on. It was more or less the end of the war—only time determined how long we would survive.[2]

Although he blustered about fighting England to the end and likewise boasted that he would fight until the Soviets were destroyed, Hitler never planned—or, perhaps more correctly, did not prepare—to fight a protracted war. In fact, Germany's early successes validated Hitler's approach. Continental Europe went down quickly, in large part because of the effectiveness of Germany's air force. Yet that air force was not unbreakable.

Following the Battle of France, the Luftwaffe was winded but still flush with success after having destroyed a modern and substantial French air force that was so poorly organized and led that it was almost criminal. But the Luftwaffe's next adversary, Great Britain's RAF, was not poorly organized or led. The Luftwaffe began operations to prepare for the German invasion of England immediately after the fall of France in June 1940. Although it nearly defeated the RAF over British territory in the seminal air clash that is remembered as the Battle of Britain, "nearly" was not enough. In fact, the Luftwaffe had been beaten.

Nevertheless, the Germans did nothing much to grow their air force. The failure of the Luftwaffe against the RAF was considered an aberration. Great Britain was a nettlesome vexation that would be reengaged after the Soviet Union was defeated—at least according to plan—the following year. The coming campaign, to Hitler's way of thinking, would take only a few months and likewise necessitated no great increase in the Luftwaffe's strength.

As it developed, the invasion of the Soviet Union during 1941 was another case of "nearly." Hitler's *blitzkrieg* sent the Soviets reeling east in near defeat. But the onset of winter found the Germans stretched to the very gates of Moscow, still wanting victory. And yet the Nazis did little on a meaningful scale to grow the Luftwaffe. This was the case even though it was ordered to support Rommel's operations in North Africa earlier that same year, not to mention other adventures in the Mediterranean and the Balkans, particularly the invasions of Greece and Yugoslavia.

Incredibly, not only did Hitler do nothing to increase his air force, he instead ordered aircraft production reduced. By the end of 1941, the Luftwaffe was thin everywhere. Instead of leading lightning strikes against weak and ill-prepared adversaries, units of the German air force were shuttled from one front to another to buttress increasingly strapped German army elements.

In fact, the Nazis found themselves in a war of attrition. Germany alone had little realistic hope of matching the global resources and massive human and manufacturing capital of Great Britain and the Soviet Union combined. But as Germany controlled virtually the whole of Europe and all its considerable resources, it was not unreasonable to believe that Germany might be able to muster enough materiel and manpower to fight both its adversaries to an interminable standstill or at least until some sort of armistice was arranged that would let Germany keep some of the territory it had conquered.

The Nazis certainly acted as if Germany could carry on indefinitely. In 1941, Germany was still producing consumer goods at close to prewar levels, and its factories were working only one shift each day. Moreover, its leadership had not fully mobilized the nation's women into the workforce, a failure that would be costly.

All these factors notwithstanding, the calculus changed for good when the United States entered the war. It was the most industrialized nation on earth, and Germany could not hope to out-produce its current adversaries together with its newest. This was especially true of aircraft production because no one in the German high command felt compelled to increase the size of the Luftwaffe commensurately, despite the fact that the United States was building long-range heavy bombers and had a doctrine that would in time bring the war into the very heart of Germany.

And so Germany wasted time as 1942 began. It was not as if it did nothing at all to increase the capability of the Luftwaffe. Hitler reversed his earlier decision, and production was increased while adjustments and reorganizations boosted the throughput of the aircrew training programs. New equipment was also introduced. But it was nothing on the scale of what Germany needed when it is considered that, to say nothing of the industrial capacity of Great Britain and the Soviet Union, the United States was now mobilizing to destroy it.

If Hitler's leadership was tragically bad, so was that within the Luftwaffe, which had officially been formed by Hitler on February 26, 1935, and placed under the command of Hermann Wilhelm Göring, already Germany's air minister since 1933. Born in 1893 to a minor diplomat of a connected family, Göring lived a somewhat privileged childhood supported by the largesse of his godfather, a family friend who happened to be a Christian of Jewish descent.

Göring began World War I with the infantry before becoming an aerial observer and subsequently a fighter pilot. In the air, Göring was an instinctive and aggressive hunter who scored steadily and was wounded in combat. For his fighting achievements, he was awarded command of Jasta 27, and toward the end of the war, he commanded Manfred von Richthofen's famous flying circus, Jagdgeschwader 1.

A handsome, gregarious, and vital young man, he was nevertheless an arrogant bully and was very much disliked by many of his peers.

Moreover, beyond his accomplishments in aerial combat, there was nothing about his performance that was particularly noteworthy; although he was patently clever, he never exercised the discipline required to develop his obviously keen intellect. Nor did the science and doctrine of aviation and air warfare seem to interest him. He excelled at actual air combat but did not appear to appreciate the intellectual capital and materiel planning that went into building and employing an air force.

Göring was exceptionally bitter at Germany's defeat in World War I and drifted a great deal following the armistice. He worked for aircraft manufacturer Fokker for a short time, tried his hand at stunt flying, flew for a Swedish airline, enrolled as a student at the University of Munich, married the wife of a former client, and signed up with the peacetime German army, the Reichswehr. He also joined the Nazis in 1922 after hearing Hitler speak.

Soon after swearing allegiance to Hitler at the end of that year, Göring was made head of the Sturmabteilung (SA), which was essentially the Nazi party's army of thugs. Thereafter, his fortunes rose and fell in concert with Hitler's. He was badly wounded during the Munich Beer Hall Putsch on November 9, 1923. It was during his subsequent escape, exile, and recovery that he became addicted to morphine, a dependence that would plague him for the rest of his life. He was subsequently hospitalized in Sweden for mental issues, and a psychiatrist described him thus: "Like many men capable of great acts of physical courage which verge quite often on desperation, he lacked the finer kind of courage in the conduct of his life which was needed when serious difficulties overcame him."[3] There followed several years of near-destitution for him and his wife.

Upon his return to Germany in 1927, he attached himself to Hitler once more and participated in practically every important event during the Nazis' rise to power. Then came a quick succession of assignments during which he accumulated wealth in the form of property, art, and money. He additionally gained power and influence as he assumed a variety of posts, including president of the Reichstag and minister of Prussia. He also became one of Hitler's closest confidantes.

Göring was not particularly well educated and was viewed as coarse and crude by many among Germany's traditional elite. His tastes were flamboyant, and he was fond of elaborate uniforms that often crossed the line into costumery. A common joke held that he wore an admiral's uniform whenever he took a bath. As time went on, he grew increasingly fat and looked more like an effete gourmand than a fighter pilot.

Nevertheless, Göring's loyalty gained Hitler's confidence in virtually every aspect of party politics and governance. Although he had been awarded the Pour le Mérite (Blue Max) and been credited with twenty-two aerial victories during World War I, Göring's chief qualification as commander of the Luftwaffe was his unbridled sycophancy toward Hitler. In contrast, Arnold had never seen combat, but his professional experience and postings together with his intelligence and work ethic shaped him into an effective leader.

The Luftwaffe that Hitler unveiled to the world in 1935 was new in concept only. Although the Treaty of Versailles had forbidden a German military air arm, restrictions were relaxed so that the intent of the treaty was abrogated by various flying "clubs" as well as unrestricted commercial aircraft manufacturing and operations. These all served as a foundation for what eventually became the Luftwaffe. In fact, by 1925, Dornier, Focke Wulf, Messerschmitt, Junkers, and Heinkel were all viable aircraft manufacturers. Deutsche Lufthansa, Germany's state-subsidized airline, put important infrastructure into place all across the country while advancing flying technologies and providing expert training.

Likewise, the postwar German army realized the importance of a military air arm and created and groomed military air experts from within its own staff. Many of them were sent to a special training facility at Lipetz in Russia, where they were given instruction in military flying. Nearly all the ranking members of the World War II Luftwaffe passed through this school. And since 1933, Erhard Milch, the head of Lufthansa and deputy to Göring, had established aggressive plans for expanding the production of military aircraft types and the aviation training infrastructure.

Accordingly, when the Luftwaffe was unveiled to a world community distracted by economic woes, it numbered almost 1,900 aircraft and more than 20,000 men. It was larger than the U.S. Army Air Corps and would remain so for several more years.

Under Milch's stewardship—and Göring's enthusiastic, if inexpert, advocacy—the German air force burgeoned during the next couple of years. When Hitler made demands of the Luftwaffe, Göring simply passed those demands to Milch, who delivered, although he often played favorites and used his position to settle personal vendettas. It was Milch's competence that compelled Göring to protect him when it came to light that Milch's father was a Jew. Göring directed the drawing up of sham certificates that had Milch's mother testifying that Milch's father was not his biological sire. The episode is said to have been behind Göring's famous quote: "I decide who is a Jew." Regardless, the incident underscored Milch's value to the growth of the early Luftwaffe. Indeed, Hitler acknowledged his competence in 1936 by promoting him to general and moving him permanently to the Luftwaffe.

Perhaps the brightest star in the new German air force, at least from a cerebral viewpoint, was Walther Wever, the Luftwaffe's first chief of the general staff. Wever had distinguished himself as a field and staff officer during World War I, and following the war, he was closely associated with aviation as part of the Reichswehr. He was universally noted as a man of great intelligence and professional and moral integrity. His assignment to the air ministry from the army in 1933 was recognized as a windfall of the highest order.

Indeed, unlike Göring and other ranking Luftwaffe officers, Wever was one of the few who studied and understood airpower doctrine. He and his staff put together the document that guided Luftwaffe operations from the time it was published until the end of World War II. *Luftwaffe Manual 16: Conduct of Aerial Warfare* was released in 1935 and was a relatively balanced and well-considered treatise that had no major failings, especially when the date of its publication is considered. Unfortunately, it was not regularly updated and, judging by the development of the Luftwaffe, was not widely read or heeded.

One of its recommendations, reflecting a view strongly held by Wever, was the development of a long-range strategic bomber force. Wever believed that such a capability would serve as a deterrent against attack by a host of potential enemies. This belief lost its strongest proponent when Wever crashed and was killed on June 3, 1936, at the controls of an He-70 after having failed to remove the aircraft's aileron gust locks. Although the Luftwaffe struggled to produce a viable long-range bomber through the end of World War II, it was a struggle that had little chance—technical and resource issues aside—without the powerful advocate that Wever had been.

In August 1936, Germany sent its first air units to support Franco's Nationalists during the Spanish Civil War. This force initially consisted of about 200 aircraft, including fighters, bombers, and observation aircraft. The Condor Legion fought primarily against Soviet aircraft, with Soviet pilots flying on behalf of the Republican forces, and gained valuable experience in tactical operations.

On the other hand, despite the bombing of civilian populations in cities such as Guernica, few strategic lessons were taken from the conflict. If anything, the successes of its dive-bombing operations and those of its medium bombers tilted German leadership toward those sorts of aircraft rather than long-range heavy bombers. After all, medium bombers were less costly to produce and maintain. The prevailing thought was that for the same amount of money, three medium bombers were better than two long-range heavy bombers. This mistake, among others, would make itself manifestly apparent during the Battle of Britain.

All told, through April 1939, when the fighting ended, a total of nearly 20,000 German servicemen served in Spain, although a small percentage of those had served with ground and antiaircraft units. Aside from experience, the German air force also took advantage of the conflict to prove its equipment. It was in Spain that many of the aircraft that would carry the Luftwaffe during World War II, including the Me-109, were first blooded.

In the meantime, Milch continued to build the Luftwaffe. It numbered nearly 3,000 aircraft by the end of 1938, and aircraft production exceeded 700 monthly by 1939. However, Milch's successes, beginning with his promotion to general in 1936, aroused jealousies in Göring and drove him to dissipate Milch's responsibilities at the same time that the German air force was racing to supersede every other.

Consequently, Göring appointed Ernst Udet as the director of the technical department at the air ministry. Udet had been an extraordinary fighter pilot during World War I and was credited with sixty-two aerial victories, second in Germany only to Manfred Von Richthofen. He was a popular, well-liked man who had spent many of the years since the war flying exhibitions or hiring out to wealthy clients for special projects. He also had brief stints in aircraft manufacturing and as an airline pilot, and his stunt work for films took him to California. A hard-drinking, fun-loving favorite, Udet counted friends of many different nationalities and never lacked for female company, nor failed to show friends a good time.

James "Jimmy" Doolittle, the famous airplane racer and aviation pioneer, met Udet several times during the 1930s and considered the German a friend. Doolittle, a reserve officer with the U.S. Army Air Corps and a technical specialist with Shell Oil Company, visited with Udet during a business trip to Germany in 1937. He recalled that Udet "was still the fun-loving, good-humored, dashing pilot who had a great disdain for politics and discipline." Doolittle further recollected that "Udet detested Hitler and his aviation boss, Göring. In the privacy of his apartment he liked to imitate Hitler. He would take a small black comb, put it under his nose and do a Nazi stiff-armed salute with hilarious, unprintable comments."[4]

All the same, a likeable, womanizing fighter pilot did not make for a great air force leader. Göring, still intent on diluting Milch's power, gave more of that power to Udet when he made him the director-general of air force equipment in 1939. Udet was now charged with the design and production of all air force aircraft and equipment.

It was a hopelessly poor assignment. Udet was much like Göring in that he understood and excelled at the application of tactical airpower at the small-unit level, but he did not have the interest or intellect to effectively do his job. In other words, he loved to fly and fight but cared little about the what, how, and why. Nor did he have the technical acumen or patience for the sort of planning and administration that was so important to aircraft design, development, and production. Rather than do the work that needed doing, he put blinders on and buried himself in dive-bomber development while Germany went to war.

As it developed, the Luftwaffe's wartime requirements underwent rapid and continuous changes that Udet did not have the capacity to understand, much less meet. Subsequently, when Hitler began to demand the impossible from the German air force, Göring turned around and buried Udet with those demands. Udet foundered. His situation went from bad to worse when the Luftwaffe was defeated during the Battle of Britain, and the pressure did nothing but increase when Hitler invaded the Soviet Union.

Rather than protecting and helping Udet, Göring saddled him with blame. Unable to cope and increasingly debilitated by alcohol dependence,

Udet shot himself in the head on November 17, 1941. Göring and the Nazi state hid his suicide and declared instead that he had been killed while testing a new aircraft. He was given a hero's memorial and interment.

Again, the comparison between Arnold's staff and Göring's is stark in its contrast. First, Arnold would not have put a playboy like Udet in charge of party planning, much less the building of his air force. Second, as stressful as serving on Arnold's staff was, its officers did not commit suicide. The two staffs lived and worked in completely different worlds.

Udet's suicide had significant, second-order side effects. Werner Mölders, a young and highly successful fighter ace, had recently been made inspector-general of fighters (*General der Jagdflieger*) and was responsible for leading the Luftwaffe's operational and strategic development. He was killed on his way to Udet's funeral when the aircraft in which he was a passenger crashed at Breslau on November 22, 1941. Mölders's replacement was another equally talented and young fighter ace, Adolf Galland. Galland was an intelligent, outspoken, and aggressive leader who, like Mölders, was credited with more than 100 aerial victories. Perhaps less sensitive and politic than Mölders, Galland was steadfastly honest, upright, and loyal to his men. He would clash violently with the Nazi leadership as he struggled to align Germany's defenses to the reality of air warfare against the Allies.

Just more than two weeks after the attack on Pearl Harbor, beginning on December 23, 1941, President Roosevelt and his military chiefs met with Prime Minister Churchill and his own military leaders in Washington, D.C. The Arcadia Conference lasted until January 14, 1942, and the work that was completed—with an eye toward defeating two formidable enemies on opposite sides of the globe—was by necessity comprehensive and wide-ranging. The diversity of the topics is illustrated by a partial list: garrisoning Iceland; the defense of Singapore and the Dutch East Indies; the security of northeast Brazil; American warships and aircraft for Great Britain; securing lines of communication in the Atlantic; the Irish; the invasion of North Africa; the defense of the

American west coast, Alaska, and Hawaii; the Soviet fight against the Nazis; and a possible German move against Portugal.[5]

One of the most vital issues to the British was the establishment of USAAF heavy bomber units in England. Arnold noted that Churchill, echoing his staff's views, "emphasized the necessity of sending U.S. bombers to England at the earliest possible moment to bomb German forces and industries, and French ports used by the German raiders." That fact notwithstanding, an agreement was reached to invade North Africa in the near term before undertaking a cross-Channel invasion of Europe. The British rightly believed that bringing the Americans into the North African fight would put an end to the German adventure there. Still, although it was not apparent at the time, allocating the air units necessary to support a North African invasion would undercut the buildup of the American air forces in England.

After the British departed for home, the military leaders of both nations, now known as the Combined Chiefs of Staff (CCS), maintained regular contact. This was done via cables and letters, staff surrogates, government and industry delegates, and, at greater intervals, face-to-face meetings and formal conferences. The continuous and earnest high-level engagement between the two nations was virtually unprecedented. It was a significant contributing factor to the ultimate success of the Anglo-American alliance.

The principal instrument of American airpower in Europe through the entire war was the Eighth Air Force, which did not even exist at the time of the Pearl Harbor attack. Hastily activated in Savannah, Georgia, on January 28, 1942, it was originally intended to be the air task force for the invasion of North Africa. However, as that offensive was deferred, the Eighth endured a short, sharp period of organizational tumult that was characteristic of practically every organization formed during the early part of the war. It gave up aircraft for a variety of missions, including Doolittle's Tokyo raid and antisubmarine patrols along the eastern seaboard. Ultimately, by March, it had passed all its aircraft to the U.S.-based Third Air Force and was made ready for service as a strategic bombardment air force in England.

As a strategic bombardment air force, the Eighth revolved around bombers. Ultimately, the defeat of Nazi Germany would depend to a significant extent on the air campaign that the Eighth would be tasked with running. Consequently, the command of that air force's bomber component could be entrusted only to an individual of extraordinary capability: Brig. Gen. Ira Eaker, an officer noted not only for his administrative and political savvy, but also for his expertise as a pilot and his dedication to the American precepts of strategic aerial bombardment.

Eaker was born in Field Creek, Texas, on April 13, 1896, to a cowboy-turned-farmer and his wife. His parents were the quintessential hard-working folk of the American prairies who scratched barely more than a subsistence living out of what had been an Indian wasteland only a generation earlier. Eaker recalled that "We were as a family very poor by any modern standard, but we didn't know it."[6] His childhood experience was typical for that time and place. He and his two brothers did farm chores when they were not studying in a one-room schoolhouse. In their spare hours, they chased small game around the countryside. When the family moved from Field Creek to Eden, Texas, nine-year-old Ira was charged with herding the family's livestock at a pace of twenty miles per day for five days.

Eaker's father was a strong and tireless, if undereducated, man. Likewise, his mother had no more than a grade-school education. However, they were not so ignorant that they did not recognize the disadvantages that their lack of schooling imposed on their lives. Consequently, Eaker's parents sought not only to improve themselves, but also to encourage their boys to learn. Eaker's mother spent many evenings reading aloud stories from the Bible and the classics. She was also a fastidious woman, insisting that the boys stay washed and well-groomed.

In 1909, drought forced the family to Kenefic, Oklahoma, where Eaker's father found what work he could. Ira matured into a driven, hard-working, and temperate adolescent with clear ambition to be something beyond a farmer, cowboy, or craftsman. He eventually enrolled at the Southeastern Normal School in nearby Durant and graduated with exemplary marks and at the top of the debate team. A favorite professor recalled Eaker's dedication: "I remember Ira Eaker as a slender, modest young man who practiced the principle of the second mile. If we told him to read one reference book, he read two . . . always doing more than was asked of him."[7]

The United States entered World War I on April 6, 1917, and the following day, every boy at Southeastern Normal enlisted in the Army. Eaker was just a week shy of his twenty-first birthday; he stood five feet, eight inches, and weighed just 115 pounds. After officers training school, he was commissioned a second lieutenant and sent to Fort Logan H. Root in Arkansas.

Assigned to the infantry, Eaker had his first hands-on contact with military aviation when a pilot on a recruiting mission landed his sick airplane near where Eaker was drilling on the parade ground. After a short chat, Eaker reconnected a sparkplug wire to fix the ailing engine. Eager to make the young lieutenant one of his first recruits, the pilot gave Eaker a form to submit for assignment to aviation training. That same day, while the two of them were riding their horses back from the parade ground, Eaker's commanding officer duped him out of the form and completed it for himself. Eaker had to wait another six weeks for a duplicate. He finally completed flight training at Kelly Field, Texas, and was posted to Rockwell Field near San Diego when the war ended in November 1918.

It was there that Eaker started a pair of associations that helped define the rest of his life. Col. Henry Arnold, with his executive, Maj. Carl Spaatz, took command at Rockwell to out-process more than 8,000 men who were no longer needed for military service. Eaker was immediately taken with the two higher-ranking officers; he noted and emulated their bearing, their leadership styles, and their calculated ways of getting things done. More than forty years later, Eaker remarked on his first impressions of Arnold: "He impressed me as a tremendous personality. He always had a glint in his eye, sort of a half-smile. He won your complete admiration and support just by being there." For his part, when Arnold left Rockwell later that year, he wrote Eaker: "I am glad I was not disappointed in you and wish you all the best of luck in the world."[8]

Luck and skill took Eaker a long way, as did his enthusiasm for meeting and associating with men of power, intellect, and capacity. The

Army's aviation community was a tiny one, and Eaker's career saw him assigned to numerous postings that could not help thrusting him into contact with virtually all the great aviation names of that era. Of course, Arnold and Spaatz were among them, and Eaker served with those two officers in the headquarters of Maj. Gen. Mason Patrick, the chief of staff of the U.S. Army Air Service, the Air Corps' antecedent. Alongside Arnold and Spaatz, he also did instrumental trench work for Billy Mitchell during the latter's famous trial.

Eaker's peers included Jimmy Doolittle and others. He knew Charles Lindbergh, Howard Hughes, and other luminaries of flight. But his acquaintances and relationships extended beyond aviation. He was Douglas MacArthur's pilot for several years, was well-liked and respected by George Marshall, and was personally awarded the Distinguished Flying Cross, a newly authorized medal, by Calvin Coolidge for his accomplishments during the Pan-American Goodwill Flight in 1926; this event also earned him a share in the Mackay Trophy.

Besides regular flying to maintain his skill and currency, Eaker was involved in many attempts to set or break aviation records as well as other flying exploits that drew the attention of the press. One of these was the Army's controversial takeover of the airmail routes at the direction of President Roosevelt following the discovery of fraud and collusion in the post office in 1934. Eaker was a principal player during the hasty organization and execution of this effort. Another accomplishment was the first cross-country flight flown completely on instruments during 1936. He was also part of Spaatz's crew when the *Question Mark* set the refueled airborne endurance record in 1929.

Eaker's career alternated among staff, command, and school assignments, but as his responsibilities grew, his relationships with Arnold and Spaatz grew closer. The three of them often flew together from March Field in Riverside, California, during the 1930s. With Arnold in particular, Eaker grew ever closer; the two of them collaborated on a series of three books. The first, *This Flying Game*, was published in 1936 and gave a public face to Army aviation, particularly its strategic implications. The writing served good purpose as it outlined the strategic potential of the Air Corps during a period when both the Navy and the Army's archaic senior ground generals sought to limit it.

Inside Army aviation itself, there was considerable turmoil during the decade before World War II over how the flying establishment ought to organize itself and for what mission. Billy Mitchell excepted, tradition held that Army aviation ought to be a defensive tool used offensively only to support ground forces. Broader-minded thinkers, Arnold and Eaker among them, believed that the best defense was an effective offense and that the strategic bomber was the ultimate offensive weapon. This doctrine of long-range, precision strategic bombing was evolved at the Air Corps Tactical School at Maxwell.

Thinkers there took a holistic approach to the study of warfare that included the motivations of a nation at war, its strengths, and its vulnerabilities. Their analysis motivated them to categorize elements of an enemy nation that, if destroyed, would most favorably impact the conduct of a conflict. These elements included military, government, and industrial targets. The Air Corps Tactical School doyens ultimately came to believe that the appropriate tool for attacking these sorts of targets—and achieving victory—was the high-altitude, self-defending precision daylight bomber.

During this period, the Army Air Corps was split into two doctrinal camps, bomber advocates and fighter proponents. Since the early 1930s, the bomber backers had been ascendant as their aircraft grew larger and more powerful. This was due in large part to the fact that more development money was put against bombers, while fighter improvement languished. Moreover, the research that was being conducted to improve the performance of commercial transports was more directly applicable to bomber aircraft.

In truth, by the early 1930s, the latest bombers outstripped their fighter contemporaries in terms of raw performance. For instance, the Martin B-10 introduced in 1933 was an all-metal twin-engine design with enclosed crew positions, defensive weaponry, retractable landing gear, and a top speed of 213 miles per hour. Its range of 1,200 miles gave it unprecedented reach, a fact that alarmed the Navy since the aircraft offered the potential to infringe on its mandate to protect the nation's sea approaches.

The B-10's fighter contemporary was the Boeing P-26, also delivered in 1933, which had fixed landing gear, an open cockpit, and a top speed of 230 miles per hour. Its range was only 600 miles. Aside from not having nearly the range required to escort the B-10 to distant targets, the P-26 could barely keep up with it. Consequently, bomber advocates believed that designing a fighter with the range and speed not only to keep up with the bombers and reach the target, but to effectively fend off enemy interceptors, was impossible. Therefore, long-range bombers would have to be armed well enough to be self-defending over enemy territory, while fighters would be relegated to the defense of important targets or friendly troops on the battlefield.

This was a conceptual failure that was addressed only incrementally once American airmen had the opportunity to observe the air war in Europe. It was not until the United States entered the war and established its objectives that the thinking of the bomber and fighter types, together with their equipment, came into confluence.

Although he stumbled on the way, Eaker would help guide that confluence and would also benefit from it. He did consider himself a fighter pilot although he was comfortable behind the controls of virtually any aircraft. His intellectual capacity was such that he did not limit himself to an exclusively fighter or bomber perspective. Rather, he advocated the use of the appropriate aircraft types, be they bomber or fighter, for getting a given mission accomplished. This mindset would serve him well in the years to come.

Moreover, during this period there was a continuous undercurrent of tension over the notion held by many inside the Air Corps that the service ought to be separate and distinct from the Army and Navy. In general, Arnold, Spaatz, and Eaker advocated this concept although none of them was vociferous about it. As a practical matter, the Air Corps was still young, and Arnold, for one, believed that the Air Corps of the 1930s was far from ready for such a break. Regardless, all three of them believed that accomplishing such a thing ought to take place through a measured and structured process.

Although Eaker had written extensively on the subject of modern air warfare up to and through the start of the war in Europe, his perceptions were further sharpened when he was sent to England in late August 1941 to replace Spaatz as an observer there. He was charged with investigating the latest aircraft communications technologies, determining the feasibility of putting searchlights aboard aircraft for nighttime operations against bombing raids, and ascertaining the latest in fighter escort procedures.

He did much more. During his one-month stay, he maintained an exhausting schedule as he visited with a number of technical experts as well as important RAF leaders. He also took time to fly some of the latest RAF aircraft, like the Spitfire and Typhoon. He was particularly impressed with the way women had been integrated into the armed forces and spent considerable time detailing the need to develop a long-range fighter suitable for escorting long-range bombers. He further examined the difficulties associated with doing this. The document he delivered to Arnold following his return a month later was the most comprehensive to come from any observer sent overseas.

Following the Japanese attack on Pearl Harbor, Eaker was put in charge of the fighter defenses on the west coast. The units he had were pitifully small in number, and he had little choice but to spread them pathetically thin. He put a unit each at Portland, Seattle, Los Angeles, and San Francisco. Even three years after Roosevelt had called his watershed aircraft meeting, there were still precious few assets.

While Eaker managed the handful of units he had, he enviously watched a procession of officers pass through the west coast to the Pacific. There, he imagined, they would be getting into the fight immediately. Having missed the last war, he wanted to make sure he got into this one. He wrote a letter that, in part, outlined his concerns at being left behind. The note was returned to him. On the reverse, Arnold had written a one-line response: "Keep your shirt on, son."[9]

CHAPTER 3

Spaatz and Eaker Go
to England

E aker was promoted to colonel at the end of December 1941. Three
weeks later, on January 18, 1942, Arnold told him that he would be
put in charge of American bomber operations in England and that
Spaatz would follow him a few months later to take over the entirety of
American air operations. Eaker was excited but reminded Arnold that
he was a fighter pilot by trade. Arnold responded that he needed to
infuse his bomber operations with fighter-pilot spirit. Eaker was ready
to go, and Arnold promoted him to brigadier general a week later on
January 25.

Eaker left for England via Bermuda, Portugal, and Ireland on February 4, 1942. Along the way, delayed by weather, he played golf in
Bermuda for nearly two weeks. After arriving in neutral Portugal, he was
struck at the irony of RAF and Luftwaffe aircraft parked peaceably alongside each other at the Lisbon airport. Overnight, his luggage was searched
by Nazi agents, and the next day, his transport aircraft, a chartered DC-3
of the Dutch airline KLM, crossed paths with an ill-intentioned Luftwaffe
Ju-88 over the Bay of Biscay. Eaker remembered that "The German came
in fast from quartering astern. The transport pilot jockeyed slightly from
one side to the other in an effort to throw off the aim of the German if he
opened up on us."

As the range closed, one of the German's engines suddenly puked a
great plume of black smoke and failed. The enemy pilot's priorities

rapidly shifted to self-preservation, and Eaker's aircraft was left unmolested to continue on to Ireland. Safely on the ground there, he made for England and, upon arrival, wasted no time in establishing VIII Bomber Command on February 23. Several weeks later, his staff set up shop at High Wycombe, a beautiful, tree-shaded girls' school.[1]

Eaker started work immediately—and at a frantic pace. It was a tempo he maintained through virtually the entire war. Although he technically was in command only of VIII Bomber Command, he actually oversaw everything until Spaatz arrived. Incredibly, to help him stand up the American air establishment, he started with a staff of only six. It was not enough to crew even a single B-17. Of this handful of men, two were Regular Army, and the remainder were reservists. Nevertheless, they were among the best and brightest, the core of a staff that would multiply itself many times over as the USAAF in England grew into the greatest air force ever fielded.

Eaker's staff increased itself in an unorthodox fashion. In just more than a year's time, the Eighth Air Force was scheduled to have more than 3,000 aircraft in England. They were to be serviced, supplied, and crewed by nearly a quarter million men. Someone had to organize and oversee the arrival of such a force, and six men, no matter how intelligent, were not enough. Indeed, in February 1942, there were not enough personnel of the right type in the entire Army to put together such a force. Accordingly, at Arnold's insistence, Eaker and his tiny staff had canvassed the United States and recruited the most intelligent and dynamic men they could find from government, industry, the arts, and academia. The new recruits were given direct commissions; a brief exposure to military procedures, courtesies, and customs; and transportation to England. It seemed almost preposterous on the face of it, but it proved brilliant in the end.

While Eaker and his staff laid the groundwork for the USAAF in Great Britain, Spaatz prepared to assume command. On February 2, even before Eaker had left the States and despite the fact that Spaatz himself had not left, Arnold made Spaatz a major general and commander of USAAF forces in England. Spaatz officially assumed command of the Eighth Air Force on May 10, 1942. On Arnold's direction, the commander of the Eighth was also charged with ownership of all USAAF forces in the entire European theater.

When Arnold gave him the Eighth, Spaatz made it clear to Arnold, his friend and superior, that he intended to send his men into battle only when they were truly ready. Doing otherwise, committing them piecemeal and untrained, would surely bring material and moral disaster on American air operations in Europe. He made the same point to the Army's chief of staff, Gen. George Marshall, only four days later. Spaatz intended to build an air force large and strong enough to defeat the Luftwaffe in a battle of attrition. Once the Germans were destroyed in the air, the way would be clear for a cross-Channel invasion of Europe.[2]

That Spaatz made it a point to tell his bosses that he would not be pushed into action too early showed that he possessed not only a thorough understanding of the two men, but also remarkable political savvy and maturity. Obviously, during the more than two decades since he had known Arnold, he understood the man's dynamic, yet impatient personality. But beyond that, he also was aware of the pressures that Arnold would be put under to make something happen—and quickly—with the air force in Europe. If Arnold was impatient, the American public was even more so. Spaatz knew that public impatience would make itself felt through Roosevelt, who in turn would pressure Marshall and Arnold. It would then pass to Spaatz.

Pressure or not, Spaatz the military commander understood what a disaster it would be to commit his airmen before they were ready. If they failed in their first few missions, not only would morale in the service—and indeed the nation—suffer, but his job, and more importantly, the concept of daylight precision bombing would be at risk. Were the Americans then forced to join the British in nighttime area bombing, the Luftwaffe might never be defeated.

It was also during this period that Spaatz floated the idea of creating two American air forces in Europe. One would be strategic in nature and would hit vital military and industrial targets deep in the heart of Germany. The second would have a tactical emphasis, striking military targets in support of ground forces. This notion of separate strategic and tactical air forces was a foreshadowing of what would come.

Work continued apace on both sides of the Atlantic, Spaatz in the United States and Eaker in England. Part of that work included a reorganization of the Eighth Air Force that more clearly delineated its different components. No good military leader ever discounted the value of a clearly defined organization. Specifically, over the next several months, the Eighth was arranged into four different commands: VIII Bomber Command, VIII Fighter Command, VIII Air Support Command, and VIII Service Command. Bomber Command—Eaker's organization—controlled the B-17 and B-24 heavy-bomber groups; Fighter Command oversaw the fighter groups; Air Support Command owned all the medium- and light-bomber groups; and Service Command managed the inglorious but absolutely essential supply and maintenance activities. This basic arrangement persisted through the end of the war, with some refinement as necessity dictated.

Progress was made quickly, chiefly because the British were exceptionally gracious hosts. If the Americans wanted something and the British had it to give, it was theirs—food, installations, clothing, and equipment. The British handed over five established bases in East Anglia and committed to building sixty more; in the end, there would be hundreds of American installations. Certainly, it served the British interests to do so as the Americans were there to help them win a war they could not win alone, but their graciousness was also extended in personal ways beyond what might normally be expected. For instance, after arriving, Eaker stayed as a house guest of Air Marshal Arthur "Bomber" Harris. Both men benefitted from the opportunity to carry their professional discussions beyond the workplace.

Camaraderie aside, the two allies still had significant differences on the professional front. As they had previously done and would continue to do for some time, the British did their best to dissuade their American friends from daylight bombing for the same reason that they had given up the concept: prohibitive losses. Still, Eaker resisted for a number of reasons. First, American doctrine had, for years, been developed around the concept of daylight precision bombing. The British had not practiced it in the way the USAAF planned, and therefore, it had not been disproven. More practically, the USAAF's bomber force was already being built and trained for daylight operations. Changing course at that point would cost time, money, and effort.

Additionally, British bombing results to that point in the war had been anything but spectacular. A report commissioned by the British war cabinet the previous summer had shown that only a third of the bombs dropped by the RAF during nighttime operations hit within five miles of the intended target. Against targets in the Ruhr River Valley region, only a tenth had done so.[3]

The British seemed to view the American air force as simply an adjunct to their own. That is, they saw it almost as a reinforcing element rather than a wholly distinct entity with its own special capabilities. They desired that USAAF bombers operate alongside them in the same operations they flew, and they wanted the American fighters to fill the same role as their own—chiefly air defense of the United Kingdom. Through Eaker, the Americans resisted this rigorously. They would not surrender their doctrine, men, and aircraft to the RAF. They adamantly refused to dilute their forces by parting them out to the British and instead declared unequivocally their intent to keep them together as a single force designed to execute USAAF doctrine. American bombers would fly strategic daylight precision bombing missions escorted by American fighters.

In this, the USAAF leadership was intractable. The RAF office in Washington noted in a message back to its leadership: "You are up against a very strong determination on the part of Arnold, Spaatz, and others to concentrate the training and employment of their forces in the U.K. entirely upon proving the daylight bombing offensive can be made a success."[4]

While Eaker was setting up shop in England, the Germans finally moved to improve their air defenses. With the wholehearted support of *General der Jagdflieger* Adolf Galland, Milch proposed increasing the production of all fighter types to 1,000 aircraft per month by June 1943. Hitler was initially opposed, believing he would have to sacrifice the manufacture of offensive bomber types to meet the new production numbers. He grudgingly authorized the plan when Milch convinced him that he could increase bomber numbers at the same time as he grew the fighter forces.

For his part, the chief of the Luftwaffe's general staff, *Generaloberst* Hans Jeschonnek, was not won over. Jeschonnek, like Göring and Udet, had been a fighter pilot during World War I, but unlike them, he had remained in the military and advanced quickly through the ranks, getting a professional education along the way. A stereotypical stiff-mannered Prussian, he nevertheless had a quick mind and a great deal of energy; he was one of the few Luftwaffe leaders who was qualified, at least in part, for the position he held.

It is because of his qualifications that it is difficult to understand why he resisted Milch's plan. With a lack of prescience that was stunning, he declared that he could not possibly use more than 360 new fighters each month. It is true that Germany was not obviously losing the war at that time. It is also true that there were not enough pilots to use so many aircraft. Still, Jeschonnek should have understood that with the Americans readying their air forces, he would need many more of both very soon and ought to have been working hard to get them.

To help pave the way for the units he was sending to England, Arnold traveled there on May 23, 1942. The neverending issue of more American aircraft for the RAF was raised again. When Churchill asked why the Americans resisted giving the British 5,000 aircraft per year when the U.S. had a productive capacity of 60,000 per year, Arnold did his best to explain that the United States, the arsenal of democracy, had obligations to a number of allies other than Great Britain, chief among them the Soviet Union. Arnold asserted that with so many needy and deserving friends, it was difficult to build his own air force with what was left over.

The chief product of Arnold's visit was a tentative agreement he penned with RAF Air Chief Marshal Charles Portal that dealt primarily with allocation and basing of aircraft, both British and American. Another meeting with Sir Henry Tizard brought Arnold up to date on the very promising progress the British were making with jet engines. The first flight of a Gloster jet-propelled test aircraft had taken place only a week earlier on May 15. Arnold also shared in the British excitement at the first 1,000-aircraft raid that hit Cologne on the night of May 30–31.

After several months of preparations on the American side of the Atlantic, Spaatz was finally ready to join his command in England. He departed Washington on June 10, 1942, but capricious weather along the route through Maine, Labrador, Greenland, Iceland, and Scotland caused considerable delays. Although he found the holdups extremely frustrating, the trip gave Spaatz some appreciation of the sorts of conditions that crews ferrying aircraft along the same path would encounter starting later that month.

In fact, the route on which Spaatz embarked during mid-June had been completed only a few months earlier. An airfield on the west coast of Greenland, Bluie West One, was finished in January 1942 and another in Labrador, Goose Bay, was made operational during March. The inaugural ferry flight was composed of eighteen B-17s destined for England and the Eighth Air Force. The formation took off from Goose Bay for Bluie West One on June 26, but six aircraft aborted for various reasons shortly after getting airborne while only nine of the bombers actually made it to Greenland. The other three B-17s crash-landed, but miraculously, all the crews were rescued. It was not an auspicious beginning for a route that was supposed to support the buildup of the USAAF in Europe.

Still, it was used through the end of the war. Except for a few P-38s early on, it was not used by fighters because it was considered too dangerous for smaller aircraft. Instead, they were dismantled in the United States and sent via ship. However, thousands of bombers followed in Spaatz's traces, and although the route never took a toll high enough to force its shutdown, it remained treacherous.

Bob Popeney, a pilot with the 416th Light Bombardment Group, recalled flying an A-20 from Labrador to Greenland later in the war: "We hit solid weather and became separated. My aircraft began to ice up and I tried to get above it but it was no use. I was burning fuel like it was going out of style, had already passed the point of no return, and there was no way I was going to make it to Greenland at that rate. So I dropped back down toward the water to get rid of the ice. When I finally broke out of the clouds, I was flying among, through, above, and below icebergs. Some of those bastards must have been three or four hundred feet high."[5]

Popeney made it into Bluie West One, which was situated at the end of a fjord marked by a sunken freighter. The 5,000-foot pierced steel plank runway angled up a fifteen-degree incline straight into a box canyon. It was a dangerous setup, but it was the only one the USAAF had. Popeney landed safely and stayed overnight. "When we left for Iceland," he recalled, "we had to take off downhill and dodge an incredibly beautiful greenish-blue iceberg that had floated right up to the end of the runway. Once I got airborne and over the ice I must have counted thirty or forty wrecked airplanes. The place was littered with them."

Still, the danger was not over until the aircraft were safely parked and shut down after landing in the British Isles. Popeney's arrival at Prestwick, Scotland, made that point clear: "It was raining like hell when we got to Prestwick, and two of the guys who got there before me screwed up and landed downwind. They ended up going off of the end up the runway, breaking their nosewheels off, and flipping 'fanny over breakfast.' The airplanes were ruined. Now I'll tell you what—that was very expensive overseas transportation!"

In the end, the loss rate on the route averaged just more than 5 percent, which was higher than the total average loss rate that the Eighth experienced during combat. On the other hand, the expected loss rate had been 10 percent.

Spaatz's aircraft safely negotiated the route and finally arrived in Prestwick on June 18, 1942, where he was personally greeted by Eaker. The following day, the pair of them took a car south to London, where, after a day of rest, Spaatz gathered the staff. He remarked on the superb work they had completed up to that time, and he advised that he would not reverse any arrangements that had already been reached with the British. Then, just as Eaker had done four months earlier, he went immediately to work. His driver during this period, Kay Summersby, remarked on his grave demeanor, saying that he was "serious to the point of grimness" and was the "hardest working man" in all of the USAAF.[6]

Spaatz liaised with his British counterparts and addressed logistics and training matters not only because those tasks needed doing, but also because he had, in effect, no aircraft to command. On July 2, 1942, he had only two B-17s and a single C-47 transport.[7] However, this paucity of assets apparently meant nothing to Arnold back in the United States, as he directed Spaatz to put American airmen into combat on Independence Day, July 4. This was something that Arnold had promised Churchill before Spaatz had even gotten to England, and Spaatz was on the hook to execute.

Spaatz did not like it, but he delivered—despite the promise he had made less than two months earlier not to send his men into the fight over Europe before they were ready. Under pressure from Arnold, Spaatz authorized the execution of a mission that was not only stupid, but wholly unnecessary. It was an uncharacteristic lapse of leadership and common sense on the part of both men.

The raid was to be made up of six American crews, together with six British crews, flying twelve RAF Boston light bombers. They were under orders to hit four German airfields in the Netherlands during the early-morning hours of July 4, 1942. The results were underwhelming as four of the American bombers failed to drop their bombs anywhere near their targets. Additionally, two of them were shot down with seven dead; one crewman survived to become the Eighth's first POW.

Nevertheless, the spectacle of USAAF airmen striking the Nazis while flying alongside their British allies made good newspaper copy and seemed to satisfy a public itch for action. The next day, newspapers across the United States carried the event as front-page news. Even the tiny *Waterloo Daily Courier* in Iowa noted: "U.S. Sends Fireworks for Europe." A bit less clever was the *Wisconsin State Journal*'s banner atop its lead story: "U.S. Fliers Bomb Nazis in Holland."

Although they performed poorly, the USAAF airmen flew bravely. The lead ship, flown by Capt. Charles Kegelman, was so badly shot up that it lost a propeller and dragged a wingtip across the ground. Nevertheless, Kegelman brought the aircraft back across the Channel to England and was subsequently awarded the Distinguished Service Cross. Although the raid could hardly be characterized as anything other than a bust, one fact that the Americans could point to with rightful pride was that the Bostons were RAF variants of the Douglas A-20 and had been built in the United States. Sadly, one of the surviving crewmembers committed suicide a few weeks later.[8]

This event was the start of a regular pattern that had Arnold pressing—and pressing hard—on Spaatz and Eaker to do more than they were capable of doing with the forces they had on hand. For almost the next two years, it was practically as sure a thing as the British insistence that the USAAF switch to night bombing.

That there were criticism and acrimony among institutions and individuals in the United States during the war is often forgotten. Early on, Arnold was vexed by the press's condemnation of American warplanes. He recalled that newspapers regularly printed stories asserting that "Not only were the P-38s, the P-39s and the P-40s 'terribly inferior' to the Jap Zero, but even our P-47s and P-51s would never stand a chance against the Luftwaffe's Messerschmitt 109 and the Focke-Wulf 190."[9]

Arnold was frustrated not only because the stories were wrong, but because the people who read those stories were the mothers and fathers, friends and families, of the men who flew the supposedly second-rate aircraft. Misinforming and frightening them did no one any good. It is a testament to Arnold's powers of persuasion that it took only a few face-to-face meetings with a handful of the most prominent writers to convince them that they were wrong. The tenor of their stories changed accordingly.

CHAPTER 4

First Mission and the Move to North Africa

Although Roosevelt, Churchill, and the Combined Chiefs of Staff had made a commitment to the invasion of North Africa during the Arcadia Conference, American enthusiasm for it subsequently ebbed. The American military leadership did not want to be distracted by a sideshow and feared, with some justification, that a North African invasion would bleed away the vital manpower, equipment, and shipping needed to strike the Germans in Europe. They wanted to hit the Nazis where it would do the most harm, and none of them thought that North Africa was that place. Accordingly, they lobbied hard for a cross-Channel invasion from England.

Indeed, Gen. George Marshall's staff put together a plan to do just that, and he traveled to England in April 1942 to try it out on the British. It became known as the Marshall Memorandum, which called for establishing an Allied foothold in France as early as the fall of 1942, but certainly no later than the spring of 1943. The British slow-rolled him. Without directly saying so, they knew there was no chance that the two nations would be able to put together a real invasion force in such a short time. Moreover, Churchill lobbied Roosevelt almost continuously to stay committed to the North African invasion; his commanders needed American help there. The British were still reeling from the loss of Singapore and Burma, and Churchill's government might not have survived if the British Army was also pushed out of North Africa.

Still, Marshall enthusiastically promoted his plan, citing the many advantages it offered and listing the reasons why it ought to be carried out. One portion of the document demonstrated his naivete—or more specifically his staff's—with regard to the relative strength of Allied air-power against the Luftwaffe. He highlighted the advantage of invading Europe from England because "It is the only place where the vital air superiority over the hostile land areas preliminary to a major attack can be staged by the United Powers."[1]

This was essentially true in the context of a cross-Channel invasion, but the Allies would not be able to establish that air superiority by the spring of 1943. That he was advised that it might be possible in 1942 was absurd. It is unknown how closely Arnold or his staff corroborated with Marshall on this point. In fact, the RAF demonstrated the challenge ahead a few months later during the raid on Dieppe on August 19, 1942. It was a disaster during which the British failed to achieve even local air superiority.

Even before the Dieppe raid, it became apparent to the Americans that they would not be able to assemble the necessary forces in England quickly enough to meet their desired timetable. An indicator of this on the airpower side was the fact that even as late as July 8, 1942, the Eighth Air Force had in England only eight B-17s, seven P-38s, and five C-47s—twenty total aircraft.[2] Later in the war, the USAAF in Europe would more than once lose multiples of that in a single day.

It was only after Marshall made another visit to England during July 1942 that he finally accepted that a successful invasion of Europe in the near term was impossible. He wrote, "[I]t became evident that the only operation that could be undertaken with a fair prospect of success that year was TORCH, the assault on North Africa."[3] It was not what he or his staff or the American public wanted, but it was something—and it was possible.

It could be made possible only at the expense of the nascent strategic-bombing campaign that Spaatz and Eaker were trying to get underway with the Eighth Air Force. Arnold, who knew that beating the Germans was the nation's, and his, top priority, bemoaned the fact that he "would shortly have to tell Tooey Spaatz, in London, and Ira Eaker . . . that not only must the original schedule be abandoned, but this very bomb group with which they were about to begin, the 97th, would soon be taken away from them and sent to Africa."[4] The 97th Bomb Group (H), the first of what would be dozens more, had recently arrived in England, and everyone was looking forward to getting it into the fray.

Still, secrecy kept Arnold from immediately divulging TORCH. In their ignorance, Spaatz and Eaker kept pushing ahead. The 97th's B-17s finally arrived, and after a false start, Eaker canned its commander, assigned another, and got it training in earnest. Eaker kept the impatient Arnold apprised of preparations during this period with a series of letters outlining not only the training, but also his and Spaatz's appreciation of the operations they were about to start: "The tempo is stepping up as we approach the zero hour. Tooey's and my theory that day bombardment is feasible is about to be tested where men's live are put at stake."[5] Arnold was unimpressed and, eager to get American bombers into the fight, wrote Spaatz a letter in which he, in so many words, told him not to err on the side of caution.

The United States operated two types of heavy bomber in Europe during the war, the Boeing B-17 and the Consolidated B-24. Both types were four-engine, all-metal, long-range bombers with multiple defensive gun positions. The B-17 was the older of the two, having first flown in July 1935. From the beginning, the B-17 exceeded expectations in virtually every regard. It was faster than the Army's original requirements, it was reliable and easy to maintain, and importantly, it was easy to fly.

Nevertheless, the original prototype crashed. Although that accident was caused entirely by human error, when combined with cost considerations, political vacillation, and development issues, it was not until just before the war that it was being produced in meaningful numbers. Still, at the time of the attack on Pearl Harbor, there were fewer than 200 of the type in service.

Early versions of the B-17 saw service in very small numbers with the RAF. The results achieved were lackluster and had to do more with the RAF's tactics than with any significant shortcomings in the type. The B-17E was the variant first put into combat over Europe by the USAAF, but the model first used in large numbers by the USAAF was the B-17F, which had eleven .50-caliber machine guns for defensive armament, a range of more than 2,000 miles, and a bomb capacity exceeding 8,000 pounds.

The definitive variant was the B-17G, which entered service late in 1943 and included an additional two guns in a chin turret under the nose of the aircraft along with other improvements informed by experience in combat. These included staggered waist gun positions so that the gunners would not bump into each other, as well as windows over the waist hatches to provide a measure of protection from windblast.

When compared to the B-24, the B-17 was slower, could not range as far, and could not carry as much payload. Nevertheless, it flew higher and absorbed battle damage that was absolutely incredible. It evoked great devotion from its crews and was the iconic heavy bomber of World War II. Nearly 13,000 were produced.

The B-24 was a newer and more modern aircraft, having been produced in a hurried response to a U.S. Army Air Corps requirement issued in early 1939. It first flew later that year, an incredible achievement on the part of Consolidated. On paper, it was more capable than the B-17. It was faster and longer-legged, and it could carry more. Its design included a more modern tricycle landing gear arrangement, as well as cutting-edge Davis wings that appeared much too thin and delicate to carry its fat, slab-sided body. Like the B-17, it was heavily armed with .50-caliber machine guns.

Nevertheless, it was not as reliable as the Boeing aircraft, and it was more difficult to operate and fly. Its fuel system was notably complex and problematic—a Rube Goldberg arrangement of tanks, tubes, pipes, and valves that vexed even the most studious flight engineers. It was said that one did not so much fly the aircraft as bully it. If the B-17 was a draft horse, the B-24 was an ox. And although it was rugged, it could not absorb nearly the punishment that the B-17 could; its thin Davis wings were its Achilles' heel. Finally, it had that one unfortunate characteristic that was difficult for anyone but a mother to forgive: it was ugly.

Still, men do form bonds with the machines in which they go to war, and although it had its detractors, the B-24 also had its defenders. "In some ways I really enjoyed the B-24," recalled Art Hodges of the 491st Bomb Group (H). "Sure, it seemed that there was always gas leaking into the interior, but it was a pretty good airplane." Hodges's observations also aligned with those of others who declared that it took a muscular man to fly the B-24 well. "You had to have strong legs to fly that airplane—and I did. It made it much easier to fly in formation if you were big enough to handle it; I actually enjoyed flying formation."[6]

The B-24J, which included an earlier-introduced nose turret, was the definitive model, and more than 6,000 of that variant alone were produced. Ultimately, as experience was gained with the type, it proved to be up to the strategic-bombing role and more. In fact, specially equipped variants of the B-24 operated by Great Britain's Coastal Command, the U.S. Navy, and the Royal Canadian Air Force were credited with helping to finally shut down the German U-boats during the Battle of the Atlantic. By war's end, 18,482 B-24s were produced. No other American type has ever been produced in greater numbers. In practice, although both air forces used both types, the B-17 made up the majority of the Eighth's bombers, while the B-24 made up the majority of the later-formed Fifteenth's.

The Eighth finally flew its first strategic-bombardment mission on August 17, 1942, when the 97th put twenty-three bombers into the air. The first group in the air was a diversionary force intended to confuse German defenders; it turned back to England after crossing the Channel. The actual attack force of twelve bombers was led by Col. Frank Armstrong, with Eaker farther back in the formation as an observer. Spaatz had wanted to go as well, but because he had been briefed that the British were decrypting German Enigma messages, it was considered too risky from a security standpoint in the event his aircraft was shot down. This knowledge would keep him from ever participating in a wartime mission.

The target was the Sotteville railroad marshaling yard in Rouen, about forty miles inland from the English Channel. The twelve bombers, escorted by British Spitfires, met tentative resistance from Me-109s and FW-190s, together with indifferent antiaircraft fire. Two B-17s were slightly damaged by flak, and credit was awarded to one gunner for the destruction of a single fighter. Bombing results, from about 23,000 feet, were promising: the bombs from all but one aircraft fell within a half-mile circle. In fact, Spaatz made the claim to Arnold that the bombing accuracy of that particular mission surpassed that of any British or German mission flown to date. Of course, the raid was too small to do much lasting damage, but it still showed the potential of the daylight precision-bombing concept to which the Americans were so wed.

The mission drew great press coverage and hearty congratulations from all quarters. Eaker was especially enthusiastic after the flight and remarked, "Why, I never got such a kick out of anything in my life!"[7] In the coming months, as men were blown apart on similar missions, the comment would seem to be careless and adolescent, but he surely could be forgiven: the mission was a significant culminating point in a career lived for just that sort of action.

Ebullience and bravado aside, Eaker carefully noted details of every sort during the mission. He observed that takeoff and rendezvous procedures needed to be polished. These were critical mission phases that would be improved and refined throughout the entire war. He also believed the mission demonstrated that point targets could be hit with precision. In this, he, Spaatz, Arnold, and the other acolytes of daylight precision strategic bombardment were vindicated. On the other hand, Eaker recognized that the mission did nothing to prove that the bombers could operate without fighter escort. However, he did say that he thought that the Germans respected the defensive armament of the bomber formations and would in the future attack "very gingerly."[8] On this point, he was very, very wrong.

Into the first week of September, the Eighth put eight more raids up without a single loss. It was an extremely busy period as not only did the 97th Bomb Group turn in all its B-17Es for new B-17Fs, but two new bomb groups, the 301st and the 92nd, started operations. The dribble of USAAF units into England had turned into a trickle.

In terms of seminal moments in the air war between the German air force and the USAAF, this period was perhaps the most important. For the Luftwaffe, it was a fantastic opportunity lost. The first American missions were small, tentative operations that were tests of the daylight-bombing concept as much as anything else. Had the Germans met these first raids with overwhelming fighter forces—and they could have—the USAAF might have been forced to dramatically reconsider its approach for taking the air war to Germany.

For instance, had that first piddling raid to Rouen been smashed, had four or five or six of the bombers been downed, the blowback within the USAAF and the press might have been ruinous. Indeed, it was possible that Eaker's plane could have been shot down. Rather than stepping from his aircraft smiling and rubbing his hands with self-satisfaction, he would have been dead or captured. Or had Eaker's ship been badly hit, his personal confidence in daylight bombing might have been badly shaken. A press conference amidst a backdrop of bodies being pulled from his bomber would have catalyzed intense introspection by the American leadership, the USAAF, and the public.

Had the Luftwaffe done this a few times during this period—and it is not unreasonable to assume it could have—then the pressure for the Americans to join the British in night bombing might have succeeded. If that had happened, the course the air war would have taken is unknowable. What is knowable is that the war would have been prolonged.

But the German leadership did not take the notion of a huge American buildup seriously. Galland noted that "They took it as so much bluff."[9] Neither did the Germans stage adequate numbers of fighters to meet the first American daylight bombers. It is true that Luftwaffe fighter forces were spread thin against the Soviets and against the British in North Africa and the Mediterranean. However, given the seriousness of the impending American bombing campaign, a focused plan for crushing the formations when they started operations should have been crafted; the fighter forces to execute that plan should also have been formed and staged.

The Germans did nothing worthwhile. Galland warned his superiors of the danger from the impending bombing offensive, but all his efforts to alert them "miscarried." He declared that "They did not want to see the danger, because they would have had to admit their many omissions and neglects."[10] Consequently, although the first American raids were small and ineffectual, so too was the German response. The best opportunity the Luftwaffe would ever have to derail the American daylight offensive was squandered.

The 82nd Fighter Group, a P-38 unit, was part of the trickle of USAAF units headed across the Atlantic. In late September 1942, it was sent from southern California to Camp Kilmer, New Jersey, and from there, it was embarked with 11,000 other servicemen aboard the *Queen Mary* for the trip to the British Isles. "I remember as we approached the Irish coast on October 2, we were met by two Royal Navy light cruisers," remembered John Walker, a pilot with the 82nd.[11] "As they tried to fall into our zigzag pattern, one of them ran right in front of us and was cut in half." The cruiser was the HMS *Curacoa*. Of its crew of 430, only 99 survived.

Upon making landfall in Ireland, Walker and the other pilots were staged at a Royal Air Force base at Maydown, while their P-38s were assembled in Belfast, where Lockheed had an assembly facility. At the same time, they were provided with four Spitfires to maintain their flying proficiency. "We ground looped and destroyed them all in about three weeks," Walker remembered. "The P-38 was a tricycle geared aircraft, and we weren't used to flying aircraft with tail wheels. Out of all that time, I got one flight in the Spitfire."

Walker also remembered the cavalier attitude that many of his peers held toward their British hosts. Put off by the genteel bearing, educated manners, and thick accents of the RAF pilots, many of the Americans dismissed their British counterparts as sissies. "I used to tell the guys that they ought to pay attention," Walker said. "Those Brits had seen combat and a lot of them had aerial victories." In fact, Spaatz said something similar at the same time when he noted that USAAF crews sometimes had a tendency to denigrate their RAF counterparts. He made the point that the RAF was the only entity in the world that was "pounding hell out of Germany."

It was not until the Eighth put up its tenth mission, on September 6, 1942, that it suffered any losses. On that day, two bombers went down, the first of what would be thousands. Although every raid had been escorted by Spitfires, there was no good way to determine how or why losses to that point had been less than anticipated. There was a feeling among many, even among a few of the British leaders, that perhaps the USAAF was on to something good. That feeling would be sorely tested during the coming months.

Just as Eaker's VIII Bomber Command was getting off to a slow start, so was VIII Fighter Command under Brig. Gen. Frank "Monk" Hunter. Like Eaker, he had precious few units in the fight during the summer of 1942. It was ironic that for all the aircraft the United States had sent to Great Britain, the few units that Hunter had fully operational were flying British Spitfires. The flyers of the 4th, 31st, and 52nd Fighter Groups were absolutely enamored with the nimble little fighter. The pilots of the P-38 groups that had recently arrived, the 1st and the 14th, were fond enough of their own mounts but had just started their first few tentative operations as summer turned to fall. The first P-47 groups had not arrived yet, and the P-39 and the P-40 were never slated for operations out of England as they simply were not suited for high-altitude bomber-escort duties.

It was also paradoxical that a significant batch of Hunter's pilots also came courtesy of the British. The three RAF Eagle Squadrons were made up of Americans who had come to England, usually via Canada, to fight for Great Britain before the Japanese attack on Pearl Harbor. The first of the squadrons was formed in September 1940 and became operational with Hurricanes in January 1941. A total of 244 men eventually served with the three different squadrons; more than 70 of them were killed. After stiff negotiations with both the British government and the individual flyers, most of the pilots were transferred to the USAAF on September 29, 1942. They became the initial cadre of the 4th Fighter Group.

The last raid by the Eighth during September 1942 was flown on the seventh. Foul weather ruined the USAAF's mission plans for the next three weeks, and it was not until October 2 that conditions improved enough to permit another mission. Back in Washington, Arnold was beside himself. His frustration was almost childlike; he insisted that Spaatz and Eaker send out more missions but seemed to refuse the excuse that the weather was too poor. This may have been due in part to the fact that the British continued to fly. In fact, during the period from September 8 to October 1, when the Eighth flew no missions at all, the British flew raids of one sort or another on nineteen different days. But in keeping with British doctrine, their crews were not required to see their targets in order to drop their bombs; they attacked through the nighttime weather with poor accuracy.

Of course, the British raids were covered by the press, and when American citizens read that the RAF's Bomber Command was killing Germans almost nightly, they naturally wondered what the USAAF was doing. After all, the USAAF was something they were paying for, not to mention the fact that they were manning it with their sons and brothers. To their minds, it was quite reasonable to expect that it ought also to be killing Germans. As the service's top man, Arnold was on the hook to answer those expectations, and he grew weary of it.

However, by early October, the point was rapidly becoming moot. The day after the Rouen mission, on August 17, Spaatz and Eaker had been ordered to create an air force for TORCH from units that belonged to, or were slated for, the Eighth. James Doolittle, by then a brigadier general, took command of the new air force, the Twelfth, on September 23, 1942. Eisenhower, who detested the notion of invading North Africa and considered it a waste of time, materiel, and men, had nonetheless been put in charge of it. Accordingly, as he was also the commander of all American forces in the European theater, he made certain that Spaatz gave Doolittle enough units to make TORCH a success.

This essentially boiled down to much of the Eighth. Not only were the already trained and blooded 97th and 301st Bomb Groups (H) tagged for the Twelfth, but four of the Eighth's operational fighter groups and several light and medium bomber groups that had been earmarked for service in England were also slated for North Africa. More would follow. Almost as bad was the fact that the Eighth had to give up much of its equipment and materiel. Additionally, the Eighth's staff spent prodigious amounts of manpower getting the Twelfth trained and organized, which left its own Europe-specific duties wanting.

Still, Eisenhower was not satisfied. In fact, Spaatz and Eisenhower reached an impasse during September when Eisenhower, concerned that the Eighth's fledgling bombing operations were slowing the buildup of the Twelfth, ordered that those operations cease. It was an order with which Spaatz strongly disagreed, and he readied a cable to Arnold in which he outlined his objections. He knew that Arnold, ever impatient for more results, would support him against Eisenhower. Prior to sending it, Spaatz presented it to Eisenhower for review. Ultimately, the two men reached an agreement without involving Arnold. So long as Spaatz gave priority to the Twelfth, the Eighth could continue its operations.

By the end of October, Spaatz had diverted more than 25,000 men and 1,200 aircraft from the Eighth Air Force to the Twelfth. It pained him to no end; just as the trickle of aircraft into England was turning into something more, he had to give them up. Spaatz was justified when he noted, "We find we haven't much left." His air force had been gutted, and the strategic-bombing campaign against Germany suffered a setback. Still, he continued to support the expansion of the Twelfth.

American and British naval, ground, and air forces opened TORCH with assaults on French Morocco and Algeria on November 8, 1942. Vichy French forces offered scattered resistance that ran the gamut from lukewarm to quite fierce. But the bulk of the fighting was over within a few days, and Vichy resistance officially ceased on November 11. From that point, the Allies turned their attention in North Africa to squeezing Rommel and his divisions off the continent.

The American and British navies conducted the greatest part of the air operations during the TORCH landings, but USAAF units were quickly put into place as airfields were made available. These first units were the nucleus around which the Twelfth Air Force established its bridgehead in North Africa. One of the earlier movements was an inauspicious but illustrative effort that saw the P-40-equipped 33rd Fighter

Group destroy a good portion of its aircraft because of poor leadership and the friction of war.

The 33rd was embarked aboard the small escort carrier USS *Chenango*, with more than seventy P-40Fs. Dan Rathbun, a pilot with the 33rd, remembered that the ship's complement was especially attentive to their needs and that its captain was a man of intelligence and grace who hosted a special dinner for the group's officers on the eve of the invasion.[12] He wished them the very best of luck. They were stunned and embarrassed when their own commander, Lt. Col. William Momyer, responded by saying that "he couldn't wait to get ashore so that we could show the Navy how to fight."

At mid-morning on November 10, the group's planes and pilots were readied for launch; they were to land at the airfield at Port Lyautey and prepare for subsequent operations. Rathbun was in his aircraft on the bow catapult, number one for launch. He waited for the order to go and remembered killing time by watching the aircraft's rate-of-climb indicator slowly oscillate up and down coincident with the small carrier's movement across the waves.

Still, the 33rd's launch was held up because there was no confirmation that the destination airfield had been taken and was ready for their arrival. Momyer was impatient for action and decided to satisfy that impatience with one of his junior officers. Rathbun remembered Momyer's order: "Shoot Rathbun and his wingman off and we will see what the situation is." Accordingly, Rathbun and his wingman, Harry Dowd, were launched. Doubtless, their minds quickly turned over various courses of action as their mission could only be a one-way trip because the P-40 had no arresting hook and the *Chenango*'s deck was jammed with aircraft far beyond its normal operational capacity.

The two pilots covered the hundred miles or so to Port Lyautey without incident. Rathbun remembered the scene on arriving:

When we reached Port Lyautey, we could see cruisers, destroyers, amphibious-assault and merchant ships offshore, many sending small landing craft to the beaches. The sight that interested me the most involved several bomb craters on the concrete runway, all made by our Navy planes in an effort to immobilize French aircraft. There were grass fields on both sides of the north-south runway but they had been flooded and pools of water remained on the grass. While the craters were big and the debris field on the north end of the runway covered the entire width of the runway, I decided to try to land just beyond the first crater and then slip past the crater farther down the runway.

Rathbun did not have much of a choice other than to try to put his aircraft down on the torn-up runway. Damage aside, the runway was a short one, only about 2,000 feet. Rathbun lowered his landing gear and flaps, then slowed as much as he dared as he made his approach. He slowed too much. The aircraft stalled just at the edge of the bomb crater and caught the lip with its landing gear. The undercarriage was shorn off, and the P-40 smacked down hard on the runway and skidded. Rathbun was unhurt.

Dowd noted Rathbun's failed attempt, and rather than try out the cratered runway, he opted to set his fighter down alongside the runway in the muddy grass. It was no good. Dowd's approach and touchdown were fine, but as his P-40 slowed, its wheels sank in the sticky muck, and it nosed over into the ground, damaging its propeller and engine.

Rathbun crawled clear of his aircraft and ran for the Sebou River that ran along the north and east side of the airfield. A small U.S. naval vessel was moored there, and he scrambled aboard to ask that a message be passed to the *Chenango* advising that the 33rd forego flight operations until the airfield was repaired. That task done, he ran back to the airfield and prevailed on a tank crew to try to fill the craters. The tank crew was willing enough, but their machine simply was not built for that sort of work—the effort was a bust. During this entire episode, an American cruiser lobbed shells into a fort that overlooked the city. Rathbun marveled at the experience: "I was surprised and fascinated by the fact that I could both see and hear the shells as they passed over the airfield."

It was not long before Momyer arrived overhead with a large formation of P-40s. Either he had been too impatient to await word from Rathbun or he had ignored Rathbun's message. Regardless, the American war effort was about to pay for his poor judgment. On his landing approach, he could not handle the short and battered runway and, like Rathbun, tore the landing gear from his ship. One aircraft after another followed him in with similarly abysmal results. When the last of the flight was finally down, seventeen aircraft were too damaged to fly again without extensive repairs. The enemy had not lifted a finger.[13]

Rathbun was stunned when Momyer blamed him for the debacle: "Rathbun, if you had used your head, you could have prevented all of this." During the chaos of the following days, as the 33rd limped into action, Rathbun recalled that Momyer continued to "take my breath away" with regularly questionable leadership.

The Americans were green, and Momyer was far from the only one exercising bad leadership. Still, there were enough good decisions being made and enough men and materiel being put ashore that the USAAF was able to begin operations almost immediately. The roster of USAAF units expanded quickly, and it was not long until the American fliers outnumbered their German counterparts.

Indeed, it was apparent only a short time after the invasion that despite setbacks that were often its own doing, the United States would continue to expand its presence there until the Germans were pushed out. The Twelfth Air Force, supported by the Eighth, would grow to meet the task.

John Walker was part of that expansion as a P-38 pilot with the 82nd Fighter Group. Since arriving in Northern Ireland aboard the *Queen Mary* in October 1942, the group had done little except work to get their aircraft into shape. Rather than integrating into the Eighth Air Force, they were part of the huge clot of units forwarded to North Africa to join the Twelfth. Although it was an administrative movement, it was still a movement fraught with danger.

By December 1942, the 82nd's aircraft were finally assembled, checked, and ready for the flight to North Africa. The route would take them down the British Isles, over the Bay of Biscay, around the Iberian Peninsula, into the Mediterranean, and thence to Algeria. The pilots watched with anticipation as their P-38s were hung with the large ferry fuel tanks that would give them the range for the long trip south. Walker was assigned to fly the last aircraft in a flight of eight on December 27. However, once the group got airborne and on course, he noted that his aircraft's fuel-transfer system was not working. It was a common occurrence with the primitive external fuel tanks of the day.

Compounding his problem was the horrible weather; the whole of the flight to that point had been through heavy rainstorms. "Over the

Welsh coast I finally made the decision to abort the flight and made a call that I was going to land," Walker recalled. He spotted a tiny airstrip on an islet and dropped the big, twin-boomed fighter through a break in the clouds.

"That little grass strip was covered in about four or five inches of water," Walker said. He put his landing gear and flaps down and lined up for the approach. "I came in a little fast and with that heavy Lightning on all that water, there was no braking action whatsoever." Walker stood hard on the brakes as his aircraft skidded down the tiny field. As he rocketed along trailing an enormous plume of water, he noted that it resembled a neatly groomed marsh more than it did an airstrip.

Nearing the end and with no hope of getting stopped, Walker still continued to dance on the aircraft's brakes. It was to no avail. "There was a raised embankment at the end of the runway," he remembered. "And I hit it." The P-38 came apart as it jumped the berm and hurtled toward the nearby ocean. "The landing gear was torn off and the aircraft spun around and ripped the propeller off the left engine before it skidded to a stop in a minefield on the beach."

Walker was in shock. "I just sat there for a moment with the landing gear warning horn blowing in my ears. Then a British soldier made his way over to the airplane, rapped on the canopy and said, 'Hey, Yank, get out of there.' Anyway, he had a mine detector and led me out."

Walker had crash-landed at a small RAF auxiliary airfield staffed by Polish pilots who towed practice targets for antiaircraft gunners. Over the next few days, the Poles took their new American friend under their wing, even to the point where he flew several target-towing missions in their Lysanders with them. However, after a few days, RAF officialdom found him and sent him on to Lands End, Wales. "I was shacked up," he remembered, "in an old castle with twenty-one other guys who had crashed, gotten lost, or bailed out."

CHAPTER 5

Casablanca and Fighters in North Africa

B y late 1942, when young men like Jack Walker were struggling to get into the fight, the United States had been at war for nearly a year, yet expectations still exceeded reality in the context of what the Eighth Air Force was able to do from its rapidly expanding network of bases in England. At home, the American workforce was fully mobilized, and factories were churning out ever increasing numbers of aircraft, while training schools were delivering crews, albeit green ones, to man those aircraft. But to that point, the American bombers had made only shallow forays over continental Europe—and in numbers that were trifling compared to what the RAF was putting up. Indeed, Great Britain had been at war for more than three years and, by that time, was regularly launching raids of hundreds of bombers, not to mention the thousand-plane raid against Cologne the previous May.

Everyone was still impatient for bombing results from the Eighth, including the American public and the civilian and military leadership in both Washington and London. That impatience translated into more pressure that weighed heavily on Arnold and subsequently on Spaatz and Eaker. The Eighth had flown its first heavy-bomber mission on August 17, but by the end of November, it had completed only twenty-three missions, a performance that disappointed everyone. Another frustration was that the largest of those missions numbered only 108, a figure that dissatisfied Arnold as his reports showed that the Eighth had close to 200 bombers on hand.

Although unusually poor weather was the chief reason for the dismal mission count, the inexperience of nearly everyone on the scene should not be discounted. Despite its brilliance, the Eighth's staff and most of its flyers had very little experience, and many of the maintenance men were likewise new and doing a great deal of learning on the job. Additionally, they were all dependent on the logisticians—also new to their jobs—who struggled to get unprecedented quantities of materiel across the globe and into the right hands at the right time. Finally, the bases from which the units operated and the depots that supported them were being built right under the men as they tried to figure out how to make war with the air force that they were still putting together.

Surely, Arnold understood at least some of this, but he was under pressure and tried to relieve some of it by leaning on Spaatz. It was a continuous strain he would visit upon both Spaatz and Eaker, and later Doolittle, throughout much of the war. On October 25, 1942, he sent a petulant cable to Spaatz that bordered on unprofessional:

> It is believed that some powerful reason must obtain which limits your heavy-bomber operations to an apparent average of less than one per week. Weather conditions alone are not believed the cause, nor the preparation of some of the two hundred heavy bombers under your control in England for use in other theaters. Request full information on the subject.[1]

This kind of communication was not fair to Spaatz. As much as he wanted results, Arnold could not deny the realities that existed across the Atlantic. He knew and trusted Spaatz and Eaker as friends and professionals; he just wanted more to happen, and he wanted it to happen more quickly. Eager to show a payoff from the unquestionable priority that the nation had given its air forces and naturally keen for results himself, Arnold found it difficult to exercise forbearance with his commanders.

Arnold was not the only one. Great Britain, America's closest ally and the Eighth's host, was also apprehensive about the USAAF's ability to pull its weight. And well it might be worried. The British were making an enormous commitment in resources, expertise, and trust, and it desperately needed that commitment to bear fruit.

As already noted, it is commonly accepted that the British did all they could to persuade the Americans to let go of their strategy for daylight precision bombing, arguing that losses would be too high and results too low. And although that was the case to a great extent, it was not true across the board. Winston Churchill was an early supporter of the American strategy, but when the initial short-range bombing missions failed to yield anything spectacular, he began to voice doubts that grew more strident as time went on. He came to believe that American bombers might best be used against German submarine pens and for night bombing.

Churchill's stance was certainly understandable. Germany's U-boats were blasting Allied merchant shipping to the bottom of the Atlantic almost as quickly as new vessels were being built. Where bombing was concerned, he felt that a conjoined night effort with the RAF would yield better results than two separate strategies of daylight precision and nighttime area bombing. In fact, he suggested that American production lines be optimized for producing night bombers.

There were, however, defenders of the American approach within the British government and military. The general thinking was that although the USAAF's strategy was unproven and might even fail, it should at least be given a chance, especially when the Americans were on the cusp of delivering thousands of aircraft, not to mention tens of thousands of airmen, into England. All of them were trained and prepared for daylight, high-altitude precision bombing.

Archibald Sinclair, Britain's secretary of state for air, wrote to Churchill that it "would be a great tragedy if we were to frustrate them on the eve of this great experiment" and declared further that "to force them into diverting their highly trained crews to scaring U-Boats instead of bombing Germany would be disastrous." When Churchill remained unimpressed by Sinclair's argument, he wrote again, along with Air Chief Marshal Charles Portal, chief of the air staff, advising "most seriously against decrying the American plan for daylight attack of GERMANY [emphasis in original]."[2]

Air Marshal John Slessor, the RAF's assistant chief of air staff (policy), worked closely with his American counterparts. He wrote: "I think

Generals Spaatz and Eaker are good sound commanders who know their business. Through no fault of their own it is taking longer to get going than they had hoped. But when they do get going they will, I believe, show good results."[3]

Portal was, at a minimum, game to let the USAAF have a go at it. He tended to run hot and cold at the prospects for an American success. Still, he realized that if the USAAF strategy were to succeed, the payoff would be enormous. "It is solely because of the great prizes that would be gained by success that I am so keen to give the Americans every possible chance to achieve it."[4] In any case, Portal felt that the USAAF could still be encouraged to investigate night-bombing operations at the same time they pursued their daylight strategy. Another consideration was the fear that the Americans, if they sensed a lack of support from the British, might become frustrated and divert men and equipment intended for the war in Europe to the Pacific.

Another convert on the British side was Air Vice Marshal Arthur Harris. Harris had warned the Americans immediately after they entered the war that they simply could not expect to conduct daylight bombing over Europe without incurring prohibitive losses. However, his regular dealings with Eaker and the Eighth had changed his mind enough such that, if he was not totally sure of the American strategy, he at least believed that it ought to be given a chance. He grew increasingly rankled at the criticism levied by his countrymen and even engaged Churchill with a series of acerbic letters in which he championed the American cause. Worried at what Churchill might do, he wrote the prime minister that if he did not support the USAAF concept, the joint bombing operations "will be hopelessly and fatally prejudiced within the very near future for an unpredictable period, if not for keeps."[5]

At the same time that the United States and Great Britain were sniping at each other, still finding their way, the American industrial effort was picking up a massive head of steam. However they might be directed to fight, by day or by night, the airmen from the United States would have plenty of aircraft. At the same time, the Nazis did little to prepare for the coming onslaught. Indeed, not only did the German leadership fail to react to growing evidence of the massive American aircraft production effort, it flaunted a stupid and blind conceit. On October 4, 1942, Göring noted the capacity of American industry and generously declared that "the Americans do very well in technical fields" and "produce a colossal amount of fast cars." He also underscored American achievements in radio and, of all things, the manufacture of razor blades. In the end, he dismissed the aircraft production targets coming out of the United States as only so much bluff.[6]

That very same month, American plants turned out 4,065 aircraft. A year later, they would more than double that.

Just two months after TORCH, the Allied leadership came together in the Anfa Hotel just south of the French Moroccan city of Casablanca. Taking place from January 14 to January 24, 1943, the Casablanca Conference was hosted by Churchill and included Roosevelt as well as the Combined Chiefs of Staff. Churchill wanted to ensure that the initiative gained with the invasion of North Africa and the British victory over Rommel at El Alamein was sustained and capitalized upon to ensure the quickest possible defeat of Nazi Germany. And in the near term, he also wanted to ensure that the American forces pouring into England and North Africa were put to best use.

Specifically, as Eaker's aide James Parton recalled, Churchill intended to persuade Roosevelt that the USAAF should "abandon day bombing and put all our [USAAF] bomber force in England into night operations along with (and preferably under the control of) the RAF."[7] Churchill's supposed intent to mount an attack on the USAAF strategy caught the American leadership by surprise.

It is impossible to know what exactly was going on in the prime minister's mind. Just prior to the conference, he had written Sinclair that "I have never suggested that they [USAAF] be 'discouraged' by us. . . . What I am going to discourage actively, is the sending over of large quantities of these daylight bombers and their enormous ground staffs until the matter is settled one way or the other."[8] It seems apparent that Churchill was torn between pressuring Roosevelt to force the USAAF to give up daylight bombing on one hand and giving the Americans more time to prove the concept on the other.

He called for the USAAF leadership to make its case to him in private at Casablanca. That case was made on January 20, most compellingly by Eaker, who presented a one-page memorandum he had personally prepared the previous evening. It outlined in direct terms why the USAAF should pursue its daylight strategy. Its opening pulled no punches: "Day bombing is the bold, the aggressive, the offensive thing to do. It is the method and the practice which will put the greatest pressure on Germany, work the greatest havoc to his war-time industry and the greatest reduction to his air force."[9] The paper went on to state that the two air forces, the USAAF operating by day and the RAF by night, could coordinate "to wreck German industry, transportation and morale—soften the Hun up for land invasion and the kill." Churchill decided to drop his objections.

When Eaker later credited the prime minister with saving the USAAF strategy, Churchill declined to take that credit and instead commented, "If this is true, I saved them only by leaving off opposing them." Indeed, even after the conference, Churchill was still not convinced that daylight bombing could succeed. On the other hand, Arnold was ready to get his air forces to work: "We had won a major victory, for we would bomb in accordance with American principles, using the methods for which our planes were designed."[10]

The temptation to speculate on what would have happened had the Americans been compelled to give up daylight bombing is great. It is fairly safe to say without going too far afield that the war would have gone on longer. Had it done so, the advanced weapons that Germany fielded too late might have been made operational in time to turn the air war against the Allies. Too, a German industry not driven to dispersion or ruin by precision bombing might have been a decisive factor in the Nazi fight against the Soviet Union. On the other hand, the United States still could have played its ultimate trump card, the atomic bomb.

Regardless, the decision to press ahead with the USAAF's daylight strategy was only the precursor to perhaps the most important work to come out of the conference. The British and Americans agreed to continue the war until Germany's unconditional surrender and to keep the main Anglo-American effort for the near term in the Mediterranean, with an invasion of Sicily and possibly Italy later that year. The Allied leaders also directed the USAAF and RAF to coordinate their operations against Germany. This agreement was the Combined Bomber Offensive.

The Combined Bomber Offensive was articulated by the Combined Chiefs of Staff via the Casablanca Directive. The edict directed Eaker, as commander of the Eighth Air Force, and Harris, as the head of RAF's Bomber Command, as follows: "Your primary object will be the progressive destruction and dislocation of the German military, industrial and economic system and the undermining of the morale of the German people to a point where their armed resistance is fatally weakened."

The Combined Bomber Offensive was a formal instantiation of the concept Eaker had described in his memorandum to Churchill a few days earlier. The priorities of the bombing operations were to be, in order: U-boats, the Luftwaffe, transportation, and oil. The fifth priority was a catchall that allowed the commanders to strike other targets associated with the German war industry. Eaker was pointedly directed to attack the German day-fighter force, among other objectives. Responsibility for the selection of targets for both the RAF and USAAF resided with the British, specifically Portal, although the method of operations against those targets was left entirely up to Eaker and his staff.

In very bald terms, the United States was being tasked to carry the heavy part of the load, even though at that time there was no way it could do so. The Americans, with their precision bombing, would hit the sorts of targets specifically called out by the Casablanca Directive. For its part, the RAF was just starting to field its radar-bombing capability, which would give it some ability to hit the same sorts of targets. But generally, it would choose not to do so. Indeed, the British ensured that the Casablanca Directive encompassed what they were already doing and planned to continue doing: "the undermining of the morale of the German people to a point where their armed resistance is fatally weakened."

The Combined Bomber Offensive was to be executed under the stewardship of Portal. It would get off to a slow start, and there would be friction over how it would be executed. But that was in the future. The important thing to the USAAF leadership at this point was that they no longer had to seriously fight to protect their vision of daylight precision bombing at the same time they were trying to fight a war.

The period prior to and immediately after the Casablanca Conference also produced a confusing muddle of assignments, reassignments, realignments, organizations, reorganizations, and new commands. With respect to the USAAF, Lt. Gen. Frank M. Andrews was appointed commanding general of all United States forces in the European theater of operations, replacing Eisenhower while the latter commanded U.S. forces in North Africa. Spaatz was disappointed when the Eighth was taken from him and he was made air commander for all of Northwest Africa, which included the Twelfth Air Force, the British Eastern Air Command, and the Western Desert Air Force, of which the Ninth Air Force was a principal element. He had known that such a thing was possible, if not probable, as he had by necessity gotten very close to Eisenhower during preparations for TORCH. It did not help that Arnold advocated the move.

Spaatz was put under RAF Air Chief Marshal Arthur Tedder, who was made air commander in chief in the Mediterranean. Doolittle was made commander of the Northwest African Strategic Air Force under Spaatz. Eaker dodged reassignment and, in fact, was promoted out of his position and made commander of the Eighth Air Force, Spaatz's previous command. It was a fine promotion, but Spaatz was no longer the official buffer between Arnold and Eaker. The chain of command now went directly from Arnold to Eaker, who would henceforth spend considerable time, energy, and emotion handling his old friend and mentor.

The Ninth Air Force traced its heritage to the period just before Pearl Harbor but did not start combat operations until its headquarters was moved to Cairo, Egypt, during November 1942, about the same time as TORCH. It was given a hodgepodge of aircraft, including fighters, medium bombers, heavy bombers, and transports, some of which had already been operating there in close cooperation with the British. During the next several months, the Ninth supported the British Army's offensives across Egypt and Libya through the end of 1942 and into 1943, until the German surrender in Tunisia on May 13. Together with the Twelfth Air Force, it also conducted a variety of operations across the Mediterranean.

Combat operations in North Africa progressed at an intense pace even while the Allied leadership was haggling at Casablanca. The 57th Fighter Group was part of the Ninth Air Force, and its P-40 pilots spent much of January 1943 bombing and strafing Rommel's increasingly hard-pressed army as it retreated west toward Tripoli. During these operations, the group's flyers often found themselves set upon by German fighters. Although the 57th experienced some real successes during this period, the Luftwaffe was not nearly beaten.

Lt. Richard W. Kimball was in the thick of that fighting.[11] On January 20, the 57th was assigned to hit a German column moving from Tarhuna to Castel Benito. The retreating enemy forces were found, and the P-40s wheeled around for their attack. Kimball noted a flight of four Me-109s just as he dove down on the enemy vehicles. Once his bomb was away, he made a climbing turn to clear the area as quickly as possible. It did not work. "Before we could get out of the way," he recalled, "they were on us from the rear."

The 57th's fliers were quick to react to the enemy attack. Kimball saw one of his squadron mates catch an Me-109 and send it down burning. He also reacted quickly: "Looking down, I saw another [Me-109] below me and climbing." Kimball hauled his airplane over to bring his .50-caliber machine guns to bear: "I turned in and raked him across with a three-quarter burst. He turned on his back and went down in flames." Righting his aircraft, Kimball scanned the sky and found it empty. He turned for home.

"Suddenly I found myself being shot at by another Me-109 which put three bursts into my tail and then pulled off." The German's rounds had also caught Kimball in the right shoulder, causing him to momentarily lose control of his P-40. Still, he was able to get it flying again and dove into a layer of clouds.

Kimball broke out into the clear but was hit again almost immediately, this time by ground fire. His engine and fuel tank were hit, and the rear of his aircraft was stitched once more. The P-40 started to burn. "Although the ship was now on fire, I decided I better fly it as long as I could in the direction of home. I managed to keep in the air four or five minutes," he recalled. By that time, though, the aircraft was becoming uninhabitable; flames burned through the cockpit floor, and Kimball made the decision to jump.

"I cut the switches, climbed out on the right wing and jumped." At the same time, a piece of the aircraft came loose and struck him above the left eye, knocking him unconscious. When he awoke, he found himself twisting through the air but still had wits enough to pull his parachute's ripcord.

"As I descended I remember looking at my watch and trying to plan what I should do when I landed." Kimball fell to the ground, shed his parachute, and started walking to the east until he caught sight of a military unit. "I was afraid it might be the enemy until I saw some General Sherman tanks, and some jeeps, and I knew it must be British," he remembered. "They explained that they didn't have anything going to the rear, where our landing ground was. Everything was going forward and wouldn't I like to go with them?"

Kimball allowed that rather than wander the desert alone, he would indeed like to go with them. On January 23, with his new British best friends, he was unofficially the first American into Tripoli.

One of the other American pilots in North Africa at that time was Hugh Dow.[12] He was an American who had joined the Royal Canadian Air Force (RCAF) during the summer of 1941, before the U.S. entered the war. He reached England during May 1942 and completed training with the RAF on Hurricanes by the end of September. This was the same time that the Eagle Squadrons were transferred to the USAAF. Dow was one among several hundred other Americans in the RAF but not in the Eagle Squadrons who were also invited to transfer to the American service.

After accepting and taking an oath at the American embassy in London, Dow was commissioned as a second lieutenant and immediately assigned to the 350th Fighter Group. This unit was one borne of exigencies, the only one formed in Europe that had not originally been organized or activated in the United States. Two factors brought this about. First, with the commissioning of former RAF American pilots like Dow, Hunter's VIII Fighter Command found itself with a temporary surfeit of pilots. Second, the RAF had on hand, but still in crates, a substantial number of P-39s, some of which had originally been ordered by France but were delivered to Britain after the French capitulation.

The surplus pilots were paired with the unused aircraft and scheduled for operations in North Africa. Practical matters made this pairing problematic. There were no American ground crews to service the aircraft, and the aircraft were boxed up, as they had been for a while. The British air depots were already overworked, and there was no way for them to get all the aircraft assembled and tested in time for TORCH. The few aircraft available and the miserable weather meant that the pilots would get only a handful of flying hours in the P-39 before being sent into combat.

Indeed, Dow had only twenty-two hours of flying experience in the P-39 before leaving for French Morocco from Lands End on January 3, 1943. He recalled readying for the 1,200-mile flight: "I put all my personal possessions in the ammo cans. To reduce weight, we carried only 100 rounds for each of the two .50-caliber machine guns mounted in the nose." The flight was led by a B-25 with an inexperienced crew, and although there were navigational miscues along the way, Dow reached his destination. However, many of the 350th's crews did not. Of the seventy-five pilots launched to North Africa from England during January and February 1943, only sixty-one successfully made the trip; the loss rate approached 20 percent. Fortunately, all but one of the pilots survived as most of them landed short of fuel in Portugal, where they were interned.

The 350th set up shop in Algeria, and its ground crews were shipped directly over from the United States. Dow had been in Algeria for a month when he was made part of the 346th Fighter Squadron's detachment to Thelepte in central Tunisia. He and eleven other pilots flew a dozen P-39Ls to Thelepte #2, one of the two airfields located outside the small town. "We got there on February 4, 1943. It was primitive," Dow said. "We literally slept in foxholes in the ground. Our aviation gas came to us in 5-gallon flimsies and 50-gallon drums. The aircraft had to be fueled by hand. It was cold enough that we received a couple of snow showers, and when it rained, it turned everything to mud. We had two pyramidal tents covering deep trenches bulldozed in the earth, one for the mess and one for operations. Only aircraft and vehicles were above ground."

At that point in the North African campaign, Rommel was fighting a rearguard action as he retreated west from Libya into Tunisia. Dow remembered: "As we had no bombs, our primary job was to find and strafe Rommel's columns." The Germans typically took cover in dry wadis when they were available as it made it more difficult for the Allies to find and hit them. The columns comprised tanks, half-tracks, and trucks loaded with troops. They were also accompanied by plentiful towed antitank and flak guns; the 20-millimeter cannons proved to be particularly deadly against the Allied attackers.

"We usually flew at a maximum cruise speed of 275 miles per hour, right down on the deck," Dow remembered. "When we found them we raked them with our 37-millimeter cannons and six machine guns but would only make a single pass." It had been learned the hard way that making multiple attacks against a ground unit was particularly deadly as the enemy typically was prepared and ready after the first pass. "Of course, they still shot back at us with every sort of weapon they could bring to bear: rifles, pistols, flak batteries and tank guns. There were streams of tracer rounds and the blue-white 20-millimeter flak puffs that seemed to walk across the sky toward us."

Dow's experience was typical as the USAAF used the P-39 primarily as a ground-attack aircraft. Subsequently, detractors have unfairly denigrated its usefulness as a fighter. It is true that equipped with only one supercharger, the aircraft's performance dropped off dramatically above medium altitude. Additionally, it was fairly short-legged, and combat sorties seldom exceeded one hour without a drop tank. Nevertheless, Dow recollected that the aircraft had attributes that made it a good fighter at low altitudes. "It only had one 'lung,'" he recalled of the P-39's single supercharger, "so its performance at altitude suffered drastically above about 15,000 feet. However, it actually had pretty impressive performance down low against the Me-109. The RAF tested it against a captured example of the Me-109 in July of 1941 and found that below 15,000 feet the P-39 could outrun and out dive the Me-109. It was the same against the Spitfire. On the other hand, the Me-109 could easily outclimb the P-39 at any altitude." Moreover, the P-39 also had a slight turning advantage against contemporary Me-109s.

Furthermore, the model of the P-39 that Dow flew, the P-39L, was decently armed. It fired a 37-millimeter cannon through the propeller spinner. Dow remembered: "Its rate of fire was pretty slow and we only carried 30 rounds. Still, when you hit something with it, it really made a dent." The aircraft also carried two .50-caliber machine guns in the nose with 200 rounds of ammunition each and two .30-caliber machine guns in each wing with about 1,000 rounds of ammunition each.

On February 15, 1943, Dow and the rest of the detachment were out of their foxholes well before dawn for what was scheduled to be a fairly typical mission. "We were supposed to fly over to Thelepte #1 to pick up a couple of flights of [USAAF] Spitfires as escorts for another strafing mission. We'd normally fly very low and they would fly cover for us at about 6,000 feet which was above the effective altitude of the 20-millimeter flak."

The arrangement made good tactical sense but did not always work out well in actual operations. "First," Dow explained, "it was difficult for them to keep sight of us, especially after we started smearing mud on our aircraft in an attempt to make ourselves less visible. Second, it was difficult for them to stay up with us; we flew at about 275 miles per hour on the deck. Then again, they left us on at least one occasion with no warning at all to chase after enemy fighters. A month later they did the same thing with another unit and the P-39s got slaughtered." Another factor that contributed to the difficulty of keeping track of the P-39s was the fact that the Spitfire pilots had to maintain a constant scan around their own formation so as not to be surprised by German fighters.

"We were delayed from taking off for a few minutes," Dow recollected, "while our ground crews wiped dew from the two-inch-thick glass armor plate that sat just behind the Plexiglas windshield. The space between was quite close and very difficult to access. But we got airborne as two flights of four and started a turn toward Thelepte #1 where we were supposed to rendezvous with Spitfires from the 31st Fighter Group. I was a wingman on Captain Charles Hoover's right wing." Dow did not know it at the time, but Thelepte #1 was being strafed by a group of Me-109s.

The P-39 crews did not anticipate any sort of German action at that point. It was only just after dawn, the nearest enemy airfield was more than fifty miles away, there was a two-ship patrol already airborne, and the Germans had never hit their base before. "But, all of a sudden," Dow recalled, "Hoover started climbing at a really steep angle and it was all I could do to keep up." It took a couple of seconds for Dow to discover why Hoover had started up so aggressively. "I finally spotted a pair of Me-109s only about 200 yards in front of us crossing in a turn from left to right."

The German fighters were blind to the P-39s clawing up behind them. "I lined up on the trailing aircraft on the right side," said Dow. "I opened fire and noted some hits in his fuselage, but we were climbing so steeply that I couldn't stay with him—I was running out of airspeed fast." Finally, unable to stay with the swiftly climbing enemy fighters, Dow let the nose of his aircraft drop down through the horizon in a steep dive toward the ground.

It was then that he spotted another Me-109 diving away low and to his right. "I started after him immediately—he was about 400 yards away and headed for the ground." Dow pushed his aircraft for all it was worth. The German fighter crossed Thelepte #2 about fifty feet above the ground with Dow hard after him. "It was good for the G.I.s on the airfield to see that this really was a shooting war," he said.

Closing on the German fighter, Dow positioned himself for the kill. "My 37-millimeter cannon had jammed after the first shot against that earlier set of fighters. Fortunately we could charge all the guns from the cockpit. I grabbed the T-handle that was attached to a cable fixed to the arming block and pulled it all the way up to my right ear."

Dow nearly flew up the German's tail. "He was down at about thirty feet and I was bouncing around in his prop wash and slipstream. I doubt that he ever saw me; I don't think he had a rear view mirror. Anyway, I closed up to pointblank range as he suddenly moved up to about a hundred feet before starting back down. I let loose with all seven guns."

Dow's fire shredded the Me-109. "He chopped his throttle while I did the same to stay behind him and stood the bird on in its wing tip to keep him in sight as I flew over him." It really would not have mattered if Dow had overshot. The enemy fighter was a wreck. Aside from dozens of machine-gun holes, the cannon had nearly blown its rudder off, and the pilot only barely managed to set his ship down on the flat, scrub-desert floor. Dow rolled his P-39 nearly inverted as he shot over the top of the Me-109. "That airplane just disappeared in a billowing cloud of dirt. He was probably going close to 150 miles per hour when he hit the ground. I didn't know whether he had survived, or not."

Dow wasted little time getting back to the airfield: "I was flying around by myself with enemy fighters in the vicinity—it was not a smart thing to do." As soon as the P-39s were refueled and rearmed, their pilots got them airborne again and headed out again on the original mission to shoot up the retreating German columns. When that sortie was over, Dow rounded up the squadron's intelligence officer and a jeep. Together, they bounced out through the desert scrub looking for the downed fighter.

"We found it about where I thought we would, two or so miles from our airfield," said Dow. "There was already another jeep there with four French soldiers guarding the German pilot, who was sitting on the ground with a bandage on his head. Standing back a little bit was a big crowd of Arabs in their ragged clothes."

When the German pilot was advised that Dow had been his opponent, he jumped up, snapped to attention, and popped him a smart salute. "I saluted back and then started negotiating with the French so that I could take this guy back to the airfield. They really didn't want to let him go—he was quite a prize!" Ultimately, Dow convinced the French soldiers that the German needed to be interrogated, and they agreed to let him go with the understanding that he was still their prisoner.

"I broke off the loose stabilizer and wrenched out the instrument panel clock before we took him back," Dow recalled. The French also sent along an armed guard. This German was a tall, good-looking, blond fellow and seemed nice enough. His name was Karl Reinbacher, an enlisted man, an *Unteroffizier*. "As it turned out, when we were finished with him he did have to go back to the French and they kept him until a year after the war."

Although his fighting retreat was one of desperation, Rommel's forces were able to regroup and join up with reinforcements flowing in from across the Mediterranean. Only two days after Dow had scored his first aerial victory, he joined the rest of the USAAF forces when they evacuated the airfields at Thelepte at dawn on February 17, 1943. They stood directly in the path of Rommel's forces as they advanced toward their final major victory in North Africa at Kasserine Pass. The American pilots flew another strafing mission against the approaching panzers while their ground crews put all non-flyable aircraft to the torch.

The 346th's detachment had been at Thelepte for two weeks before the German columns overran the airfields there. "During that time," Dow recalled, "We flew approximately 100 sorties and lost four P-39s shot down and another pilot wounded and grounded."

During this period, the USAAF was still building the Twelfth with green crews—there really were no other kind. While Churchill, Roosevelt, and the Combined Chiefs of Staff charted out the course of the war, Lt. John Walker, who had crashed his P-38 along the Welsh coast while ferrying it from Ireland to North Africa finally received orders to fly a photo-reconnaissance version of the P-38, an F-5, to North Africa. He flew as part of a large and varied gaggle of B-17s, B-25s, P-38s, P-39s, and B-24s, all destined for Doolittle's Twelfth Air Force. Walker did not crash during this trip, and after a grueling flight of eight hours and twenty minutes, he taxied his aircraft in front of the headquarters of the 5th Photographic Reconnaissance Group, commanded by Lt. Col. Elliot Roosevelt, the son of the president.

"The sergeant who parked me told me to hurry up with the paperwork and to go inside. I was going to be reassigned to the photo-reconnaissance outfit." Walker had no desire to join the "Photo Freddie" unit and slipped nonchalantly away from his aircraft to an adjacent hangar where he had earlier noticed some twin-engine French Dewoitine aircraft. "I found a French pilot who spoke English," he remembered, "and he told me that they delivered mail around to the other airfields and that he knew where the 82nd Fighter Group was. Well, I crawled on top of a pile of mail sacks, and a few hours later, I was back with my original unit! My buddies wanted to know where the hell I'd been," Walker said. "They thought I was dead."

Part of the Twelfth Air Force, the 82nd Fighter Group was based at Telergma, Algeria. Up to that point, after only a month in theater, the group had already lost nearly 10 percent of its pilots. "North Africa was a disaster early on," said Walker. "We got our asses kicked. The guys told me that I was fresh meat and that the Me-109 pilots were really good." An indication of the desperate mindset of the time is that Walker, separated by months from any meaningful training whatsoever, was still sent into combat the very next day.

He was assigned as a wingman to one of the squadron's few captains for a bomber escort mission. "I thought that I wouldn't have much to worry about because the captain would take care of me." Sure enough, the Germans showed up, and a twisting, turning melee ensued. Walker admitted that in his fear and confusion and in his desperation to stick with his flight lead, he never caught sight of the fight. "The only thing I saw was shell casings coming out of my flight lead's aircraft as he fired his guns. I never saw a single German aircraft." After the mission, Walker considered his situation: "I needed to get my head out of my ass if I was going to last very long."

Walker slowly built up missions and combat time. On March 7, 1943, he was part of an early-morning bomber escort. Just off the Tunisian coast, Walker and his flight lead spotted an Italian three-engine seaplane, a CANT Z.506 B. It was a type commonly used for bombing and reconnaissance. The great lumbering aircraft was crossing the flight path of the formation, from left to right. "This guy had no business in the world being where he was—just off the coast like that," Walker recounted.

Following his flight lead down to the deck in a sweeping righthand turn, Walker watched as his leader's machine-gun fire fell harmlessly into the sea behind the enemy aircraft. Careful not to make the same mistake, Walker ensured that he pulled enough lead, then watched with satisfaction as pieces flew from the enemy aircraft and it caught fire. "Just before it hit the water, I saw this guy jump out of the side of the airplane," remembered Walker. "I have no idea whether or not he lived."

Walker scored again the following month on another mission as part of a low-level sea-sweep escorting B-25s on April 5, 1943. By that time, the North African campaign was nearing a conclusion. Together, the well-blooded British armies and their newly blooded American counterparts had squeezed Rommel's undersupplied and increasingly desperate divisions into an ever-smaller piece of Tunisia.

Still, the Germans tried to hang on. Having lost most of their capacity to move materiel across the Mediterranean by ship, they relied more and more on air transport. The results had not been good, and Adolf

Galland made a trip to Tunis to inspect his hard-pressed fighter units. Along with every other task they could possibly perform, they were expected to help protect the air transports. He recalled the performance of the transport crews:

> Supplying the encircled troops by air demanded catastrophic losses. The transport planes could not be adequately protected. Of the still available aircraft more and more fell out because of the shortage of spare parts. . . . Despite this, they continued to supply the troops in Tunis right to the last. The performance of the transport crews is beyond praise.[13]

Indeed, Germany's desperation was such that the burden for supplying its armies in North Africa fell in large part to the Luftwaffe.

"As we crossed the coast of Tunisia," Walker remembered, "someone called out 'Good God, look at twelve o'clock.' I had been checking our rear, and when I turned back around, it looked like a swarm of bees. There was a huge flight of Ju-52s bringing gas to Rommel along with a bunch of other aircraft."

The B-25s made a turn to get out of the field of play while the P-38s tore into the lumbering German transports with a viciousness that ripped the enemy formation of more than one hundred aircraft into pieces. "I took one look and wondered how we were going to handle this," Walker said. "The 1st Fighter Group, flying high cover, dropped their belly tanks right on top of us. The radio chatter was horrendous. I couldn't hear anything and I couldn't call anybody. I just pushed the throttles forward and flew into the fight. I lost sight of my flight leader in the first turn."

Walker made a diving turn for the deck trying to track the action as best he could. "I thought to myself that everyone was going too fast, so I cracked a bit of combat flaps to slow myself down. I remember that the crews in the Ju-52s were firing out of every opening that they could stick a gun out of. I lined up on one and started firing. It exploded and tumbled right into the water."

Walker tried to make sense of the swirling massacre that the fight had become and saw another flight of P-38s barreling through the Ju-52s. Again, he thought to himself that they were going much too fast.

Still alone, he made a complete circle and prepared for another run on the slow transports. Just as he prepared to fire on his second victim, another P-38 cut him off, only an instant away from receiving the full brunt of Walker's guns. "I took another look," he recounted, "and right in front of this other P-38 was a Ju-88 medium bomber sitting in the middle of all these Ju-52s. The rear gunner was firing and I wanted to shoot at him but I couldn't get the other P-38 to move over." Finally, he got off a burst of gunfire and observed strikes on the enemy aircraft.

"I made another turn to follow a different Ju-52, which was trying to get out of the area. But my guns quit. I had burned them out. Instead of firing short bursts, I had been firing long bursts, which had burned them out." The M2 .50-caliber machine gun that was the primary weapon of American types during the war fired a fast, hard-hitting round at a rate of fire approaching 800 rounds per minute. However, if fired in bursts much longer than a second each, the rifling tended to degrade and accuracy suffered.

At this point, with shouts over the radio that Me-109s had now joined the fray, Walker pointed his aircraft landward and pushed it as fast as it would go. Looking to his side, he was surprised to find that he had been joined by two P-38s from the 1st Fighter Group. The neophyte wingman had become an ad hoc flight leader.

Now without enough fuel to return to his base at Telergma, Walker led the other two P-38s to a small British coastal search-and-rescue base. While they waited overnight for fuel, they and a number of other P-38 pilots called in their claims over a primitive hand-cranked telephone.

During early 1943, American military forces were still trying to figure out the best way to make war. In particular, the U.S. Army Air Forces had grown from 57,000 personnel in 1940 to more than 1.7 million by January 1943, more than a twenty-five-fold increase in three years. Consequently, almost no one had enjoyed anything close to a full military career, and many tried to apply rules and regulations that were appropriate for a training environment, but which had no place in real operations.

Hugh Dow remembered the early part of his service in North Africa: "That was when orders were still being issued by dictators the next level up, or at higher levels, that no one dared to question, whether they made any sense or not." He recalled being "appalled at the uptight culture of the U.S. Army when I transferred over from the RAF, which by that time [October 1942] had more than three years of battle experience."

Dow noted that the British had long since stopped focusing on unimportant details: "The RAF had gotten over any prewar spit-and-polish nonsense that did not contribute directly to the war effort, and they devoted their full attention to winning the war . . . about which they were deadly serious. The RAF was no pushover and those who broke the rules were disciplined, but there was no petty stuff by the time I joined them in England, in May 1942."

After transferring from the RAF to the USAAF as a new second lieutenant, Dow was sent to RAF Station Coltishall as part of the initial cadre of the 346th Fighter Squadron. He was heartily unimpressed by what he encountered: "I recall some of the second lieutenants, products of Air Corps training, trying to order around other second balloons [second lieutenants] with less time in grade than they had. They reminded me more of my days in high school ROTC than of men ready for battle. But somehow during the first year of operations we slowly overcame that pre-war attitude, at least at the squadron and group level, and began treating subordinates as grownups. But in those early days in North Africa, no one stuck their neck out to question arbitrary directives."

In fact, as the Allied situation solidified during 1943, the Germans, try as they might, could not overcome the masses of men and materiel that the Allies brought ashore in North Africa. Consequently, the USAAF found time to indulge itself in the sorts of administrative absurdities that Dow noted. If nothing else, it indicated that things were going reasonably well in the theater.

An incident that happened to Maurice Duvic is a good example. He was a B-26 copilot and part of a group of crews ferrying twenty-two aircraft from the United States to join the 17th Bomb Group in Algeria. Before he departed the States, he was given $5,000 in per diem cash and instructions to disburse it to the other members of the formation as required.

When his aircraft was destroyed in April 1943 in a takeoff incident at Saleh, Morocco, much of the money burned with it. Incredibly, while all stops were being pulled to finish off Rommel and press the Germans throughout the rest of the Mediterranean, an investigation was opened to probe the circumstances surrounding the loss of the aircraft, funds, and personal property.

"They appointed a board of second lieutenants fresh out of ROTC training," recalled Duvic.[14] The investigation was a ridiculous little affair that seemed grossly out of context considering the wartime circumstances. "When they pressed my pilot, Max Zimmerle, about whether or not I had tried to retrieve the money after we crashed, he blew up: 'Dumbass! He was trying to get out of the burning airplane!'" The investigation wasted nearly two months before Duvic, and the rest of the crew were cleared of any sort of negligence or culpability and sent to join the 17th Bomb Group.

CHAPTER 6

Romance, Submarines, and Sicily

The Americans came pouring into England in increasingly larger numbers beginning late in 1942. During the course of the war, the United States sent nearly two million men to or through the British Isles. Of these men, nearly half a million were from the USAAF. As the English population numbered only about fifty million, the impact of the Americans was significant.

But their arrival was noteworthy not only because there were so many of them, but for other reasons as well. Most important, the appearance of units from the United States was a physical manifestation of the commitment of Great Britain's dearest ally. Nevertheless, that commitment had its price. American men and equipment—and the hundreds of new bases and installations that were built to house them—stressed Britain's economy and infrastructure. Farms were displaced, roads and bridges were used hard, and small village economies were sorely disrupted.

The Americans also had a cultural influence on the British. Compared to their hosts, who at this point in the war had already endured years of rationing and deprivation, the U.S. servicemen were well-fed, healthy, and pink with enthusiasm and vigor. Their accents, which most of the British previously knew only from Hollywood movies, were exotic. Additionally, they were paid relatively well compared to their English counterparts and had access to goods that had long before disappeared from English shelves. In short, they were novel, exciting, and comparatively well-off.

Although British sentiment regarding their cousins from across the Atlantic was overwhelmingly positive and generous, there was cause for resentment from some quarters. The USAAF represented a young male population in a country that had sent many of its own young men overseas. Young British women, without young British men, naturally filled that void with young American men. As might be expected, this caused some bitterness. If a British serviceman fighting in North Africa or languishing in a Japanese prison camp was aggrieved that the girl he had not seen in a year or more had dropped him in favor of an exciting new American who was stationed nearby, it was not without some justification.

Still, it is easy to generalize and forget that these were real people with real feelings living real lives. When American servicemen flying from British bases started dying over Europe, everything became very real indeed. Whereas the British had initially engaged their allies with careful reserve, villagers and townsmen across England soon began referring to their local contingents of Americans as, "Our Yanks."

Maurice Paulk was a supply man at Molesworth, where the 303rd Bomb Group (H) was based. During his thirty-three months in England, he enjoyed tremendous hospitality from the Parkes family in Dudley. He was at a local pub one night when he was extended an invitation:

A young fellow surrounded by about four girls and a male friend of his asked us to join them. We were the first Yanks that they had been able to talk to. Made several friends that evening. Harold, the Englishman, a couple months later invited me to supper and to stay all night. They treated me as a family member and a guest too. Many is the time that I have eaten the only egg in the house, drank the last glass of milk and was given the only piece of meat. I tried to explain that we were well fed on base and please don't favor me. My words were to no avail.[1]

It was inevitable that romantic associations were also formed, as happened with eighteen-year-old Pauline "Bobby" Roberts of Northampton and S/Sgt. Joseph "Zip" Zsampar, a ball-turret gunner with the 303rd Bomb Group (H) out of Molesworth.[2] Bobby Roberts was a beautiful and vivacious girl, the daughter of a thrice-married ballerina and fashion model. Zsampar, the son of Hungarian immigrants, was an accomplished artist and sculptor. When he arrived at Molesworth in September 1942, he was twenty.

Bobby Roberts, a competitive swimmer, was an otherwise typical young woman who loved to socialize with her friends and especially liked to attend dances at the military bases that were sprouting like mushrooms across the Northampton countryside. At one of these events, she met the dark-eyed, good-looking Zsampar.

Neither of them was old enough to have previously loved long and hard. Bobby had earlier enjoyed a tender association with a Free Frenchman, but it compared not at all to the romance that developed between her and Zsampar. While the young American might fly and fight over Europe one day, the next could very well see him and Bobby walking hand-in-hand through Northampton or sightseeing in London. As Zsampar's mission count grew through the winter of 1942, so did the ardor between him and Bobby. During January 1943, they were engaged to be married.

Zsampar's combat flying with the 303rd contrasted spectacularly with his quiet courtship of Bobby Roberts. The mission—or rather the slaughter—of January 23, 1943, is instructive. The group sent twenty-one B-17s on an attack against the U-boat pens at Brest, where the Germans met them with forty-five fighters and an astoundingly heavy flak barrage. The 303rd lost five bombers over the target area, and another four crash-landed at various points in England. Zsampar's aircraft, *Idaho Potato Peeler*, was one of those that crashed. The pilot, Lt. Ross Bales, was able to belly the big bomber into a field near the village of Chipping Warden without injuring any of his crew.

Zsampar gave his English love a portrait of himself. On the reverse side, he wrote, "America lend-leased this soldier to England's fairer sex. Handle with care and return in good order." Their romance continued to develop into the spring of 1943. It included an evening at the posh Trocadero restaurant in central London during which a German bomb blew the windows out of the dining room where the two young people huddled against each other under their table.

The courtship ended tragically. A mission was scheduled against the submarine pens and yard at Kiel, Germany, on May 14, 1943. On the night before, Zsampar sent a friend into Northampton to break the date he had scheduled with Bobby. The mission was remarkable for the number of fighters—more than 100—the Luftwaffe put into the air against the group. The consensus among the crews was that they had never before seen so many enemy aircraft.

Astonishingly, especially considering the fierce German defenses, the 303rd lost only one aircraft. Sadly for Bobby Roberts, that aircraft was Ross Bales's new bomber, *FDR's Potato Peeler Kids.* Joseph "Zip" Zsampar was aboard. The B-17 was last seen spinning down to the sea. Although six parachutes were observed coming from the aircraft, no survivors were recovered.

Naturally, Bobby was devastated. There was nothing she could do. Since she was only Zsampar's fiancé and not his wife, she had no official relationship to him, and his effects were boxed and sent home. Physically and materially, the American airman was out of her life. Spiritually, he was not. The effects of his loss stretched decades beyond his relationship with the English girl. Her daughter from a later marriage, Louise Smedley-Hampson, remembered: "Two photos exist of Mum, puffy-faced from crying; she had Zip's air force wings pinned to her pink polka dot dress." Despite her rigid Catholic upbringing, Bobby Roberts went to a medium to try to establish contact with Zsampar and had no success. "The consequence of this bizarre interview," continued her daughter, "was that in later years after drinking one too many glasses of sherry, Mum would declare that Zip had not died, but swum ashore and was living in France with amnesia."

Bobby eventually married Louise's father, "a gentle, humourous, artistic soul who deserved more out of life than being someone's second choice." Louise remembered that her mother never got over the loss. "Indeed, Mum spent the rest of her life, bitter and angry, but still speaking of Zip in tones of adulation that were never used when talking about anyone else."

Some version of this heartrending calamity struck regularly in England. Nevertheless, the majority of relationships did not end so disastrously. In fact, the end of the war saw more than 70,000 British war brides leave England for the United States.

While the fighting was raging in North Africa, men and equipment intended for the Eighth Air Force in England continued to cross the Atlantic from the United States. The voyage, especially at that point in the war, could be especially dangerous as the German submarine wolf packs were still very active. Ray Marner of the 44th Bomb Group (H) recalled the scene from the deck of the British merchantman *Chantilly* as his convoy, HX-228, was hit during the night of March 10–11, 1943, by more than a dozen U-boats:

> About 6:30 P.M. we heard an explosion and the muster bell rang. We grabbed our clothes and went on deck in time to see an oil tanker on our starboard side. It was split right in two. Two other ships were sunk as well. About midnight we were attacked again. . . . I think they got two more ships. . . . About 3 A.M. we heard a terrific explosion and a munitions boat was hit. The flames grew larger and larger until they lit up the whole convoy. It was just like day outside. We were perfect targets so a destroyer shelled the ship so it would explode. . . . Flames shot thousands of feet in the air and died down quickly. All men lost their lives.[3]

Eaker could not destroy the Luftwaffe without men and equipment, and too much of it was drowning in the Atlantic. Still, he was not overly eager to send his crews after the enemy submarines or the infrastructure that supported it. Personally, his first priority was the destruction of the Luftwaffe, but there was little associated with the German U-boats that intersected with his desire to do battle with the Luftwaffe.

Some who outranked Eaker thought otherwise. Churchill was desperately afraid that England might be cut off and saw the Eighth as a weapon that might be able to help defeat the German U-boat threat. Specifically, he wanted the American bombers to hit the submarine pens in France and the yards in Germany. Moreover, Churchill was backed up by the Casablanca Directive, which listed submarine targets as the first priority. Indeed, missions related to U-boats consumed the lion's share of resources through much of 1943. In fact, 63 percent of the bomb tonnage it dropped in the first half of 1943 was expended against submarine targets.[4] To be certain, Eaker did have some interest in mitigating the submarine threat; were the Germans allowed to run wild, it was possible he would never receive enough men and materiel to prosecute the strategic air campaign.

The mission of May 14, 1943, was directed against the Krupp Submarine Building Works at Kiel. It was made up of 109 B-17s and 21 B-24s, all from the 44th Bomb Group (H). The raid was one of the largest to date and included closely coordinated diversions and attacks on secondary targets. Another unusual aspect was that part of the route was flown at wave-top level over the North Sea in order to stay below German radar. Norman Kiefer aboard the B-24 *Old Crow* remembered standing between the pilots on the flight deck: "There, spread across the sea, was the greatest armada of American aircraft I had ever seen. We had to be invincible!"[5]

Approaching the Frisian Islands, the B-17s and B-24s climbed to 25,000 feet in preparation for the bomb run. The small group of B-24s trailed the slower B-17s and S-turned to keep from running them down. Once over the target, the B-17s loosed their high-explosive bombs. The B-24s followed with sticks of incendiaries intended to burn the wreckage the B-17s created.

Paul Reed was the pilot of *Scrappy*, one of the trailing B-24s.[6] He remembered that the 44th had loosened its formation because the incendiaries tended to fall erratically, and there was concern that they might strike the trailing aircraft if a normal formation was flown. The Luftwaffe rose to meet the Americans, and Reed watched as an FW-190 attacked his ship from nearly head-on just before the B-24s released their bombs: "And as the puffs of bursting 20-mm . . . ammo came toward us, it became apparent that the line of fire would put the successive bursts right into our cockpit. Purely reflex action alone caused me to hit the wheel in a dive to try to get below the line of fire, but unfortunately, the bursts did not quite clear the plane, but hit the top turret directly behind the cockpit."

The shell of the top turret was blasted off of the B-24, and its gunner, Sgt. Adam Wygonik, slammed to the flight deck from his position at the top of the aircraft. He was bleeding from his face and upper torso and was too badly injured to tend to himself. The radio operator, Alan Perry, immediately assessed Wygonik's condition, giving the stricken man oxygen and trying to treat his wounds.

But Wygonik was too far gone. It was obvious to Perry that even if the aircraft was not shot down, the badly hit airman would not survive the flight back to England. He snapped a parachute to Wygonik and put the wounded man's hand on the ripcord ring. Then, nearly unconscious from lack of oxygen, he turned back to retrieve a portable oxygen bottle. When he clamped the mask to his face and turned back around, Wygonik was gone. The pilot, Reed, remembered: "Apparently either intentionally or otherwise, Adam had rolled off the flight deck, onto the catwalk in the open bomb bay. The bay doors were still open as we were on the bomb run. No one could say for sure that Adam's chute had opened since all attention was on fighting off the attacking aircraft."

Scrappy was in trouble. One engine was smoking, part of the left vertical stabilizer and rudder were shot away, the aircraft had been holed by multiple 20-millimeter cannon rounds, the top turret was essentially shot away, and the left landing gear hung out from the wing. Reed nosed his damaged ship over and joined a lower group of B-17s for protection. He recalled: "After the fighter attacks broke off, we flew pretty much alone back to England."

Once over the 44th's airfield at Shipdham, Reed and his crew tried to get *Scrappy* into condition to land. However, the aircraft's landing gear would come down only partway. If Reed and his copilot put the aircraft down on the runway, it would block other aircraft from landing. If they put it into the grass, the landing gear might dig in and cartwheel the aircraft. Reed recounted his decision: "I bailed the crew out over the field except for my co-pilot, George Winger. We flew the plane back out toward the coast, where I set it on automatic pilot. George bailed out first and I was close behind. After *Scrappy* crossed the coast, it was shot down by a flight of Spitfires."

As it developed, the injured flight engineer and top turret gunner, Adam Wygonik, did indeed survive. He recalled that Alan Perry actually did push him clear of the aircraft: "I landed in Kiel near the target area, was soon picked up by German troops and taken at once to a hospital where I was well-treated and confined as a patient for a few days; then sent to Sandbastel hospital just a few miles from Kiel, where I recuperated from most of my injuries. Later I had my right eye removed at a hospital in Vienna, Austria."

The strike had not been escorted all the way to the target, and it had cost the 44th five aircraft and crews. Overall, the Eighth lost eleven bombers. One of those bombers had carried "Zip" Zsampar.

By the spring of 1943, the United States was racing to meet the requirements called for by AWPD-42, which had been submitted the previous September as an update to AWPD-1. The defeat of Germany was still the overarching objective of the new plan, with the destruction of the Luftwaffe as the overriding intermediate priority and aircraft and engine factories as the top enabling priority. To achieve its stated objectives, AWPD-42 called for a U.S. Army Air Force numbering 2.7 million men. Already, in May 1943, it tallied 2.2 million personnel and would dramatically slow its growth to a peak of 2.4 million in July 1944. Essentially, by the spring of 1943, the USAAF had all the men it needed to win the war; it needed only to train and field them.

But whereas AWPD-1 and AWPD-42 outlined objectives and the manpower and materiel requirements for meeting those objectives, they did not prescribe a detailed plan for *how* the objectives were to be met. Accordingly, in the early spring of 1943, Eaker hosted a combined USAAF/RAF team to devise a plan for carrying out the Combined Bomber Offensive as ordered by the Casablanca Directive.

The Combined Bomber Offensive plan called for four phases of complementary actions between the USAAF and the RAF. The phases were generally focused on hitting German targets at ever-increasing penetration ranges with growing numbers of bombers as they came available. The plan was accepted by Eaker and his RAF counterparts and subsequently championed by Eaker to the Joint Chiefs of Staff in Washington during April 1943. It was accepted and thereafter presented to the Combined Chiefs of Staff, who adopted it on May 18, 1943, at the Trident Conference in Washington.

The endorsed plan was subsequently codified and given the name POINTBLANK, which directed that the German aircraft industry was the new priority target system and that the destruction of the Luftwaffe was the chief overriding intermediate objective. The case had been made, understood, and accepted that air superiority had to be achieved prior to the planned invasion of Europe.

If the May 14, 1943, strike on the submarine yards at Kiel had been costly and if it had failed to scratch Eaker's itch to hit the German air force, he could at least take comfort in knowing the Luftwaffe would defend important targets. At the same time, though, he knew that these operations were costing him dearly in crews and aircraft. Loss rates were running at approximately 6 percent during this period; the aggregate odds of a crew completing twenty-five missions were only about 20 percent.[7]

One of the reasons for the high loss rate was that the Luftwaffe had adapted head-on attacks by massed groups of more heavily armed fighters. Air Corps tests during the late 1930s had mistakenly shown that these tactics were too difficult to execute and had thus neglected the development of protection and defensive fire in its bombers against these sorts of attacks. Nonetheless, the German pilots were able to master the tactic. It was found to be more effective than the more natural inclination of the pilots to peck away at the rear or edges of the formations in small groups, or even as ones or twos. Ultimately, the USAAF added turreted guns to the nose sections of the B-17 and B-24 to dissuade Luftwaffe flyers from these frontal assaults. The results were middling as the Germans still practiced head-on gunnery passes until the end of the war.

The oddest events sometimes occurred on bombing missions. Walter Baker of the 487th Bomb Group (H) recounted one unpleasant, if not immediately dangerous, episode: "We were at altitude near the Zuider Zee. All of a sudden, the ball turret gunner, Kenny Brouhard, called out over the intercom, 'Hey . . . hey, I've got something all over my turret! Something just splashed all over my turret and guns!' Our pilot, Frank Chaffee, asked him, 'Well, what is it? What's it look like Ken?"[8]

"Ken hesitated a second," recalled Baker. "Then he called up, 'It looks . . . it looks like shit!' And sure enough, that's what it turned out to be. When we got back we found out that some of the officers in the planes in front of us had gotten some bad chow and ended up with really bad diarrhea. They crapped in their flak helmets, then pitched it out a hatch near the nose. That's how it ended up all over Kenny."

At the end of a mission, Hollywood often has the ragged, worn-out bomber crews stumbling out of their aircraft and into the dispensary, or the barracks, or the bar. That was not the case as there was much for them to do once they got safely back on the ground. Aside from debriefing and other tasks, the gunners were responsible for taking care of their weapons. The heavy M2 .50-caliber machine guns had to be removed from the aircraft after every mission. There were thirteen of them on the B-17G, each, with their accessories, weighing more than seventy-five pounds. Just getting them out of the aircraft was an enormous chore. Walter Baker recalled, "They had to be cleaned. We'd take them to the armory, pull them apart, clean them, put them back together and then coat them with a light application of oil. The next day we'd go back, take them apart again, clean them again, then put them back together and coat them with a special lubricant. Then they'd be ready to go."

Each crewmember was responsible for the guns at his position and would use the same ones on each mission. "We were really careful about making sure there was no moisture in or on them," Baker said. "Any water at all would freeze them solid once we got to altitude." It was typical for the crews to test fire the guns over the English Channel on the way to the target. "If we found something wrong, technically we could fix it, but it was so cold—minus 40 degrees Fahrenheit—that if a guy had to take his gloves off he risked losing fingers to frostbite. Several crewmen did."

The invasion of Sicily, Husky, was mandated at the Casablanca Conference, and planning had been going on since then. Although there had been missteps along the way, the American buildup in North Africa had been huge. The British and American armies forced the Germans and Italians who were not able to escape the continent, which was most of them, to surrender on May 13, 1943. Following that victory, the near-term goal was Sicily, with the invasion scheduled for early July.

As commander of Northwest African Air Forces, Spaatz was extremely aggressive during this period and during the Sicilian campaign and beyond. In fact, the important island fortress of Pantelleria, which was located halfway between Tunisia and Sicily and garrisoned by Italians, was heavily bombed and forced into surrender by airpower alone, a result that greatly heartened Spaatz. He meant the Mediterranean operations to showcase the effects of airpower on the battlefield and greatly resented that not only were his air units subordinate to ground commanders, but he also begrudged the command arrangements with the British. He wanted American air forces out from under both. At one point, he even discussed the notion of a separate air force with visiting senators.[9]

The A-36 Invader (the official name was Apache) was a dive-bombing variant of the Allison engine–powered P-51A. It came to exist only as a result of what was, in effect, a government contracting gimmick intended to keep the P-51 line open until funding became available for the P-51B and subsequent models. In total, only 500 were produced.

For the dive-bombing mission, aside from being structurally strengthened, the A-36 had a redesigned wing fitted with slatted, hydraulically operated dive brakes on top and bottom. These devices kept the aircraft from accelerating above about 400 miles per hour in the near-vertical dives typically favored. In practice, the aircraft was put into a dive from approximately 12,000 feet and the two 500-pound bombs—one under each wing—were released at an altitude of between 2,000 and 4,000 feet. The A-36 also carried two .50-caliber machine guns in the lower nose in addition to the two .50-caliber machine guns mounted in each wing.

The A-36 first arrived in the Mediterranean theater during March 1943 and started combat operations in June. Although the original P-51 design was never intended as a dive bomber, the A-36 proved to be quite effective in the role. Still, notwithstanding the fact that it was a derivative of the P-51, its performance was inferior to that of the virtually unequaled Packard Merlin–engined P-51s that were fielded later. Its Allison engine lacked the supercharger equipment needed for good high-altitude performance. Subsequently, although it acquitted itself well enough as a fighter at lower altitudes, it was a poor performer above about 15,000 feet. It certainly did not dominate the standard Luftwaffe types of the day.

As massive as the buildup in North Africa and the Mediterranean had been, Allied air units had yet to achieve total air supremacy in the theater during the spring and early summer of 1943. Although they had been pushed out of North Africa with the defeat of the German army there in May, Luftwaffe units still operated throughout much of the Mediterranean. And their pilots and equipment, if not as numerous as those of the Allies, were still top-notch.

Capt. Glenn Stell of the 86th Bombardment Group (Dive) learned this firsthand only a few days before the Allied invasion of Sicily on July 10, 1943.[10] This period marked the introduction of the 86th and its A-36s to combat operations. At the time, the unit operated out of an airfield at Korba along the Tunisian coast.

On July 7, the 86th was tasked with hitting a German radar installation at Marsala on the western tip of Sicily. The trip was a short one—less than 150 miles—and for most of it, the flight of A-36s stayed very low over the water to avoid being detected by German radar. Stell noted that they flew so low that their prop wash lifted a plume of spray from the surface of the sea. Approaching the Sicilian coast, he and the other pilots climbed to 10,000 feet for the attack.

Once their bombs were away, the pilots pulled out of their dives and scrambled toward their pre-briefed assembly point. As Stell scooted low across a harbor, he spotted two ships and opened fire on them with all six of his .50-caliber machine guns. Once he completed his pass, he continued toward the assembly point and was surprised to see tracer rounds arcing past his aircraft. "My first thought," he recalled, "was that they were doing a lot of firing from those ships. I looked into my rear view mirror and was shocked to see three German Me-109s sitting on my tail. They had been using the tracers to line up their 20-millimeter cannon."

The enemy pilots must have been satisfied that they were in a good position to use their cannon. Stell remembered: "They began to shoot my plane to pieces." One of the enemy shells knocked out the two guns in his left wing and set the ammunition there afire. Explosions wracked the wing, and the gun bay doors were bent up into the windstream, where they caused tremendous drag and control problems. Another round tore away his engine cowling, and two of his three propeller blades were badly chopped up. "Then," Stell said, "a shell came through the canopy and exploded in the cockpit. The shell fragments cut my face, arms and legs causing a lot of bleeding."

Through all of this, Stell struggled to keep from flying his damaged aircraft into the water while at the same time maneuvering to keep from getting blown to bits. He fought with himself, resisting the urge to snap into a wide sweeping turn away from the enemy fighters that in actuality would have made his aircraft a bigger, easier target. Instead, he made small, jinking heading changes that did not shake the Me-109s but still spoiled their aim. So low over the water, it was difficult for the Germans to position their aircraft for an accurate burst of fire.

"I kept wondering why the referee did not blow his whistle and stop this," remembered Stell. "It then dawned on me that this was for keeps." He was not the first pilot to realize the deadly nature of aerial warfare only when he was in mortal danger.

When Stell approached the assembly point, the enemy pilots gave up their chase. Perhaps they were put off by the sight of Stell's squadron mates or believed that his aircraft was too badly damaged to make it back to base or were simply out of ammunition or fuel. Regardless, they broke off their attack, illustrating how in aerial combat even the most desperate situations can change in a matter of seconds for reasons that might ultimately be unknowable.

Stell did indeed nurse his damaged aircraft back to the Tunisian coast. But whereas the Germans had failed to kill him, the aircraft almost succeeded. "On reaching the field, when starting in to land, I got careless and forgot about the drag on the left wing. I slowed the plane on the approach as I usually did and the left wing dropped. I pushed the throttle full forward and was able to pull the wing up before it hit the ground."

Shaken and bloodied, Stell was nevertheless safe. He was taken to the medical tent, patched up, and put back in the air the following day.

When his squadron commander was killed a couple of days later, he was given command of the unit.

The spring and summer of 1943 were also a period of barely veiled acrimony between Arnold and Eaker. Arnold's impatience for results from the Eighth Air Force, his ignorance of conditions in England, and Eaker's own justifiable insistence on mounting raids only when his crews were ready and conditions were right continued to create a great deal of friction between the two friends. It did not help that Arnold was hospitalized on May 10 following the second of four heart attacks that he would endure before the end of the war. He had suffered his first at the end of February, a month after the Casablanca conference, and was genuinely concerned that Roosevelt, in poor health himself, might have him step down.

Arnold began the long-distance fusillade in earnest during June when he questioned Eaker about the disposition of his staff, particularly some of its most important commanders. He continued his attack by criticizing the readiness of Eaker's combat units and their apparently slow, even lethargic, tempo of operations. This was a particularly sore topic with Arnold, who spent considerable political capital making certain that Eaker, above all his other commanders, received the greatest measure of aircraft, crews, and equipment.

Eaker replied to Arnold with a carefully considered suggestion that perhaps Arnold was not fully aware that although the number of bombers in the Eighth had increased, the ground equipment to support them was lagging, as was the state of training of the aircrews. Regarding commanders, Eaker pointed out that there were still no ranking officers with the requisite experience available to replace those who displeased Arnold. He wrote Arnold: "Neither of us has been able to accomplish ideal [*sic*] for reasons both should appreciate. We get nowhere with recriminations."[11]

Arnold did not buy it, writing back: "I am perfectly willing to take the blame for anything, but that does not correct the existing situation." He additionally schooled Eaker: "I am willing to do anything possible to build up your forces, but you must play your part. My wire was sent to get you to toughen up—to can these fellows who cannot produce—to put in youngsters who can carry the ball." The tone of Arnold's correspondence with Eaker was patronizing and obtuse, almost as if Eaker were managing a lagging regional sales district for a middling company rather than the chief war-making instrument in the air war against Germany.

The discourse went back and forth. Arnold did not like the results coming from Bomber Command and questioned the aggressiveness of Fighter Command; he was not sure that Eaker was managing his maintenance and supply organizations as best he could; and he believed that too many of Eaker's staff officers were more interested in personal advancement than they were in winning the war. Eaker took umbrage and further outlined the situation in England before standing up to Arnold: "I shall always accept gladly and in the proper spirit, any advice, counsel or criticism from you. I do not feel, however, that my past service which has come under your observation indicates that I am a horse which needs to be ridden with spurs."[12]

The rancor eventually subsided to a low simmer. As much as Arnold might have disliked the pace at which operations were advancing, there really were no gaping holes in Eaker's logic or explanations. Still, the situation through the remainder of 1943 never really satisfied him.

If Arnold, the chief of the U.S. Army Air Forces, seemed impatient and demanding, it was because he, by nature, was impatient and demanding. But the stresses under which he operated must also be appreciated. He was not responsible only to his boss, Gen. George Marshall, for Eaker's strategic operations against Germany, but he was also responsible for U.S. Army Air Forces operations in North Africa and the Mediterranean, the Aleutians, the South Pacific, China, Burma and India, the Panama Canal, and every aspect of every army air force activity everywhere else in the world, not to mention the United States. These activities ranged from training to production, construction, and relationships with other branches of the army as well as with the navy. He was particularly worn down by continuous infighting with the navy over production priorities, command relationships, and responsibilities within different theaters. Some might offer that in light of all the demands on Arnold's energy, it was remarkable that he had so much time to devote to Eaker.

The invasion of Sicily began on July 10, 1943. The success of that assault required air superiority over the landing areas just as OVERLORD, the invasion of Normandy, would require nearly a year later. Accordingly, the Allies maintained continuous pressure on the German air force. Operations around the Mediterranean continued nonstop, and whereas the quantity and quality of the Allied air forces did nothing but grow, the Luftwaffe was hard-pressed even to make good its losses, much less match the Allies unit-for-unit.

At the time of the invasion—an effort comprising more than 3,000 vessels—the Luftwaffe had only about fifty aircraft in Sicily. It was a puny force that had no hope of deterring the masses of men and equipment pouring onto the island. This is especially true when it is considered that the Allies generated more than 1,000 fighter sorties over the beachheads on the first day of the invasion.

Admittedly, the Germans had more air units on the Italian peninsula that were capable of ranging the area of operations, but even those were incapable of effectively challenging the landings. Nevertheless, the Allied leadership took no chances. Just as they had done in the weeks prior to the invasion, they continued to order daily attacks against virtually every enemy airfield on Sicily.

The USAAF's combat chronology dutifully recounts these air operations in dry, colorless phrases that do no justice to the terror visited by the bombers onto the German and Italian defenders. To be fair, they likewise describe none of butchery that the defenders inflicted on the attacking aircrews. Rather, the missions are ticked off like so many errands:

> In Sicily, Northwest African Strategic Air Force (NASAF) planes hit Milo and Sciacca Airfields during the night of 10/11 Jul and numerous tactical targets during the day, including town areas, vehicle convoys, bridges, trains and roads; NASAF B-17's bomb the Catania marshalling yard while B-26's hit Milo Airfield and Gerbini satellite airfields; and B-25's and P-38's hit Sciacca Airfield . . .

In a sense, the missions *were* errands, albeit deadly and terrifying. But just the same, they were tasks that had to be completed before the invasion could be gotten underway.

Johannes Steinhoff was the commander of JG 77, a fighter unit that had been evacuated out of North Africa and dispatched to various bases before being posted, in part, to Sicily during June 1943. He recounted a raid that typified the seemingly endless series of attacks on the island's airfields:

> From the east, over Mount Erice, came the steadily increasing roar of engines. Even as we raced for the slit trenches we could hear the whistle of bombs—a vile noise. I dived into the trench head first, landing on the back of an airman who had got there sooner than I. For a few seconds all was quite still. Then the carpet of bombs came thundering toward us with appalling crashes and explosions. The formations were releasing their bomb loads one after the other so that the carpet kept rumbling closer, unrolling to the rhythm of successive bursts. In the trenches everyone held his breath hoping that the next stick would fall on the far side. . . . Presently the sound of engines died away and for a moment or two there was complete silence, a silence that was broken almost at once by the cries of the wounded, shouted commands and calls for stretcher bearers.[13]

Maurice Duvic was a B-26 copilot with the 17th Bomb Group based out of Djedeida near the northern coast of Tunisia. The 17th's crews had been regular visitors to Sicily and returned to do business on July 11, 1943, the day following the opening of the invasion. On that day, Duvic's squadron, the 34th, led an attack on the Trapani-Milo airfield complex.

At that point, the air defense of Sicily was little more than controlled chaos. German aircraft shuttled from base to base, dodging attacks as best they could while losing aircraft both in the air and on the ground. Hangars and other permanent infrastructure had already been rubbled weeks earlier. Still, the defenders did their best to fill the craters that pocked their airfields so that, if nothing else, there was a useable surface for taking off and landing.

"Intel briefed us that the Italians were manning the flak guns," remembered Duvic. "So, we really weren't that worried. Based on our earlier missions we really had little reason to respect their shooting ability. What we didn't know was that the Germans had moved into the area."

The 17th launched six flights of six aircraft each from its base at Djedeida. Each flight was made up of two three-aircraft formations, one behind the other. "We went in at our normal altitude of about 10,000 feet," Duvic recalled. "As we got close to the target the flak began to get heavy; it started at the rear of the formation and worked its way forward." Still, the group maintained its formation and got its bombs away with little trouble. The medium bombers, flying at such altitudes, generally tended to be the most accurate of all the USAAF bomber types. They also were typically quite hard hit by flak defenses.

"The flak was very intense by the time we dropped our bombs," said Duvic. "As we left the target area, we didn't get the familiar call over the intercom from our bombardier: 'Bombs away, bomb bay doors closing.' So, I looked down through the tunnel from the cockpit down into the nose of the aircraft and caught sight of our bombardier, Ken Kirkendoll. He looked back at me and grabbed his right arm with his left hand. He couldn't move it, he'd been hit."

Duvic and his pilot, Max Zimmerle, conferred briefly before agreeing that Duvic should climb down to assist Kirkendoll. Duvic recalled: "I pulled up the rudder pedals and crawled under them and down into the nose of the aircraft. Kirkendoll was shot up pretty bad. He had been hit in the right arm and calf. His elbow was shattered. I tried to get his flight jacket off and we ended up cutting away the sleeve. Blood was pulsing out from where he'd been hit in an artery."

Kirkendoll was in mortal danger. Duvic called up for William Brown, the flight engineer, to pass down straps from a life preserver so that he could fashion a tourniquet for the bombardier's arm. "He was getting worse by the minute," Duvic recollected. "As I worked to get him patched up, everything became covered in blood." Nevertheless, Duvic continued to render first aid in the tiny blood-slicked space to keep Kirkendoll from bleeding to death.

"He was going into shock," Duvic said, "but was still in a lot of pain, so I pulled a hypodermic full of morphine that was kept in the first aid kit. I jabbed him with it, but the plunger wouldn't go down. The poor guy, he was in terrible pain already and here I had him stuck with a needle that wasn't doing him any good at all. Finally, I got the painkiller into him after Brown told me that I needed to twist the hypodermic to break the seal." It was at about that time that Kirkendoll vomited all over the compartment.

By this point, Zimmerle had dropped the green-painted B-26 to only a couple of hundred feet above the Mediterranean. His plan was to divert into the airfield at Mateur, near Bizerte. The 17th had been at Djedeida for less than a month, and the medical facilities there were not as well equipped and staffed as those at Mateur. Through the blood and vomit-spattered glass nose of his aircraft, Duvic could see two other B-26s also racing for Mateur.

By the time the airfield came into view, Zimmerle was third in line to land. Duvic remembered what happened next: "The aircraft in front of us crashed; its landing gear collapsed so we had to go around the pattern until they got the mess cleared up. I was really concerned because that boy [Kirkendoll] was about half dead from shock and loss of blood."

Finally, Zimmerle landed and taxied clear of the runway. "There were no ambulances available," recalled Duvic. "They had already been used to take other wounded airmen to the hospital. I started to get really upset; that boy was dying while we waited around for an ambulance. And then, when the ambulance finally showed up, the medical orderlies stood there and wasted time while they debated the best way to get him out of the aircraft."

Zimmerle nearly had to restrain Duvic, but Kirkendoll was finally pulled from the aircraft and taken to the hospital. In the end—in large part thanks to the actions of Duvic, Zimmerle, and the rest of the crew—Kirkendoll survived.

Not everyone was so fortunate. The flak had been particularly vicious. Of the thirty-six aircraft sent on the mission, twenty-five were damaged. Of those, two were so badly shot up they were scrapped. The flak from the Trapani-Milo complex wounded seventeen men, of whom three later died.

Back at Trapani, Steinhoff landed his Me-109 following the raid. He recorded his impressions: "The airfield, when I landed, looked absolutely dead. Nothing moved; not a soul was to be seen. Near the battered olive trees between the bomb craters, the forlorn ruins of the hangars pointed skywards. It seemed as though I had arrived on the moon or some dreadful planet."

The Luftwaffe, in Sicily at least, was very nearly dead.

CHAPTER 7

TIDALWAVE

As the fighting raged in Sicily and elsewhere in the Mediterranean and as the Eighth continued its strategic missions in northern Europe, a critical raid that many believed held great promise was being readied in North Africa. The mission to Ploesti, Romania, was one of the ancillary projects born out of the Casablanca Conference. Because it was estimated that the refineries around Ploesti provided a third or more of Germany's petroleum, the Allied leadership took a special interest in its destruction. It did not take a particular brand of genius to recognize that a German military that had its fuel supply dramatically choked would be considerably less effective. This applied especially to the Luftwaffe as aircraft without gasoline were worthless.

Planning began in Washington almost immediately. One of the biggest and most obvious challenges facing the planners was the fact that the USAAF did not possess nearly enough bombers to destroy the numerous refineries that made up the Ploesti complex. At the time, it was estimated that it would require a raid of more than 1,000 bombers to destroy Ploesti. In reality, especially in light of the effort that was mounted the following year, that number was a gross underestimate. Regardless, using conventional high-altitude bombing tactics there simply would not—could not—be enough aircraft in place during 1943 to achieve the desired level of destruction.

Consequently, the raid's chief planner, Col. Jacob Smart, decided on an approach that no one had ever seriously considered: attacking from low altitude. In fact, the bombers would attack from *very* low altitude—200 feet or less. Bombs dropped from such a height—as compared to those dropped from several miles up—could hardly miss their targets; the physics just would not permit it. Thus, the needed accuracy could be achieved. And if critical components of the various refineries were hit, good effects could be had without turning the entire complex into ruins.

Smart and his planning team identified forty-one of those critical components. Their destruction would reduce Germany's entire refining capacity by up to 30 percent. Perhaps even more important, it would reduce the production of high-octane aviation gasoline by up to 95 percent.

Aside from accuracy, a low-level attack offered other advantages. If they flew low enough, the crews could keep their bombers out of radar-detection range until they were fairly close to the target. Caught by surprise, the enemy air defenses would be much less effective. Furthermore, the bombers would be able to attack under the sorts of clouds that could typically foil a conventional high-altitude raid. And, low to the ground, enemy fighters would be denied the option of attacking from below the bombers.

Of course, the concept also presented problems. Perhaps most critical was the fact that the aircraft would be vulnerable to virtually every weapon in the enemy's defensive arsenal. And as large as they were, the aircraft would make relatively easy targets. Also not to be discounted was the obvious fact that the pilots had to keep the aircraft from flying into the ground. The big ships were not easy to control and keeping them away from terrain or tall obstacles was not a simple matter. Additionally, navigation at low level posed difficulties. Relative to high-altitude flying, landmarks passed quickly and line of sight was limited. Accurately flying the routes to the different targets at Ploesti would demand unerring navigation and superb airmanship.

As the planning proceeded, Spaatz and others expressed doubts about the mission, particularly the notion that the desired level of destruction could be attained. They also believed that the losses inflicted by the German and Romanian defenses would be very high. Winston

Churchill, of all people, displayed a keen interest in the effort and was kept abreast of the planning. Like Spaatz, he also expressed misgivings at what the mission might cost in lives. In fact, it was Churchill who prevailed on the Americans to change the code name of the operation from the randomly assigned SOAPSUDS to TIDALWAVE, believing that the former belittled an operation that might exact a horrible price against those sent to execute it.

Despite trepidation from various quarters and after two months of planning and staffing, Eisenhower and Arnold approved the concept in May 1943. Arnold assigned the mission to Maj. Gen. Lewis Brereton's Ninth Air Force. Brereton in turn put Brig. Gen. Uzal Ent, a rated balloon pilot and the leader of IX Bomber Command, in charge of the plan's execution. Brereton himself planned to fly aboard the lead aircraft during the raid.

A primary concern associated with the mission was its extreme range. Planned to be flown from primitive desert airfields around Benghazi, Libya, the round trip measured 2,400 miles, making it the longest raid ever flown. Not only would it demand an aircraft with a tremendous fuel capacity, but it would also stress the robustness and reliability of flight-critical components, such as engines.

If nothing else, the extraordinary length of the mission narrowed the choices about which aircraft to select. The United States operated only one aircraft type with the requisite range and bomb-carrying capacity, the B-24. Even then, the plane would have to be fitted with auxiliary coated-fabric bomb bay fuel tanks. Consequently, five B-24 bomb groups were assigned to the raid: the 44th, 93rd, 98th, 376th, and 389th. The 44th, commanded by Col. Leon W. Johnson, was an Eighth Air Force unit and was sent with thirty-six aircraft to Libya from its base in England. The 93rd, led by Lt. Col. Addison E. Baker, likewise was an Eighth Air Force unit and also mustered thirty-six aircraft from England. The 98th was a Ninth Air Force organization already in Libya and was headed by Col. John R. Kane; it boasted a roster of forty-six bombers. Col. Keith K. Compton's 376th, also a Libya-based Ninth Air Force outfit, operated thirty aircraft. The final group, the 389th, had never seen combat, but rather was sent to Libya almost immediately after arriving in England from the States; it was commanded by Col. Jack W. Wood and carried thirty aircraft on its roster.

Planes, people, and plans were all put into place during July 1943. Especially intensive preparations were made during the last ten days, including multiple practice missions against mock targets erected in remote areas of the Libyan desert. These practice sorties were mostly flown without the enlisted gunners and radiomen. The gunners were not needed for the practice flights because the actual mission would present them with nothing they had not already trained for; the radiomen were not needed because the mission required strict radio silence.

On the other hand, the skills needed for the low-level flying were something that the pilots had to practice. In all their previous experience, they had been prohibited from low-level flying—"buzzing"— since it was a dangerous, if exhilarating, stunt that had cost the army a great deal in crashed airplanes and personnel. But with the requirements of this special mission, it was something they were not only allowed to do, but it was something they were *ordered* to do. Wrestling the B-24's flight controls at low altitude was dangerous and difficult. At heights of 100 feet or less, the big bombers actually had to be climbed before a turn in order to keep from scraping their wings across the ground.

Aside from the pilots, the bombardiers had to familiarize themselves with the crude fixed metal sights they were issued; bombing at low altitude required little more in terms of equipment. The rudimentary little devices were nothing like the secret, sophisticated bombsights they had trained with for high-altitude operations. The navigators likewise had to get used to the notion of doing their job at altitudes of only a couple of hundred feet. Plotting and flying a course while nearly scraping the treetops was a much different proposition than navigating from miles above the earth. The flight engineers were also part of the practice sorties. Big bombers did not go flying for practice or otherwise without engineers.

Specific target assignments were made, and the date of the mission was set for August 1, 1943. The 376th, with Col. Keith Compton in the lead and Major General Brereton aboard, would head the mission. Its target assignment was the enormous Romana Americana complex (White I) on the eastern side of Ploesti. Following Compton and the 376th would be Baker's 93rd. The plan called for this group to separate into two elements to hit three targets on the southern side of the city: the

Concordia Vega complex (White II) and the Standard Petrol Block and Unirea Speranta refineries (combined as White III).

Kane's 98th was assigned as the third of the five groups making up the column. Brig. Gen. Uzal Ent would be riding aboard Kane's ship, a position from which he could monitor the progress of the mission. The group had two targets, the Astra Romana and the Unirea Orion refineries (combined as White IV) on Ploesti's southern edge. Following the 98th was Johnson's 44th, which was supposed to split into two groups to hit the Colombia Acquilla refinery (White V) on the city's southwest fringe and the Creditul Minier operation (Blue) in neighboring Brazi.

Finally, the 389th was assigned to the rear of the column. Its target was the Steaua Romana complex at Campina to the northwest of Ploesti. Accordingly, the last portion of its route would diverge from the rest of the formation. Many of the 389th's men hoped that, removed from Ploesti as it was, it would be thinly defended.[1]

The plan in its entirety called for the five groups to execute a carefully orchestrated, nearly simultaneous, multi-axis attack that would get the bomber crews across their separate targets and out of the enemy defenses in as compact a period as possible. Carrying it off successfully would demand discipline, courage, and airmanship.

Through virtually the entire preparation period, there was debate about the virtues and shortcomings of the low-altitude plan. Brereton had initially been cold to the idea but grew more enthusiastic as the practice missions proved the accuracy of the low-level tactics. However, Ent disliked the notion and nearly lost his command when he drew up a petition against it that he intended to circulate among the five group commanders.[2] At the lower levels of command, there was also dissent. Kane believed it was too dangerous and declared that the concept had been conjured up "by some idiot armchair warrior in Washington."[3] Others believed that there was too much reliance on surprise and the notion that the mission would somehow go undetected.

During the last few days of July, apprehension grew among some of the men. Rumors of expected high casualties began to spread. The anxiety was not helped when, just before the mission, Arnold forbade Brereton from participating. He felt that considering Brereton's knowledge of a number of critical war plans, the risk of him being shot down and captured was too great. Consequently, Ent was the ranking officer and would take Brereton's place in the lead aircraft with Compton.

The 389th started trickling into England from the States during June, but it flew no combat missions and was there only a short time before it was sent to Libya as part of the force being put together to attack Ploesti. "We flew down from England and spent a night in Oran before flying into our airfield near Benghazi," remembered Ernest Poulson, a copilot who had joined the group just before it left the States.[4] "There was virtually nothing there when we arrived. Our tents were folded up in stacks—we had to set them up ourselves. The runway was nothing but a section of desert that the engineers had scraped clear of big rocks. It was dirt."

The men of the 389th put things in order, and it was not long before they started operations on July 9 with a strike to Crete. They flew five more raids during the next ten days, the last taking place on July 19. "It wasn't easy," Poulson recalled. "The dust and sand were so bad that it was a real challenge for our maintenance men to keep the aircraft up and operating. Our crew got shot up over Crete on one of our missions, and our usual aircraft, the *Pistol Packin' Mama*, wasn't going to be ready for the big mission."

From July 20, the five bomb groups focused almost exclusively on the long-distance raid to Ploesti. "The practice sorties we flew in Libya against the mock targets in the desert were quite demanding physically," remembered Poulson. "The B-24s we were flying didn't have servos or powered controls. Consequently, it took both the pilot and copilot to fly the aircraft, especially while trying to maintain our position in the formation, low to the ground and in turbulence." Adding to the difficulty for Poulson and the other crewmen was the fact that it was high summer in the North African desert, where temperatures often soared well above 100 degrees Fahrenheit. Indeed, simply drinking enough water to stay hydrated could be a challenge in such conditions.

"During the time leading up to it," said Poulson, "we knew that the mission was important, but we really hadn't been officially told where we were going. It wasn't until General Ent talked to us a day or two prior that we realized how critical the effort was. He told us that so long as we destroyed the target, the mission would be worth it even if everyone was shot down. That kind of got my attention, but I was a young man and was pretty sure that if anything bad happened, it would happen to someone else."

Ent's comments were surprising for another reason. "Up to that point we had been briefed that the defenses around Ploesti wouldn't be particularly rough," remembered Poulson. "The guns were allegedly manned mostly by Romanians and we were told that they not only weren't very proficient, but also were tired of the war and not particularly motivated. We were also told that because we'd be going in at low altitude we wouldn't be vulnerable to their big flak guns—the 88s. Supposedly, they wouldn't be able to depress the gun barrels low enough to shoot at us. Of course, we found that wasn't true at all."

It was still dark on the day of the mission, August 1, 1943, when Poulson was awakened at around 0430. He joined his pilot, Robert O'Reilly, and the rest of the crew at their aircraft, the *Chattanooga Choo Choo*, shortly after dawn. "We'd never flown that airplane before; it came to us from a different group, but it seemed just fine. About the only problem we had was with our navigator, Richard Britt. He had diarrhea pretty bad, but he insisted on going."

The crew preflighted the ship and got the engines started without any difficulty. The dust roiled up by the 389th's B-24s whipped across the airfield and into the eyes, noses, mouths, and ears of all the crews as they waited for the signal to take off. It came at 0700 local time, and almost immediately, the group's aircraft started trundling awkwardly down the runway before powering themselves out of the dust and sand and into the sky. Finally, it was *Chattanooga Choo Choo*'s turn, and O'Reilly and Poulson put power to the big bomber's four dust-choked engines.

"Taking off was always the most dangerous part of flying out of that airfield," said Poulson. "It wasn't just because the runway was rough and the aircraft were so heavily loaded, but the dust cut visibility to nothing. The crew in the first aircraft had good visibility, but everyone behind them had to get on their instruments and take off nearly blind." O'Reilly and Poulson wrestled with the controls as their aircraft rumbled faster and faster across the dirt until, finally, they were able to lift the over-burdened ship into the morning sky. They were one of 177 aircraft that got airborne for the mission that morning.

"We got formed up over the water pretty quickly," said Poulson. "All of us were conscious of the fact that we were going to need every bit of fuel we had, so we didn't waste any time getting together." Once the groups were formed, they found their places in the larger formation and headed north across the Mediterranean at approximately 5,000 feet. "It was pretty uneventful except that one aircraft, for no reason that any of us could see, went into a spin and crashed into the water. It was a real mystery. There were no radio calls and no one bailed out." The plane was *Wongo Wongo*, temporarily assigned to the 98th Bomb Group. No conclusive evidence was ever produced about what caused the aircraft to fall into the sea.

After crossing the Mediterranean and reaching the island of Corfu, Compton turned the stream of bombers slightly east of north. By now, the formation was significantly smaller than it had been earlier that morning because, aside from the loss of *Wongo Wongo*, several other aircraft had aborted for various reasons. For instance, six of Kane's aircraft from the 98th returned to base. Another had crashed on takeoff, killing all but two of its crew. It is estimated that 167 aircraft comprised the formation as it turned over Corfu.

At the head of the 389th, the last group in the formation, Wood started climbing the group even before it reached Corfu. "We could see a heavy bank of clouds in the mountains immediately beyond the island," said Poulson. "We didn't penetrate them, but rather stayed above them."

The next portion of the route took the crews across Albania, Yugoslavia, and a corner of Bulgaria before crossing into Romania. Although the plan called for the five bomb groups to fly as a continuous column until reaching the initial point in Romania, they began to string out early. This would prove to be one important factor in the disastrous undoing of the carefully crafted attack plan.

Another of those factors was the fact that the mission, which counted on surprise as a chief component of its success, was not a secret. Radar stations along the route detected what was, at that time, the largest American raid ever assembled and launched from North Africa. Additionally, ground observers spotted the formation, as did pilots who happened to be in the same piece of sky at the same time. Indeed, Bulgarian pilots flying outdated Czech-built Avia B-534 biplanes made abortive attempts to intercept the formation. As slow as they were, however, they just could not get into a position to do so. At any rate, if the target was not apparent to German and Romanian forces during the early portion of the mission, it became rather more obvious as the mission progressed and position reports continued to be received.

Kane, leading the 98th, fell behind Compton and the first two groups, the 376th and the 93rd. The reasons for this are unclear and have been debated for some time. Compton, leading the mission from his bomber, *Teggie Ann*, had briefed that he would be using higher power settings than what had traditionally been used by the Libya-based units during their previous operations. The higher power settings would increase fuel consumption but would also increase the formation's airspeed, with the net result being more miles covered per gallon of fuel consumed. Kane was against this and argued that the higher power settings would increase stress on the engines while consuming too much fuel. It is unclear whether Kane fell behind because he refused to use higher power settings or for other reasons. Regardless, the fact remains that he failed to keep up with the two groups in front of his own. Subsequently, the 44th was trapped behind him.

Poulson remembered that the 389th lost visual contact with the other groups after Wood took the group up to altitude following the turn at Corfu. Nevertheless, it was not crucial as the formation's target, the Steaua Romana refinery at Campina, was well northwest of the main refinery complexes at Ploesti. Unlike the rest of the groups, the 389th's attack was a solo effort that did not depend on detailed coordination with the other formations.

Once across the Balkan Mountains that ran along the border between Bulgaria and Romania, Compton started the column of bombers down to low altitude. At the same time, realizing that the rear half of the bomber stream had fallen badly behind, he executed a small series of S-turns, hoping that Kane and the two groups behind him would close the gap. His efforts were for naught; Kane never came into sight.

Compton pressed across the Danube into Romania and pushed the throttles of *Teggie Ann* forward. The B-24s of the 376th and the 93rd, now only 500 feet above the ground, raced along at 190 miles per hour.

Below them, the crews watched the rural landscape of Romania unfold like a tourist film. But the actors in that film, the peasants, stopped playing their roles mid-script. Instead of tending fields or flocks, they stared up moonfaced at the unprecedented sight of the big bombers. Some of them waved tentatively at the men they could see manning the strange flying ships, and some of the crewmen aboard the B-24s waved back.

Later, when O'Reilly and Poulson and the rest of the 389th reached the Danube, they did not do much waving. Frank Kees, their flight engineer, had been keeping a keen eye on their aircraft's fuel quantity. Because of the extreme range of the mission, there was not an engineer aboard any of the big ships that was not hawking his bomber's fuel situation. Kees passed bad news to O'Reilly and Poulson. According to Poulson, "We had already burned through half of our fuel, and we were still about thirty minutes from the target. It was apparent that even though we were carrying an auxiliary tank in the bomb bay, we didn't have enough gas to get back to Libya. By the time we got across the Danube, we'd already decided that we would divert to Cyprus after the attack rather than try to make it all the way back to Libya."

If Kane had caused the greater formation to disintegrate into two separate groups, willfully or not, Compton made a mistake that was at least as bad. Rather than hitting the initial point at Floresti, he turned too early—on direction from his navigator, Harold Wicklund—over the town of Targoviste. Consequently, instead of heading for their targets at Ploesti, the 376th and 93rd flew straight for the capital city of Bucharest. The carefully orchestrated mission was coming apart.

The two groups flew on the errant heading for several minutes before Compton realized his mistake. By that time, the formation was hopelessly off course, and there was no way to salvage the attack as it had been planned. Compton conferred with Ent and asked for permission to turn the groups loose to attack targets of opportunity. It would be better to hit something rather than nothing at all. Ent gave his approval, and Compton made the call over the heretofore silent radio. Behind him, Addison Baker had already recognized Compton's mistake and decided on his own to turn his formation north toward Ploesti.

The enemy had more than 300 heavy- and medium-caliber antiaircraft guns ready and waiting. High above the ground-hugging bombers, German and Romanian fighter crews scanned the sky, looking for the inbound Americans. Tethered around the city were dozens of sagging barrage balloons, some of them rigged with explosives. The shooting and killing part of the deadliest mission in USAAF history was only moments away.

Baker led the 93rd toward the Colombia Acquilla refinery, which had originally been assigned to Johnson's 44th. It was not long after he broke formation with Compton that the enemy guns opened fire on him and the men who followed his lead. Heavy shells and medium-caliber rounds savaged the low-flying B-24s from virtually every quarter as they raced to unload their bombs. The enemy fire ripped through the skin of the big bombers, knocked engines from their wings, and slammed aircraft into the ground, where they were swallowed in great clouds of dirt and smoke and flame. Men were shot dead at their crew stations while others jumped from damaged ships. Because the aircraft were so low, some of the jumpers hit the ground before their parachutes had a chance to blossom. The carnage was horrendous.

At the same time, the American gunners returned fire with their .50-caliber machine guns. The heavy slugs smashed into the enemy gun positions and tore men apart. It was a crazy, pointblank, high-speed shootout the likes of which had never been seen before.

Baker's aircraft was slashed by a balloon cable and, immediately after, was hit in the nose section and caught fire. With his ship failing, Baker jettisoned his bombs in an effort to stay airborne. Still afire but also still flying, he led what was left of his group to the target, where they dropped their bombs and turned the complex into a wicked mass of choking flames and smoke. Bursting clear to the other side of the refinery, Baker's aircraft was targeted again. With the ship little more than a flying mass of fire, he lifted its nose for altitude to give his crew a chance to jump. It was for nothing. The aircraft fell off on a wing and crashed to the ground.

While Baker was leading the front element of the 93rd against the Colombia Acquilla refinery, the trailing element hit the Astra Romana complex. The enemy fire there was equally gruesome. Indeed, of the thirty-nine B-24s that the 93rd put into the air that day, only fifteen managed to make it out of the target area.

Compton did not take his group after the refineries, possibly not wanting to disrupt the attacks of the groups behind him. Instead, the

376th pecked at targets of little consequence on the edge of Ploesti. The exception was Maj. Norman Appold, who led a flight of only five aircraft against the Concordia Vega complex. Those five B-24s hit the refinery so hard that nearly half of it was destroyed.

In the meantime, Kane's 98th, together with the 44th, finally crossed into Romania and dropped down to low altitude. They were approximately twenty minutes behind Compton. Nevertheless, their navigation was good, and they hit the correct initial point, Floresti, just as planned.

Tragically, the separation between Compton's half of the force and what had become Kane's half had given the men manning Ploesti's defenses—among the very heaviest in the world—plenty of time to prepare. In fact, the previous two groups had made whatever attacks they could, little of it according to plan, and were already on their way out of the area when Kane arrived on the scene.

Kane wheeled the 98th around in a righthand turn toward the southeast and White IV, the Astra Romana and Unirea Orion refineries. As he did, the forty-one aircraft that made up the group spread out in the prebriefed attack formation of five rows. Each row was made up of from six to ten aircraft, line abreast. Johnson's 44th likewise deployed in its attack formation.

A railroad track paralleled their path into Ploesti. On that track, a flak train, bristling with small- and medium-caliber antiaircraft guns, had a head of steam and raced to keep up with the big bombers. Although the train could never hope to keep up with the formation, the shells its guns fired more than made up for the mismatch in speed. The train's guns let loose wicked streams of fire that tore into the thin-skinned bombers with horrific effects. The slow relative speed between the bombers and the train, together with the fact that the aircraft were so closely bunched, made it so that the German gunners could hardly miss. Fixed gun positions on the ground along the route added to the ferocity of the fire. As if that were not enough, ten German-flown Me-109s attacked from above. Aircraft started going down immediately.

None of this was apparent to O'Reilly and Poulson aboard *Chattanooga Choo Choo* as Jack Wood led them and the rest of the 389th to their turn point. Wood was vexed by the confusing series of cloud-shrouded look-alike peaks and valleys that passed under the nose of his bomber. Finally, concerned that he might fly past his turn point, he banked the twenty-nine-aircraft formation toward the southeast.

"But we weren't set up correctly," remembered Poulson. Wood had turned too early but recognized his mistake soon after and put the formation back into a wide circling turn to the right that took them west, then northeast and into the next valley. "It seemed to take forever—I was really unhappy about that. It was a costly delay that gave the enemy gunners more time to get ready." While Wood got the big formation turned around on course, Poulson and the rest of the men aboard the bombers sneaked glimpses of the target complex beyond a small foothill that partially blocked their view. Anticipation grew aboard the big ships.

"Our airspeed increased to about 210 miles per hour as we descended to 200 feet," Poulson recalled. When Wood finally rolled out of the wide right turn, he had the group pointed nearly south and straight at the target. The formation, a column of six pairs of three-ship elements line abreast, was still in good shape. Regardless, the enemy gunners had had plenty of time to prepare for the big gaggle of B-24s, and they engaged the Americans with a ferocity that was terrifying. "Tracers arced up from everywhere—they shot at us with everything they had," remembered Poulson. "I even saw people shooting at us with pistols!"

Poulson was struck by the ferocious noise of the fight as much as by anything else. The four big engines on the B-24 made enough racket in any case, but the sound of enemy shells ripping into the ship, the chattering roar of the bomber's own .50-caliber machine guns, and the crew's shouts over the intercom swirled together into a nearly overwhelming cacophony. All of it resonated through the steel infantry helmet Poulson wore especially for this mission.

That clamor and the sight of the fearsome fight around them stoked the crew's adrenaline. Poulson was struck by chunks of shrapnel in his right calf and under his left arm. "I had no idea I had been hit until much later." The flight engineer, Frank Kees, clambered down from the top turret and shouted over the din at O'Reilly and Poulson that he had been hit in the leg and that the left outboard engine—number one—was on fire. "We were able to get the engine shut down and feathered," said Poulson, "but it was still on fire."

Still, the burning engine was the least of their problems at that moment. Horsing the big aircraft through the hail of enemy fire and toward their target, while keeping it from crashing into the ground, demanded the strength of both men at the controls. "Right about that time," Poulson said, "I spotted a large cable strung across our path. I shouted at O'Reilly but I'm not sure he heard me. Anyway, I hauled back on the yoke and fortunately we had enough airspeed to clear it."

"We put our bombs into our assigned target—I was impressed by that," said Poulson, "but somewhere during that time our aileron and rudder cables were shot away. We had no control over either, no directional control at all." Coming off target the plan called for the group to make a slight right turn. Without their ailerons and rudders, O'Reilly and Poulson could not turn their aircraft anywhere. Horrified, Poulson watched as the aircraft on the other side of their three-ship formation crossed underneath *Chattanooga Choo Choo* from left-to-right and avoided hitting both the ground and their aircraft by only the barest of margins.

That they were going to crash was a foregone conclusion. The best that O'Reilly and Poulson could hope for was that they could control it somewhat. "I shouted up at the bombardier, Albert Romano, and the navigator, Richard Britt, to get up out of the glass nose and prepare for the crash," recounted Poulson. "At about that time, I found out that we still had a bomb hung up in the bomb bay and I told Romano, the bombardier, to get back there and get rid of it."

In the meantime, O'Reilly and Poulson performed miracles to keep the aircraft aloft. The left wing dipped earthward and failed to respond to any of their inputs. If it hit the ground, it would likely cartwheel the big bomber into a massive ball of flaming wreckage. According to Poulson, "Then O'Reilly cut the throttles of the engines on the right side to idle and ran the number two engine on the left side to full power and brought the aircraft's wings level."

Behind them another crew fought for their lives. A B-24 piloted by Lloyd Hughes had been badly shot up prior to the target. Fuel gushed from the stricken ship in a torrent so heavy it nearly obscured the rear of the fuselage. Nevertheless, Hughes and his copilot, Ronald Helder, kept their place in formation and plunged into the blazing cauldron that the target had become.

The crew's fate was sealed when the bomber's left wing ignited in a great fiery blaze. The bombs fell from Hughes's aircraft and into the target. Seconds later, the aircraft exited the target area—a great airborne torch. Still, it was flying, and Hughes and Helder managed to guide it down a shallow valley just above a dry riverbed while they looked for a place to set it down.

They did not make it. A wingtip caught the ground, and the aircraft somersaulted in a gruesomely spectacular explosion. Miraculously, two of the crew survived. Hughes was ultimately awarded the Medal of Honor for his heroism. His citation reads in part:

> Approaching the target through intense and accurate antiaircraft fire and dense balloon barrages at dangerously low altitude, his plane received several direct hits from both large and small caliber antiaircraft guns which seriously damaged his aircraft, causing sheets of escaping gasoline to stream from the bomb bay and from the left wing. . . . With full knowledge of the consequences of entering this blazing inferno when his airplane was profusely leaking gasoline in two separate locations, 2d Lt. Hughes, motivated only by his high conception of duty which called for the destruction of his assigned target at any cost, did not elect to make a forced landing or turn back from the attack. Instead, rather than jeopardize the formation and the success of the attack, he unhesitatingly entered the blazing area and dropped his bomb load with great precision.[5]

Almost simultaneously, O'Reilly and Poulson prepared to put *Chattanooga Choo Choo* into the dirt. Like Hughes, they were flying down a dry riverbed. Poulson recollected, "To slow our speed, we took a gamble and put the flaps down full." Doing so was dangerous because as shot up as the aircraft was, there was a chance that the flaps on one wing might extend while those on the other might not. Were that to happen the aircraft would go into an uncontrollable roll and crash.

Fortunately, the flaps came down together. Poulson remembered: "We hit the ground almost immediately. The sound—the ripping and rending and tearing of metal—was mind numbing. We bounced and skidded and rocked and I waited, almost hoped, to lose consciousness."

Poulson did not lose consciousness and endured the violent shaking in his seat while the bomber tore itself apart. When it finally ground to a halt, the aircraft was nearly broken in half, and the top of the fuselage above him and O'Reilly was ripped completely off. Poulson's left wrist and right shoulder were both broken, and he struggled to get clear of the ruined bomber. "I managed to get unstrapped from my seat and parachute, but each time I tried to get up and out of the aircraft, someone stepped on me as they hurried to climb out of the wreckage through the topless cockpit. I finally scrambled clear, and we got together outside the aircraft—there were eight of us. The other men said that Richard Britt had been killed and that Frank Kees was also dead. The top turret had broken loose during the crash and crushed him. Anyway, we broke up into three groups. I stayed with Louis Medieros, our tail gunner and Clell Riffle, our radioman. Medieros's legs were horribly bruised and battered and I pretty much carried him up into a cornfield where we tried to hide."

The three men hunkered down in the field hoping to escape attention. It was no good. "We'd been spotted," Poulson said, "and the local Romanian militia or gendarmerie surrounded the field and started shooting into the corn; that was more than a little unnerving. I had a .45-caliber pistol, but the other two men were unarmed. I decided it wasn't a situation that called for any sort of heroics. We put a white handkerchief up in the air and surrendered."

Their Romanian captors found it hard to believe that Poulson and the other two men were Americans. To this point in the war, the United States really had not figured into their part of the fight. "They were terrified," Poulson said. "They were convinced that we were Russians. They saw the big white star on our aircraft and confused it with the Soviet red star. We'd been taught a few phrases in Romanian, to include, 'I am an American,' but they just didn't believe us."

Still, the Romanians did not overly abuse Poulson or his two comrades. "They tied us together with me in the middle—I was quite a bit bigger than the other two men. Then, as they marched us off, they shouted a lot and kicked me in the butt several times, but other than that, the Romanians didn't really hurt us."

As it turned out, nine of the ten crewmen aboard *Chatanooga Choo Choo* survived the raid. "Britt actually hadn't been killed," remembered Poulson. "He was trapped in the wreckage, but still alive. The Romanians cut him out and took him to the hospital to treat him for the burns he'd suffered from being soaked in high-octane gasoline."

The 389th's attack on the Steaua Romana refinery was the most successful of the strikes against the Ploesti complex that day. The facility was absolutely devastated and did not return to operation until after the war. It had cost the 389th six of its twenty-nine aircraft; four of them were shot down while another two diverted into Turkey where they were interned.

While Poulson and his crewmates were being led away, the hell that the mission had become was still being played out. Wounded men died at their positions; gunners fought off or succumbed to enemy fighters; crews struggled to keep damaged ships airborne; others, low on fuel, worked desperately to reach airfields in Turkey or Cyprus. The lucky ones who managed to clear the continent with enough fuel had a ride of several hours during which they could contemplate what they had just accomplished.

The last bomber to make it back to Libya banged down onto its dirt runway after dark, sixteen hours after it had gotten airborne. *Liberty Lad* had two engines out, no hydraulics, and no brakes, and it rolled for a mile before crunching to a halt. The hulking, shot-up ship was the ideal metaphor for what had been the bloodiest bombing raid in U.S. history.

Overall, the raid on Ploesti had been extraordinarily costly, especially considering the early phase of the war when individual aircraft were still precious commodities to the USAAF. Accounts differ, but of the approximately 177 aircraft that got airborne out of Libya that day, 54 were lost. Of that number, 46 were destroyed, and 8 were interned in Turkey. An indeterminate number of others were so badly shot up they were written off following their return.

But the loss of so many aircraft was only part of the hurt. Those bombers were manned by nearly 500 men, of whom 310 were killed, 108 captured, and 78 interned. The death rate was a record for missions of comparable size because of the low-altitude nature of the raid. Because the big aircraft were so low during the attack, there was little opportunity for the crews to parachute to safety when their ships were hit. Rather, many of them perished in the fiery explosions that their aircraft became when they smashed into the ground.

Although the losses had not been as horrific as many had feared, the raid had been botched, and there was plenty of blame passed around afterward. Compton was furious with Kane for failing to stay with the leading two groups, but his own missed turn to the target had caused at least as much harm. Among some of the men, there was anger that their leadership had sent them on such a bloody mission. The intelligence failings were also obvious to everyone who participated.

In the end, there were no official punishments or recriminations. Instead, an unprecedented five Medals of Honor were awarded, along with a great number of Distinguished Service Crosses and Silver Stars. Every man who flew the mission was awarded the Distinguished Flying Cross.

The mission received a great deal of publicity, and the bravery of the crews was roundly praised. Air Chief Marshal Tedder congratulated the men in a letter to Brereton: "The gallantry and determination with which the attacks were pressed home are beyond all praise and will be an inspiration to all Allied air forces. A big job, magnificently done." Arnold's commendation was more guarded: "[Y]our preparation and training for Tidal Wave satisfactorily bore fruit, and we all are immensely proud of the showing you made. The impression prevails that Tidal Wave dealt a blow that will materially contribute to the defeat of the Axis."[7]

Although the mission had not gone according to plan, the effects were spectacular and greatly alarmed the Germans. Still, the audacious raid failed to achieve the desired objective of taking the refineries out of the war. Classifying damage to infrastructure as multifarious as a refinery is a mushy business, but intelligence estimates determined that approximately 40 percent of Ploesti's production was taken out of action. This was not an unimpressive achievement, particularly when it is considered that significant parts of the mission were bungled and that the very considerable defenses had plenty of warning.

But the effects of the damage were not long lasting. The Germans immediately tapped into their reserves. Simultaneously, they put thousands of slave laborers to work clearing the wreckage, then began repairing the damage with remarkable resourcefulness. Rubble and debris were cleared; damaged sections were replaced or cannibalized for parts; previously idle equipment was put into service; and new components were manufactured and installed as required. Within a period of only several weeks, Ploesti was producing more oil than it had before the raid. The effects of the mission on German combat operations, if there were any, were negligible.

That the Germans were able to effect repairs so quickly was in large part due to the fact that the USAAF did not have the wherewithal to follow up the strike with more attacks. Instead, the groups borrowed from the Eighth were later returned to England while the Ninth turned its attention to other targets. Subsequently, there were not enough aircraft to maintain a consistent bombing campaign against Ploesti. Otherwise, the story of Ploesti might have been a much different one. As it developed, it would be many more months before the source of oil so essential to the German military would again figure prominently in the USAAF's operations.

The German air force was still a powerful force in the summer of 1943. Although it had been pushed out of North Africa and was losing its grip on the rest of the Mediterranean, it still often inflicted grievous hurt on the Americans and British in the West, and it nearly always prevailed when it met the Soviets in the East on anything like equal terms. All the same, the Americans, British, and Soviets were growing stronger, whereas the Luftwaffe was slowly bleeding to death.

This fact was not lost on the German hierarchy. The Germans were excellent fingerpointers, and their fingers were increasingly aimed at *Generalmajor* Hans Jeschonnek, the chief of the General Staff of the Luftwaffe, and at Hermann Göring, who had lost touch with the realities of the air war and had no good plan for mitigating the pressures under which his flyers were increasingly operating. More and more, he hid behind the trappings of his office and deflected blame onto others. On the other hand, Jeschonnek, the proud Prussian peacock and devoted follower of Hitler, could not hold up under the pressure. On August 16, he, like Udet, killed himself.

CHAPTER 8

The Gunners

When the self-defending bomber concept was developed during the 1930s, most fighters carried two or four rifle-caliber machine guns. A single .50-caliber Browning provided about the same firepower as three rifle-caliber machine guns, so a pair of them had about the same firepower as three 1930s-era fighters. Moreover, at the time, it was thought that because flexible and turret-mounted guns could move independently of the aircraft, well-trained gunners could achieve greater accuracy than fighter pilots with a battery of fixed weapons.

The concept of self-defending strategic bombers such as the B-17 and B-24 depended on manned .50-caliber machine guns arranged on the aircraft singly and in pairs in order to provide—within a formation of other bombers—a withering density of firepower against attacking fighters. The key to the effectiveness of those guns was the training of the men who manned them. Well-trained aerial gunners maximized the defensive firepower of the bomber formations while poorly trained gunners bankrupted the self-defending bomber concept and rendered meaningless the massive amount of resources spent to field it.

Therefore, operating bombers with ineffective gunners was not an option. Although Eaker would eventually be forced to concede that the bomber formations could not survive unescorted against large groups of expertly coordinated and aggressively flown fighters, those bomber formations would be even less survivable with ineffective aerial gunners.

Even when the bombers were escorted, enemy fighters sometimes broke through that escort. Accordingly, common sense dictated the gunners be as well trained as possible.

The level of training that was possible early in the war was not as great as what was achieved later. In fact, at the time of the Pearl Harbor attack, although three flexible gunnery schools had been formed, none of them had started to train students. Even when they began to produce trained aerial gunners, it soon became apparent that the demand was nearly insatiable, far exceeding what they could provide. Accordingly, the USAAF opened four more flexible gunnery training bases. In the meantime, the training crank was turned as fast as it would go.

It was not until late in 1944 that the supply of trained men began to meet the need. This is easier to understand when it is considered that depending on model, the B-17 and B-24 had upwards of six dedicated gun positions. And although it was these two aircraft that demanded the most gunners, the needs of the medium and light bombers, as well as the later B-29, also had to be met.

The scope of the task was colossal. First, of course, no one had experience that even remotely resembled what was going to happen over Europe. In fact, few people had any experience at all. Certainly, there were personnel who had served as gunners on earlier bombers, like the B-10 and B-18, but that experience with simple turrets mounting single .30-caliber guns was not seamlessly transferable to the much more advanced, multigun turreted systems that were being fielded in increasingly large numbers.

In fact, just getting enough instructors trained to staff the gunnery schools was extremely problematic. The training establishment had to rely somewhat on schooling and materiel provided by the manufacturers who built the turrets, gunsights, and weapons. Nevertheless, the schools managed to bootstrap themselves into operation during 1942.

Aside from expertise, ammunition and aircraft were also in short supply. Early on, because of a shortage of .50-caliber ammunition, gunners were trained on .30-caliber weapons. And training aboard or against operational aircraft was infrequent until later in the war.

The gunnery courses were initially four weeks in length and were later extended to six weeks. "During the first week or so we spent a lot of time in ground school," remembered Henry Hughey, a B-17 ball-turret gunner who served with the 487th Bomb Group (H). "It was lots of books. And then we started our practical training when they gave each one of us a brand new Browning M2, .50-caliber machine gun still covered in Cosmoline. They taught us how to take that thing apart and clean it. It was a great hands-on introduction for us."[1]

Once the student was introduced to the .50-caliber machine gun, the training intensified immediately. "They made us learn all the specifications for it and trained us so that we could take it apart piece-by-piece, blind-folded, and then put it back together again," Hughey recalled. "This was important and useful because a lot of the time during actual operations, depending on what position or turret you manned, you couldn't see where your hand was on the gun; you had to do whatever needed doing by feel."

The training quickly moved to the field. To introduce the students to the basic principles of aerial gunnery, they learned to shoot shotguns against clay pigeon targets. This shotgun training also included shooting at the same clay pigeon targets from a moving truck. This more readily replicated aerial gunnery although it was still far from the real thing. "We were put in the back of a pickup truck," Hughey remembered, "and it would follow a horseshoe-shaped track, and as it moved, they'd launch clay targets from various points along the track and we'd shoot at them. The last target launched was always a zero deflection shot right over the top of the truck; we'd make the instructors mad by just sticking the gun barrel up in the air and whacking the target as it flew by."

Similar training was done from trucks mounted with actual gun turrets equipped with .50-caliber machine guns. The trucks followed a predetermined track while the students fired at raised canvas targets mounted atop a railcar towed by a jeep or pickup. The vehicles were protected by raised earthen berms. Hughey described how the students were assessed: "Before we went to the range we'd roll up our ammunition belt then dip the tips of the bullets into paint of a specific color, then we'd dip them again in hot wax." The paint and wax combination transferred to the target when it was hit and thus enabled the instructors to score a student's performance.

"We also had to learn to handle gun malfunctions," said Hughey. "We'd go to the malfunction range where they had guns attached to mounts in fifty-five-gallon drums filled with concrete. The guns were set up to have certain faults. They might fire only a couple of rounds, or none at all, or more than they were supposed to. We were required to identify and sometimes fix the problems."

And it was not just the guns that the students were required to learn. They also had to become familiar with gun turrets, turret breakdowns, and the different types of sights. There were a variety of different sighting devices, ranging from simple iron-ring arrangements to sophisticated lead-computing equipment. Learning how to use them was integral to effective gunnery as oftentimes, because of the unique dynamics of shooting from an aircraft moving in three dimensions against another aircraft also moving in three dimensions, the correct firing solution was counterintuitive. "To hit a target," Hughey said, "sometimes required us to aim *behind* it."

The final portion of the course included gunnery from a small aircraft such as an AT-6 against a target towed from another aircraft. Once the student successfully completed that portion of the training, he was awarded silver aerial gunner wings.

Training did not end there, however. Upon graduation, the newly minted gunners were shipped from their schools to bases, where they were matched with an aircraft crew. Generally, they were sent to an aircraft that used the type of turret the gunner had trained with. But it was not unusual, particularly early in the war, for gunners who had been trained on one particular type of turret and gunnery system to be sent to an aircraft type that had completely different systems. In these instances, the gunner learned his new turret on the job with help from his new comrades.

Once paired with a crew on a particular aircraft, the gunners learned to work as part of a team on that aircraft. They studied what they needed to know about the new ship's systems and received additional gunnery training. "We used to shoot against targets towed by a B-26 [AT-23]," said Hughey. Indeed, as more resources came available, the assets devoted to aerial gunnery became more sophisticated, including specially armored, orange-painted P-63 Kingcobra fighters at which the gunners shot with frangible .30-caliber bullets.

Once assigned to a crew, the gunners melded with the other airmen as they completed several months of training on the actual aircraft type they would take into combat. On both heavy bomber types, the B-17 and the B-24, gunners made up about half the crew, and most of the rest of the crew had some gunnery training as well. It was during this period that the men developed the bonds and teamwork they would take into combat—bonds that, after being strengthened by the shared terror of combat, were described by many men as greater than any they had ever known.

Henry Hughey recalled that his training continued through his entire combat tour. "The leadership was really smart about the way they used our time. If we weren't flying we were in class, or we were in the books. We spent a lot of time reading in the combat library. There, they kept classified accounts from first-person experiences. These were from guys who had survived really dramatic situations or who had been shot down and successfully evaded. We benefitted a lot from lessons that had been learned before we ever got there. One bit of advice that stuck with me was that if you had to bail out at high altitude you shouldn't pull your ripcord right away otherwise there was a chance that you might get shot up by a German fighter pilot."

Once overseas, the experiences of the gunners differed little from those of the rest of the crew. They endured the same psychological hardships that were part of being separated from families and loved ones. They put in brutally long hours not only flying long missions, but also preparing for them, and then standing down their equipment and participating in debriefings. During the missions themselves, combat aside, they endured the same brutal cold.

"That was one thing they never could really prepare us for in gunnery school," Hughey remembered. "The cold, minus forty or fifty degrees, was not like anything that we'd ever experienced. If you had a gun malfunction and tried to fix it without having any protection on your hands you were going to lose some skin and flesh. Your fingers and hands would literally freeze to the metal—frostbite was a real problem." Aside from their electrically heated suits and felt boots and gloves, the gunners wore silk glove liners that enabled them to work on their guns in the event of a malfunction at high altitude. Still, the cold was so severe that the silk gloves permitted only seconds of work at a time.

As ferocious as the cold was, it did not blast bombers out of the sky. Fighters and flak took the greatest toll on the bomber formations, and the gunners existed to kill, or at least dissuade, enemy fighters. Every bit of training they received, together with the nation's enormous invest-ment in that training and their equipment, and the faith that a generation of air corps strategists had put into the theory of self-defending bomber fleets, hinged on the gunners. If they did not perform, everything was for naught.

Essentially, the nation's grand strategic interests coincided with the very basic survival interests of the gunners. If a bomber's gunners were unable to hold off the enemy fighters, the bomber was shot down, and its gunners, along with the rest of the crew, were captured or killed. If the gunners deterred or defeated the enemy fighters and survived the enemy's antiaircraft fire, the bomber reached its target, the greater strategy was advanced, and everyone survived to do it again.

Still, the responsibility for holding off the enemy fighters did not belong entirely to the gunners. The self-defending bomber concept did not hold that a single aircraft would fight off groups of fighters, but rather that formations of bombers flying in close formation would project virtually impenetrable, concentrated cones of fire. If the bomber pilots flew good, tight formations, the density of the fire the gunners could deliver was much more effective than if the pilots flew sloppy, more relaxed formations.

Of course, the type of formation was very important to the effec-tiveness of the defensive fire. The goal was to find a workable arrange-ment that brought the most guns to bear in the most directions. Additionally, any formation that was considered for defense also had to be workable for bombing. These formations underwent continued refinement throughout the conflict.

Col. Curtis LeMay, the commander of the 305th Bomb Group (H), pioneered the first widely accepted formation, the one on which most subsequent arrangements were based. The basic formation included three aircraft in a wedge shape, with two of these wedges making up a squadron. The three squadrons making up the group were in turn arranged in a wedge shape, with one squadron as the lead, one squadron stacked slightly higher on one side, and the final squadron stacked lower on the other side. This concept was first tried late in 1942 and was adapted by other units as it provided concentrated and overlapping fields of fire for the gunners while still being reasonably easy to fly.

Changes were constant because of new tactics by enemy fighters, larger group formations, modifications to bombing techniques, changes in leadership, and a seemingly neverending pursuit of the perfect arrangement. B-24s also flew different formations than B-17s, primarily because they were more difficult to handle in formation. The Fifteenth Air Force flew different formations than the Eighth Air Force for reasons that are not clear; it is not evident that one was better than the other.

There were dangers associated with operating so many big aircraft with so many guns so closely together. Among these hazards were midair collisions. Although it was infrequent, it was not unheard of for two or more aircraft to inadvertently collide and chop each other out of the sky. Another risk was that in the heat of combat, gunners would inadvertently shoot into neighboring bombers while shooting at an enemy fighter. This was obviously not supposed to happen, and it did not happen within a well-disciplined formation. "We were supposed to stop shooting if the Germans went through the formation," recalled Hughey. "Our formations were designed so that we put maximum firepower to the outside of the formation, not inside. And in reality, if an enemy plane got through us and into the formation, he was moving so fast that he wasn't there for very long."

The truth of the matter was that later in the war, antiaircraft fire (flak) brought down the greatest numbers of aircraft. Against this threat, the gunners were powerless. Just like every other crewman, they had no choice but to simply endure and watch. If the flak was heavy and accurate, their positions simply became seats to mortifying theater. When a ship was hit and knocked down—often in flames—it was the unusual crewman who did not consider that but for luck, it could have just as easily been his aircraft that was hit. "It was a common joke," said Hughey, "to say that we were 'gunners today and goners tomorrow.'"

Hughey was a B-17 ball-turret gunner; reviewing his position and the Sperry ball turret is instructive as it helps to underscore the complexities of the equipment and the job. "The turret was too small to accommodate the gunner with his parachute, so I kept mine on a small shelf just in front and above the turret. My G.I. shoes were tied to it because the electrically heated felt boots we wore would have flown right off if I'd had to parachute. Even if they had stayed on my feet, they would have been worthless for walking, or evading."

Because of the gun arrangement, it was not possible to get inside the turret until the aircraft was airborne. Then the gunner, from outside the turret, manually cranked the guns straight down, opened the hatch, and lowered himself into the glass and metal bubble. "Once I got in, I'd turn on the electrical and hydraulic power. An electric motor drove the hydraulic pumps that actually powered the turret. I was essentially on my back, looking through my legs which were actually a little bit higher than my head. My torso was protected by a padded section of armor plate. It was pretty tight in there with ammo boxes and the ammunition chutes that fed the guns [250 rounds per]. The sight was between my knees and my face. It was a Sperry K-4 automatic computing sight which projected an illuminated firing solution on a glass plate so long as I set it up correctly."

The turret was equipped with two of the ubiquitous M2 .50-caliber machine guns. "There were two handles above my head," Hughey said. "Pulling back on them raised the guns, pushing forward lowered them. If I pushed them to my right the turret rotated to my left, and vice versa. There were buttons on top of each handle that fired the guns. We were supposed to keep the turret in a constant turn so I worked with the guys from the armament shack to adjust the turret so that it was always in a slow, steady turn. Otherwise, I would have had to keep my arms above my head the entire time and that could really wear a person out."

The B-17 ball turret's guns provided near-hemispheric coverage around the lower half of the aircraft. This let the gunner fire against fighters attacking from level or below the aircraft. Cutoff solenoids ensured that the gunner did not shoot the aircraft's propellers. "To communicate with the rest of the crew, there was a press-to-talk footswitch on the right side," said Hughey. "There was another footswitch on the right side that let me adjust the diameter of the sight reticle."

It happened occasionally, but the gunners usually did not swap positions on the aircraft. "Our tail gunner was Jimmy Spurlock—he was from my hometown." Hughey remembered. "We had enlisted together and gone through all our training together and got assigned to the same aircraft. Anyway, that tail position was the worst. The gunner had to sit on a bicycle-style seat; it could get really uncomfortable, especially after eight or nine hours—I didn't want anything to do with manning that position!"

How effective were the gunners aboard the big bombers? The answer is difficult and will never be satisfied in quantifiable terms. The reasons are manifold. First, if a German fighter was engaged by one gunner, it was likely that it was also engaged by at least several more. If that fighter was obviously destroyed, for instance, if it lost a wing or exploded in midair, it was likely—and understandable—that more than one gunner would claim an aerial victory.

Moreover, it was difficult for the gunners, especially in the heat of battle, to distinguish between enemy fighters that were mortally damaged and those that were only slightly so. Aircraft often had significant pieces shot away—wing and fuselage panels or even engine cowlings—but were still quite flyable. Nevertheless, aircraft that were significantly damaged were going to do no more fighting, at least not until they were repaired.

Claims against the Me-109, the Luftwaffe's most numerous fighter, were likely overinflated because its engine belched smoke when pushed quickly to full throttle. As a German pilot added power and dived away from his attack on a bomber formation, he quite often trailed a plume of smoke that could be interpreted as proof of damage. This might then erroneously be submitted during debriefing as a claim for a destroyed enemy aircraft.

Although it might appear that an enemy fighter was damaged to a point where it could not possibly fly, it could not truly be confirmed as destroyed unless it exploded or came apart in midair or was seen to crash to the ground. That a gunner, in the middle of a fight and moving away from the scene at more than 150 miles per hour, had the opportunity to watch an enemy fighter fall four or five miles to the ground is doubtful. Further, layers of clouds below the fight often made it impossible to see the ground.

Debriefing officers had their hands full trying to sort out who shot what, when, and where after missions that witnessed significant fighter opposition. There simply were no good means to accurately sort all the conflicting and overlapping claims. Typically, awards for aerial victories far exceeded the losses the Germans actually sustained. Everyone knew it. Still, it did no great harm. When USAAF planners estimated Luftwaffe losses, there was some accounting for the excessive claims made by the bomber crews. If allowing more claims helped the morale of the crews, that was not a bad thing. Additionally, the inflated claims made for good news copy.

But regardless of the fact that it is impossible to measure precisely the number of German aircraft shot down by the gunners aboard the heavy bombers, there is no debating the fact that they were effective to a very great extent. Although the gunners put in claims for more aircraft than they actually destroyed, they *did* shoot down significant numbers of German fighters. The Luftwaffe pilots hated and feared the streams of fire that lashed out from the bomber formations, which no doubt influenced the aggressiveness of at least some of the enemy fliers.

One German pilot quite candidly described his fear on taking part in his first formation head-on attack against a group of B-17s: "My heart dropped into my boots. . . . I was so nervous that I forgot everything. I just flew straight ahead, firing." But having survived the headlong attack through the American formation, that same pilot recovered his wits enough to down a straggling bomber. A single bomber was much easier prey than a coherent, mutually supporting formation—a truth that was proved over and over throughout the war.[2]

The trepidation at attacking the bomber formations was expressed by another Luftwaffe flyer, *Oberstleutnant* Hans Philipp, an FW-190 pilot and the commander of JG 1:

Against 20 Russians trying to shoot you down, or even 20 Spitfires, it can be exciting, even fun. But curve in towards 40 Fortresses and all your past sins flash before your eyes. And when you yourself have reached this state of mind, it becomes that much more difficult to have to drive every pilot of the *Geschwader*, right down to the youngest and lowliest NCO, to do the same.[3]

This quote, dating from the fall of 1943, came from an ace with more than 200 aerial victories against the Soviets. The difference in the tenor of the fighting between the Eastern Front and the Western is illustrated by the fact that after six months at the head of JG 1 fighting the RAF and the USAAF, Philipp shot down only a single P-47, a single Spitfire, and a single four-engine bomber. He was killed within a week of making the observation above.

The common perception of the bomber crews was one of young men bonding closer than brothers. In some cases, this was true. "We depended on each other, literally, for our lives," said one veteran." Another offered: "The most difficult thing I've ever done, in all my life, was saying goodbye to my crew after the war. I've never been so close to anyone—it was more than family."

But to think this was the rule is absurd. The odds were small that ten different men from a broad spectrum of backgrounds would get along well all the time. Certainly, they could perform as a trained team, but they could not be forced to embrace each other in every situation. One veteran's recollection supports this. For a variety of reasons, he had lost respect for his pilot and had had a series of unpleasant encounters with another of the crewmen. Finally, after completing twenty missions, he felt he could no longer work with his own crew:

> So I went to the Chaplain. This was late in the evening, after debriefing, and I told the Chaplain exactly what happened, and I told him I would like to fly with another crew that's more professional than what this crew was. And sure enough, the next mission, I was on another crew. I flew with different crews [for his final five missions], and man, it made a big difference. They had respect for me, and I had respect for them.[4]

When asked about the typical perception of closely tied crews, the same veteran replied: "Maybe some of them were, [but] not me. It seems like everybody was looking out for themselves and a lot of horseplay around." His observation has some merit and certainly is consistent with human nature, especially when it is considered that most of the men were only a year or two removed from pushing and shoving on the schoolyard.

Although the medium and heavy bombers were mostly flown from the States to their bases in England, nearly all of the fighters were transported by ship and assembled and flight-tested upon arrival. Robert "Punchy" Powell, a P-47 pilot with the 352nd Fighter Group at Bodney, remembered that their replacement aircraft were shipped over and assembled at the depot at Burtonwood before being flown into the airfield. "A lot of times these aircraft were brought in by WASPs [Women Airforce Service Pilots]."[5]

"On one particular day," he said, "one of these gals flew into the pattern with a new P-47. Well, she cut off one of our guys, and he ended up having to abort his landing and go around." The female pilot landed safely and parked her aircraft while the affronted squadron pilot made another trip around the circuit before landing. "That guy was mad as hell at this woman pilot," Powell recalled. "Of course, he had no idea it was a female flying the other plane. He taxied right next to where she was still filling out paperwork in the cockpit. Anyway, he shut his engine down, climbed out of his airplane, and stomped up to hers and shouted up, 'You get your ass out of there—I'm gonna kick your balls off!' She smiled down at him and pulled her helmet off, and all of her hair came tumbling down around her shoulders. 'You just go ahead,' she said, 'and give it a try!'"

CHAPTER 9

Black Thursday and Long-Range Fighters

The combined USAAF and RAF day and night raids on Hamburg from July 24 to August 3, 1943, turned the city to ashes. The devastation was staggering and on a scale unlike anything the Germans had experienced. Firestorms with temperatures exceeding 1,000 degrees centigrade morphed into massive, hellish, self-feeding monsters that literally sucked the air out of the city and used it for fuel. The chief of the city's civil defense, *Generalmajor* Kehrl, filed a report on the devastation:

> Trees three feet thick were broken off or uprooted, human beings were thrown to the ground or flung alive into the flames by winds which exceeded 150 miles an hour. The panic-stricken citizens knew not where to turn. Flames drove them from the shelters, but high-explosive bombs sent them scurrying back again. Once inside, they were suffocated by carbon-monoxide poisoning and their bodies reduced to ashes as though they had been placed in a crematorium, which was indeed what each shelter proved to be.[1]

The raids killed 40,000 people, injured nearly 100,000 more, and made a million people homeless. It was the wakeup call that Germany's leadership needed to fix the air defense of the Reich. And for once, they seemed resolved to do something about it. Galland, for one, believed that a massive fighter-production program could prevent future attacks of this sort. At a meeting in Göring's office at Hitler's Wolf Lair in East Prussia, it appeared that, for once, everyone in the Luftwaffe high command was in agreement. Galland recalled that he had never seen, and would never again see, everyone so committed to a cause: Hamburg must never happen again.

Following the discussions, Galland remembered that Göring summarized the consensus: "The Luftwaffe . . . must now change over to the defense against the west. It should be possible to stop the Allied raids against the Reich by concentrating all forces and their effects on this one aim."[2]

The crowd of ranking officers waited while Göring left their company to report their resolution to Hitler. In his absence, they continued to discuss and develop their plans. When Göring returned, he walked wordlessly through their ranks and straight into an adjoining room. It did not bode well. Galland was called into the room a short time later along with Dietrich Peltz, the *Inspekteur der Kampfflieger*. They were embarrassed to find Göring crumpled over his desk, his head facedown in his arm.

The *Reichsmarschall* was a ruined, pathetic wreck. Hitler had rejected everything Göring offered. He berated Göring and the Luftwaffe and declared that the only way to deal with the attacks from the west was with even greater and more devastating counterattacks. On his orders, the Luftwaffe was to direct every effort toward burning England's cities to the ground. It was an absurd notion. Germany had neither the numbers nor the types of aircraft needed for such a thing. It was too late. It had not been in 1936, when Wever was killed and the U.S. Army Air Corps was flying early models of the B-17. But in 1943, it was beyond hopelessly impossible.

Galland recollected his incredulity: "It is difficult to describe how I felt at that moment. Annoyance and revolt were mixed with a failure to understand and a wish to resign. What was left of the leaders' unanimity on the question of air defense? What could I do here now? Should I not have asked to be relieved of my post?" In the end, Galland left with the rest of the leadership, hopeful that Hitler's decision might be altered.[3]

It was not.

The size and frequency of the Eighth's raids increased through the summer of 1943. At the same time, the Luftwaffe improved the tactics and equipment of its fighters. Modifications were made that gave both the Me-109 and FW-190 more armament, making them better able to knock down the heavy bombers. Likewise, they adjusted their tactics such that they attacked in larger formations. Consequently, the loss rate among the American bomber groups climbed precipitously, especially as many of the raids went beyond the range of fighter escorts. Indeed, 148 bombers were lost on just four raids from August 8 to August 14. To put the 148 lost bombers in context, it had been less than four months earlier that the 115 bombers the Eighth sent on the April 17 raid against Bremen were a record.

The dual raid against Schweinfurt and Regensburg on August 17 was even more telling. Unescorted for much of their route, the 376 B-17s the Eighth put in the sky that day were utterly savaged: 60 were shot down, and at least that many more were heavily damaged. A significant number of them were never returned to service. Still, Eaker continued to put his men into the fight.

The butchery did not abate as summer turned to fall. The attack on October 10 was particularly costly. The Eighth put 206 bombers over Munster. Of that number, 30 were shot down, including 12 of 14 aircraft from the 100th Bomb Group (H). Eaker was alarmed; the notion of self-protecting strategic bombers was at risk.

Even so, the American bombers came doggedly on. Despite the losses they took, they inflicted grievous damage, and the Luftwaffe's leadership was increasingly at a loss about what to do. Too often, the solution was to hurl insults and exhortations at the flyers. It was an indication of desperation. Göring, who endured Hitler's tirades, had no compunction against turning right around and insulting his fighter pilots, those responsible for defending the Reich from the Allied bombers. An especially egregious example was his declaration on October 7, 1943:

I have laid aside my decorations. I shall not put them on again until the German Luftwaffe starts to fight with the kind of dedication it fought with when I won them. This is final, however, the *Jagdwaffe* is going to give battle to the last man. If it does not, it can go and join the infantry. The German people doesn't give a damn about the *Jagdwaffe*'s losses.

If there was any doubt that the Schweinfurt mission of October 14, 1943, was of preeminent importance to the USAAF leadership, it was dispelled by the dispatch read to the crews scheduled for that day's mission:

This air operation today is the most important air operation yet conducted in this war. The target must be destroyed. It is of vital importance to the enemy. Your friends and comrades, that have been lost and that will be lost today, are depending on you. Their sacrifice must not be in vain. Good luck, good shooting and good bombing.

Lt. William C. Heller—the wood lath and wire boy—was now a B-17 pilot with the 303rd Bomb Group (H) based at Molesworth.[4] He remembered the disquiet from the group's officers at 0500 when the curtain was pulled away from the map marking that day's target. "It was a DP raid—deep penetration. The line went far into Germany, and when we saw that it was Schweinfurt there was certainly some anxiety and concern. The group had been there a couple of months earlier in August and it had been a tough one." However, the weather was poor. "It was misty and raining, and there was some talk that the mission might get scrubbed." No doubt, there were crewmen who hoped the mission *would* be cancelled even though they knew full well that sooner or later, the target would have to be hit.

Those hopes were not realized. The crews climbed aboard their aircraft and readied them for takeoff. Once the engines were started, the pilots of the big ships taxied to the runway while keeping an eye out for the flare that would signal their launch. The signal came, and Heller watched as the lead bomber rumbled down the runway. In only a few minutes, it was his turn: "Visibility was still so bad that we couldn't see the end of the runway. But we took off and transitioned to instruments until we broke out into a brilliantly clear sky at 7,000 feet."

The 303rd managed to form in good order, but elsewhere, the miserable weather caused problems. The 305th Bomb Group (H), a B-17 outfit based out of Chelveston, could not find its place in the bomber stream and attached itself as best it could to another wing. However, its formation was ragged and barely recognizable as such; this fact would cost it dearly in the coming hours. None of the B-24s planned for the raid—all from the Second Air Division—was able to join the effort. They were subsequently directed to execute an unplanned diversionary raid to Emden, well north of the target area.

"We made our way east in a nice, tight formation," remembered Heller of the 303rd. "Our Spitfire escort left us about mid-channel and the P-47s turned back as we reached western Belgium. From that point, we were on our own." And the Luftwaffe pilots took advantage of that. Although they did mix it up with the P-47 escort before it turned for home—and lost seven aircraft while scoring only one victory—the bulk of the German fighters saved their fuel and ammunition for the bombers. It made little sense to throw themselves against the combined defenses of the fighters and the bombers when they only had to wait until the fighters, low on fuel, turned back for England. Once the protective escort was gone, there was plenty of time for them to orchestrate and execute their attacks on the bomber stream.

"The Germans were there just as soon as the P-47s departed," recounted Heller. "They started hitting us immediately and never really let up." The Luftwaffe pilots generally started their runs with head-on attacks and then reconstituted for additional attacks from multiple directions. Heller remembered skidding his aircraft to spoil the aim of the enemy pilots: "My aircraft was an older model without servos [to help power the controls] and my legs got so tired from stepping on the rudder pedals that I had to use my hands to push down on my legs."

Heller continued to dance the big aircraft within the constraints of its place in the formation. His copilot, Jack Coppom, had been trained as a fighter pilot and signaled exactly when Heller should skid the ship. Heller recalled one particular attack: "Just after following his motion to skid left, a great cluster of 20-millimeter shells burst right where we had been."

Likewise, Heller responded to calls from his gunners as attacks came from quarters that were outside his line of sight. "Just as sure as I'd slip or dive the ship within the formation, shells would burst in clusters all about us, usually in the same spot where we had been. It was wonderful crew coordination; there's no wonder I loved those men."

Wilbur Klint, a copilot in another part of the 303rd's formation, noted the wild maneuvering of the big ships. He and his pilot were also "at the controls almost all the time, trying to get the most evasive action possible without ramming one of our own planes."

The ubiquitous flak guns were also at work. Black bursts pocked the formations, and although they did not knock down as many bombers as the fighters, the enemy guns still took their toll. Atypically, the German fighters did not appear to pull back while the flak gunners worked. Rather, they pressed their attacks almost without interruption. "There were so many of them," Heller said, "that I don't understand how they didn't shoot each other down, or run into each other."

Because the mission was such a long one, the B-17s were fitted with extra fuel tanks in their bomb bays. They carried 410 gallons each and added much-needed range. When Heller's tanks emptied, he tried to jettison them, but they failed to fall away. This was dangerous. The tanks never emptied completely, and the small amount of fuel remaining combined with the air in the tank to create a mixture that, if it were struck by an enemy incendiary or cannon round, would explode with all the fierceness of a purpose-made bomb.

Heller's crew wrestled unsuccessfully to get the stubborn tanks to drop clear while the fighting around them continued without a break. "Everywhere I looked," Heller recalled, "there were B-17s on fire, enemy fighters being blown out of the sky and parachutes. It was particularly horrifying to see parachutes on fire and know that those men were falling to their deaths." It was especially upsetting for Heller because these were men whom he knew. These were men with whom he worked, dined, and played. These were men who had wives and children and families. These were his friends.

The fighting was so violent that Heller did not immediately notice when a 20-millimeter cannon round smashed through the windscreen in front of him, passed over his shoulder, and punched through the fuselage. Heller reported: "I didn't really notice it until sweat and the condensation inside my oxygen mask started to freeze."

Pilots of the 353rd Fighter Group wish each other luck before they take off from their base in England to escort the heavy bombers on a mission over enemy installations. The plane is Lt. Col. William B. Bailey's North American P-51 *Double Trouble Two*. USAAF

An A-36 dive bomber of the 86th Fighter Bomber Group. A derivative of the P-51A, the A-36 gave a good account of itself in North Africa, the Mediterranean, and Italy. USAAF

The underside of a 361st Fighter Group P-51 painted with invasion stripes. The seventy-five-gallon external fuel tanks greatly extended the P-51's already impressive range. USAAF

Twenty-year-old Barrie Davis flew P-47s and P-51s with the 325th Fighter Group out of Lesina, Italy. He was credited with six aerial victories.

BARRIE DAVIS

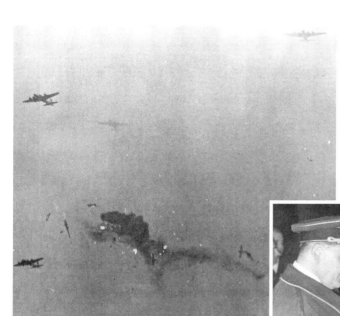

Flaming wreckage
marks the point where
two B-17s collided
over an English base
as their bomb group
recovered through
heavy clouds. USAAF

Hermann Göring and Ernst Udet, 1938.

BUNDESARCHIV, BILD 183-H08192 / CC-BY-SA

P-39 pilot Hugh Dow of the 350th Fighter Group scored an aerial victory over
a German Me-109 on February 15, 1943, while flying out of Thelepte #2 in
Tunisia. Following his success, he drove into the desert and picked up the
German pilot. Dow scored two kills over Me-109s while flying the P-39.

HUGH DOW

For the gunners, the day continued long after their bombers returned to base. Among other tasks, the guns had to be taken out of the aircraft and thoroughly cleaned. USAAF

Adolf Hitler and Hermann Göring, 1938. BUNDESARCHIV, BILD 183-2004-1202-504 /

A flight of P-47s from the 56th Fighter Group at the start of their formation takeoff roll. USAAF

Fifteenth Air Force bombers such as this B-24 often had to clear mountains en route to and from the target. Doing so could be a challenge with one or more engines shot out. USAAF

The Me-109G was the Luftwaffe fighter most often encountered by USAAF crews. BUNDESARCHIV, BILD 1011-676-7974-13 / KEINER / CC-BY-SA

Mechanics from the 78th Fighter Group service a P-47. Note the size of the fighter relative to the men working on it: the "Jug" was the largest single-engine fighter of the war. USAAF

A P-51 ground crewman of the 361st Fighter Group signals the aircraft's pilot.
USAAF

Good formations enabled gunners aboard bombers to protect the group with effective, overlapping fields of fire. USAAF

FW-190s based in the Netherlands dogged USAAF crews through much of the war. BUNDESARCHIV, BILD 101I-619-2664-07 / KESTNER / CC-BY-SA

An He-111 crew—and friends—surrenders at the end of the war. The Luftwaffe had fallen a long way since the *blitzkrieg* days. USAAF

Joseph Zsampar was a ball-turret gunner with the 303rd Bomb Group, based at Molesworth. The romance between him and his pretty English love, Pauline Roberts, ended tragically. LOUISE SMEDLY-HAMPSON

The Curtiss P-40 was a stalwart during the early fighting in North Africa and the Mediterranean and was able to hold its own against contemporary German fighters. USAAF

The B-17 could absorb massive amounts of damage and still return to base.
USAAF

An Me-109 assembly line during 1943.

Art Fiedler was a twenty-year-old P-51 pilot with the 325th Fighter Group. He was credited with eight aerial victories. ART FIEDLER

Armorers from the 1st Fighter Group reload the four .50-caliber machine guns and the single 20-millimeter cannon of a P-38. USAAF

A B-17 crew bails out of its stricken aircraft. Note the crewman behind the aircraft as well as the crewman immediately behind the aircraft's right wing. USAAF

An FW-190 (right side of photo) downs a B-24 over Austria. USAAF

A B-17 formation (foreground) and a B-24 formation (background) come together. Midair collisions were a real danger when great numbers of bombers joined. USAAF

A German twin-engine fighter takes a B-17 under fire. USAAF

The B-26 was used extensively against tactical targets such as airfields. USAAF

The distinctive profile of the P-38 meant that it was less frequently mistaken for an enemy fighter. USAAF

B-17s from the 99th Bomb Group of the Fifteenth Air Force. Note the "Mickey" radar set in the leading aircraft in place of the ball-turret gunner.
USAAF

The P-38 possessed excellent firepower, as well as good range and maneuverability, especially in its later iterations. On the other hand, it was expensive and more difficult to fly and maintain. USAAF

Ground personnel and crews not flying "sweat out" a mission as they wait for their comrades to return. USAAF

Gen. James Doolittle. USAAF

Henry H. Arnold following
the Allied triumph in
World War II, circa 1947.
BUNDESARCHIV, BILD
183-19000-1047 / CC-BY-SA

The B-17G was the iconic heavy bomber over Europe from late 1943. This
particular aircraft has had its ball turret replaced by a "Mickey" radar bombing
set. USAAF

Fatigue shows on the faces of this bomber crew during post-mission debriefing in early 1944. USAAF

A right waist gunner aboard a B-17 ankle-deep in spent shell casings. Note the flak apron and other protective gear. USAAF

Fred Christensen Jr. of the 56th Fighter Group scored more than twenty aerial victories. The nose art of his P-47, *Miss Fire*, was among the comeliest in the Eighth Air Force. USAAF

Heller was not hurt by the shell because he had had the bulletproof glass that was initially installed in the windscreen removed. "I didn't like the bulletproof glass," he said, "because it iced up so easily and I'd spend as much time scraping away ice as I did flying. So I asked the crew chief to replace the glass with a silicon-wafer windscreen." When the heavy 20-millimeter shell struck the lighter windscreen it didn't meet enough resistance to trigger its fuze and explode. Had it impacted the heavier, bulletproof windscreen it would likely have detonated, injuring or killing Heller.

Sometime during the run to the target, two of the engines on Heller's aircraft began to lose power. Heller and Coppom worked to stay in formation but it was difficult. They coddled the sick engines and relied on increased power from the two remaining good engines to hold their place. It was a dicey game, as running the power up on the good engines put them under increased stress and consequently made them much more susceptible to failure. It was not until they jettisoned the ship's bombs that they were able to hold their position in the formation without struggling.

That they were able to stay within the protection of the formation was a bittersweet triumph for Heller and his crew. Without their bombs, their mission was an empty one. The terrifying trip into the heart of Germany and into the full fury of the Luftwaffe would see them drop no bombs on the target.

Nevertheless, regardless of whether they had bombs or were able to hold formation, the crew was still in mortal danger. Heller recalled: "I saw a Fort up ahead start to smoke—the next instant a sheet of flame, then nothing!" But it was not only the bombers that fell over Europe that day. German fighters also went down. Heller recollected that his crew bagged three of the enemy aircraft: an Me-110, an Me-210, and an FW-190.

Those aircraft that still had their bombs were greeted with a break in the clouds directly over the target, and they released their loads of general-purpose and incendiary bombs. But the Germans did not let up just because the bombers had dropped their loads. Rather, the attacks continued with the same intensity. In fact, many of the enemy aircraft that had attacked the raiders on their way to the target landed to refuel, rearm, and take off again. The Luftwaffe flew more than 800 sorties against the American bombers that day.

That the Germans made the interception of the bombers an all-out effort is indicated by the varied types of aircraft they sent aloft. Those in greatest numbers were the FW-190s and Me-109s, but twin-engine types, some of them night fighters, were also put into the fight. These included Me-110s, Ju-88s, and Me-210s. There were even reports of attacks by the slow and venerable Ju-87 Stuka.

The Luftwaffe flyers also employed some of their latest weapons. This was the biggest effort ever flown by twin-engine aircraft against the American bombers, and many of them, together with a smaller number of single-engine aircraft, carried 21-centimeter rockets. These projectiles were wildly inaccurate but could be fired from greater than 1,000 yards, outside the effective range of the bombers' .50-caliber guns. In the unlikely event that one of these weapons found its mark, the big warhead almost certainly guaranteed the bomber would go down. Even if a kill was not achieved, damaged bombers often fell out of formation and became easy prey for conventionally armed fighters.

The weather over the German coastal bases grew steadily worse, and the fighters finally gave up their attacks as the bombers retreated out over the water. They had been under constant fighter attack for more than three hours. Heller and his crew had survived to that point although their ship had been badly hit. Aside from the two lame engines, the left horizontal stabilizer had been badly holed, as had the vertical stabilizer and the leading edge of the left wing. Elsewhere, the ship had sustained random hits that were not as critical.

Heller's instrument panel had also been badly shot up, and he had no airspeed indicator or artificial horizon. These instruments were absolutely critical for penetrating bad weather, and bad weather still blanketed the English countryside. Heller recollected:

Twenty minutes before the fuel would have been exhausted, a small hole appeared, and we were able to spiral down at a rate of descent that frosted the instrument panel. We found RAF Henley just outside of London. The RAF immediately gave us a clear runway. A doctor and a chaplain met us at the flight line. We needed neither, thank God, but these actions boosted our admiration of the RAF. Women mechanics (WAAF) repaired the battle damage temporarily and provided fuel from their meager stores to get us back to base at Molesworth. Our RAF hosts served us tea and dinner and provided beds for us. Before going to bed the gunner's cleaned and oiled their guns. By 9:00 P.M., after a good day's work, I went to bed with a word of thanks to Our Lord for our preservation.

October 14, 1943, came to be known as Black Thursday. The USAAF sent 291 B-17s to Schweinfurt that day, and 60 had been shot down. Another 7 badly damaged aircraft were beyond repair and had to be scrapped. The loss rate was a staggering 23 percent. Some individual units were absolutely savaged. The 305th, the group that had never found its proper place in the bomber stream, had put 15 aircraft over the continent. Its ground and support crews waited in stunned disbelief as day turned to dusk and only 2 of the bombers returned to base. It took the unit months to fully recover.

When word got back to the States, the reaction was dark. The second raid on Schweinfurt, if no other mission had, drove home the point that unescorted bombers, even heavily armed bombers, could not operate over Germany during daylight without being savaged. Still, Arnold tried to project an image of confidence and perseverance. To anyone familiar with the facts, his statement seemed uninformed, a mixture of bravado and ignorance: "Regardless of our losses, I'm ready to send replacements of aircraft and crews and continue building up our strength. The opposition isn't nearly what it was, and we are wearing them down. The loss of 60 American bombers in the Schweinfurt raid was incidental."[5]

In fact, the losses on this second Schweinfurt raid, in combination with the grievous losses sustained during the previous three months, reverberated through the core of the USAAF's strategy.

Despite the tragic losses, Eaker's report to Arnold the following day was spirited rather than defeatist. After describing in detail the composition and tactics of the German fighter formations, he characterized their operations as "perfectly timed and coordinated and skillfully executed." He then tallied the Eighth's losses and called the bombing results "excellent," which was actually quite accurate. Albert Speer estimated that 67 percent of ball-bearing production capacity was destroyed. Eaker further underscored his belief that the losses "did not represent disaster," but rather showed "that the air battle has reached its climax."[6]

Eaker then asked Arnold for more bombers and crews, "every possible fighter," and drop tanks for the fighters. He closed with an expression of steadfast determination:

> We must show the enemy we can replace our losses; he knows he cannot replace his. We must continue the battle with unrelenting fury. This we shall do. There is no discouragement here. We are convinced that when the totals are struck yesterday's losses will be far outweighed by the value of the enemy material destroyed.

The raid marked the apex of the Luftwaffe's successes against the USAAF. Regardless of how Arnold or Eaker might have tried to qualify what had happened during the previous several months, the truth was that their dearly held precept—unescorted daylight bombardment of Germany—was untenable. In blunt terms, notwithstanding the bravery and skill of its men, the Eighth had been sorely beaten over Schweinfurt.

Even the United States, with its ability to produce unprecedented numbers of aircraft and crews, was unable to sustain the loss rates experienced during the period. Even if it could have, the public might not have supported such enormous casualties. In plain terms, each heavy bomber that was shot out of the sky took what was practically a high-school baseball team with it. Every member of that team had mothers and fathers, families and friends. Sacrificing them wholesale in a campaign that seemingly had no end would have been difficult for Arnold to sell in the long term.

Although Arnold outwardly projected an attitude of bravado, the Black Thursday raid surely must have motivated him to reflect on the seemingly endless string of debates he had had with his British counterparts since before the U.S. entered the war. The earlier British insistence—indeed, their certainty—that the United States would never be able to execute a daylight bombing campaign against the heart of Germany was more credible than ever. As much as he might bluster, Arnold did not have a crystal ball, and from where he sat, he had no firm evidence about whether the USAAF in Europe was winning or losing the bombing campaign, especially in light of the latest losses.

It was now clear that several of the key assumptions underlying the campaign were flawed. While the USAAF bombers were faster and more heavily armed than the British or German bombers of the early-war years, fighter performance and firepower had increased even more quickly. In addition, the effectiveness of the bombers' defensive guns had been overestimated. Finally, the ability of a resourceful, competent foe like the Luftwaffe to conceive and adopt innovations of its own—such as the head-on attack, air-to-air rockets, and massed attacks—was probably underestimated.

Arnold was certainly human enough to question his own beliefs, and there is little doubt that he retraced in his mind the events that had gotten his air force to that critical juncture. He surely must have recalled Eaker's eloquent defense of daylight bombing to Churchill at the beginning of the year in Casablanca. He might even have recollected one of his first conversations with RAF Air Vice Marshal Arthur Harris a year before Casablanca. At a social engagement in Washington in January 1942, Harris told Arnold: "The Boche have too many fighters, too much flak, too much bloody power against that West Wall to make it worth the losses. God knows, I hope you can do it, but I don't think you can. . . . Come join us at night. Together we'll lick them."[7]

Despite any misgivings he might have had, Arnold urged Eaker to communicate words of encouragement to the flyers: "The cornered wolf fights hardest, and the German air force has been driven into its last corner."[8]

Ultimately, it took Luftwaffe cannons and guns to make the point that British pleading and counsel could not. Notwithstanding Arnold's bluster and swagger, Eaker no longer sent his bombers without fighter escort. Until procedures and equipment extended the range of the American fighters, there would be no American bombing campaign beyond the peripheries of Germany.

Eaker's wartime aide and biographer took issue with the notion that Eaker forbade raids into Germany beyond the range of fighter escorts:

What halted deep penetrations from October 15 to the end of December was not the lack of long-range fighters . . . but simply

the atrocious run of bad weather. No orders were ever issued by
Eaker . . . to refrain from deep attacks. Nor is there any indication that such a deliberate holdback was considered. The statement that air superiority over Germany had been lost can only
be chalked up to ivory-tower superficiality.[9]

Perhaps, but it is difficult to believe that there was not a single day
during the period when the weather over worthwhile German targets—
beyond the range of fighter escorts—was not forecast to be good enough
for visual bombing.

From Black Thursday until early 1944, the Eighth returned to Germany, but only along the margins and always with fighter escorts. Missions were also less frequent as the miserable European winter weather
precluded operations on most days. It was a time of relatively subdued
activity during which both sides made ready to reengage with vigor.

The USAAF made good use of that time. For one, it created a new
strategic air force. The Fifteenth Air Force was officially formed on
November 1, 1943, under Doolittle in Tunis. By the end of the month,
Doolittle, by now a major general, had moved the new air force's headquarters to Bari just above Italy's southern heel. The Italian government
had surrendered on September 8, 1943, and the Allies had invaded the
following day. Still, the German armies in Italy had not capitulated and
would hold much of the country until the end of the war. Nevertheless,
the territory under Allied control by November 1943 was more than adequate to host a new air force.

The creation of the Fifteenth had been in the planning stages for
months, and for months, Eaker had lobbied against it. It was just one
more burden in a long string of peripheral distractions and demands that
had bled his operations and prevented him from bringing the Eighth up
to its full strength. Almost since its arrival in England, the Eighth had
been a continuously pilfered piggy bank of aircraft, crews, and materiel.

But this time, rather than sending units to support a campaign as had
happened with North Africa or lending a few groups for discrete missions as had occured for the Ploesti raid, he was being robbed so that a

complete and separate strategic air force—in essence, a competitor—could be built. The initial cadre of bombers came from units already in the Mediterranean, although many of those had originated from the Eighth the previous year. But the majority, fifteen of the twenty groups that eventually made up the Fifteenth, had been slated for Eaker's Eighth.

The creation of the Fifteenth had been debated for a while. Arnold had initially been critical of the notion. Like Eaker, he was resistant to any plan that diluted the Eighth and detracted from the rapid escalation of the bomber offensive. However, he was slowly won over to the idea by the advantages extolled by its advocates including Spaatz, Tedder, Portal, and Eisenhower.[10]

Spaatz in particular was a promoter of the idea. He had not wanted to leave his command of the Eighth to come to the Mediterranean. There he had no real role in the strategic air war that his friend Eaker was directing from England. Spaatz craved command of a strategic air force and was a likely candidate to get one if such a force was put together in the Mediterranean. In fact, Spaatz had earlier made the very ambitious observation to Arnold that the region offered superb basing opportunities for the gigantic B-29, a purely strategic aircraft that dramatically eclipsed the B-17 and B-24 in every regard.

If more infrastructure had to be built to support the Americans in England, even more was needed in Italy, where existing airbases had to be extensively lengthened, enlarged, and otherwise engineered and additional ones had to be built. On the other hand, Italy did offer markedly better weather. Although fog and rain and cloud might shut down operations in England on any given day, there was a fair chance that missions could be flown that same day from bases in Italy. This was a very important factor when it is considered that air superiority had to be unequivocally established in the few short months remaining before the invasion of Europe scheduled for late the next spring.

Italy also featured a geography that allowed the heavy bombers to range into territory that the Eighth could not reach from England. For instance, the critical campaign that was eventually waged against Ploesti by the Fifteenth during the spring and summer of 1944 could never have been executed from England. Indeed, some would argue that the destruction of Ploesti alone was worth standing up the Fifteenth.

Finally, faced with two strategic air forces on separate flanks, the Germans would have to split their defenses; split defenses would be weaker defenses.

Spaatz used all of these points to justify his objective to Arnold in a letter dated June 24, 1943: "If we can establish ourselves in Italy, much of Germany can be reached from there with better weather conditions at our airdromes than prevail normally in England. This would immediately, when applied, force a dispersion of the German fighter and anti-aircraft defenses."[11] Later, he held up the examples of the Ploesti raid and a very effective mission to Wiener Neustadt on August 13. There, single-engine fighter factories were hit with devastating effect by the same bomb groups that had raided the Romanian oil fields. Certainly, if such telling blows could be delivered from bases in North Africa, much more might be done from bases in Italy that were much closer to Germany.

Aside from creating a new strategic air force during this period, the USAAF fielded new equipment that would change the air war. Following Black Thursday, when the USAAF leadership accepted that its bombers could not range deep into Germany without fighter escorts, it did not give up. Rather, it adapted technical and procedural advancements that allowed its fighters to provide the needed escort. Simply put, if fighters with longer range were required, then fighters with longer range would be fielded. In fact, on June 22, 1943, Arnold bluntly directed his deputy, Barney M. Giles, to find a long-range escort solution: "You have got to get a fighter to protect our bombers. Whether you use an existing type or have to start from scratch is your problem."[12]

When it flew its first operational missions from bases in England during March 1943, the P-47, as it was designed, built, and operated, had only marginally better range than the notoriously short-legged British Spitfire. It was hardly capable of taking the bombers deep into Europe. Two months after its introduction, Eaker noted this in a letter to Arnold: "The P-47s are doing all right. We are well pleased with their performance in combat. . . . The P-47 is, of course, of little more use than a Spitfire IX to accompany long-range bombers until the long-range tanks are provided."[13]

The problem had been recognized even before the massive fighter flew its first operational sortie. Work was performed on a number of fronts, one of those being the externally carried fuel tanks, or drop tanks, that Eaker had mentioned. They were an initial and partial solution that continued to be developed until the end of the war.

The notion of carrying additional fuel externally was not new to World War II. Spaatz had experimented with external tanks in Michigan during his early biplane fighter days in the 1920s. Germany had used external tanks on its aircraft during the Spanish Civil War. In fact, the P-47C—the variant being used at that time—already had provisions for carrying a 200-gallon conformal tank beneath its belly. However, that particular type of tank was designed for long-range ferry operations rather than combat; it was not pressurized, and above 20,000 feet, it failed to feed the engine.

Although some operational experimentation was done with the conformal belly tank, it was a relatively diminutive, teardrop-shaped seventy-five-gallon affair that first saw extensive operational use at the end of August 1943. This tank increased the range of the aircraft somewhat, but not to the extent required. It was followed by a British-manufactured 108-gallon fuel tank only a month later that increased the big fighter's range even more.

These British tanks were remarkable designs. Truly disposable, they did not use critical wartime materials but instead were manufactured of resin-impregnated, laminated paper. They were extremely lightweight and, when empty, were easily handled by a single man. In operational use, after being jettisoned from the fighter and falling to the ground, they burst open so that any remaining fuel could not be salvaged by the Germans. Moreover, because they were made of little more than paper, their broken husks were of little use to the enemy. Their most significant drawback was that they tended to "melt" if kept full of fuel for too long. Still, that was a niggling shortcoming that was easily planned around.

As time went on, aircraft maintenance improved, as did pilot techniques; both factors added small increments of extra range. Finally, escort procedures were adapted that did not force the big fighters into fuel-sucking, bomber-hugging formations. The results of all these factors in the aggregate were remarkable. Whereas the early P-47s penetrated only barely beyond the English Channel in March 1943, a year later they were protecting bombers deep into Germany.

And it did not stop there. Variants of the P-47 were introduced during the spring of 1944 which, along with many other features, included nearly 20 percent more internal fuel. Aside from the increased internal fuel, the newer model's wings were plumbed to carry external fuel tanks. So, with more internal fuel and two 108-gallon drop tanks—one slung under each wing—the P-47 was finally able to range over a great part of Germany. The availability of 150-gallon steel drop tanks by mid-1944 made it that much better.

By early 1944, the USAAF had the tool it needed to get the job done. The P-47 not only had the performance to meet its Luftwaffe counterparts on similar terms, but it finally had the range to escort the bombers deep into Germany. Furthermore, in addition to the big ungainly fighter, the USAAF had an ace in the hole. That ace was the North American P-51 Mustang.

The P-51 almost did not happen. During late 1939, when the British were eager to purchase American combat aircraft, North American Aviation president James "Dutch" Kindelberger, a World War I pilot, approached a British purchasing commission with an offer to sell what ultimately became the B-25 medium bomber. The British demurred and instead asked Kindelberger if his company would be interested in producing the Curtiss P-40 under license; Curtiss was running at full capacity at the time. Kindelberger countered that the bureaucratic work involved, along with the time it would take to get the tooling in place, would take longer than it would for him to design and build a better aircraft.

Intrigued, after reviewing a preliminary design, the British agreed to fund the project. A contract was awarded on May 29, 1940, with the stipulation that the production aircraft cost no more than $50,000. Although not contractually bound, North American was asked to produce a prototype in less than 120 days. The designers, one of whom was German, went frantically to work. Together with the production staff, they produced the prototype, without an engine, on September 9, 1940, only 102 days after the contract had been awarded.

The aircraft, officially the NA-73X was beautiful. Designed for the inline Allison V-1710 engine, its advanced features included a thin NACA laminar flow wing, an advanced radiator concept, and an airframe that was spectacularly streamlined in virtually every detail. That airframe was constructed almost entirely of aluminum, except for the fabric-covered rudder and elevators. And notably, despite being similar in size, the aircraft carried almost double the amount of fuel as the contemporaneous British Spitfire.

The prototype underwent a variety of technical fixes while waiting for its engine to be delivered. Its maiden flight on October 26, 1940, was a success, and although it crashed and was badly damaged less than a month later, the British had already placed orders for several hundred of the new aircraft before the prototype had even been built.

The initial design and prototype work went quickly, but the subsequent development of the aircraft was more typical. The new type, dubbed Mustang by the British, did not reach operational RAF units until February 1942. The plane was well-liked, handled superbly, and was especially suited to low-altitude armed reconnaissance missions over France and the Low Countries. However, its first major clash with the Luftwaffe was particularly inauspicious. During the Dieppe raid on August 19, German pilots claimed three Mustangs while P-51 pilots claimed a single FW-190. An additional six Mustangs were lost to ground fire.

The American equivalent of the British variant was the P-51A and differed only in armament and other minor details. The type did not have a built-in advocate within the USAAF, and its development lagged as a consequence. On the other hand, the P-47 and the P-38 were designs that had been developed and produced in response to air corps specifications, and as such, they had promoters within the service whose careers were intertwined to some degree with those types. The P-51 was given only passing attention for the better part of a year.

One reason that the Mustang failed to attract any champions early in its career was the fact that its Allison engine, fitted with only one lackluster supercharger, could not deliver enough power at high altitude. Above approximately 15,000 feet—just as with the P-40 and P-39—the aircraft's performance fell off sharply. In its early form, it offered no promise as a high-performance bomber escort. That being the case—and with an eye toward future development—the USAAF bought 500 examples, modified them as dive bombers, and redesignated them as A-36s. Another 310 P-51As were purchased and used in ground-support and reconnaissance roles. Both variants enjoyed modest success overseas.

It was the British who first acted on the question that they and others had asked: what sort of aircraft might the Mustang become if it were re-engined with the better-performing Rolls Royce Merlin? Equipped with a two-stage supercharger arrangement, the Merlin was designed for high-altitude operations, and at approximately the same size and weight as the Allison powerplant, it was recognized as a potential cure for what ailed the P-51. The British got to work on the Merlin installation in the spring of 1942 while North American Aviation engineers started a month or two later with a Packard-built variant of the same engine. Both modifications were designed to turn a four-bladed propeller rather than the original three-bladed types.

The British got their modified aircraft airborne in October while the Americans flew theirs in November. Performance of the re-engined aircraft was spectacular and included a stellar climb rate and a top speed of 441 miles per hour at 30,000 feet. The concept was proven, and production—with Packard-built Merlins—went into high gear. It was a good thing: the USAAF, confident in the engineering predictions, had ordered 400 P-51Bs two months earlier, and orders for thousands more followed.

The new type flew its first operational sorties with the Ninth Air Force's 354th Fighter Group on December 5, 1943. On loan to the Eighth Air Force for escort duties, the 354th took the bombers on an uneventful and relatively short-range mission into France. Only eight days later, on December 13, the P-51 flew the USAAF's longest escort mission to date when it took bombers all the way to Kiel. On that same day, the P-51B saw its first combat when 1st Lt. Glenn Eagleston was credited with the probable destruction of an Me-110. The first official credit for an aerial victory while flying the P-51B was awarded to 1st Lt. Charles Gumm for downing an Me-109 on December 16 during a bomber-escort mission to Bremen.

Armed with two .50-caliber machine guns in each wing, the type was well loved from the beginning. Still, it did have its share of teething problems, one of which was the tendency of its guns to jam during aggressive maneuvering. Because the P-51's laminar wing was so thin, the guns were installed at an angle rather than upright. Thus arranged, the ammunition-feed arrangement was quite serpentine and prone to blockages. These difficulties were addressed in various ways, electric-feed motors being one, but were never fully mitigated until the intro-duction of the P-51D, which had its guns mounted upright.

Another aspect of the aircraft that demanded respect from its pilots was its handling under certain conditions. Later versions of both the P-51B and P-51C (virtually identical aircraft, with the P-51B being built at North American's Inglewood, California, plant, and the P-51C in Dal-las, Texas) were built with an additional eighty-five-gallon fuel tank behind the pilot's seat. This added greatly to the type's already impres-sive range, but at the cost of flyability. Because the aircraft's center of gravity was dramatically shifted by the weight of this additional fuel, maneuvering was greatly restricted until the tank was empty. Indeed, in practice, the tank was typically filled with only sixty-five gallons rather than its full capacity.

Arthur Fiedler, a Mustang ace with the 325th Fighter Group, recalled how the extra fuel tank gave the aircraft some problematic han-dling characteristics:

Initially we were unaware of the stability problem with a full fuselage tank and so in an effort to make sure we used all our fuel we would use the drop tanks first. The problem was that in steep turning contests . . . our guys were reporting that once the turn had been established, they found themselves pushing *for-ward* on the stick with all their strength to prevent the turn winding up. Some succeeded, some did not. Those that could not prevent the turn from getting increasingly tighter reported that the bird whipped over into the most vicious high speed stall snap roll they could imagine. This often culminated in a spin. To the best of my knowledge most were able to recover in the 30,000 feet or so they had available; however, it is possible that some who did not return might have failed to recover. Within a couple of weeks we were given orders that after takeoff, we would burn the fuselage tank down to 35 gallons which would prevent that sort of thing from happening . . .[14]

Finally, although the airframe itself proved to be quite rugged, the cooling system for the engine did not. Any damage that caused the cool-ing fluid to empty itself was guaranteed to cause the engine to overheat and fail. This was a deficiency that would cost many aircraft and lives; it would never be overcome.

Regardless, most of the Mustang's pilots did not give much thought to those shortcomings. Everything else about the aircraft was so positive that its pilots fell in love with it instantly. Most of them felt that it was easy to fly and equal to or better than any German fighter. In many cases, it gave them the confidence to press attacks when they might otherwise have gone home. An example is the engagement described by 1st Lt. Allen Bunte of the 4th Fighter Group. On March 29, 1944, near Magdeburg, Germany, his squadron bounced a group of FW-190s that were pressing an attack on the bombers that the 4th was charged with protecting. Bunte recalled: "Due to there being a P-51 on the tail of practically every Hun, I couldn't immediately find a target, so I dove for the deck, got under the approximate battle area, and waited."

Bunte did not have long to wait. A group of four FW-190s broke through the clouds and hurtled past him nose-to-nose, but he lost contact with them before he could get turned around. He also lost his wingman somewhere along the way, yet still continued trolling alone over the German countryside looking for something to shoot. After a few minutes, he spotted a large group of FW-190s coming toward him from the west at low altitude. He decided to ambush the German flyers:

Taking what advantage I could, of trees, hills and buildings, for hiding, I made a large circle and came in behind what I was now certain were Huns. There were eleven of them flying very good formation at about 800 feet. I was then several miles behind and it took me about ten minutes, balls out flying, to get in range. As I began to close noticeably, I throttled back to what I thought was a small closing speed, adjusted my trim, estimated my range, picked my Hun, and waited until I was about 150 yards away, still about 500 feet below and unnoticed by anyone, eased back gently on the stick until I was directly behind him. Fired about a three-second burst and broke violently for home—full bore.[15]

Bunte threw a hurried look over his shoulder and watched his victim, aflame, falling toward the ground. In his combat report, he justifiably asserted: "I claim one FW-190 destroyed and one hell of a lot of intrepidity." Bunte finished the war a prisoner of war. On April 5, 1944, he struck a high-tension wire while strafing a German airfield near Gardelegen. In flames, he put his Mustang into a lake and was subsequently dried out and delivered to the Luftwaffe.

In truth, the Mustang was easy enough to fly that the USAAF did not exercise a great deal of concern about introducing it directly into combat. Robert "Punchy" Powell was a P-47 pilot with the 352nd Fighter Group based out of Bodney. He remembered the arrival of the group's first P-51s on April 7, 1944, as a complete surprise: "We were coming back from a mission and as we got close to the field we could see large numbers of P-51s parked all over the place. To that point, most of us had never even seen a P-51." After landing, Powell's crew chief climbed up on his wing. "He told me that the group CO said I was going to fly thirty minutes in the Mustang that was parked next to my bird. Well, we had no training, no manuals, no nothing. I said, 'The hell I am!' Well, of course that's exactly what we did. For my 30-minute introduction to the Mustang, after getting our engineering officer to show me how to start it, I took it up to about 5,000 feet, noting that it climbed like a homesick angel. To get the feel of it I did some really tight turns, a chandelle in both directions and a barrel-roll. I wanted to see how it reacted in a stall before I took it back for a landing, so I put the wheels down, cut the power and pulled the nose up until it stalled. I was surprised by how stable it really was. I think this is about what most of our pilots did on their introductory flight to the P-51. Then we had a mission in our new airplanes the very next day. We were lucky that it was a milk run because we still had very little idea how those airplanes worked. As time went by though, we really grew to like the P-51."

Production of almost 4,000 P-51B's and P-51C's was nearing completion when the definitive version of the Mustang, the P-51D, was flown on November 17, 1943. This variant included many improvements, the most noticeable being the reduction of the fuselage behind the pilot to allow the installation of a bubble or tear-drop canopy. Whereas the rearward visibility of the earlier Mustangs had been merely acceptable, the new canopy permitted an unobstructed view in virtually every direction. Another improvement was the addition of one more gun to each wing, giving the aircraft a total of six .50-caliber weapons. All the improvements were well worth the price; the changes introduced minor instability and decreased top speed by only a couple of miles per hour. The P-51K was a Dallas-built version of the P-51D with an Aero-products propeller rather than a Hamilton Standard. Visually, the differences between the two aircraft were so small as to be dismissed. In practice, they were generally all identified as P-51Ds.

Although the Mustang's performance attributes alone made it a superb aircraft, its price made it an exceptionally attractive value. The army was billed only $59,000 for the P-51, whereas the P-47, at $104,000, was almost twice as dear. Other reference points include the P-38 at $106,000, the P-39 at $71,000, and the B-17 at $270,000.

The Mustang was for all practical purposes the best all-around fighter of the war, but the USAAF could have prevailed without it. At the same time as the P-51 was arriving in England in numbers great enough to make a difference, the P-47's range was being improved to the point that it could escort the bombers virtually anywhere they needed to go. Indeed, although it never saw service in Europe, the ultimate operational variant of the Thunderbolt, the P-47N, had a longer range than even the P-51, an attribute that served it well in the closing months of the Pacific War. Had the need been an imperative, its development could likely have been accelerated.

Finally, the P-38 Lightning should not be left out of the long-range fighter discussion. Although it had originally been conceived as a high-speed interceptor, it had the longest range of any of its early contemporaries. Indeed, because of that long range, the Lightning was the fighter most in demand in the Pacific, a theater characterized by a vast geography where long range was crucial and where a second engine provided a difficult-to-quantify measure of safety and peace of mind. Like the P-47, the P-38's range was steadily improved through the addition of more internal fuel as well as drop tanks. Again, similar to the Thunderbolt, the Lightning's range was increased to the point that is also could escort the bombers across much of Germany.

Still, the P-38 had a mixed record while operating out of England. Its speed and maneuverability were roughly equivalent to its contemporaries on both sides of the fighting; in fact, its later iterations were more maneuverable than the P-51. And its guns, concentrated in the nose, provided massively effective firepower. Although his was not a universal opinion, when asked which Allied fighter he felt was the most difficult opponent, the great Luftwaffe ace Johannes Steinhoff declared: "The Lightning. It was fast, low profiled and a fantastic fighter, and a real danger when it was above you. It was only vulnerable if you were behind it, a little below and closing fast, or turning into it, but on the attack it was a tremendous aircraft."[16]

But the P-38 was not easy to fly, and its reliability in the cold and wet that characterized northern Europe was not as good as the P-47 and P-51. Fully half of the P-38s lost over Germany succumbed to engine problems rather than enemy fire. Too, twice the number of engines required twice the amount of engine maintenance. And of course, although only marginally more expensive than the P-47, it was almost double the cost of the P-51.

In plain terms, the P-38 really offered no compelling advantages over the other two fighters, a fact the USAAF readily recognized. In fact, as the P-47 and the P-51 became more widely available, the idea of removing the P-38 from service offered practical advantages. Although the task was not completed during the war, retiring the Lightning would have reduced the number of fighter types and subsequently simplified the maintenance, logistics, and training pipelines. That simplification alone would have provided considerable cost savings aside from the fact that the P-38 was the service's most expensive fighter to procure. The USAAF recognized all of this, and in fact, there were very few active P-38 groups in Europe at the time the war ended.

Nevertheless, had it been required, the P-38 had the capacity to not only hold its own in the skies over Europe, but perhaps even to dominate them. Taking a cue from the dramatic improvements imparted to the P-47 when it was tested with hydraulically actuated Hamilton Standard "paddle blade" propellers in 1942, Lockheed sought to similarly improve the performance of the P-38. Slightly more powerful variants of the standard Allison V-1710 engines were installed in a test aircraft, which was then fitted with the new propellers. To accommodate the changes, larger propeller spinners were mounted, and the engine cowlings were likewise adjusted. Whereas the engine, spinner, and cowling changes did not stand out to the untrained eye, the longer and broader propeller blades were immediately apparent.

Tests began in February 1943, a month before the P-47 even began combat operations from England, and the results were dramatic. The modified aircraft's top-end speed of more than 450 miles per hour, its climb rate of nearly 5,000 feet per minute, and its maximum altitude of more than 45,000 feet exceeded the capabilities of both the P-47 and the Merlin-powered P-51. The modification also increased range by at least 10 percent.

In a move that is still a "head scratcher," the USAAF declined to move forward with production of the variant that came to be designated P-38K. Although the changes to the aircraft were not too extensive, at that time the service did not want to disrupt the production flow for the several weeks that it believed would have been needed to adapt the assembly lines to the new design.

The decision can be debated, and it is. Yet the USAAF cannot be faulted in the larger context of the war. It did not need to spend the money and materiel on the P-38A. It could, and did, win the war without it. Whether it knew this or not when it took a pass on the P-38K is open for discussion. At any rate, the Lightning soldiered through the end of the fighting without ever having realized its full potential.

In discussions about aircraft range, it is tempting to reference unqualified specifications to compare one aircraft against another. This is an amateur's trap. The varieties of factors that can affect an aircraft's range are so great as to defy definition by a single number. For instance, a popular reference book lists the range of the P-47C at 550 miles. Yet it does not declare if this number includes a drop tank and, if so, the size of the drop tank used. Further, it is unknown whether this value delineates an operational range that includes reserves for such real-world requirements as a rendezvous with a bomber force, extra fuel for combat, and the fuel necessary to divert to an alternate airfield in the event that the home base is weathered in. It could be a number derived from flying a maximum range profile at air speeds and altitudes that have little relevance to actual operations.

The same book references an almost equivalent range of 528 miles for the Me-109G, an aircraft considered to be relatively short-legged. Again, the same considerations apply, and there is no good way to make a reasonable comparison between the two aircraft simply based

on the numbers listed. Engineering reports and exploitation evaluations, usually not available to the casual enthusiast, are the best basis
for comparing one aircraft against another. However, the most germane
indicator of an aircraft's useful range is a review of how it was actually
used in operations. Ultimately, all three major USAAF types, the P-51,
P-38, and P-47, were long-legged enough to fly escort missions deep
into Germany.

When a newly trained pilot finally reached combat, he was in the
game for keeps. The enemy did not care if he was new, and his squadron
mates expected him to perform as the mission required. That newly
arrived American crews were able to do so is a testament to the training
they received. "I was on my sixth mission," said Bob Powell, a P-47
pilot with the 352nd Fighter Group. "We had only been flying combat
operations since September. On this date, December 24, 1943, we had
completed our bomber-escort responsibilities and were making our way
home at about 10,000 feet. I was feeling pretty proud of myself at that
point as I was flying as wingman to Col. Everett Stewart and had maintained my position really well and had kept sight of everyone just as I
was supposed to do."

Keeping his head on a swivel, Powell continued to scan the sky for
enemy fighters. "Then I looked back and Stewart was gone!" It took a
second or two for him to catch sight of Stewart's aircraft in a split-S, and
it took only an instant more for him to give chase.

"I caught up with him pretty quickly, and in fact had to pull back on
the throttle and start fishtailing to keep from overrunning him," Powell
said. "I wasn't even sure what we were chasing until I saw his guns firing
and all of a sudden I saw a gray-black twin-engine airplane with big
black crosses on it."

Powell was equally surprised when "out of the corner of my eye I
caught sight of another plane—it must have been the first one's wingman. It essentially flew right out in front of me. I wasn't real composed
or anything. In fact, this was the first time I had fired my guns in combat. I just pulled the trigger and started firing short bursts and he went
down in a burning, spiraling dive."

Back safely on the ground at Bodney, Powell remembered that "Stewart asked me what kind of aircraft we had shot down. I told him that I didn't know. I just saw those big black crosses and knew that they were German." The enemy aircraft were later identified as Me-110s.

CHAPTER 10

Doolittle, Phased Escort, and Freedom for the Fighters

Arnold sent a cable to Eaker on December 19, 1943: "Conference at SEXTANT provided for changes in command Mediterranean Theater and a commander for OVERLORD."[1] Just as the Casablanca Conference of January 1943 had codified major organizational changes for the Allied air forces, so had the Cairo Conference at the end of 1943. Sweeping changes were made in December that were intended to better streamline command relationships in preparation for the invasion of Europe the following year.

Most important, above and beyond the air forces, Eisenhower was named the commander of the Allied forces for the invasion. Until very shortly before the decision was made, the assumption was that Marshall would be given that posting. It was generally agreed that he would be an excellent choice for the command; however, Roosevelt relied heavily on his counsel and expertise in Washington and wanted him to stay put. Where the air forces were concerned on the American side, Spaatz was put in charge of a new organization, the U.S. Strategic Air Forces (USSTAF); the commanders of both the Eighth and the Fifteenth would report to him. Those two air forces were slated for change as well. Doolittle was to be relieved of the Fifteenth and replaced by Maj. Gen. Nathan Twining. For his next command, Doolittle was headed for England to take Eaker's Eighth.

Eaker was stunned and confounded by the change. He had not been in attendance at Cairo, where Arnold had roundly criticized the Eighth. On December 4, at a meeting of the Combined Chiefs of Staff, Arnold was especially critical of the 50 percent readiness rate of the Eighth's bombers and of the fact that the largest raid sent the previous month numbered only 600 bombers. His patience had run out. It was quite likely that he had made up his mind long before. For his part, Spaatz had earlier learned of the change and agreed with Arnold.

Despite their disagreements earlier that year, Eaker still felt surprised and betrayed because Arnold had promised that he would make it clear to Eaker if he was dissatisfied with Eaker's performance. Eaker responded immediately: "Believe war interest best served by my retention command Eighth Air Force: Otherwise experience this theater for nearly two years wasted. If I am to be allowed my personal preference having started with the Eighth and seen it organized for major task in this theater, it would be heart-breaking to leave just before climax."[2]

There followed a series of exchanges involving Arnold, Eaker, Eisenhower, Marshall, Spaatz, and others. The decision was questioned and reviewed and assessed anew, but when the cables and letters stopped, nothing had changed. Eaker was to give up the Eighth on January 1, 1944, the same day that Spaatz was to stand up his new command. Eaker was sent to the Mediterranean, where he was made commander of the Mediterranean Allied Air Forces (MAAF). It was a new command that combined Spaatz's North African Air Forces with the Mediterranean Air Command. Technically, it was a promotion, and at that time, the units comprising the MAAF combined to make it the biggest air force in the world. It included the RAF's Desert and Balkan Air Forces—the latter supported partisan operations—as well as the Twelfth Air Force and the Fifteenth. In practice, Spaatz passed orders to the Fifteenth through Eaker. Eaker, in turn, had authority to alter those orders only as exigencies beyond Spaatz's immediate knowing dictated. It could have been a disaster, but because of their like-minded perspectives and friendship, it worked well in practice.

Moreover, it should be noted to Arnold's credit that the changes he made worked. Aside from the obvious fact that the Allies won the war, the coordination between the USAAF and the RAF was generally good, and the Allied armies by and large received the support they desired not only for the invasion, but during subsequent operations as well. This included a protracted period during the summer of 1944 when strategic bombers were used directly overhead the battlefield.

It had been nothing two years earlier. However, supported by the world's greatest industrial engine and an aviation training machine second to none, Spaatz and Eaker had stewarded the men and materiel entrusted to them into the most potent air force in history. Although several other USAAF numbered air forces were organizational peers, no one pretended that the Eighth was anything other than America's preeminent strategic weapon in Europe.

And it was still growing. Whereas, especially early on, Spaatz and Eaker had enthusiastically tallied every bomber and fighter that arrived in England, numbers of aircraft were no longer the worry they had been. By January 1944, American industry was just hitting its stride; factories in the United States were producing quantities of aircraft that greatly exceeded what Germany or any other nation manufactured. For instance, during the entirety of 1943, the Luftwaffe accepted 25,500 aircraft. This stands in remarkable contrast to what plants in the United States produced: deliveries in just the previous month, December 1943, totaled 8,761. Moreover, Germany's production was heavily focused on single-engine fighters, whereas the American manufacturing effort produced large numbers of complex, resource-intensive, four-engine types.

Many of those aircraft rolled off the factory floors and, within weeks, sometimes days, were paired with newly trained crews and flown across the Atlantic to England. There, a growing infrastructure composed of vast, coordinated supply and repair depots stood ready to support the new aircraft as they were pitched into the fight over Europe.

By January 1944, the Eighth was ubiquitous across all of southeastern England; there really was no way for it not to be. Even then, more than two years after the U.S. entry into the war, new airfields were being carved out of the English countryside because there simply were not enough existing bases to accommodate the enormous masses of men and equipment that were pouring into the country daily. Nearly every village or town had some sort of American airbase nearby, and many of those belonged to the Eighth.

Of course, the Eighth Air Force should not have been anything other than the chief instrument of American airpower on that side of the world. The Allied war effort, by design, was directed against Germany first and Japan second. Consequently, the preponderance of the nation's men and materiel was sent to England, from which the cross-Channel invasion, a necessary precursor to the total defeat of Germany, was planned for the coming spring. Before that operation could be started, the Allies had to grind down Germany's military and the industry that supported it. Much of that responsibility fell to the Eighth. And now, effective on January 6, 1944, the one man responsible for its success or failure was Maj. Gen. James H. Doolittle.

Whereas Arnold, Spaatz, and Eaker were generally known to the casual followers of the air war in Europe, Doolittle had already been the contemporaneous equivalent of a rock star for a decade or more. Born in 1896, the same year as Eaker, Doolittle grew up in Alaska and southern California and had a reputation as a particularly dogged and feisty boxer. He left college to join the army in 1917 during World War I and spent the war in the States, first as an aviation cadet and subsequently as a flight instructor.

Following the war, he stayed in the army as a pursuit aviator, finished his degree, and then earned advanced degrees at MIT in the fledgling field of aeronautics. There followed a period of intensive experimentation during which he immersed himself in the science of flight while simultaneously serving as a very public test pilot. He represented the army in the immensely popular air races of the day, setting many records and winning a host of trophies, including, like Arnold and Eaker, the Mackay Trophy. Doolittle's name was all over the newspapers of the 1920s.

However, his greatest contribution to flight was the pioneering work he did on instrument—that is, blind—flying. He was credited, in 1929, with the first flight executed totally on instruments from takeoff to touchdown. He was instrumental in the development of the artificial horizon, and the follow-on development of equipment and techniques helped pave the way for safe operations in all sorts of weather. Doolittle's work was a significant contributor to reliable and safe aviation operations worldwide, and practically every pilot who flew during World War II used equipment derived from his efforts.

Doolittle resigned his regular commission during 1930 but stayed active with the reserves. Employed as a technical expert by Shell Oil Company, he urged the development of 100-octane aviation gasoline. Eventually embraced by the U.S. Army Air Corps as its standard aviation fuel, it was one reason behind the high performance of American aircraft. German aircraft engines were designed to use a lower-octane fuel and subsequently did not realize the performance advantages conferred by the more potent stuff.

Recalled to active duty just after the U.S. entry into the war, Doolittle achieved immortality in the public eye when he led sixteen B-25 medium bombers from the decks of the USS *Hornet* on a raid against Japan on April 18, 1942. The tiny force inflicted inconsequential material damage with its bombs and, low on fuel, was scattered and lost in its entirety. Doolittle was crestfallen and feared a court-martial. Instead, the raid proved an enormous boost to public morale, and Doolittle was proclaimed a public hero and awarded the Medal of Honor. At the same time, it caused the Japanese to hold back more forces for home defense than it otherwise would have and to reconsider their strategy for Asia and the Pacific.

Following the famous raid, Doolittle was called for service with the Eighth, but was subsequently given command of the Twelfth Air Force in North Africa. Eventually, he stood up the Fifteenth Air Force and moved it to Italy during a command posting of barely more than a month. It was during this short period that he was given the nod to take the Eighth.

Although Doolittle was on the hook for what the Eighth did or did not do, there was little doubt that he would get plenty of direction from Spaatz and Arnold; their own professional fates and legacies were closely tied to the conduct of the air war over Europe. Still, Doolittle was the man directly in charge, and he would ultimately be credited with the organization's successes or failures. And in that respect, taking command of the Eighth was a double-edged sword.

For one, considering that the Eighth Air Force was receiving the lion's share of the USAAF's resources, Doolittle was being dealt the strongest hand possible. Succeeding with such a powerful force, one that was growing stronger every day, was considered by some to be a fore-gone conclusion. On the other hand, at the head of such a magnificent air force, underperformance would be immediately met with censure. Eaker, the Eighth's previous commander, knew that better than anyone.

Simply put, Doolittle might receive little credit if he succeeded, but a failure would permanently diminish the extraordinary accomplishments that already marked his career. Of course, infinitely more important than his reputation was the ultimate necessity to win the war. If the Eighth failed to perform, the fighting might be prolonged at the cost of many more lives.

Doolittle appreciated the complexities of his position. Responding to a congratulatory letter from Gen. George Patton, he wrote of the differences between commanding the Eighth and commanding in the Mediterranean theater: "Down there, where you are not 'under the guns,' any modest success was apparently appreciated. Up here miracles are confidently anticipated. Have been a little slow in getting my Miracle Department organized but hope for the best."[3]

Curiously, in the same note, he seemed almost to complain at his wealth of assets: "Up here it requires an equal or greater amount of ingenuity to effectively utilize the almost unlimited resources at one's disposal." This statement makes it obvious that Doolittle was at least somewhat overwhelmed with the vastness of the enterprise that was the Eighth. At that time, it included 1,774 B-17s and B-24s, nearly as many fighters of various types, and tens of thousands of men who supported, maintained, and flew them. It was larger than all but the greatest commercial corporations, and that Doolittle might be at least a little intimidated upon taking command, despite the fact that he had already commanded two numbered air forces, is understandable. There was no way that one man could immediately know all its trappings and workings, much less become intimately familiar with everyone who made it work. Less capable men would have been stultified at the prospect of shouldering such responsibility.

Aside from the difficulties associated with learning his new job, Doolittle encountered friction from his British peers and superiors. He was a stranger to some, and many of them met his assignment with at least some circumspection. His first meeting with Air Chief Marshal Arthur Harris, Eaker's friend, was less than inspiring. Harris's staff, rather than making time for the important American, advised Doolittle that he would have to make an appointment. He took the slight and dutifully complied. He recorded Harris's response to his arrival: "Sitting at his desk, he nodded and went back to shuffling some papers. After a minute or two, he finally motioned me to sit down and we exchanged brief comments. I left after a few minutes but not without saying that he would always be welcome to see me in my office at any time—without an appointment."[4]

That he was able to, early in his tenure, schedule an audience with King George VI at Buckingham Palace gives some measure of the importance of his position. However, at the outset of the meeting, the monarch met him with a protracted silence that Doolittle finally broke with platitudes about the excellent relationships he was enjoying with his British counterparts and his certainty that the positive rapport would hold through the successful prosecution of the war. He was understandably dismayed when the king met his offerings with, "We're certainly sorry to lose Eaker."[5]

The implications associated with replacing Eaker, as evinced by the king's remarks, may have been what troubled Doolittle most about his new command. As noted earlier, Eaker was very displeased, if not bitter, that the command he had worked so doggedly to build was taken from him and given to Doolittle just as it was reaching maturity. That the two were friends made the situation that much more prickly. It was obvious that Doolittle recognized he benefitted from his friend's good work when he wrote: "I inherited the 8th Air Force at a natural turning point in its history. Ira had left me a 'going concern' that he had practically built from scratch."[6]

Taking command of the Eighth in a basic military sense required no magic. As an already-proven commander, Doolittle only had to give orders and guidance as he saw fit. His officers and men would then execute those orders and follow that guidance. The Eighth was a military organization like most others, and Eaker had already staffed it with capable and, in many instances, top-notch officers. They had done well for Eaker and probably would have performed at least competently under any reasonable leader.

Still, Doolittle was under the magnifying glass, and he wanted—and needed—more than competent performance for the coming campaigns;

he spent considerable time with his subordinate unit commanders to ensure he got it. Aside from making his basic philosophies and expectations known, he reached out to his men, as any good commander might, for new proposals or ideas. Some of those solicited notions were worthwhile, and after vetting by him and his staff, they yielded a number of adjustments to the way the Eighth conducted its business. Just as Eaker and his staff had experimented with the most effective way to use the bombers, Doolittle, using much of that same staff, continued the practice. This pattern of changes and reiterative fine-tuning continued especially as new equipment arrived.

One innovation that was introduced on January 7, 1944, the very first day following Doolittle's assumption of command, was the phased-escort concept. The idea had been discussed for months, well before Doolittle's arrival. Up until that time, the fighters joined with the bombers and stayed with them until low fuel required them to return to their bases. It was a practice that failed to maximize the fighters' range. Tied to the bomber formations, the escorts wasted fuel at almost every step. Once they got airborne and into formation, they had to burn precious gas finding and forming with their assigned group of bombers. If the bombers were late, as was sometimes the case, more fuel was needlessly burned waiting for them.

The real waste began once the fighters joined the big aircraft and turned for the target. Because the optimum airspeed of the fighters was so much higher than that of the bombers, they had to weave or fly S-turns to stay in position. Consequently, for every mile the bombers advanced toward the target, the smaller fighters flew that distance and more, albeit in turns rather than in a straight line. Essentially, the concept cut the effective maximum ranges of the escorts dramatically when compared to their straight-line maximum ranges. For instance, even the early P-47s had the range to fly well into Germany, but constrained by close escort tactics, they could not escort the bombers nearly so far.

The phased-escort concept was designed to mitigate this dissipation of the fighter escort's capabilities. It had the fighters fly directly to a rendezvous point and then stay with the bombers until another group of fighters rendezvoused with the formation farther along the route. Because the second group of fighters was able to fly more directly to the deeper rendezvous point, rather than S-turning, it had more fuel and could take the bombers farther than the original escort group. These phased groups, or relays, of fighters were able to accompany the bombers much farther along their routes than were single groups tied to the bombers by close-escort procedures.

The phased-escort notion was also tailored to the capabilities of individual fighter types. The initial legs were flown by the shorter-ranged P-47s or even by RAF Spitfires until more American aircraft became available. The intermediate route segments were escorted by the longer-range P-38s, while the farthest handoffs were taken by the wide-ranging P-51s that were only then starting to arrive in numbers.

The new concept provided a badly needed enhancement to the Eighth's strategic reach. The system enabled missions against a range of targets that had previously been safe from escorted attack. Ultimately, the phased-escort doctrine—together with the greater availability of the P-51—was refined so well that the bombers were able to range virtually all of Germany with fighter protection.

The assignment of Doolittle as their new commander, not to mention the other high-level leadership changes that had been made during the previous weeks, meant very little to the individual USAAF men whose job it was to actually fight and organize and supply the war. Their day-to-day duties remained largely unchanged, and it did not matter to them who was in charge; the characteristics of the aircraft they flew remained the same, engine repair procedures did not change, fuel and supplies still had to be moved to the airfields, men still needed to be fed, and so on.

And, of course, more missions had to be flown. That fact was highlighted on January 7, 1944, the day after Doolittle took command and the same day that the Eighth implemented the phased-escort concept. Just more than 500 B-24s and B-17s and nearly 600 escorting fighters were sent against the enormous I. G. Farben chemical complex at Ludwigshafen in western Germany.

The various plants there manufactured a broad spectrum of products that were subsequently used to produce everything from explosives to plastics and synthetic rubber. If they could be neutralized, the downstream impact on Germany's combat units, including the Luftwaffe, would be substantial. At more than three miles in length, the interconnected composite of factories presented a massive target. It was also important because there was a good chance the German air force would rise to defend it.

Robert Sweatt was a B-24 waist gunner with the 389th Bomb Group based out of the airfield at Hethel.[7] The twenty-one-year-old Texan had initially been tagged for training as a cook after being drafted during 1942, but service as an aerial gunner promised the excitement of combat flying, better pay, and better opportunities for promotion. Of course, those better promotion opportunities existed primarily because so many gunners were lost in combat.

The inherent dangers did not dissuade Sweatt from taking gunnery training and a subsequent assignment overseas. By January 1944, he was already an experienced crewman, a veteran of sixteen missions, and no stranger to combat. The mission to Ludwigshafen would make him even less so.

Sweatt's crew originally had not been scheduled for the mission. The men had earned some well-deserved time off and were looking forward to a rest and relaxation period in Scotland. They never got there. Instead, they were called in and assigned to Maj. Kenneth Caldwell, one of the group's squadron commanders. He was charged with leading the group that day. The 389th, in turn, would be at the head of the 2nd Combat Wing made up of two additional B-24 bomb groups, the 93rd and 445th. That Sweatt and the rest of the crew were specifically selected for the lead ship was no doubt a credit to their expertise. It is likely, though, that the tribute did little to salve the disappointment of having their passes cancelled.

Following breakfast, the officers attended the briefing while Sweatt and the rest of the enlisted crew prepared their ship, *Trouble*, for the mission. At engine start, Caldwell was seated at the copilot's position while Capt. David Wilhite, the crew's regular pilot, took his normal seat. They were airborne just after nine, and Caldwell and Wilhite maneuvered their bomber so that the twenty-three aircraft that made up the 389th's contribution to the mission could assemble in their assigned positions.

Cloud layers at around 13,000 feet made it difficult to bring the entire force of more than 500 bombers together, but eventually, most of the aircraft were joined and the stream of big ships crossed the coast over Holland and headed for Germany. Unable to join the main force, two bomber groups totaling about fifty aircraft returned to their bases.

On this mission, the B-24s were assigned to follow the B-17s. Because the best cruise airspeed for the Liberator was faster than the B-17, Caldwell and Wilhite led their formation in gentle S-turns in order not to overtake the wide-winged, Boeing-built bombers. Although the turns themselves were not difficult, keeping several groups of bombers together, each including more than twenty aircraft, was not easy. As Caldwell and Wilhite carved lazy arcs through the clear sky at 23,000 feet, Sweatt had a good view of much of the raiding force. From his waist-gun position, he described the scene succinctly: "The sky looked like it was filled with blackbirds."

Antiaircraft fire on the route into and over the target was characterized by the official record as "both barrage and predicted type, from moderate to intense and inaccurate to accurate." Sweatt's description of the flak was more matter-of-fact: "The sky was black." The official record also described fighter activity: "Some enemy aircraft opposition from IP [initial point] to shortly after target; 10 Me 109s and 10 Fw 190s pressing attacks fairly close, all from 5 to 7 o'clock low and level. Enemy aircraft attacking both singly and in coordination." Together, the defenses around the target were deadly enough to knock down a handful of the American bombers.

The target itself was obscured by clouds and was bombed using radar. Although less accurate than visual bombing, dropping the bombs with the aid of radar was better than not dropping them at all or dropping them blindly through the clouds. The I. G. Farben complex was so huge that if the targeted point were not hit, the chances were good that something else of value would be. Still, the results were not what they would have been had the factories been visible. The Eighth Air Force would visit Ludwigshafen several more times.

The rally plan following the attack called for the entire force to stay together and take up a course northwest across France and then north to cross the English Channel. Caldwell abandoned that scheme and asked the navigator for a direct course to England. Wilhite, the crew's regularly assigned pilot, reminded Caldwell that they were supposed to lead their formation in trace of the B-17s. Caldwell would have none of it and continued to angle away from the main formation. Perhaps he believed that once he got the wing formation clear of the slower B-17s, he could fly at a higher air speed and get back to friendly territory more quickly.

Leading the 445th Bomb Group (H) behind Caldwell was Capt. James M. "Jimmy" Stewart. At this point, the Hollywood star already had several missions under his belt and was universally respected in his unit as a courageous airman and genuine leader. Noting that Caldwell was deviating from the plan, he called out the error. Caldwell was heard over the radio, "I know what I'm doing. Get off the air."

Stewart could have left Caldwell and continued on the correct course, closing with the larger formations of B-17s and sharing the protection their greater numbers offered. Further, the proper route was the same one that the fighter escorts were covering. Leaving Caldwell to follow the prescribed plan was a safer—and also defensible—choice.

Stewart chose to stay with the headstrong Caldwell. First, Caldwell was the leader of Stewart's part of the formation, the 2nd Combat Wing. Second, Stewart knew that there was protection in numbers and that a larger formation was more difficult for enemy fighters to attack than a smaller one. Alone, Caldwell and the 389th would be very vulnerable. Perhaps Stewart had the well-being of Caldwell's men in mind when he called out over the radio: "Padlock Red leader to Padlock Green leader. We're sticking with you." Ultimately, the flight lead of the 93rd Bomb Group also made the same decision as Stewart, and the three-group force of B-24s pressed west across France.

If it was Caldwell's intent not to attract attention, he failed. A gaggle of fighters, identified as P-47s, appeared and the bomber crews watched with relief as the pilots of the smaller aircraft positioned themselves for the escort back to England. It was at that same time that the navigator realized the course he had given Caldwell earlier was wrong. Rather than approaching the English Channel as they should have been, they were crossing south of Paris. He shouted over the intercom: "Make a 90-degree turn! We're 100 miles off course."

At almost the same time, someone else called out, "Enemy fighters-twelve o'clock." Their escort of P-47s was actually a group of FW-190s and was turning to make a head-on firing pass. George Hammond was the bombardier in an aircraft off the left wing of *Trouble*. He watched horrified as 20-millimeter cannon fire smashed into its cockpit shredding Caldwell and Wilhite where they sat at the big aircraft's controls. "I was transfixed as Caldwell reared back, taking the yoke with him. The bomber made a complete loop from level flight."

Sweatt recoiled with revulsion as the same firing pass that rent Caldwell and Wilhite to bits sent cannon rounds into the ball turret where S/Sgt. Max Snyder was instantly killed in an explosive spray of blood and bone and glass. With the bomber out of control, Sweatt reached for a parachute. His left arm refused his command, and it took an instant for him to realize that it had been shot up. He lunged out again, this time with his right arm, and snatched the parachute from where it was hanging. He struggled inside the careening bomber but finally got the parachute strapped across his back.

As the big ship shuddered, nearly out of air speed and at the top of its loop, the wings came off. What was left of the bomber started down in a spiral. The resulting centrifugal force pinned the men who were still alive against the fuselage. "I felt like I was 500 pounds," Sweatt recalled. "I was trapped."

An explosion blasted what was left of the bomber into pieces and knocked Sweatt unconscious. When he woke he found himself alone, miles above the ground. All around him, falling with him, were parts of what had been *Trouble*. "It was like a junkyard," he recalled.

He was struck by the eerie quietness of it all. It was a marked but still frightening contrast to the cacophonous hell that had, only a moment before, been his aircraft. Gone was the roar of the four engines that had powered the massive bomber. Gone were the booming rips of machine-gun fire. Gone were the frantic shouts over the intercom. Instead, there was nothing but the soft whistle that he and the pieces of *Trouble* made as they fell toward earth.

Among those pieces was a terror that Sweatt never forgot. It was a fellow crewman falling past him, a friend. He and the other man had played together, made war together, and shared stories together. Now they were falling together. The other man had no parachute, and there was nothing Sweatt could do for him.

Sweatt clawed at his parachute's ripcord with his right hand, but his heavily gloved fingers could not grasp the ring. He used his teeth to pull the gloves free; his left arm was still useless. An instant after yanking the ripcord, his parachute streamed out of its casing with a cracking flutter and snapped him almost to a halt as it caught air. The rest of the debris sped away toward the earth.

Suspended above the frozen French countryside near the town of Chartres, his arm shot up, his body battered, his friends gone, Robert Sweatt hardly considered James H. Doolittle and the changes he had in mind for the Eighth Air Force.

At about the same time that Sweatt was descending in his parachute, four P-47s of the newly arrived 367th Fighter Group loped in a loose echelon over the farm-checkered countryside. They had been part of the phased-escort effort to Ludwigshafen that day. Now, low on fuel and having just bored down through the carpet of clouds that covered much of that part of Europe, they made ready to land.

They were attacked by eight FW-190s. In almost no time, three of the four rugged Thunderbolts were shot into the ground. The fourth pilot escaped by climbing back into the clouds, no doubt surprised to have been attacked over the heart of England.

In reality, as he later learned, he and his comrades had been torpidly cruising over German-held French Normandy. Their navigation had been poor and was further complicated by the clouds that kept them from visually confirming their position over the ground. The landscape over that part of France nearly mirrored that of southeastern England, and pilots from both sides had made the same mistake on both sides of the Channel and would again.

Regardless, three of the four Americans had paid for their carelessness with their lives. The end of the Luftwaffe was still a long fight away.[8]

Arguably the most far-reaching of Doolittle's changes was one that was immediately embraced by the fighter pilots. Until early 1944, even for a few weeks following the introduction of the phased-escort concept, the Eighth's fighters, once they had joined with their assigned bombers, were under orders to fly close-escort tactics. They were directed to stay almost in formation with the bombers and forbidden to give chase to German fighters or engage them unless the bombers were under direct attack. The orders were intended to ensure that the bombers were never left unprotected.

In practice, the concept did not work well. If the German pilots chose, they could usually orchestrate their attacks before the escorting fighters could get into position to defend against them. The orders to stay put chafed and were more than many American fighter pilots could take. Instances in which they left the bombers to pursue German fighters often resulted in severe admonitions or even official discipline.

Doolittle issued a new directive that markedly changed the way the escorting fighters protected the bombers. This transformation of doctrine accelerated the already tipping balance of air superiority away from the Luftwaffe and toward the Americans. Doolittle recalled it as an anecdotal, almost accidental decision. Early in his tenure, while visiting the head of the VIII Fighter Command, Maj. Gen. William E. Kepner, he noted a sign that declared, "THE FIRST DUTY OF THE AIR FORCE FIGHTERS IS TO BRING THE BOMBERS BACK ALIVE." When queried by Doolittle, Kepner said that the sign had been there when he arrived. Doolittle ordered him to replace it with one that stated, "THE FIRST DUTY OF EIGHTH AIR FORCE FIGHTERS IS TO DESTROY GERMAN FIGHTERS." When Kepner asked Doolittle to clarify that he was "authorizing me to take the offensive," Doolittle replied, "I'm directing you to."[9]

Doolittle recalled that "tears came to Bill's eyes." Kepner was overjoyed that his men would finally be given free rein to go after the German air force. It was something that they had agitated for almost since the beginning. Certainly, the idea did not originate with Doolittle and came naturally to anyone tasked to operate under the constraints of close escort. In fact, Doolittle's fighters in the Twelfth Air Force had been freed from close-escort restrictions during his command in North Africa and the Mediterranean. No doubt he surmised that if the idea had worked there, it should work over Germany.

Official records are more prosaic than Doolittle's recollections. The minutes from a meeting on January 21 note Doolittle's declaration that "the role of protecting the bombardment formation should not be minimized" but that the escort fighters "should be encouraged to meet the enemy and destroy him rather than be content to keep him away." In other words, the Luftwaffe formations would no longer have the luxury of assembling and formulating their attacks within sight of the bombers and their escorts. Doolittle was giving his pilots the initiative.

The news could not have been better received by the fighter units. Up until that point, they had been fighting at an enormous disadvantage, like a dog forced to fight while chained to a post. Now they were free, within reason, to range away from the bombers and hit the German formations before they could get into position to strike.

The effects were immediate. The Luftwaffe units were most effective when they massed their attacks, but assembling large numbers of fighters and getting them into position were problematic on the best days, requiring experienced flight leaders and disciplined and skilled wingmen. However, the task became impossible when under attack by even one or two fighters. When the newly empowered Americans struck, the large German formations invariably broke down into many smaller, less effective packets. Ultimately, the change in tactics produced more dead German pilots and better-protected bombers.

However, the bomber crews did not embrace the change. After all, there was great comfort in actually seeing their protectors nearby, and they feared, perhaps with some justification, that they would be deserted as soon as the first Luftwaffe aircraft appeared. To say that they hated Doolittle's new edict would be an understatement. Many of the men transferred those feelings directly to their new commander.

But what the bomber crews could not always see were the distant swirling dogfights. German aircraft that were engaged when the escorts charged ahead or to the far flanks stood little chance of making attacks against the boxed bomber formations. Nor could the crews see the aerial frays that occurred when the phased-escort relays, en route to or from the bomber streams, tore into the enemy fighters they met.

Still, when the Luftwaffe pilots managed to slip past the escorts—and it occurred often enough—the bomber crews decried the new tactics as ineffective. The result was that they never fully embraced the abandonment of close-escort tactics. In the end, largely in response to the outcry from the bomber men, the actual practice was to turn loose the bulk of the escorts while keeping smaller reserves close to the bomber streams. The rancor never really subsided until the Luftwaffe had been ground down so badly that the sight of German fighters became a rarity.

Although the Luftwaffe was occasionally scoring some impressive tactical successes even in early 1944, its end was becoming more certain, despite the fact that the Germans still had experienced men flying very good aircraft and the American airmen who would ultimately destroy the German air force were still relative newcomers or had not even arrived from the United States. The fault was in prior German planning.

The German air ministry had delivered a study more than a year earlier on December 16, 1942, that recommended tripling fighter production, but the difference among what was called for, what was needed, and what was delivered to its fighter units was a giant chasm. At the end of 1942, the Luftwaffe had approximately 1,400 single-engine fighters in its frontline units. A year later, six months prior to the invasion of Normandy, that number had grown to only about 1,600 aircraft. Production had indeed increased somewhat, but so had American daylight operations. Subsequently, although the Luftwaffe received more fighters than it otherwise would have during 1943, it lost many more fighters than it had at any other point in the war to that time. Those losses had been sustained not only against the USAAF bombing campaign in the West but also against the Soviets in the East and against the British and Americans in the Mediterranean.

The Germans simply could not keep up with the Americans, British, and Soviets. In the context of the American strategic missions out of England, where the average size of selected missions by the Eighth was only about 80 bombers at the start of 1943, those raids averaged approximately 500 bombers by the end of the year—more than a sixfold increase. Dedicated to the protection of these bombers was an escort fighter force that grew similarly in size. On the other hand, the number of German fighters intercepting the bomber formations was also about 80 at the start of 1943, but only about 240 at the end of the year—

merely a threefold increase. Therefore, the Luftwaffe's disadvantage in pure numbers versus the bombers and fighters deteriorated from about 1:2 to about 1:4.

Despite the numerical disadvantage, the Luftwaffe pilots enjoyed total respite from the escort fighters when they were forced to return to their bases because of fuel considerations. It was then that the Germans were able to inflict massive casualties on the bombers as they had during several raids prior to the stunning tragedy that was the second mission to Schweinfurt in October 1943. And it was losses like those that had forced Eaker to suspend unescorted bomber missions, which meant that much of Germany was out of reach. For a brief period, it seemed as if Germany had successfully negated the daylight bomber threat.

But it was only a short interlude. By February 1944, the longer-range P-51 had entered service in numbers great enough to make a contribution, and the P-47 and P-38 had been fitted with drop tanks that, when coupled with other modifications and more efficient procedures, enabled them to range deep into Germany. Perhaps most importantly, Doolittle had freed the fighters from close-escort duties and ordered them to chase down and kill their German counterparts whenever the situation presented itself.

Luftwaffe losses in aircraft and pilots soared.

CHAPTER 11

Big Week, Interns, and Flak

With the start of a new year, a new set of commanders, new tactics, and a burgeoning wealth of new aircraft and crews, Spaatz looked for new opportunities. By February 1944, the staffs of the USSTAF and the RAF were ready to kick off an aerial offensive they reckoned would yield them double results. Their analysis held that a concerted series of large, around-the-clock raids against the German aircraft industry would not only inflict serious damage to Nazi aircraft production, but would also force the Luftwaffe to come up and fight. If it fought, it would bleed. The operation, dubbed ARGUMENT, would go a long way toward establishing Allied air superiority over Europe if it were successfully carried out. Constrained by weather, it was executed by the Eighth and Fifteenth Air Forces, together with the RAF's Bomber Command, during the brief period from February 20 to 25, 1944.

On the last day of the effort, February 25, the 457th Bomb Group (H), based out of Glatton, England, put fifty-five B-17s airborne for a strike on the Messerschmitt plant in Augsburg. Piloting one of those bombers, *Straight Shot*, was Lt. Archie Bower.[1] His crew had been stood down the previous day in preparation for being sent to London for some much-needed rest. "The crew, however," remembered Bower, "wanted to fly another mission before we went on leave and asked that we volunteer for the Augsburg mission."

The B-17s of the 457th got airborne with little difficulty and climbed through layers of clouds before heading southeast at an altitude of more than 27,000 feet. The flight into southern Germany was unremarkable until the bombers approached the target. Bower recalled: "On the bomb run we encountered heavy flack [*sic*]. Number two engine was hit and lost oil pressure rapidly." Aside from the number two engine, the number three engine had also been damaged and holes pocked the aircraft. Nevertheless, Bower and his copilot, William Baxendale, held *Straight Shot* in formation until the bombardier, Richard Cooke, released the ship's bombs.

Soon, however, it became apparent that the bomber could not stay with the rest of the group, and *Straight Shot* was left alone, a straggler. Nothing attracted German fighter pilots so much as a lone bomber because, rather than the combined defensive fire of a formation, they had only to deal with the guns of a single aircraft. "All of our gunners began firing heavily," recounted Cooke, the bombardier. He operated the two .50-caliber machine guns in the aircraft's chin turret, but only one of them was working. "I got off a burst at a Bf-109 attacking our nose. He came in head-on firing and barrel rolling. I was dazed by how fast he flew by."

The number two engine began to run away, and Bower ordered Cooke and Lee Hoskins, the navigator, out of the nose of the aircraft. Cooke recalled that Bower "was afraid that if the prop disconnected, it would take the nose with it." The two men crawled out of the front of the aircraft past the flight deck, across the bomb bay, and into the radio room where Cooke manned the single gun there as the radio man, John Popowitz, stayed at his station. Almost immediately the ball turret gunner, Wesley Schneider, crawled up out of his position; his guns had stopped working.

The enemy fighters continued to savage the lone B-17. Bower called over the intercom for Hoskins to come back forward and plot a course for Switzerland; *Straight Shot* was never going to make it back to England. "Lee Hoskins looked over at me," recalled Cooke, "and said, 'See ya later Cooke,' and started over the catwalk back to the pilot's compartment. That's the last I saw of him."

It was at about that time that a pack of FW-190s attacked from the right side; cannon fire ripped through the fuselage and set the midsection of the aircraft on fire. It tore the men there apart. Wesley Schneider, who had left his inoperative ball turret guns to help man the waist guns, was dead, as was one of the other waist gunners, Jesse Hirschberg. Cooke described the rest of the carnage: "John Popowitz was blown across to the other side of the radio room with a bad hip wound. Joe Snyder [the other waist gunner] was badly hit in the body and both legs. One of his legs especially was all chewed up. I was hit in the legs with shrapnel." It was at about that time that the tail gunner, John Woskovich, crawled up from the rear of the aircraft. He found a mess of hot, bloody brass shell casings and bodies.

The front of the aircraft was likewise in chaos. Baxendale, the copilot, had left to check the situation in the rear. Fire was coming from the nose of the bomber onto the flight deck where it was burning Bower. Moreover, *Straight Shot* was becoming uncontrollable. Bower recounted: "We started to drop. I ordered the crew to bail out at 17,500 feet. Then I pulled the emergency release for the bomb doors, which was my emergency exit. Unfortunately, the cable came loose in my hands apparently damaged by the flack." Bower left his position, headed back to the bomb bay, and threw his body against the doors to no avail. In the meantime, Hoskins, the navigator, and Frank Giardano, the flight engineer and top-turret gunner, jumped out of the ship uninjured.

The bomber fell to earth in a slow spin, and the men inside found it nearly impossible to move. At one point, its flight steadied, and Woskovich and Snyder managed to jump from the waist. At about the same time, Baxendale made his way over to Cooke, threw his arms around Cooke's neck and torso, and shouted at him to jump: "Let's go Dick! I'll see you on the ground!" The pair, wrapped tightly together, fell clear of the bomber. Cooke described their fall:

I didn't understand why Baxendale jumped with me like that. I thought he was going to stay together with me to get free of the plane. We jumped and free fell for several thousand feet. He never spoke. He never let go. As I pulled my chute at about ten thousand feet, the impact broke his grip, and he fell away. I watched him, waiting for his chute to open. It never did. "Oh, god," I thought, "he doesn't have a chute!" All the time we were clinging together, I thought he was wearing a chute. It wasn't until I saw his chute not open that I realized he didn't have one. He had been trying to ride my chute down with me. He had not said anything to me. My chest tightened up. Bill was my friend, a good friend, and a good man. Our wives were friends.

Failing to clear the aircraft through the bomb bay doors, Bower crawled to the radio room, where he grabbed the injured Popowitz and dragged him into the waist section. The aircraft had by that time started a series of stalls and recoveries against which Bower struggled. He checked the bodies of the dead men and finally managed to shove Popowitz out of the bomber. He threw himself clear just before the aircraft hit the earth.

Above him, the mortified Cooke was still floating down in his parachute. He heard the sound of a fighter engine and spun around in his harness. An Me-109 was fast approaching: "I tried to swing on my chute and make as small a target as I could. Rather than open fire, the pilot rolled his plane and saluted as he flew past. He was so close I could see his face. This was one of the men who had taken us down. As I followed his plane, I saw him engaged by a P-51. It was over quickly. His fighter exploded in the air."

Of the original ten-man crew, Cooke, Woskovich, Snyder, Popowitz, Bower, Hoskins, and Giardano reached the ground alive. Hoskins was never seen again and was probably killed by German civilians. Popowitz died untended in a German clinic later that same day. The rest, some injured, survived the war.

Bower recalled an encounter with one of his German counterparts: "Later that night, I was visited by one of the pilots who shot us down. He told me that we had downed two of his comrades. He rolled a piece of paper around the end of a cigarette to keep the smoke away from my burns and held it while I smoked. He also brought me a bottle of cold beer."

ARGUMENT, better known as Big Week, was costly, but it did produce results. The USAAF lost an unprecedented 247 bombers and 38 fighters, and the RAF lost 131 bombers. While the losses stung, they were readily replaced. On the other hand, the German aircraft factories were hit hard, and nearly 400 Luftwaffe fighters were downed. But most important of all, nearly 100 German fighter pilots were killed. The Germans could and, despite the damage to their factories, did replace their aircraft losses. Pilot replacements came more dearly, and when they came, they were of poorer quality. Indeed, the operation is often defined as the seminal turning point in the air war over Europe.

Still, Adolf Galland was unimpressed: "Allied propaganda . . . considerably exaggerated the effects of these raids. The Big Week was for several days the sensation of the Western press. The Allied Command also overrated the effect of the raids and underrated the resilience of German industry, as they admitted later."[2] There was some truth to Galland's point of view as German aircraft production soared later that year.

Indeed, at the end of 1943 and into 1944, while the United States hurried to ready its fighters for long-range escort duties into the heart of Germany, the Nazi leadership put new urgency into upgrading their fighter defenses. Their assumption was that the American bombers would be back in greater numbers, albeit still unescorted; technical experts in Germany had always declared that a long-range, single-engine fighter capable of meeting the Me-109 and FW-190 on even terms was impossible. That fact notwithstanding, the bombers were tough enough to knock down even when they penetrated without an escort. The Luftwaffe knew it would need every fighter it could get its hands on when the Americans went deep again.

It was during this period that the responsibility for aircraft production in Germany was reshuffled, and Erhard Milch, by then the director-general of air force equipment, was organizationally placed under Hitler's minister of armaments, Albert Speer. Whereas Milch had enjoyed some modest successes in increasing Germany's aircraft production during 1943, Speer's organizational brilliance, combined with strong backing from Hitler, generated a tremendous increase in aircraft manufacturing.

One of the key factors in the success was the decision to disperse enormous aircraft factories into smaller plants and workshops that were difficult to locate, much less bomb with any efficiency. For example, a small machine shop in one town might produce aircraft components that were brought together with parts from a plant in a neighboring village that formerly crafted, for instance, agricultural implements. These elements would then move through the country along a fabrication web until all the disparate pieces were assembled into complete aircraft that were immediately sent to operational units. Although the practice was less efficient than traditional, single-site manufacturing it was also less vulnerable to Allied bombing. Another contributing element to the plan's achievement was the incredible fact that, up to that point, the German war industry had not yet been fully mobilized. Indeed, there was still spare capacity in the form of excess factory space, older but serviceable equipment, and idle labor. Speer found that spare capacity and put it to work.

The results were extraordinary. Although the Big Week operations at the tail end of February 1944 dropped aircraft production to 1,700, down from January's number of 2,100, production during March exceeded 2,300. Totals increased month-over-month until peaking in September 1944, months after the Normandy landings, at more than 3,700 aircraft. This is compared to December 1943, when less than 1,400 aircraft were manufactured even though Eaker had called off deep-penetration raids more than a month earlier.[3] Although manufacturing began to slip after September, production numbers continued to exceed 2,500 aircraft each month until January 1945, when the collapse of manufacturing across all of Germany began to accelerate under the Allied bombing onslaught.

This astonishing increase in production was achieved despite the inefficiencies associated with scattering manufacturing nodes across a wide geographic area. Furthermore, it gives a hint about the size of the air force Germany could have had in 1943 or even 1942. Had an aggressive manufacturing scheme been implemented before the aircraft factories were shattered, it is quite possible that a much larger Luftwaffe would have ruined the American daylight bombing campaign soon after it started.

Producing more aircraft was one thing, but training enough pilots to fly them was quite another. By the time Speer's efforts bore fruit, it was already too late since it took much more time to train skilled pilots than it did to crank out aircraft. When it is considered that it typically took about eighteen months for Germany to produce a well-qualified fighter pilot, it is easy to see that drastic action should have been taken during late 1942 or early 1943 to match pilot numbers with the increased aircraft production numbers of mid-1944. No such effort was made.

In fact, Germany's short-sighted leadership resorted to disastrous stopgap measures. Instructors were pulled from flying schools and sent to frontline fighter units. Bomber and transport pilots were likewise given quick fighter conversion courses and ordered into combat. Student training courses were shortened, and the new pilots arrived unprepared for combat. These were foolish acts that not only robbed the bomber and transport commands of the personnel they needed to meet their own missions, but also gutted the pilot training efforts. Still, the time was too late for anything to have worked. Regardless of whether it had aircraft, without trained pilots, the Luftwaffe was in a war it had little hope of winning.

Ultimately, the numbers tell the story. From 1940 through 1944, the Luftwaffe produced just under 15,000 fighter pilots. Those pilots declined in quality as the war wore on. On the other hand, during approximately the same period, the USAAF alone, not including Great Britain or the Soviet Union, produced nearly 200,000 pilots of consistently excellent caliber.

Galland might have been unimpressed by Big Week, but the truth was that the dynamic between the American daylight bombers and the Luftwaffe had changed for good. American bombers had the escort fighters they needed to go wherever they wanted whenever they wanted. If there was any doubt in Galland's mind, the Eighth Air Force surely must have removed it when, after weather broke up a pair of raids on March 3 and 4, it hit Berlin hard on March 6, 1944, only nine days after Big Week. Although the RAF's Bomber Command had been bombing the Nazi capital for years, the Americans were there not just to terrorize the city's populace, but to destroy its industry.

Although it was actually the 55th Fighter Group flying P-38s that put the first fighters over Berlin, Hermann Göring was famously quoted as saying, "The day I saw P-51 Mustangs flying over Berlin, I knew the jig was up." Indeed, although the ranges of both the P-47 and P-38 had been improved to the point that they could penetrate far into Germany, the P-51 was given responsibility for escorting the bombers on the deepest segments of their penetrations. And they had good success in doing so as indicated by the encounter report of Glendon Davis of the 357th Fighter Group, who, with his wingman, dove on an FW-190 that was attacking a straggling B-17 west of Berlin:

> We dove down on the E/A [enemy aircraft] but couldn't close on him as the tail gunner of the bomber was firing at him. We broke to the side of E/A and at that time he saw us and broke into us. . . . We were forcing him to keep a tight spiral by cutting on the inside of him when he tried to widen it out. At 10,000 feet, he dropped his belly tank. At 5,000 feet, his plane appeared to be stalling as he tried to pull out. His canopy flew off but the plane went right on into the ground without the pilot ever getting out.[4]

With a fighter escort that the German air force was incapable of defeating, the Eighth returned to Berlin whenever it wanted throughout the remainder of the war.

Even as late as February 1944, Arnold was anxious about the perceived role and value of his strategic air forces. He was especially fretful that they might be overshadowed by RAF's Bomber Command. He wrote Spaatz: "Already, the spectacular effectiveness of their devastation of cities has placed their contribution in the popular mind at so high a plane that I am having the greatest difficulty in keeping your achievement . . . in its proper role not only in publications, but unfortunately in military and naval circles, and in fact, with the President himself."[5]

Despite the successes gained against the Luftwaffe during early 1944, the strategic fight over Europe was still a fearful one, and the crews of both the Eighth and the Fifteenth were under tremendous strain. Indeed, keeping morale high challenged the USAAF's leadership at every level. Because the operations were so dangerous, one of the most contentious issues was the number of missions required to complete a combat tour. Early on, Eaker let crews from the Eighth go home after they completed twenty-five missions. This was during a time when the odds of actually doing so were quite long. As the loss rate declined—but more importantly as the need to execute the strategic air campaign became especially compelling in the period before D-Day— Doolittle upped the requirement for the Eighth's crews to thirty missions during February 1944. A few months later, in July, he increased it to thirty-five. In Italy, airmen in the Fifteenth were justifiably upset when their required mission count was set at fifty.

The entire situation vexed both Arnold and Spaatz, who needed every airman he could get, regardless of mission count. Arnold was especially bothered by reports that crews that had completed their missions and returned to the States were bad-mouthing the tour-length policies. He wrote Spaatz: "Reports reaching me from trustworthy sources, as well as my own personal observations, lead to the conclusion that the behavior of returned combat personnel does not always reflect credit upon the AAF."[6] Arnold believed that there was a morale problem, and he naturally wanted it fixed.

Measuring morale was a squishy science, and fixing it when it was bad was a prickly challenge. Doolittle recognized the importance of informing and educating his men about the impetus and motivations behind his decisions. It was February 1944 when he addressed his commanders: "During the next few months it is mandatory that we secure complete air superiority over the German Air Force in this Theater . . . we must adopt every expedient to improve the effectiveness of the Air Force."[7] One of those expedients was extending the tours of the aircrews. In fact, Doolittle made it clear that completion of thirty missions was not a guarantee that a crewman would be taken off of combat operations. Rather, completion of thirty missions made a crewman *eligible for consideration* for removal from combat operations. In practice, most commanders did pull their men from flight duties once they had completed the requisite number although, by the summer of 1944, about 4 percent had exceeded the count. Of this small percentage, however, some were volunteers.[8]

That being said, it should be understood that all aircrew were volunteers. They all had the option to decline flying duty for reassignment elsewhere. Accordingly, if it wanted to maintain the volunteer aircrew concept, the USAAF leadership had to ensure that what it demanded of its men was not so onerous that it would drive masses of them to quit. It was a fine line that they logically did not want to test.

One metric that Arnold considered as a measurement of morale was the number of aircraft that flew into the neutral countries, Switzerland and Sweden. As 1943 turned into 1944, the number of crews diverting into these two nations increased, a fact that greatly alarmed him. An obvious reason for crews to land in either place was that their aircraft were incapable of returning to either England or Italy; landing in a neutral country was better than going down in enemy territory or into the sea. In truth, this was the primary reason for these diversions. But the fact that he might have had crews intentionally turning themselves over to the Swiss or the Swedes in order to sit out the rest of the war bothered Arnold. He believed it was a reflection on morale, which in turn was a reflection on him and the rest of the USAAF.

Moreover, the numbers of aircraft flown into the neutral nations was not inconsequential. During May, June, and July 1944, they totaled ninety-seven.[9] Arnold wrote Spaatz, urging "that great care be taken not to hold combat crews in the theater until war weariness provokes an uncontrollable urge to grasp release by the action [landing in neutral countries] indicated." For his part, Spaatz replied with some indignation that he was aware of the issue and was balancing the requirements to prosecute the strategic campaign against the mental state of his aircrews.

Bearing in mind what happened to the airmen of a 44th Bomb Group (H) B-24, it was not unreasonable that the crews aboard damaged ships considered diverting into either Switzerland or Sweden. On May 25, 1944, the group's primary target was the Belfort marshaling yards in France, not far from Switzerland. The ship captained by 2nd Lt. Frank Tomer was hit by flak and fell out of the formation with one engine out and another badly damaged.[10] Sgt. Eldon Anderson, the tail gunner, recalled, "After we left the formation, we flew around a bit trying to decide what to do with our bombs. We finally found a big, open space and let them go. We then discussed what to do—to go on to Switzerland, which wasn't that far away, or to attempt to make it back to England."

Tomer and his crew decided to try to get back to the 44th's base at Shipdham. "By that time," Anderson said, "we were down to about 10,000 feet due to those ailing engines, but thought that with luck, we could get back to base. We flew at this altitude because we couldn't get any higher—and were prime targets for the German flak batteries. Eventually we were hit again by flak, and this time I believe it was the nose section because the plane started falling at once." There was no communication from the cockpit to the rear of the aircraft, but the bomber started out of control, and it was obvious that it was time to leave. Anderson bailed out along with two other crewmen. The rest of the crew, seven men, went down with the stricken bomber and were killed.

It is unreasonable to believe that there were not at least a few bomber crews that diverted into the neutral countries under the flimsiest of pretenses or under no pretenses whatsoever. After all, despite the successes achieved in early 1944, the sky over Germany offered excellent opportunities to die. For instance, the bomber loss rate per mission in the Eighth Air Force averaged only 1.5 percent in May 1944. Nevertheless, math was a cruel mistress as even that small number put against a tour of thirty missions produced odds guaranteeing that more than a third of the crews would be shot down. With that frightening fact in mind, it would be ridiculous to believe that every crew that was interned had no other choice than to crash in Germany.

Still, testimony indicates that most of the crews that were interned did arrive aboard mortally stricken ships. Sam Barrick, a pilot with the 100th Bomb Group (H), had his B-17 badly shot up by fighters on a mission to Berlin on March 16, 1944, before landing in Sweden.[11] Aside from serving on a team that repaired, scrapped, or salvaged the stricken bombers (for eventual return to the United States), he sat on an evaluation board that was tasked with determining how many of the crews that came into the country did so in order to shirk their duties: "Only one was found to be questionable," he stated. "No action was taken against the aircraft commander."

To those who questioned the motivations of the crews that landed in the neutral nations, Barrick had this to say: "Too bad these writers could not have been there to attend the funerals in Sweden, visit the wounded in the hospital, and see the extensive battle damage most of the airplanes had received. Too bad they didn't know about the long hours spent under field conditions, repairing aircraft and some that would have been junked back in the UK."

In fact, the circumstances surrounding Barrick's decision to save his crew by diverting into Sweden were typical. His waist gunner, William Sapp, recounted the fierce combat over Berlin: "We had two engines hit in the initial attack and would not have been able to keep up with the formation except that there was no formation to keep up with—we had lost 14 planes and, including our plane, this left seven planes flying." With one engine afire, Barrick wrestled the aircraft over the Baltic.

Sapp remembered that Barrick's decision really was a foregone one: "The navigator said we didn't have enough fuel to make the North Sea, which was understandable to me because I could see right through one of the wing tanks. As a result, we headed for the Baltic Sea and Sweden." Ultimately, Swedish fighters intercepted the bomber and escorted it to a field where Barrick was able to bring it safely to the ground.

Aircraft diversions into Sweden and Switzerland declined following D-Day, when airfields were established on continental Europe. Furthermore, as the Soviets closed on Germany from the east, bomber crews had the option of continuing in that direction with their wounded ships. Nevertheless, aircraft continued to trickle into Sweden and Switzerland; it was a fact with which the USAAF had to reconcile itself. In total, the interned aircraft amounted to a significant number, perhaps 300 or even more. But in reality, many of them were so badly damaged that they would have been lost or written off anyway. Regardless, the Eighth and the Fifteenth were able to absorb the losses and soldier on.

In the end, as Allied successes continued to mount through 1944, aircrew morale—both real and perceived—improved. That it was good enough, considering the outcome of the war, is obvious.

Hollywood depictions of bomber combat during World War II are valuable in that they help kindle the public's interest, but ignorance and the limitations of the film medium sometimes combine to render a less-than-perfect picture of what the experience was actually like. "When there was a lot of flak," remembered Walter Baker of the 487th Bomb Group (H), "it wasn't like in the movies. You didn't hear it explode. It was more of a shooshing sound: SH-VUUMMP! Then, when the shrapnel hit the fuselage, it was like someone threw marbles against a bunch of tin. It was a rattling sound."

When an aircraft was pockmarked by shrapnel farther out on the wings, there was no sound. "I can remember looking out over the left wing," said Baker. "And a set of holes appeared in the wingtip just as fast as I could blink. One instant they weren't there and the next they were. There was no noise and the aircraft didn't lurch or anything. There was nothing but those holes. That was just the small stuff, though. One time we took a direct hit in the fuel tank on the right wing, directly between the number three and four engines." The impact from the big enemy shell nearly flipped the bomber over. "But it didn't fuze properly. It didn't explode."

Although the shell had not detonated, the ship was nevertheless in mortal danger. Once the pilots got the aircraft back under control, the ball-turret gunner called over the intercom: "Man, there's fuel streaming all over the number three turbo." The "turbo," or turbocharger, fed compressed air into the engine and was extremely hot. The crew held its collective breath until the flow of fuel from the wrecked wing tank was exhausted. By all odds, the extremely inflammable gas should have caught fire. And if that had happened, it would have been only a short time until the wing failed. "We were pretty lucky that day," Baker said—an understatement.

But tens of thousands of airmen were not so lucky. Flak (*Fliegerabwehrkanone*) guns knocked down American and British aircraft by the thousands. The type most used against the strategic bombers—and with devastating effect—was the iconic 88-millimeter (*acht-acht*) gun designed and produced by Krupp beginning in 1933. It was evolved and improved, and as demand for the weapon increased, its production was spread among different manufacturers.

Although Germany's flak defenses included relatively small numbers of larger weapons such as the 105-millimeter and the 128-millimeter, it was the 88-millimeter that destroyed the most bombers. It could fire approximately fifteen twenty-pound rounds per minute up to an effective altitude of just more than 30,000 feet. The high-explosive rounds were fitted with mechanical time fuzes, and their casings were scored or segmented so as to separate into sizes and shapes that would inflict maximum damage. Later in the war, the shell casings were manufactured with an incendiary component that virtually guaranteed devastating fires when they penetrated fuel tanks.

The Luftwaffe operated a vast and complex system for controlling their air defenses. This system included radars, ground and aerial observers, and the headquarters and communication elements required to coordinate and control them all. Flak defenses, which were organizationally part of the Luftwaffe, ringed cities and other important targets and were also laid out in geographic belts or along obvious avenues of approach. The basic organizational element was the battery, which was typically made up of two or three groups comprising up to six or eight guns each. The batteries were cued either visually or by radar for both direction and height finding.

Later in the war, the most common method for engaging the bombers was with barrage fire. The batteries set their guns to fire into an area or "box" through which it was determined the targeted aircraft would fly. The shells were fuzed to detonate within that box. On command, all guns within a given battery fired at once. The objective was to put an intense concentration of shells into a given area at the exact moment a bomber formation was traversing it. It was an inexact art: three to four thousand shells were expended for each bomber shot down.

The flak defenses came at a very heavy cost; aside from the guns and ammunition, the manpower requirements were intensive. Gun crews, depending on the phase of the war, ran from six to ten or more, not including the headquarters and technical staffs assigned to each battery. In fact, approximately a million personnel were assigned to the Luftwaffe's flak arm through much of the war. As the conflict dragged on and German fortunes fell, the guns were increasingly manned by Home Guard personnel, women, teenagers, forced laborers, and even prisoners of war.

The 88-millimeter guns were not purpose-built for antiaircraft work alone, but in fact, they proved to be exceedingly effective for ground combat, particularly as antitank weapons. That the Germans had nearly 11,000 of them defending against Allied bombers during the height of the Soviet offensives in 1944 was significant. There is little doubt that even half that number could have had some impact on the fighting on the Eastern Front.

Heavy bombers, B-17s and B-24s, were the classic targets for the big flak guns. And in fact, in the Mediterranean and European theaters, antiaircraft fire brought down more heavy bombers than did fighters (3,752 bombers attributed to flak versus 3,299 bombers attributed to fighters).[12] Nevertheless, other aircraft types were also devastated. Bob Popeney, an A-20 pilot with the 416th Light Bombardment Group, recalled a mission he flew to Duren, Germany, during October 1944:

The flak was very intense, and I happened to look down at Nordstrom, who was flying in the slot—the number four position. Just at that instant, he took a hit right behind the wingroot and broke in half. The metal of the fuselage was curled the same way a firecracker does to a tin can. I could see the inside of the airplane—zinc chromate green. And I could see Nordstrom's eyes. He looked confused. I presume it was because he couldn't feel the stick or the rudder. He had no controls. And then immediately his aircraft flipped up and then went tumbling down. All of this happened in just a split-second. I told my gunner to watch; to follow it down and watch for parachutes. He saw nothing. We never heard from Nordstrom again.

The smaller fighters were also vulnerable. Joe Black of the 357th Fighter Group recalled an episode: "We were on a big mission to Berlin and were flying in solid overcast. We got too close to Helgoland where they still had a lot of flak batteries and a shell burst right next to my plane. It shattered my canopy and my wingman's as well. A shard cut my chin and started it bleeding."

The two fighters eased out of the formation and made their way safely back to base. "There was talk of giving me a Purple Heart Medal for that one," Black said. "I rejected that idea. There were guys on the ground doing real fighting. The wound I had was tiny by comparison; I'd done things to myself that were almost as bad while shaving."[13]

Countering the German air defenses was a top priority, and a variety of countermeasures were fielded during the war. Both the British and the Americans used window, or chaff, to confuse German radars. The RAF pioneered the concept and first used it on a grand scale—with great success—during the Hamburg raids of July 1943. Made up of thin metallic strips, it was cut to specific lengths to jam particular radar frequencies and bundled in small packages that held thousands of individual lengths. "It was one of my duties to dispense the chaff," remembered Walter Baker, a B-17 radioman with the 487th Bomb Group (H). A truck would come around to all the different aircraft before a mission to leave us our allotment. It came in cardboard tubes, and I'd usually be able to talk the guys into giving me one or two extra tubes—I'd use them for flak protection."

The chaff was supposed to be released at particular points along the route. Baker recalled: "When it was time to put it out, I'd pull the cap off a tube and then hold the tube upside down in a special chute in the radio compartment that was open to the outside. Then, the slipstream would just pull it out."

"The Germans used chaff [*Düppel*] too," recounted Baker. "They cut it a little wider than we did, but it was essentially the same." He recollected one morning after a late-war German harassment raid: "I was walking to the mess hall and on the way I noted that the snowy ground seemed to be especially shiny and glittery. It took me a moment to realize that what I was looking at was chaff—German chaff!"

A similar episode was recorded by Joseph Dell, a P-47 pilot with the 86th Fighter Bomber Group. He was shot down on March 22, 1945, and spent several days trying, ultimately unsuccessfully, to evade capture. "One thing that amazed me was that I had noticed in travelling throughout this remote, immense, sprawling fir forest that silver icicles like the ones we had used to decorate Christmas trees at home were on the branches of every single tree. I couldn't believe the Germans would do this." It was only later that he learned that the "decorations" were actually chaff from Allied bombers.[14]

Much is made of what impact the Me-262 jet fighter would have had on the course of the war had the Nazi's fielded it earlier than they actually did. The Me-262 possessed tremendous performance and outstanding firepower. That being said, the Germans missed an opportunity to knock down the Allied bombers in much greater numbers for significantly less cost.

That opportunity was a proximity fuze for large antiaircraft rounds such as the 88-millimeter. The ammunition the Luftwaffe flak units typically used not only had to be aimed so as to arrive in the middle of the Allied bomber formations, but it had to be fuzed with timing devices so that it detonated at the correct altitude. It was a difficult problem. However, a proximity fuze would have eased the problem by detonating the warhead whenever a round passed close to an aircraft.

The Germans tried to create such a device and failed. The Allies undertook the same task and succeeded. Using British research and experiments as a springboard, the U.S. Navy funded an intensive development effort that leveraged expertise across government, industry, and academia beginning late in 1940. By early 1942, the navy was testing early prototypes. The fuze worked by transmitting a continuous wave radio signal in all directions; when a nearby aircraft reflected that signal back to the fuze's tiny receiver, the shell was detonated. The navy named its new device a VT fuze—for "variable time," which actually was more descriptive of the type of fuze it replaced. Yet because the experiments were classified, the misleading nomenclature was believed to be appropriate.

The first tests against real aircraft were scheduled from the USS *Cleveland* for a two-day period beginning on August 12, 1942. Success was realized when the three remotely piloted aircraft intended as targets were all destroyed during the first morning by only four rounds of proximity-fuze antiaircraft ammunition. The new technology was subsequently rushed to the Pacific. It first scored when the USS *Helena* used it to down a Japanese bomber on January 5, 1943.

Secrecy surrounding the new fuzes was intense for obvious reasons. The Allies feared that the Germans might get their hands on an example and reverse engineer it. It was estimated that the new fuzes made antiaircraft artillery seven times more effective.[15] Had the German flak gunners been able to increase their effectiveness so greatly, it is quite likely that the Allied bombing campaign would have ground to a halt until countermeasures were developed. Such a halt could have prolonged the war.

Ultimately, the Allies used the proximity fuze for a wide range of applications. It was instrumental in stopping V-1 missile attacks on England; the vast majority of the flying bombs never made it through the British antiaircraft belts because of the effectiveness of the fuzes. In fact, the last day of the V-1 attacks saw 100 of 104 of the flying bombs shot down, most of them by proximity-fuze antiaircraft shells.

As preparations continued for the invasion of Europe, it was recognized that the Eighth would have difficulty sustaining a strategic campaign while simultaneously supporting army units on the battlefield. Subsequently, it was decided to make the Ninth Air Force a tactical air force and move it to England. That move was made in September 1943.

For its new role in England, the Ninth took on new equipment that would eventually include B-26s, A-20s, A-26s, P-51s, P-38s, and P-47s. Close cooperation—and no small amount of friction—was maintained between the Eighth and the Ninth. The Ninth, particularly in late 1943 and into 1944, provided P-51 and P-47 units as escorts for the Eighth's bombers. In fact, the first P-51s to serve in the bomber escort role belonged to the Ninth. For its part, the Eighth would give over its heavy bombers for tactical strikes in support of Allied ground forces before and after the invasion.

CHAPTER 12

Pilot Training

B eginning in early 1944 and through the end of the war, the USAAF crushed the German air force not just with greater numbers of aircraft, but with good pilots to fly them. That it was able to do so was because its leadership had years earlier exercised a level of foresight that was missing in the Luftwaffe. Even in 1940, more than a year before the United States entered the war and when the U.S. Army Air Corps had fewer than 4,000 flyers, a seemingly absurd annual pilot training goal of 30,000 was established. By 1944, the American investment toward that objective was paying off. Good numbers of well-trained pilots arrived overseas ready for combat.

If an air force could not field well-trained aircrews, it did not matter how highly developed its aircraft might be or how many of those advanced aircraft it produced. In the hands of poorly trained crews, they were little more than wasted resources. This was not a secret. Every nation realized the importance of good training and, for the most part, at least at the beginning of the war, ensured that its crews were well prepared for combat. And as lessons were learned from the fighting, the best air forces adjusted their training to ensure that the flyers they produced were as skilled as possible.

The United States steadily improved the quantity and quality of its aircrews. Improving the quantity of the aircrews it produced required a Herculean effort because, prior to the start of the fighting in Europe, the training output of the air corps was only a tiny fraction of what was eventually needed. The reason was simple: the U.S. Army Air Corps was a little air force that enjoyed minimal turnover, and up to that point, there simply had been no need for a huge training apparatus capable of stamping out tens of thousands of flyers per year.

Numbers aside, upgrading the quality of its aircrews was a different challenge. Although the skill sets of its aircrews at that time were certainly adequate, the air corps pilots did not stand out as especially superior compared to those of the other major belligerents, especially Great Britain, Germany, and Japan. This was particularly true as the flyers from those other nations gained fighting experience while the Americans sat on the sidelines.

Robert Stanford Tuck, a distinguished RAF fighter pilot, noted this inexperience during a technical tour of the United States before the Japanese attack on Pearl Harbor. A veteran of the Battle of Britain and subsequent operations from England, Tuck had been credited with more than twenty aerial victories by the time he arrived in the United States in October 1941. At that point, the U.S. Army Air Corps was racing to ready itself for a war that seemed certain to overtake the United States. Tuck's visit was part of the army's effort to learn about the most recent tactics to come out of the fighting in Europe. It was a mutually beneficial arrangement: while the Englishman would have a chance to assess the latest American equipment and the air corps's operational personnel, the Americans would have the opportunity to pick his brain.

Tuck was assigned to fly in exercises with the 1st Pursuit Group based out of Spartanburg, South Carolina. The unit operated the Republic P-43 Lancer, an operationally short-lived predecessor to the P-47. He summarized his impressions of his American counterparts:

Their flying was of a very high standard—precise, neat and quite flashy at times. But right at the start I found one serious omission in their work: very few of them had been up above fifteen thousand feet, even though the P.43 could operate at twenty-five thousand and even higher. They just didn't appreciate how important an advantage height was in modern air-fighting. It shook them when I told them about dogfights at over thirty thousand![1]

Tuck also noted shortcomings in the air corps' oxygen equipment, formations that were too tight and unsuited for combat, a lack of radio discipline, and a dearth of experience in nighttime operations. Nevertheless, he did appreciate the enthusiasm of his American friends as well as their ability to receive and offer criticism. He also had the opportunity to test U.S. aircraft and came away with positive impressions of both the early P-51 and P-47. The air corps took advantage of assessments like Tuck's to develop not only its equipment, but also its training.

As the situations in Europe and Asia deteriorated and the prospect of war became more likely, Roosevelt and the military services fretted not only about the size of the American air forces in terms of aircraft numbers, but also about the limited number of trained pilots. Their anxiety was well founded. In 1938, the U.S. Army Air Corps had fewer than 4,000 pilots, more than half of whom belonged to the reserves or National Guard.

Accordingly, on December 27, 1938, the month after Roosevelt's momentous meeting on aircraft production, the Civilian Pilot Training Program (CPTP) was announced as part of the Civil Aeronautics Act of 1938. It included provisions for training up to 20,000 pilots a year with instruction initially located on or near eleven colleges and universities. Each trainee, drawn from local universities, was given extensive ground schooling and up to sixty hours of flight instruction.

As 1939 turned into 1940 and the situation abroad deteriorated, the CPTP expanded rapidly. Its inclusive nature was remarkable for the time and included Negro schools that graduated nearly 2,000 pilots. Initially, it also included women, and approximately 10 percent of the program's enrollees were female. However, as it was recognized that females would not serve as combat pilots and because combat pilots were so desperately needed, there was little sense in expending scarce resources to train them. Subsequently, women were excluded from the program, but not before more than 2,000 had been graduated.

The program was a success. Following the attack on Pearl Harbor, the United States had a much greater pool of trained military pilot candidates from which to draw than it otherwise would have. Although the CPTP graduates were still required to complete the military training programs, their pass rate was measurably better than that of the raw recruits.

During 1942, the CPTP program morphed into a quasimilitary one, and its name was changed to the War Training Service (WTS). The students taking part were compelled to commit to military service following their graduation. In the end, the CPTP and WTS were administered by more than 1,100 educational institutions and nearly 1,500 flight training schools that provided instruction to more than 400,000 people. The program was phased out during 1944 when the military's own training programs were at their peak and it became apparent that the WTS was no longer required to win the war.

At the same time as the CPTP was put into high gear, the U.S. Army Air Corps dramatically increased its own training capacity. During 1939, 800 new pilots graduated, which was a significant increase over previous years. However, production improved tenfold the following year, when 8,000 pilots were trained. The next year saw even more gains as 27,000 new pilots were produced. Still, the USAAF realized—even before the United States entered the war—that many more pilots would be needed.

Such a marked expansion in pilot production was not easily achieved. Chief among the difficulties was recruiting enough qualified candidates. In the years before the war, the requirements for pilot training were kept especially stringent simply in order to cull the enormous number of applicants. Young men were required to have a minimum of two years of college credit and exceptional physical qualifications. However, upon the country's entry into the war, the Army realized that it would need to ease its requirements.

Among the least popular of those prerequisites was that which called for college credit. It had nationwide attention, and an editorial in the New York *Daily News* voiced opposition: "The possibility that we may pick up some pilots who don't know a cosine from a dodecahedron, or the proper way for a gentleman and an officer to navigate a teacup, is of very minor importance. We bet there are a lot of taxicab drivers who could be turned into swell combat pilots." Spaatz also felt that the college-credit requirement was excessive as it put too much emphasis on learning that was paid for, rather than on innate intelligence and ability.

On December 10, 1941, just three days after Pearl Harbor, the college requirement for flight training was abolished. Applicants had to produce only a high-school diploma, and from that point, they were screened with aptitude tests. Additionally, the minimum age was lowered from twenty to eighteen, but the maximum age of twenty-six was maintained. Married applicants, who up to that point had been prohibited, were accepted.

The pool of eligible recruits increased immediately by more than two million. But although there were literally millions of young men eager to prove their mettle as pilots, simply sorting through them, much less training them, was an enormous task. Accordingly, the USAAF created a nationwide network of several hundred Aviation Cadet Examining Boards to screen the applicants. There, young hopefuls who met the most basic requirements were given the Aviation Cadet Qualifying Examination. Those who successfully completed that test were subsequently required to pass rigorous physical examinations.

The thoroughness of the flight physicals had been relaxed somewhat in recognition of wartime exigencies, but the examinations were still quite comprehensive. John Walker eventually flew P-38s out of North Africa and Italy, but he almost did not make it. He had been denied entry into the Navy's flight-training program because of a bad ankle. On advice from the Navy's examining officer, he subsequently tried to hide it from the Army when he applied for pilot training with that service: "There we were, in a line, all naked except for me—I had my socks on." The Army took no notice of his ankle but turned him away because he had blocked sinuses. It was only after he had a corrective operation that he was accepted for training.

For virtually the entire war, very few who passed the written and physical examinations were sent immediately to flight school. The capacity to push everyone through as they became available just never existed. At the end of 1942, the USAAF's pilot training machine could take 10,000 new aviation cadets each month, but there was a pool of well more than 50,000 qualified candidates. That pool was never drained, and subsequently, throughout the entire war, virtually every qualified candidate was told to "Go home and wait."

During part of the war, the Army experimented with college training detachments and sent some of the "poolees" to one of several colleges where they received basic military instruction, some classroom training, and about ten hours of flight instruction. But the experience of Ken Barmore, who eventually became a B-24 copilot and was shot down over Ploesti in 1944, was more typical. He had passed the aviation cadet examination board's aptitude and physical tests in June 1942. It was more than half a year before he was finally called for training:

> I left Verona [New Jersey] very early in the morning of February 8, 1943 with orders to report to the armory in Newark. I said goodbye to the folks and took the trolley to Newark—it was very cold and dark. At the armory there was a very large group of us intended for the Army, but none of us knew where we were going. Ultimately we were told that we were going to the classification center at Nashville, Tennessee, to determine if we would be selected for training as navigators, bombardiers or pilots. When we arrived and walked onto the installation—our home for the next month—we could hear the cadets that were already there yelling "you'll be sorry!" But we were already in the Army and it was too late to turn back.[2]

Indeed, when the call came, young pilot hopefuls like Barmore were directed to one of three (Nashville, Tennessee; San Antonio, Texas; and Santa Ana, California) Army Air Forces Classification Centers, where they were once again subjected to a wide-ranging battery of physical, psychological, and aptitude tests. They also received basic military training and drill as well as their first uniforms—the same kit that was issued to a private. If they were not washed out, the candidates were down-selected for pilot, bombardier, or navigator training.

Although the U.S. Army Air Corps had been selecting pilot candidates for some time, it had never before screened so many. Consequently, it explored all methods to get the job done. Barmore recollected one of the more unusual examinations:

> One test had you holding a needle-like object straight out in front of you. Each end had a joint you could move in any direc-

tion. Lifting the front end up caused the far end to go down, etc. The far end had a needle-like metal end and that was to be kept inside a small hole but without touching the sides of the hole. Each time it touched the side a buzzer went off. You also had to keep count of each time the buzzer went off while behind you there was a sergeant yelling and trying to distract you.

After successfully passing through the rigors of the classification center, the young men were designated aviation cadets and sent to pre-flight training, where they were given extra privileges and better pay, along with more officer-like uniforms. Preflight was typically an eight-week course with emphasis on military indoctrination, physical conditioning, and aviation-related academic studies, including meteorology, physics, Morse code, aerodynamics, and engineering.

Because the training effort was so large, virtually everyone, including instructors, was new to the military, and the instruction was sometimes spotty or thin. Accordingly, students who had progressed to a certain point in their training were used to oversee those in the classes that followed. This had a dual purpose of providing additional oversight of the newer trainees while at the same time giving the more senior students some experience with military leadership. Individuals who were caught committing small infractions were given "gigs" or demerits that they were compelled to work off, oftentimes by marching.

However, the system was sometimes little more than sanctioned hazing and predictably had drawbacks that occasionally resulted in silly but sometimes serious abuses. Barmore described one such episode when he was suspected of breaking the honor code:

There was an upperclassman that didn't like me for some reason because he was always on me at every formation. One day he asked me if I had shaved and I told him that I had and he replied that I was lying because it didn't look like I had. I had to report to one of the officers and have a miniature trial. It turned out okay because several cadets near my bunk said that they had seen me shave. If I had been found guilty, I could have been washed out.

Aviation cadets who successfully completed preflight training were introduced to flying during the primary flight training phase at one of more than sixty bases. Because this beginning phase of training was so elementary and especially because there was a limited number of military instructors, the students were taught by civilians who were supervised by a handful of military officers. The period of instruction usually lasted eight weeks. The typical aircraft used were the Stearman PT-13, PT-15, or PT-17 Kaydet; the Fairchild PT-19 Cornell; and the Ryan PT-22 Recruit. These aircraft were chosen because of their docile, forgiving natures, their ability to be mass-produced, and their low costs to purchase and operate. Aside from flying, academic, physical, and military training continued, but flight-related activities dominated the program.

Again, the USAAF's training effort was so enormous that every instructor in every discipline could not be the very best. This was the case with Barmore's primary flight instructor. Barmore was one of five cadets assigned to him and only one of two that actually completed primary training. Still, it was a near thing:

> The check pilot asked me to do a chandelle, which is an aerobatic maneuver. I had no idea what it was. My instructor had never had us do that. This check pilot also wrote me up and said that I was afraid of the plane and flew bent over under the glare shield. I told him that since my instructor was from the South I'd had a difficult time understanding him through the Gosport tube and that crouching down out of the wind was the only way I could understand him.

Students who experienced difficulty were not coddled or given much extra instruction. The phrase that was repeated often in training circles was "We're getting them ready for this war, not the next." There is no doubt that many cadets with extraordinary potential were washed out when an aberration in their own performance or some shortcoming or misunderstanding in instruction got them into trouble.

Students who completed primary flight training accrued approximately seventy hours of flight time, depending on the aircraft flown, the location of the training, and the phase of the war. Primary flight training was followed by basic flight training, usually in the Vultee BT-13 or BT-15 Valiant, at one of more than thirty bases. The similar North American BT-14 Yale was also used, but in much fewer numbers. Both trainers were low-wing monoplanes with fixed landing gear, an enclosed cockpit, and a radial engine that gave the aircraft much more performance than the trainers the students had flown during the primary phase.

Military pilots provided training during basic. Many of them were young lieutenants who had completed flight training themselves only months earlier. Their talent and aptitude for flight were such that they were immediately plowed back into the training organization as instructors. The need for military instructor pilots was so great that there really was no other good option. Many of these instructors were bitter at having the opportunity for combat denied or delayed. On the other hand, the experience they gained as instructors made them much better pilots when they actually did reach the operational theaters.

Barmore's instructor, Lt. Forrest Chilton, was one of these. He remembered Chilton with fondness and respect:

> I felt that this instructor would jump all over me and force me to learn, and I believed that was exactly what I needed, especially when compared to my primary instructor who didn't seem to care that much; he loved to get the plane upside down and glide down. Lieutenant Chilton was the opposite and was all business. . . . I really liked him; he always looked like he loved every minute that he was in the air. He sure jumped on us for dumb errors, but then he told us when we did something good, too.

The basic phase of flight training, like the earlier phases, included intensive academics and physical instruction, but the emphasis was on flying. Introduced for the first time were instrument flying techniques that would prove to be life-saving to so many pilots in the foul weather that dominated northern Europe. Formation and night flying were also introduced, and it was during this phase that the determination was made about whether the individual cadet would proceed on a multi-engine course of training for ultimate assignment as a bomber or transport pilot or a single-engine syllabus for fighters.

A number of factors influenced a cadet's selection for multi-engine or single-engine training. The needs of the service were always given the greatest consideration. Still, this was a bit of a crapshoot since it was difficult for the planners to project operational needs in a war whose future could only be guessed at. Physical size and strength was also a factor. Bombers and transport aircraft required muscle to fly well; the B-24 was especially notorious for being heavy on the controls. Moreover, the larger aircraft could accommodate bigger men, and consequently, taller cadets were more likely to be selected for multi-engine training. Psychological evaluations also played a role in the selection process, whereas the final—and least important—consideration was the desire of the student. It was generally true that the number of fighter pilots required was less than the number of cadets who wanted to be fighter pilots. Accordingly, it was not uncommon for students to be assigned to fly something other than what they had hoped for.

The syllabi in the basic phase diverged depending on what type of aircraft a student was selected to fly. Those tagged for fighters flew more formation and aerobatics while those designated to fly the big aircraft had more instruction in cross-country and instrument flying. In total, depending on a number of factors, the average student logged about seventy hours of flight time in approximately nine weeks during the basic phase.

The advanced phase followed basic flight training. Multi-engine students typically flew the Beechcraft AT-10 Wichita or the Cessna AT-17 Bobcat, while the single-engine cadets flew the North American AT-6 Texan. The training was a logical extension of what the students had previously learned with emphasis on multi-engine operations, navigation and instrument flying for the multi-engine flyers, while the single-engine cadets practiced more complex formation flying, aerobatics, and basic gunnery. Like the primary and advanced phases, the cadets logged about seventy flight hours during advanced.

Toward the end of this training, the students were queried about which model of aircraft they wanted to fly. Barmore recalled the process:

We had to sign up for the plane we would like to fly once we got our wings. I put down A-20 first, B-26 second, and P-38 for third. For fields, I picked Orlando, Florida (an A-20 base), then

Macdill, Florida (a B-26 base), and last, P-38, but they didn't have any locations listed for P-38, so I just said East Coast. They made you feel like you were getting a choice, but from past experience we knew, we didn't have any chance of getting what we wanted.

Barmore was correct; he was assigned to fly B-24s.

Upon completing the advanced phase, the cadets were graduated from training and commissioned as second lieutenants, while a few were given the lesser rank of flying officer. From that point, they received orders to train in operational aircraft, in which they typically received a hundred or more additional flight hours, usually in the model they would take into combat.

Although the overall training program was not perfectly tailored to take advantage of the strengths of every individual, it was effective in turning out huge numbers of trained aviators in a minimum period of time. Again, Ken Barmore serves as an example. He left his home in Verona, New Jersey, on February 8, 1943, virtually ignorant of all things aviation and military. He graduated from advanced flight training as a winged aviator and second lieutenant on November 3, 1943, less than nine months later. He subsequently was trained as a copilot on the B-24—a large and complex aircraft—and was en route to Italy with a brand new bomber only four months after having received his wings. And each month the USAAF produced thousands of pilots just like him. In total, the army trained 193,000 pilots from 1939 to 1945

One very telling statistic of the army's commitment to aviation training is the percentage of hours that were flown to support it. From January 1943 until victory was achieved over Japan, the USAAF flew a total of 107,886,000 hours. This number encompassed all the hours flown by all types in all theaters in all operations, including combat. Of that total, 49,060,000 hours—more than 45 percent—were flown by training aircraft. Had the records reached back to the U.S. entry into the war, that percentage would have increased since there was relatively little operational flying taking place at home or abroad during that period.

One coarse metric for measuring whether the USAAF achieved the desired effects against Germany was the number of combat sorties it flew. Obviously, it required serviced and ready aircraft to generate those sorties, and no nation produced as many aircraft and combat-ready crews as the United States. The numbers bear this out, and the meteoric increase in the USAAF's ability to send aircraft against Germany was nothing less than astonishing. During January 1943, the Americans generated 5,097 sorties over Europe, North Africa, and the Mediterranean. Just more than two years later, that number increased more than twentyfold. During April 1945, the USAAF flew 120,897 combat sorties in Europe, most of them over Germany. Although good records for the Luftwaffe do not exist, its sortie count was only a tiny fraction of the crushing American effort.[3]

The massive production of aircrews came at some cost in efficiency. The USAAF was compelled to find a middle ground of what it could accept in terms of the quality of its flyers versus the quantity of the flyers it needed. In other words, it could have chosen to field exquisitely trained and capable aircrews, but at the cost of numbers. On the other hand, it could have stamped out more flyers than it actually did, but at a price in quality.

In the end, the choice it made was obviously good enough—the Allies won the war. But the loss rate in accidents was extraordinary. During the war, the USAAF lost 65,164 aircraft to all causes. Of that total, an astounding number, 21,583, were lost within the United States. In other words, 33 percent of the aircraft destroyed during the war were lost at home to causes that had nothing to do with enemy action.

Only the imagination limited the different ways that aircraft were destroyed while Stateside. Jack Walker was part of the first cadet class that was groomed specifically for the P-38. After earning his wings in March 1942, he was assigned to the 55th Fighter Group at McChord Field near Tacoma, Washington. Lack of experience with the new airframe and a high accident rate fed the apprehensions of many of the new P-38 pilots. "We had two test pilots from Lockheed with us and they said that the P-38 on a single engine during takeoff was deadly," Walker recalled. "They had a lot of guys scared, me included."

The aircraft was new to the service, and Walker and his peers were new to flying altogether. A lack of experience and a poor understanding of the handling characteristics of the aircraft resulted in frequent takeoff and landing accidents that often were fatal. In that area of the Northwest, the runways were typically bounded by trees, which exacerbated even more the danger of dealing with an engine-sick P-38 on takeoff or landing.

One accident Walker recalled occurred during this time. Unlike most mishaps in the P-38, this one was unrelated to the engine or the handling qualities of the twin-boomed fighter. He was number three in a flight of four aircraft engaged in an aerial tail-chase off of the Washington coast. Walker watched in horror as the lead aircraft started a turn around a towering cumulus cloud and plowed head-on into a navy PBY Catalina. The two aircraft disintegrated in a huge explosion that claimed the lives of the PBY crew and the P-38 pilot. Air traffic control was essentially nonexistent at that time, and as America's skies began to fill with unprecedented legions of warplanes, accidents of this sort became more commonplace.

Of the 43,581 American aircraft destroyed overseas, 22,948—more than half—were lost because of pilot error or mechanical failure, rather than to enemy fire. Therefore, 68 percent of the aircraft destroyed in USAAF service during the war were wrecked at the hands of its own crews and maintenance men.[4] That is a direct indictment of the quality of their training.

The training received by USAAF pilots was still markedly better than what was given to their Luftwaffe counterparts during the period when the USAAF was vigorously building its strength in Europe. Whereas newly minted American pilots arrived in theater with well more than 300 flying hours, their German opposites in the latter half of 1943 and early 1944 were put into the field with only about 170 hours. By the end of 1944, young German fighter pilots were sent to their operational units with only about 135 hours of total flying time. The difference is greater when it is understood that the Americans averaged 165 hours in the type of aircraft they actually took into combat, whereas the Germans averaged only about 30.[5]

The paucity of training afforded the Luftwaffe trainees was a harsh contrast to the richness in resources and leadership afforded their U.S. counterparts. Often, American pilots did not know enough to appreciate it. The statement of six-victory ace Frank K. Everest concerning the training that he and his comrades received is illustrative: "Most [USAAF pilots] went into combat with very little flying time—upon checking my own logbook, I found I had 225 hours in the P-40 when on my first combat mission and shot down my first two aircraft with 246 hours."[6] Although he did not realize it, Everest's flight time in his combat aircraft alone was double the total flight time of the average Luftwaffe pilot thrust into combat during 1944.

Put at the controls of complex and advanced fighters with such little experience, the odds that newly trained German pilots would suffer mishaps were considerable. The typically poor flying weather characteristic of northern Europe made the chances greater still. Subsequently, the likelihood that the neophyte Luftwaffe flyers would survive the much more dangerous and demanding milieu of aerial combat against vastly more numerous and better trained rivals was not good.

Indeed, it is worth considering the mindsets of these inexperienced German pilots. They were among their nation's finest young men and were given some of the best flying machinery in the world, yet they were not provided the skills to operate it. Still, their orders were not only to operate it, but to defeat the increasingly numerous American and British fighters that challenged them not only in the sky, but also, particularly later in the war, as they took off and landed at their own airfields.

These young flyers dealt not only with the expectations of their people, the dogma and orders of their leaders, and the complex nuances of high performance aircraft they were not qualified to fly, but also with their own demons and fears. A fiery death either at the hands of the Allies or from their own lack of experience was not only a distinct possibility, but rather a real probability. Indeed, orders, expectations, propaganda, and pride notwithstanding, young German men were not predisposed to throw their lives away, and they became increasingly disillusioned at their odds of living through the war, much less making a difference in it. This dissatisfaction manifested itself as early as 1944. One surviving German pilot declared:

> My requests in III/JG 26 that I be taught the specific skills I needed fell on deaf ears. The answer to all my questions was the same—"Stick close to your Number 1, your Rottenfuehrer, for if you lose him you are as good as dead!" . . . This showed an arrogance that was every disillusioning. . . . I felt rotten. In such a fought-out, war-weary shop, how could I gain the instinctive skills so necessary for my own survival?[7]

This pilot's take on the real situation was accurate. German fighter losses for 1943 were marginally greater than USAAF fighter losses, but their loss rate for the whole of 1944 was horrific. The monthly aircraft loss percentage of the operational Luftwaffe single-engine fighter units posted to northern Europe and the Mediterranean was 82 percent.[8] It almost defies belief that of every 100 operational aircraft carried on the average unit's roster at the start of any given month, all but 18 of them would have been destroyed by the end of that month. When it is considered that it took about two to three "shoot downs" to kill a German pilot, it is easy to understand that it was the rare pilot who survived more than a few months of air combat in the West.

This fact was borne out to *Generalfeldmarschall* Hugo Von Sperrle during July 1944 when he surveyed the fighter units of Luftflotte 3. In general, he found that only the group and squadron commanders had greater than six months of combat experience. There was only a small smattering of individuals with three months or more experience in the field. In fact, the majority of the fighter pilots had less than thirty days of operational time.[9] No air force in the world could have hoped to maintain any sort of effectiveness with so high a turnover rate. The German air force was no exception, and its very organization began to disintegrate from this point. In fact, if a Luftwaffe pilot was not fortunate or skilled enough to survive the war unscathed, his next best chance at living through the fighting was to be wounded only just badly enough to be removed from service.

The average Luftwaffe pilot early in the war was a superbly trained air combatant. This was proven during the various *blitzkrieg* campaigns across Europe and in the Battle of Britain, where he fought at a disadvantage. It was true even in North Africa and the Mediterranean through most of 1943. Even when the Americans started operating from England over northern Europe in greater numbers during late 1943, they accorded him great respect. Still, the blooded Luftwaffe veterans who had started the war were killed, and their places were taken by less skilled flyers. And those replacements were subsequently also killed and replaced by even less capable airmen. This death spiral continued until the German air force was no more.

The lack of skill of the German flyers late in the war was apparent to the American pilots who shot them down, sometimes quite easily.

One example was the encounter of 1st Lt. James Fowle, a P-51 pilot with the 364th Fighter Group. He was about fifteen miles northwest of Trier on December 23, 1944, when his wingman "called in a gaggle of fifty-plus Me-109s at three o'clock to the bomber track. I broke right and closed on a 109 that still had on a belly tank. I gave him a short burst observing many strikes on his cockpit and wing roots."[10] The German aircraft went down in flames.

Fowle next turned his attention to a second Me-109 and put bullets into that fighter's cockpit and wing roots. "I closed on him so fast that I thought he had cut his throttle." Fowle likewise reduced his power and slid up to the enemy aircraft's left side. Its propeller had stopped and the plane was on fire. It spun earthward out of control and Fowle recalled, "I think the pilot was killed."

There were still plenty of targets, and Fowle took on a third Me-109: "I closed slightly and framed him with my K-14 [gunsight] and gave a long burst, observing strikes on his wings and cockpit. . . . He started down in a dive and bailed out, his canopy hitting my left wing." A fourth Me-109 presented itself: "I closed on him from dead astern, but before I could get my pip on him, he bailed out. I did not fire a shot at him."

Although Fowle's skill should not be discounted, the German flyers did not seem to fight so much as they presented themselves as targets. The pilot of Fowle's first kill had not even jettisoned his external fuel tank, a routine task prior to engaging in air combat (although Göring sometimes forbade it because of its cost). None of Fowle's victims did any maneuvering, and his final victim simply abandoned his aircraft before even being taken under fire. Those pilots were a far cry from the skilled veterans so often encountered during the early part of the war.

No nation's air arm produced as many high-scoring pilots as did the Luftwaffe. Through the war, more than 100 German pilots were officially credited with 100 or more aerial victories. The highest tally was logged by Erich Hartmann, who achieved 352 kills flying primarily against the Red Air Force. On the other hand, the highest-scoring American pilot in Europe, Francis Gabreski, achieved only 28 aerial victories.

In truth, the majority of the high-scoring Luftwaffe flyers achieved their successes against poorly trained Soviet pilots operating second-rate equipment, especially early in the war. Another considerable factor behind the extraordinary aerial victory credits of these individual Germans was the fact that their leadership failed to field an adequately staffed force capable of defeating the ever-increasing numbers of Allied aircraft. Because there was no adequate plan to train the required number of flyers, the Luftwaffe grew in size only very slowly. Not only were there not enough new pilots to sufficiently increase the force, but there were not enough to relieve those who needed respite from extended combat duty. Indeed, as the war wore on, there were not even enough fresh pilots to take the places of those who were wounded or killed.

In many cases, once a German pilot was put in the field, he stayed operational, with very brief respites, until he was killed. Flying nearly daily and sometimes multiple times per day, he simply had more opportunities to encounter Allied aircraft. A few Luftwaffe pilots flew more than 1,000 sorties, while it was rare for a USAAF pilot to log more than 100. As the war continued into its last year, Allied aircraft became so numerous—so ubiquitous—that encounters became increasingly frequent. In other words, there seldom was a lack of action for the average Luftwaffe pilot. Conversely, some American fliers never so much as saw a German aircraft.

Essentially, the Luftwaffe had so many pilots with so many aerial victories simply because those pilots had so many opportunities. But to be fair, those pilots became exceedingly skilled, which was necessary in order to survive frequent clashes with an enemy that grew ever more capable and overwhelmingly numerous as the war went on.

During the single month of March 1944, the United States produced 9,068 aircraft. It was more aircraft than the combined air forces of the United States, Great Britain, and Germany had possessed only five years earlier.

In fact, the United States eventually had more aircraft than it could use. Bob Popeney of the 416th Light Bombardment Group made the point when he described what was done with the unit's A-20s when new A-26s were received toward the end of 1944:

> We were ordered to fly our A-20s into Blackpool, on the west coast of Scotland. When I landed, they were waiting for me. A crew chief crawled up on my wing and we taxied about halfway down the runway. The runway at Blackpool was up on a sort of palisade, about three hundred feet above the water. Once we got settled on the runway the crew chief told me to get what I wanted out of the airplane and to get out. Then he lined the airplane up on the runway, put the RPM full forward, gave it about twenty inches of manifold pressure, and jumped off the wing. The plane just went down the runway, dribbled off the end, flipped over on its back and went into the drink. That's how we got rid of our A-20s. It broke my heart.

CHAPTER 13

Ground Attack
and Bomber Bailouts

Although they were encountered less and less frequently over Italy as 1944 drew on, the German fighter units there could still be deadly. This fact was underscored on March 13, 1944, when the 86th Fighter Bomber Group lost five A-36s, derivatives of the early P-51 Mustang, to German fighters. The 526th Fighter Bomber Squadron lost four of those aircraft. Its diary records that day's events:

> The mission our squadron flew today proved to be the most disastrous we have experienced. The four pilots who were flying cover were attacked by enemy fighters, outnumbered 5 to 1, and all four failed to return. Lts. Buchman, Mudrick and Warren were last seen north of Rome, and Lt. Forster, after returning to the field and being cleared twice for a crash landing, announced he was going to bail out in the sea. He was last heard of over the Bay of Naples, but a search failed to reveal his whereabouts, and it is believed he may be the victim of drowning.

The invasion of Italy that began in the late summer of 1943 provided the Allies with airbases in the boot heel region from which to attack Axis targets that were out of the range of the England-based Eighth Air Force. However, the wisdom of the slogging, oftentimes murderous ground campaigns up the Italian boot was questioned then as it has been ever since. During March 1944, the Allies were stalled in central Italy, and there was great debate about how to most effectively break through the German defenses that made up the Gustav Line.

It was agreed that the best means to dislodge the Germans was to smash and starve them through a concentrated air campaign against their lines of communication. Although this had been going on to a lesser degree during the previous months, this new effort was to be a more concerted one. The scheme agreed to was code-named STRANGLE and was announced on March 19, 1944. Specifically, it targeted railroads, especially marshaling yards and their concentrations of rolling stock. Later, it focused on bridges, aqueducts, and tunnels. Eaker, now the commander of the MAAF, believed in its effectiveness. In an April 7 letter to Arnold, he stated: "My personal belief is that our communications attack will make it possible for the [U.S.] Army to move forward when they next make an effort."[1]

Operations over most of Italy during that time were at a phase that USAAF leaders were trying to replicate over France in preparation for OVERLORD. Essentially, the Luftwaffe had been defeated, or pushed out, and Allied air commanders were able, for the most part, to support their ground counterparts whenever, however, and wherever they needed.

But only for the most part.

John Blair Watson starting flying A-36s with the 86th Fighter Bomber Group beginning in October 1943. By April 18, 1944, Watson had flown more than fifty missions and was flying more often as an element, or flight, leader and less often as a wingman. On that particular day, he was scheduled to fly as his squadron's (525th) airborne spare on a group mission to break railroad tracks along the Rome-Orte route. If an aircraft aborted the mission for whatever reason prior to crossing into enemy territory, Watson was to take its place.

This airborne spare was frequently needed. Watson recalled that some individual pilots dropped out of missions repeatedly while others never seemed to abort. He remembered: "I had a roommate about whom we began to worry because he turned back often."[2]

The 86th scheduled the mission of April 18 as a three-squadron effort, with each squadron providing eight aircraft, plus airborne spares. It was not necessarily typical for the group to fly as a whole. However, Watson remembered that "Our intelligence section informed us that German fighters had been appearing more and more frequently in skies which we had foolishly come to consider our own." As a result, the group leadership wanted to present strength in numbers.

The group formed and set a course up Italy's west coast soon after takeoff from its base at Pomigliano. It was not long before Watson's squadron commander dropped out of the flight. Leadership of the eight-plane formation now fell to Watson. As he added power to slide into the newly vacant squadron leader's position, the original wingman refused to ease back and give him room. "Things were getting a little uncomfortable until someone in the rear of the squadron . . . broke radio silence and said, 'Get the hell out of there, Brinley, Watson's supposed to be leading!'"

Watson's flight of eight was positioned low and to the right of the lead squadron at 12,000 feet. He saw that clouds were building ahead, potentially blocking the route into the primary target. Accordingly, he noted to himself that his squadron's secondary target at Viterbo, about ten miles inland, appeared to be clear. In the event that the group aborted the primary mission, he was determined to take his flight to Viterbo.

This determination was the product of earlier frustration. "I was conscious that my decision was . . . influenced by the fact that on several missions I had felt that we had not been aggressive enough, that we had aborted missions for flimsy reasons. If the leader wanted to abort, no pilot was likely to object, for another mission would have been accomplished as far as the record was concerned . . . I had vowed to myself that, if I were leading, we would attack any target which seemed at all reachable."

As it developed, the lead squadron started a sweeping lefthand turn out over the sea, where the aircraft could safely jettison their bombs before returning to base. It was aborting the mission. The second squadron followed suit. Watson did not follow, but rather swung his formation around in a righthand turn toward Viterbo, through which a road and railroad ran.

Approaching the town, Watson spread the formation and started the group down in a shallow dive to pick up speed. "Almost directly over the target, I pumped my stick back and forth to signal that I was about to open my dive brakes, and then did so." He rolled his aircraft nearly inverted and let the nose fall through the horizon and down toward the target. "I picked out the railroad yard in my gunsight."

Rather than following Watson, the rest of the formation scattered when his wingman, seemingly confused, arced away in a different direction. "Blind to what had happened," Watson remembered, "I dropped my bombs, firing my guns at the same time, hoping to scatter any German gunners who were lining us up in their sights." Watson passed through 2,000 feet before he wrestled his aircraft out of its dive and pointed it skyward. He closed the dive brakes and steepened his climb. "It was always like getting a kick in the pants when the dive brakes closed." He recalled. "The plane seemed to slide ahead as if the sky had been greased." Watson started a wide lefthand turn after arriving at the off-target rendezvous point. Beyond his shoulder, he could see black smoke swelling up from the rail yard at Viterbo. He and at least some of the rest of the squadron had struck two separate strings of box cars.

What he did not see was the rest of his flight. After a turn or two, he was joined by another A-36, but the remaining planes were nowhere to be seen. "There were some other aircraft in the sky," he remembered, "but they were much higher and too many to be the rest of my squadron." Watson noted that the other group started toward him, and he supposed that it might have been the other two squadrons; perhaps they had decided to hit the same target.

"Suddenly, tracer fire began to cut across the circle we were making," remembered Watson. The other group was obviously not friendly. He noted that the radio frequency was suddenly clobbered with the sound of Americans cursing and shouting. An instant later he caught sight of a group of P-40s in a melee with enemy fighters. At the same time, pairs of Me-109s flashed past, jockeying to get into position behind him and the other A-36.

Watson wrenched his aircraft through a series of brutal maneuvers, hoping that his new wingman would be able to hang on. Desperate to shake the far more numerous enemy fighters, he pulled hard over into a righthand turn and dove into a heavy line of clouds. A moment or two later, he was out the other side, where, almost surrealistically, there was nothing to be seen. "It could have been a fine spring morning anywhere," he recalled. In his new happy place, there was no one who wanted to kill him. In fact, there was no one at all.

Watson started south down the friendly side of the line of clouds and encountered nothing. He reversed course and continued back north until he came to an opening through which he could still see smoke rising from the rail yard at Viterbo. Anxious to rejoin his friends, Watson darted though the gap and started looking. What he found was the same large group of Me-109s milling around a couple thousand feet above him. And in the distance, the P-40s were still preoccupied with their own fight.

The enemy aircraft, numbering about sixteen, dove down on Watson in pairs. The first two Me-109s began firing at him from very long range. "I chopped my throttle and pulled the nose around as tightly as possible. I looked down my left wing and saw them sweeping by underneath me, standing out clearly against the cloud floor below."

It was about that time that Watson heard a radio call from the P-40 fight: "Look at that poor son of a bitch down there with ten of them on his tail!" It took an instant or two for him to realize that he was the poor son of a bitch.

The next pair of German fighters also failed to hit Watson and flashed by his right wing, close aboard. He hauled the nose of his aircraft up and left, then reversed direction to the right. He caught sight of one pair of Me-109s climbing for altitude, another diving on him, and another just about ready to drop down on him. At just that instant, another fighter overshot him to his right: "I could clearly see the pilot's face, pretty well hidden by goggles and helmet, looking at me."

An instant later, the German's wingman streaked in front of Watson's aircraft and climbed away. In the distance, Watson saw that the P-40 fight—apparently the longest in recorded history—was still ongoing. "More tracers whizzed by. I jinked left, then right. I kicked the stick forward, banged my head on the canopy, then grabbed the stick by both hands and hauled back, forcing me down on my seatpack so hard I could feel the solid articles within sinking into my buttocks." A violently moving target was difficult to hit, and Watson sought to move his aircraft as violently as possible.

That Watson had survived as long as he had against so many aircraft was improbable. Still, he kept his wits and anticipated the flight paths of his next two attackers. The first one climbed in front of him, and Watson started his own aircraft up waiting for the other German. Just as he expected, the enemy wingman arced in a climb just in front of his A-36. "I relaxed on the stick and began firing my guns just as he came into the line of fire." Watson's rounds found their mark. "My bullets started to strike his nose and drifted back along his fuselage as he came higher. Parts began to fly off his plane." Tracers from another Me-109 flashed past Watson's aircraft and kept him from confirming the destruction of the fighter he had just shot full of holes.

He gave his aircraft a bootful of rudder and spiraled away to the left. His maneuver did not work. A pair of sharp explosions rattled his aircraft. "The panes of the canopy were pockmarked with little spots," he remembered. Watson noted a hole in his left wing and wondered at the damage caused by an explosion that he had felt under his seat.

Still, after the exchange of fire, it seemed that the enemy pilots pressed their attacks less aggressively. Perhaps Watson's shredding of the one Me-109 had tempered their enthusiasm. Noting that the German fighters had become strung out, he raced toward the west, jinking slightly to spoil their aim as they continued increasingly desultory gunnery runs against his damaged aircraft. Finally, he found a deck of clouds and ducked below them to outdistance the Me-109s. At 2,000 feet, with his throttle jammed to the stop, he noted that his airspeed was 315 miles per hour.

At last, the Germans gave up the chase. Watson made it safely back to Pomigliano, where, unsure of how badly his aircraft had been hit, he executed a wide approach to landing and then carried a little extra air speed to ensure that he did not stall. Once he was safely parked, he crawled out of the cockpit to survey the damage to his A-36. Aside from the hole in his left wing and the pockmarked canopy, he was surprised by what he found on the lower left side of his fuselage. There, an enemy shell had perfectly sheared a line of rivets along a skin joint. The panel subsequently peeled back, leaving a two-by-four-foot section of the fuselage structure exposed to the elements. The margin between fortune and disaster in the air battles above Europe could be very fine indeed.

That margin had not been enough for the squadron mate that had joined Watson just before the fight had started. The process of elimination revealed that it had been Milan Vukovich. Vukovich was never seen again and presumably was shot down and killed sometime while Watson was fighting for his own life.

Whereas Watson's unit was part of the tactical Twelfth Air Force, the heavy bombers assigned to the Fifteenth Air Force were likewise hitting Italy's transportation nodes, but not without cost. The 450th Bomb Group (H) was one of the new Fifteenth Air Force units intended to execute Combined Bomber Offensive missions out of Italy. It was based at Manduria, and its target on April 25, 1944, was the railyard at Varese in northern Italy. "We had just gotten back from a raid on Ploesti the day before," remembered William H. Harvey, a B-24 bombardier who was nineteen at the time.[3] "We felt that if we could get through *that*, well, we could handle anything."

The heavily defended refinery complexes at Ploesti were among the most important targets in all of Europe, yet they did not have a monopoly on the Fifteenth Air Force's attention. Indeed, the Fifteenth was often called to hit targets that supported the campaigns in Italy. Varese, only five miles west of Switzerland's southern tip, serviced a network of rail lines that made it important in the context of Strangle. Still, it was not the sort of target the Luftwaffe typically defended with any kind of vigor at this point of the war, and planners likely gave little thought to the notion that German fighters would be much in evidence.

"So we took off on what we thought was going to be a milk run," Harvey recounted. Harvey's plane, *Maiden USA*, was one of twenty-nine aircraft that the 450th sent on that "milk run." The pilot, Harmond Dessler, flew in a slot position near the rear of the formation.

"Somewhere around Florence, we got into some clouds as we climbed, and the formation came apart somewhat," Harvey recalled. "We broke out at about 14,000 feet and started to regroup as we regained sight of each other. Above us, there was another deck of clouds at about 22,000 feet." It was then that, almost 200 miles short of Varese, the Germans struck with a force of Me-109s that was estimated at more than two dozen. "We got hit pretty badly," Harvey said. "The first pass, they came at us head on."

"Pretty badly" was an understatement. That first pass destroyed *Maiden USA*'s left inboard engine, hydraulics, and radio equipment. Worse, both the copilot, Wayne Sullivan, and the nose gunner, Anthony Raffoni, were shot dead. "Raffoni was killed," recalled Harvey, "but I remember that he shot down the guy that killed him." Aside from Raffoni and Sullivan, William Kelly, the navigator, was badly wounded.

Dessler put the damaged plane in a diving turn to the southeast in a bid to get low to the ground and, hopefully, away from the enemy fighters. It did not work. The Luftwaffe fighter pilots overwhelmed the straggling B-24. "They continued to come at us from all directions," Harvey recounted. "Still, everyone was doing their job and performing just as we had been trained. Raffoni was dead, but all the other gunners were putting up a good defense. The radioman, Clifford Davidson, was at his secondary position, manning the right waist gun. I went back to the radio compartment to connect an oxygen fitting for our flight engineer and top turret gunner, Francis Miliauskas." It was then that the tail gunner, Jim Mays, called out that more fighters from a different group were attacking from behind. "An instant later," Harvey remembered, "I got hit in the back and shoulder and the panel in front of me blew up in my face."

Already badly crippled, *Maiden USA* was increasingly targeted by the enemy fighters. A particularly vicious attack from the bomber's right side is likely what killed Miliauskas. "I didn't ever see him again," remembered Harvey. Through it all, Dessler did his best to keep what was essentially an unflyable aircraft airborne. "He had no hydraulics and his copilot [Sullivan] was dead," Harvey said. "He was doing a damned fine job."

By that time, it was doubtful that the plane would stay airborne, and there was certainly no way that it was going to make it to the target at Varese. Dessler salvoed the bombs in an effort to lighten the ship. But with the hydraulic system shot out, there was no way to close the bomb bay doors. The aerodynamic drag they created was almost as bad as the weight of the bombs had been.

"I got my chest pack [parachute] on and went back to manually crank the doors down," Harvey recalled. It was a difficult and dangerous task when conditions were good; the bombardier had to stand out in the bomb bay on a narrow catwalk open to the sky while wrestling with the handle of the cranking mechanism. Performing the same task while wounded, under fire, and aboard a plane that was falling out of the sky was a considerably greater challenge.

Ultimately, it did not matter. "We were only about 1,500 feet above the mountains and still coming down when we started to bail out," Harvey recounted. "By now, Vernon Coil was climbing out of the ball turret. At the same time, Clifford Davidson and Bruce Hanson, the left waist gunner, got Jim Mays out of the tail turret. Mays's skull had been creased by a 20-millimeter cannon shell; the shell didn't explode but Mays was in really bad shape anyway."

Hanson and Davidson rigged a length of cord from Mays's ripcord handle to the aircraft so that when they pushed him clear of the aircraft, his parachute opened automatically. Then Hanson followed Mays out the hatch through the floor of the fuselage, just behind the ball turret.

Harvey did not wait long to follow them. He leapt clear of the aircraft from where he was standing in the bomb bay. But as if his existing wounds were not bad enough, he added another injury when he struck one of the bomb bay's cross members with his face and broke his nose. "I didn't even realize it until I got on the ground." Dessler also abandoned the aircraft. "I'm not sure if the airplane blew up before it hit the ground or not," Harvey said. "If it did, that might explain why Davidson and Coil never jumped. My flight boots were blown off as soon as I left the airplane, and I only had a short time in the parachute before I landed on a ledge on the side of a steep hill. It was pretty tough to get out of my harness and up off that slope. I ended up tossing my Mae West and my heavy flying jacket—I missed that flying jacket later."

On the road in the valley below where he landed, Harvey spotted two German soldiers on motorcycles. He gathered himself together as best he could and quickly limped away. Although he did not know it at the time, Dessler and Hanson made it to the ground safely. Kelly, wounded as he was, died during the jump or soon after. Mays's wound was so bad that when he was recovered by the Germans, he was repatriated almost immediately. Harvey entrusted himself to the local Italians, who handed him over to the Germans. He spent the rest of the war in a prisoner of war camp.

Among the most effective changes that Doolittle made following his assumption of command at the Eighth was one that took the war right to the Luftwaffe's front doorstep. The bomber-relay system was arranged so that groups of fighters relieved other groups of fighters as they escorted the bomber formations to their targets. Subsequently, the fighters that were newly relieved often had fuel and ammunition with which to do mischief. Although they had very occasionally done some free-lancing before it was officially sanctioned, Doolittle gave them free rein to shoot up whatever warranted it, either in the air or on the ground.

The effects of Doolittle's orders were immediately apparent to the German fighter crews. Whereas previously, the American fighters had left them alone so long as they were not harassing the bombers, that was no longer the case. Following Doolittle's abolition of the earlier restrictions, the USAAF pilots were chasing the German pilots down, following them home, shooting them up as they took off and landed as well as on the ground; they were ruthlessly aggressive. Galland recalled that his fighter crews were forced to "skulk on our own bases."

It was a particularly bitter pill especially because Göring had issued orders that his fighter pilots were to refuse combat with the American fighters and instead concentrate wholly on bringing down the heavy bombers. Such a concept was wholly unrealistic as it was often necessary to attack through the American escorts to get through to the bombers. Moreover, it sapped the aggressive spirit and effectiveness out of the German pilots; they were forced avoid the escorts, creep around the bomber formations, find an opening, launch an ambush, and run.

Air-to-air combat demanded skill, finesse, courage, and some amount of luck. It was a deadly aerial dance that, to a point, could be forced or refused by its practitioners. On the other hand, strafing enemy airfields was all about guts and luck. Robert "Punchy" Powell of the 352nd Fighter Group had plenty of guts but nearly ran short of luck on April 18, 1944, the same day that William Harvey's B-24 was shot down on its way to Varese.

On that day, as the Eighth was busy pounding the Luftwaffe in preparation for the invasion, the group had been tasked with escorting

B-17s on a raid against the German airfield at Avord in central France. It was part of the plan to clear the Luftwaffe from the invasion area. After being relieved of their escort duties, the 352nd's squadrons continued over France, trolling for targets of opportunity. The small German airfield they spotted at Herbeville in northcentral France fit that description perfectly.

On that day, Powell was the two-ship element lead in Capt. Robert Sharp's flight of four. They dived down on the enemy airfield at more than 350 miles per hour before leveling off only fifty feet or so above the ground. Their arrival had not gone undetected, and they were met by an antiaircraft fusillade made up of guns of all sizes. Shells latticed the air just above the airfield and presented an almost impenetrable curtain.

The attack consisted of only one pass and lasted only a few seconds, but it was enough time for Powell to destroy a Ju-88 at the far end of the field. "It blew up just as I let off the trigger." He stopped firing with only enough time to barely clear the hangar that housed it.

The short-lived attack was also long enough for the defending Germans to exact a price from the blue-nosed P-51s. "My aircraft started an uncommanded roll to the left," Powell recalled. "At the same time it wanted to do a zoom climb which would have been disastrous around all that antiaircraft fire." Low to the ground, Powell's Mustang was a difficult target as the German gunners could not fire indiscriminately across the airfield for fear of hitting their own people or equipment. On the other hand, a sharply climbing fighter would present a target for virtually every gun.

"It was all I could do," Powell recalled, "to hold the nose of the aircraft down." Just behind him, his wingman, Jamie Laing, had been hit in the cooling system. His engine would not last much longer.

The right horizontal stabilizer on Powell's aircraft had been badly torn up by a 20-millimeter cannon round. "The hole was as big as a washtub," he remembered. "It pushed up a chunk of metal that acted like a control surface and that was what was causing me so many problems." Powell made ready to bail out of his difficult-to-handle aircraft. "I took off my oxygen mask and started to unstrap, but as the aircraft slowed it became more controllable, so I decided to stick with it."

Powell set a course for home and was soon joined by Sharp and his wingman, Bill Furr. Laing had bailed out just moments earlier after his engine had given up. He had only gotten about fifteen miles from the airfield. There is little doubt that all of them questioned the worth of their attack.

"We got back to Bodney okay," recounted Powell. "As I got close, Colonel Joe Mason, the group commander, called me over the radio and asked if I intended to stay with the airplane or to bail out. I told him that I thought I'd tried to bring it in." Mason directed him to wait until the rest of the group landed; he did not want Powell to crash on the airfield and disrupt the recovery. "That was a real confidence builder," remarked Powell.

"As everyone started getting down on the ground, I did a controllability check at about 5,000 feet," said Powell. "I wanted to make sure that I had enough altitude to either recover or bail out if the plane went out of control." After lowering his landing gear and flaps, he noted that the aircraft handled well enough. He subsequently made his approach to Bodney, carrying a bit more airspeed than usual, and made an otherwise uneventful landing.

While the Twelfth and Fifteenth Air Forces were pounding the Germans in Italy and while the Ninth was beating up German forces in preparation for OVERLORD, the Eighth's bombers continued their strategic strikes almost right up to the time of the Normandy invasion. "We had several missions under our belt by the spring of 1944," remembered Foster Heath, a B-17 tail gunner with the 305th Bomb Group (H), based out of the airfield at Chelveston, in central England.[4] "In our experience, we had seen several aircraft catch fire while under attack either by flak or fighters. What often happened was that the crews who waited too long to bail out never had a chance. Their aircraft would go out of control and they'd get trapped inside and go down with the ship."

Heath's crew decided not to run that risk. Headed by their pilot, Edward Kass, the men met to discuss what their actions would be if their aircraft caught fire. "We decided that if we caught fire, and couldn't put it out right away, that we would jump immediately," Heath said. "We weren't going to die in a bomber that couldn't be saved."

This decision had been made before the crew flew its fifteenth mission against an aircraft component factory at Cottbus in eastern Germany. The date was May 29, 1944, and Heath remembered that the morning was wet and misty. The sad weather matched their bomber assignment: "We were given a ratty old aircraft," he recounted. "It had been belly-landed just a few days earlier and was patched up and given to us for that day's mission. It was a mess."

The mission was scheduled to be a very long one as the straight-line distance from Chelveston to Cottbus and back was nearly 1,300 miles. At the B-17's cruising speed of 150 miles per hour, this distance translated into a flying time of more than eight hours. Of course, the bombers rarely flew direct routes, so the distance would be greater. Additionally, it took time, often more than an hour, to get the group airborne, formed, and started on its route. Accordingly, the mission duration would span eleven hours or more. This pushed the upper limits of both the B-17's range and the endurance of its crews.

It was just before sunup when Kass got the tired ship off the ground. "We were leading our squadron, the 366th, within the group formation," Heath recalled. The ingress to the target was largely uneventful until the group of nearly fifty B-17s approached Cottbus. Heath recounted that portion of the mission: "We had been briefed that the flak would be bad, and it was. We had also been briefed that the fighters would be bad, and they were. Still, prior to the target we hadn't been hit and we started down in a very slight dive from 26,000 feet to get a little bit of extra airspeed; we got our bombs out okay."

Once their bombs were away, the B-17s made a lefthand turn to the north. The route took them in between Berlin and Frankfurt, then over the Baltic Sea. "The plan was for us to get down to about 14,000 feet once we got over the Baltic," said Heath. "That way we could relax a little bit and get off of the oxygen before climbing again over Denmark where they had a lot of flak batteries." As it developed, there was no relaxing. Heath recalled: "I spotted an FW-190 climbing very steeply. He leveled off at our altitude, behind us and slightly to one side. It was odd, because he didn't shoot at us."

From where he sat in the tail of the aircraft, Heath was the most vulnerable of the crew. He did not wait for the enemy fighter to open hostilities, but rather initiated the engagement with fire from his two .50-caliber machine guns. His shots found their mark, and the FW-190 fell earthward, apparently out of control. "I shot him down," he said, "and the waist gunner confirmed it."

Aside from some random and uncoordinated flak bursts, the group remained unmolested as it crossed the coastline and headed out over the Baltic before turning for Denmark. "It was then," Heath recalled, "that our navigator, Robert Kiernan, came up on the intercom and shouted at Kass that there were bright blue flames shooting into his compartment. We weren't taking any flak, and there were no fighters, so it was probably damage from something that had happened earlier. Kass asked him if he could put the flames out and then Kiernan said, 'Whoa, here they come again!'"

Kass wasted no time. Just as they had discussed earlier, he was not going to let the crew get caught in a burning deathtrap. "Kass rang the bailout alarm," Heath recalled, "and everyone started to jump." Heath did the same. "There was a little hatch right in front of the tail gunner's position," he said. "I got out of my compartment and put on my chute, then grabbed my shoes." The heated flying suit that he was wearing had integral flying boots. They were no good for walking in the event that a crewman parachuted into a situation where he stood a chance of evading or even if he was captured and made a prisoner of war. For that reason, Heath held tightly to his shoes.

"I opened the hatch and tried to push myself through, head first," Heath said. "But I got caught up on something and couldn't get out." He pulled himself back out of the opening and into the fuselage for a moment to catch his breath and reconsider his situation. "I tried again, but got caught up once more." As he hung, suspended in the bomber's slipstream, he saw the blossomed parachutes of several of his crewmates.

"Finally," he continued, "I just frog-kicked like crazy and got myself free." Heath had not realized it, but it was his parachute's ripcord handle that had been catching up in the hatch. Consequently, once he was through the opening, his parachute deployed immediately. "I went from 150 miles per hour to a dead stop in about two seconds," he recalled. "I had bruises in my groin for two months after that. But I still had my shoes!"

Heath recalled the silent hush as the crewless bomber motored off to the west. "I had never experienced silence like that." The only noises—

and they were very slight—came from the air that slipped through his parachute shrouds and from the rustle of his clothing and gear when he moved. "It was quiet," he said, "but it was also very, very lonely."

Nevertheless, he forgot his loneliness a moment or so later when his plane, now without a crew, circled lazily back toward him. "I thought that plane was going to kill me yet," Heath remembered. He watched helplessly as the B-17 settled on a course that appeared certain to inter-sect with his descent. However, after Heath gave his parachute's risers a few tugs it became apparent that the bomber would miss him. It nosed down, passed below him, dipped a wing into a lazy spiral, and fell toward the sea.

As he floated down from 14,000 feet, Heath could still see several parachutes far below him. "I tried to steer my chute. I pulled on it one way, then another, but it didn't really matter. I couldn't tell that I was making any difference in where it was taking me. Through it all though, I was pretty proud that I had managed to hang on to my shoes. As I got close to the water, I got ready to get rid of my chute, and I also inflated one half of my Mae West." Water landings were particularly dangerous since the parachute could drop on top of its wearer and entangle him in the long shroud lines connected to the canopy. Then, as the whole sod-den mess sank, it could drag the crewman down with it. "I got lucky," Heath said. "There was a slight breeze and my chute fell off to one side. I was able to get out of my harness without too much trouble."

But he was shocked at the frigidness of the water. "I had no idea it was going to be so cold! It was literally bone-numbing and it caused me to finally drop my shoes. The last I saw of them, they were floating too far away for me to get them."

Quite by luck, Heath had managed to fall fairly close to the crew's two waist gunners. "I could hear them, but I couldn't see them—the water was too choppy. One was from South Carolina and the other was from Tennessee. I'd hear one of them shout in a classic southern drawl, 'I'm freezing my ass off!' Then, the other would answer in an accented twang, 'I'm freezing my balls off!' It was almost funny except that we were going to die. I shouted back and forth with them for a little bit, but stopped after a short time because it was sapping my energy."

Heath was a good swimmer: "I started kicking for the shoreline. I could see it in the distance, and there was also a ship in between me and the coast. I found that if I kicked hard enough my legs would get up close to the surface where the water was considerably warmer. I kept my arms close to my chest, otherwise really cold water would rush into my suit and down my body."

Nevertheless, despite his efforts, Heath failed to close the distance to the shore. "I think there was a current pulling me out," he said. "And then the ship turned away in the wrong direction, and I almost gave up hope. From that point, I just concentrated on staying afloat and warm as best I could."

Still, after a time, the cold water became too much to bear. "I decided that there was no way I was going to make it," Heath recollected. "I figured that I ought to just end the misery myself. I stuck my head below the surface trying to drown myself. Three times I tried it, but my face just kept bobbing up out of the water."

Ultimately, the icy water rendered him unconscious. Debilitated by the near-freezing temperature, his body started to shut down. "And then," he recollected, "something bumped me on the shoulder and woke me up." Heath forced his mind out of its cold-induced stupor. "I looked up and blinked, and blinked again and focused. There were two German sailors rowing a dinghy right next to me. I threw an arm up and hooked it over the edge, but I couldn't lift myself out of the water." Balancing against the choppy sea, the two Germans grunted and gasped and puffed until they were able to drag the heavy, water-soaked mess that was Heath out of the sea.

"They were from the ship I had earlier seen in the distance," Heath said. "When they rowed me back to the ship, I still wasn't strong enough to get up the stairs of the gangway they extended down to us. One of them had to get behind me and push, while the other pulled; I was absolutely exhausted!"

Heath was hypothermic—and a prisoner—but he was alive. He was taken, shivering, below decks. "I couldn't even take my own gear off; my hands wouldn't work. They helped me out of my flying suit. They even hung it up—I still remember that." He was given two scratchy gray wool blankets, and after an hour or so, he started to warm to a normal temperature. "Then I heard voices," he recalled, "and realized that I recognized one of them."

That voice was Kiernan's, the navigator who had discovered the fire in the aircraft. He and Heath exchanged stories: "I learned from him that he and the copilot, Gioffe, had jumped out of the aircraft together. They fell toward the water almost side-by-side and as they got close, Kiernan pulled his ripcord and his parachute opened. Kiernan didn't know if Gioffe froze, or if his parachute didn't open, or what, but he went straight into the water and was killed."

The captain of the ship came down to speak with the men. "He spoke English and talked with us for a few minutes," Heath said. "Then he told us to come up on the deck; they had found two bodies. We went up, and there were our radio operator and one of our waist gunners. They were both dead. They were blue from the cold." Heath learned later that he and Kiernan were the only survivors and that the bodies of all the other crewmen were eventually recovered.

Heath remembered that "Kiernan was kind of a mischievous and resourceful type. He tore apart his escape kit and pulled out the money that was in it—it had denominations of currency from all sorts of countries in it. Anyway, he waved it in front of the captain and started shouting, 'Sweden! Sweden!' The captain wasn't too impressed by that, and he certainly didn't take us to neutral Sweden."

"That same day they took us back to the little seaport at Swinemünde, just north of Stettin," Heath remembered. There were some Luftwaffe guards and a 'committee' of townspeople there to meet us." The mob of civilians, having endured years of Allied bombing, was ready to lynch Heath and Kiernan. "They would have literally torn us from limb-to-limb. They were cursing and shouting and spitting on us. We were very, very happy to have those German guards. They loaded us into a truck and as they drove away, I remember, one of those civilians grabbed a board and started beating on the truck. They were angry!"

Newly arrived crews were understandably anxious to learn what they could about actual operations before they started flying themselves. One crewman with the 100th Bomb Group at Thorpe Abbotts in England recalled going out to the ramp to watch the unit's B-17s return from a mission: "Here's one coming in with two red flares shooting. It got to the end of the runway and the meat wagons headed in. When we got there, the windshield was cracked and a couple of fellas came up and were crying. The ambulance fellows came out with a body, and I thought, what in the hell am I doing here?"[5]

CHAPTER 14

The Oil Plan

One of the most vicious battles of the war took place during the late winter and spring of 1944, and it was waged between and among American and British leaders and airmen without consideration for national loyalties. At issue was how best to use the Allied air forces, beyond the POINTBLANK objectives, to ensure the success of the coming OVERLORD invasion. The assault on Nazi-held Europe had been anticipated for years and promised to be an operation not only of unprecedented magnitude, but also of enormous consequence. At the time, its success was by no means a foregone conclusion, and its failure might have quite literally meant the end of hope for a free Europe. Accordingly, a great deal hung on the Allied air forces hitting the right targets and hitting them well.

Deciding what the right targets were was at the heart of the issue. On the one side, there were the proponents of what became known as the transportation plan. In the main, it proposed to emasculate Germany's ability to turn back the invasion through the destruction of coastal defenses, Luftwaffe airfields in the vicinity of the landing beaches, and transportation and communications targets. Transportation targets included railroads, marshaling yards, junctions, bridges, roads, canals, and other infrastructure. It was believed that the destruction of these sorts of targets would deny the Germans the ability to get men and materiel where they were needed.

The chief architect of the plan was professor Solly Zuckerman, a South African–born zoologist and British public servant who had come to notice following his studies of bombing and its effects on the human body. The detailed calculations he generated to buttress the transportation plan won over much of the RAF hierarchy, including Portal, Tedder, and later, to a lesser extent, Harris. There were also American supporters, like Louis Brereton, the head of the Ninth Air Force. Notwithstanding the scheme's endorsement by a significant faction of leading RAF men, its execution counted on significant USAAF participation.

The transportation plan had many critics, especially among the Americans, although there was also no shortage of detractors on the British side below the highest levels of leadership. Spaatz was a vocal opponent of the idea and his staff supplied him with arguments against it. First, the bulk of the railroad targets were in France. Attacks by high-altitude strategic bombers against railroad targets nearly always produced collateral damage. Collateral damage was an unemotional term that meant the unintentional destruction of nonmilitary property and the accidental killing of civilians. Such a campaign would surely kill more French—on a more regular basis—than was already the case. The railroads also carried a great deal of civilian traffic. Their destruction would have effects beyond those intended.

Second, the Germans had exhibited an extraordinary talent for not only rerouting around broken rails and busted bridges, but also for quickly repairing them—often in a matter of days, if not hours. This meant that the same targets would have to be hit at frequencies that were greater than normal. Additionally, Spaatz wanted to keep pressure on the Luftwaffe by forcing it to fight. If it fought, he could kill it. It was not going to fight with any vigor to protect French marshaling yards. Further, there was just too much infrastructure; northern and central France was laced with roads and rails. Spaatz argued that there were not enough resources to execute Zuckerman's concept while simultaneously conducting operations consistent with Pointblank.

The American leadership had a separate proposal. In early March 1944, Spaatz presented what came to be known as the oil plan. In truth, it was a reshuffling of the Combined Bomber Offensive priorities with oil at the top. Spaatz's staff calculated that the Eighth and Fifteenth would need only fifteen days with weather good enough for visual bombing to hit twenty-seven different plants and refineries. The missions would cut the provision of fuel to the German military by more than half. Starved for fuel, the Nazis would be greatly hamstrung not only at the invasion beachheads, but on every front.

Spaatz believed his plan was quite executable and highlighted the fact that oil targets were generally quite compact. Refineries were almost entirely above ground, virtually impossible to harden, and quite vulnerable to aerial bombardment. Unlike other production plants, they were impossible to disperse, and very importantly, they were likely to be rigorously defended by the Luftwaffe.

The oil targets presented, in quite coarse terms, more opportunities to kill German pilots. However, because of their condensed nature and generally remote locations, they were difficult to find and bomb with radar equipment. Rather, raids against these targets required clear weather, a condition far from predominant in Europe.

Critics argued that the concept had long-term potential but that it would take too long for the effects to be felt. Certainly, they believed that it would have little impact on the German forces defending against the invasion; the Nazis would tap their strategic fuel stocks to fill any gap that an attack on the refineries might create in the few months remaining before the invasion.

Neither side was inclined to give way. Churchill became involved in the discussions when a study stated that French civilian casualties might exceed 150,000. This was political and moral anathema to the prime minister and created a sticking point that was never resolved, although Eisenhower, after discussions with Tedder, advised Churchill that the estimate of casualties was far too high. At the same time, Spaatz brought influential RAF staffers into his camp, and it looked for a short time as if the oil plan might emerge as the favored concept.

The one man he failed to convince was Eisenhower, the man who would ultimately make the decision. Eisenhower had as his deputy, RAF Air Chief Marshal Arthur Tedder, and Spaatz had, as his operational superior, Air Chief Marshal Charles Portal, chief of the air staff. Portal and Tedder were both for Zuckerman's transportation plan, as was Air Marshal Trafford Leigh-Mallory, the commander in chief of the Allied Expeditionary Air Force, who was charged with air planning for the invasion force Eisenhower would take across the Channel. Spaatz had always gotten along reasonably well with Portal and Tedder, and even Zuckerman, but not so Leigh-Mallory, and he played the air marshal down to Eisenhower.

In truth, responsibilities, political allegiances, and command relationships during the period were awkward and confusing. This was to be expected when two mighty nations combined their militaries as the United States and Great Britain had. As also might be expected, personalities came into play. Tedder felt underutilized as Eisenhower's deputy and schemed to take control of Leigh-Mallory's duties. No less a personage than Churchill felt compelled to make suggestions about how the air forces ought to be organized for the invasion and who ought to be doing what. For his part, Eisenhower, who had effectively been given control of all the air forces preparatory to the invasion, was particularly jealous of his control of Spaatz's strategic air forces—the Eighth and Fifteenth—during the period before Overlord. And the theater commander in the Mediterranean, British General James Maitland Wilson, tried to jump across chains of command to exercise direct control over the Fifteenth Air Force, very much to Spaatz's annoyance.

With this disharmony simmering in the background, the meeting to decide between transportation targets or oil targets was held on March 25, 1944. First, it was agreed that all other priorities and target types aside, the destruction of the German air force was the overriding imperative. The real debate was over the next priority. Ultimately, on Portal's recommendation, Eisenhower decided on the transportation plan.

Still, Spaatz did not give up. He pressed for opportunities to not only prove his point, but shorten the war. Less than a week after Eisenhower made his decision, Spaatz offered that he could execute not only his share of the transportation plan, but could also mount a campaign against vital oil targets. He was particularly eager to mount a series of raids against the refineries and production facilities at Ploesti, to be followed by a concerted effort against the synthetic oil industry in Germany. Depending on who was doing the tallying, Ploesti provided anywhere from a quarter to a third of Germany's oil and was well within reach of the now firmly established Fifteenth Air Force in Italy.

Spaatz received no endorsements to his suggestions, nor were there any rebukes. On April 5, 1944, 230 bombers of the Fifteenth Air Force struck marshaling yards—transportation targets—at Ploesti. Curiously, nearly all the bombs fell directly on the adjacent Astra Romana Refinery. Spaatz's oil plan was underway.

The Fifteenth went back to Ploesti two more times in April while simultaneously supporting the transportation plan. Still, Portal was no idiot and called Spaatz to task for his shenanigans. It was during May that the British commander ultimately gave Spaatz permission to execute his oil campaign as long as sufficient weight was given to transportation targets.

The Fifteenth sent its fourth raid against Ploesti on May 5, 1944. It was a large one that included more than 600 B-24s and B-17s. Ken Barmore was part of that day's effort as a copilot on *Devil's Duchess*, a B-24 with the 451st Bomb Group (H) based out of Castellucia, Italy.[1] It was only Barmore's third mission, but he was already a blooded veteran; he and his pilot, Paul Krueger, had been badly shot up by flak on only their second mission, a raid against Orbetello, Italy. "We barely managed to bring the plane back and, in fact, got chewed out by our commanding officer for not bailing out. He didn't realize at the time that both our waist gunners' parachutes had been ripped up by flak."

In a press interview following the mission, one of the waist gunners, Maurice Kelly, was quoted: "The next time I go up, I'll have two chutes with me, and that's for sure." Barmore was unsure about it all: "I was so new that I thought getting shot up like that was just normal." As it would turn out, it would indeed be normal for Barmore.

He remembered the May 5 raid on Ploesti: "It didn't seem particularly extraordinary or dangerous until we got close to the target. Then, in front of us, we could make out what was an enormous black cloud." That cloud was not weather, nor was it made up of smoke from the already burning target. "It was an enormous cloud of flak bursts." As threatening as the flak was, it had to be penetrated to get to the target, and the 451st did just that.

"We got our bombs away with no problem," said Barmore, "and then started a lefthand turn to the rally point. It was then that we were hit." Although the flak was heavy, the official report attributed the damage *Devil's Duchess* received to enemy aircraft. Regardless, the aircraft was doomed as three of the engines were badly damaged. The pilot, Paul Krueger, realized his oxygen had been shot out, rang the bailout bell, and passed the aircraft's controls to Barmore before heading back to the radio room for a portable oxygen bottle.

"When I took the controls, I realized there was no way that we were going to make it back," remembered Barmore. "The nose started down, and I couldn't bring it back up. I looked up and saw that the group was leaving us behind." In the meantime, the bombardier, nose turret gunner, and navigator parachuted from the front of the aircraft. Krueger was gone as well.

"Charlie Joines came down from the top turret with blood all over his face and hands," Barmore continued. "I got out of my seat and cleaned him up some and found that even though he was bleeding a lot he had only suffered small cuts from the turret's shattered glass. Then the ball turret gunner, Lyle Clark, came up and told me that the waist had been badly hit and that he needed help back there."

Barmore started back toward the aircraft's midsection. "Whereas most other guys had backpack parachutes that they'd put somewhere next to them, I always wore a seat pack parachute that I kept strapped to me. I sat on it when I flew. Well, it got caught up on something as I was crossing the catwalk through the bomb bay." There, in the stricken bomber's belly, Barmore was doused with a spray of hydraulic fluid and gasoline. "I would have gone up like a match if we had caught fire."

After what seemed an eternity, Barmore broke free and passed through the bomb bay. Lyle Clark and Charlie Joines had already jumped clear of the spiraling aircraft during this time. "When I reached the waist, George McDonald, our tail gunner, was working on Arch Eakins, one of our waist gunners. Eakins had been hit very badly. George was able to get Eakins pushed out of the camera hatch, and I told him to jump as well. Things happened so fast that it was amazing that we were able to think at all."

In the meantime, Barmore worked on the other waist gunner, Maurice Kelly. It was Kelly who, after the crew's second mission, declared that he would always carry a second parachute. "He was pretty mangled," Barmore remembered. "There wasn't much left of his legs. I got his parachute on and asked him if he could pull the ripcord if I pushed him out and he said that he could." Barmore got Kelly out the camera hatch and made ready to jump. "I looked through the hatch and saw the ground spinning up at me and thought, for just an instant, that it reminded me of practicing spin training in the BT-13 Valiant."

Barmore waited almost too long before he jumped. "I pulled the ripcord immediately and the chute jerked me to a stop. The aircraft hit the ground and blew up right below me. I was really scared; I was sure that I was going to fall into the fire." Barmore was in his parachute for just a few seconds before he fell to the ground, barely missing the burning wreck that had been *Devil's Duchess*. He had jumped so late that despite the fact that he was the last one out, he was the first one down.

"I saw Kelly come down and got out of my parachute and went to him first," Barmore recounted. There was not much that he could do for the badly injured gunner. "I gave him some morphine and tried to make him as comfortable as I could. By then, we had attracted quite a crowd of Romanian peasants and one of them brought some water for Kelly. George McDonald came up limping as well." At about that time, two German soldiers arrived on the scene, talked with a few of the Romanians, then departed.

The Romanians were generally friendly and quite mindful of the men. Barmore persuaded them to load Kelly into a cart, and they helped him to cushion Kelly's legs with his parachute. They were then taken to a village police station. "Kelly was very ashen," Barmore remembered, "and I didn't see how he could live very long. He talked to us some and didn't seem to be in any pain."

Barmore and McDonald were being interrogated when a man motioned them to come outside where Kelly was still in the cart. "Kelly was almost gone, and he passed away about 1700 [5 P.M.] with McDonald and me at his side. A very old woman put candles in his hands and blessed him and cried as though he was her own."

There were twenty more raids against Ploesti throughout the spring and summer of 1944. The RAF (205 Group) flew four of those missions, although they made up only 4 percent of the sorties. The last mission was flown on August 19, 1944. By that time, the Fifteenth was simply bouncing the rubble. When the Soviets arrived later that month, the oil infrastructure at Ploesti was little more than ashes. Spaatz and his USSTAF had successfully executed one of the most important elements of the oil plan and one of the most effective air campaigns in history.

Still, the Germans continued to produce oil elsewhere and the USSTAF and Bomber Command continued to make strikes against a large list of those targets to the end of the war. In hindsight, Spaatz's belief in the oil plan was justified to a great extent. Indeed, the effects of the oil attacks were emphatically validated by Adolf Galland:

> The most successful operation of the entire Allied Strategical [*sic*] air warfare was against the German fuel supply. This was actually the fatal blow for the Luftwaffe! Looking back, it is difficult to understand why the Allies started this undertaking so late.[2]

Radar bombing was a relatively new capability in early 1944, and the Fifteenth used it occasionally during the Ploesti campaign that same year. Its use became increasingly common by both the Eighth and the Fifteenth throughout the rest of the war. That aside, much has been made of the fact that the USAAF adhered to its policy of precision daylight bombing whereas the RAF, almost exclusively, practiced area bombing at night. The implication is that the American bombing was accurate and selective and that it inflicted relatively few civilian casualties.

When compared to the British, this was generally true; however, the reality was that weather quite often obscured targets, and USAAF bombers were compelled to use radar to drop their loads through the clouds with an accuracy that was no better than what the RAF bombers achieved at night with their radar attacks. In other words, USAAF bombers killed plenty of civilians and destroyed a fair share of nonmilitary infrastructure.

Dropping bombs through the clouds was discouraged over occupied countries, especially France, but over Germany, if neither the primary target nor any others could be found, it was considered better to dump the bombs and hope they hit something worthwhile by virtue of luck rather than to haul them back to England or Italy. In any event, fuel considerations occasionally made it impossible to bring the bombs back from distant targets anyway. Furthermore, aircrews were understandably nervous about landing an aircraft with bombs aboard. Consequently, thousands of tons of American munitions were dropped virtually arbitrarily across enemy cities and towns, where they exploded with deadly effect.

Blindly dumping the bombs was not only ineffective and morally problematic, it was also wasteful. Aside from the fact that it took an enormous amount of effort to plan and fly a mission, it was also dangerous. It was bad for morale to lose crews and aircraft for no reason other than to toss bombs haphazardly across the German countryside.

Nor should the squandering of the fuel it took to fly a mission be overlooked. The folks back home lived their lives as best they could on stingy gasoline rations. They expected the fuel they made available for the war to be carefully stewarded. Getting just a single bomb group in the air consumed tens of thousands of gallons of gasoline. Wasting that fuel on ineffectual missions undid their sacrifices.

Accordingly, finding a better way to strike through the clouds was imperative. After some success with line-of-sight-limited, beacon-based systems, namely "Oboe" and "Gee-H," the British pioneered the way with their H2S radar which was able to map large ground features. Matching the features on the radar against those of the intended target allowed the RAF crews, beginning on January 30, 1943, to bomb at night with an accuracy that was much better than they had previously achieved. As the equipment and training were improved, the accuracy of radar bombing occasionally rivaled that of daylight visual bombing.

What radar did for British operations at night was directly applicable to USAAF bombing operations through an undercast of clouds or haze that obscured the target. The Americans borrowed the British H2S beginning September 27, 1943, and then fielded their own H2X, or "Mickey," radar sets on November 30, 1943. These new devices, technically designated AN/SPS-15, were carried in aircraft at the front of formations and enabled the bombers to hit large targets through the clouds with at least some effect, whereas earlier the bombs would have gone wide or perhaps the mission would have been scrubbed.

Practically, as the RAF night missions became more successful because of radar and as the USAAF flew more missions because they could bomb with some effect through weather, the distinction in accuracy between the day and night campaigns became less marked. It is true that although the British sometimes attacked distinct industrial and military targets—and occasionally during the day later in the war—they generally continued to deliberately target cities for the terror and destruction such strikes caused. When the Americans struck through clouds to hit discrete targets within cities, the effects were much the same because many bombs still fell outside the intended target area. And outside the intended target area were men, women, and children who were blasted, sundered, and burned just as surely as if they had been hit by British bombs at night. In effect, then, when forced by weather, the Americans practiced area bombing that was little different from that performed by the British.

Moreover, the Eighth Air Force, just like the RAF's Bomber Command, occasionally designated city centers as targets, and thus, some USAAF missions had no specific target other than the city itself.[3] This was often done when the weather was anticipated to be poor and there was no real chance of precisely striking a discrete target. Essentially, again, these raids were no different from the nighttime area bombing raids of the RAF.

It should also be understood that the art and science of navigation and bombing—particularly from long distances—was not perfect. Mistakes could and did happen. A dramatic example is the fact that elements of the Eighth Air Force mistakenly bombed neutral Switzerland on several different occasions. Rather than hitting a specific target in a particular city, the crews bombed the wrong country entirely.

CHAPTER 15

D-Day

While the Fifteenth was getting its campaign to destroy Ploesti underway, the Ninth Air Force, the Eighth, and the RAF continued to fly tactical and strategic missions in final preparations for the Normandy landings. Since late March 1944, Eisenhower had exercised close control of the air components in England, and as June approached, the heavy bombers were hitting targets in northern France as well as deep inside Germany. Much to Spaatz's satisfaction, the Luftwaffe's pilots were usually beaten whenever they showed. Adolf Galland, the commander of the German fighter forces, reported that Luftflotte Reich, the organization responsible for fighter defense over Germany, lost almost 40 percent of its fighter pilots during April. To the west, Luftflotte 3 lost nearly a quarter of its pilots. There were not enough replacements, and those that existed were of increasingly poor quality.[1] The Allied plan to beat down the German air force prior to the invasion was working.

And then came June 6, 1944, and the Allied assault on Normandy. Galland recalled: "From the very first moment of the invasion, the Allies had absolute air supremacy."[2] The Combined Bomber Offensive had worked. When the invasion forces broached the cold, gray shoals of Normandy just after daybreak on June 6, 1944, the Luftwaffe was nowhere to be seen. Whereas the Americans and British put 14,674 sorties into the air that day, the Germans mustered just 319.

The one overriding reason to destroy the Luftwaffe had been the invasion of Europe. If the German air force was still extant, it might be able to stymie the Allied troops on the beaches or even before they could cross the English Channel. And even if the Allies were able to establish a foothold on the continent, fighting across France and into Germany without air superiority would have been a gruesomely bloody endeavor, if it could have been done at all.

"We flew two missions on D-Day," remembered Robert Hansen, a B-24 pilot with the 458th Bomb Group (H).[3] "The crews were brought together the night before and briefed to the overall plan, and of course they were given stern warnings to maintain absolute secrecy. Anyway, we were up at two in the morning and airborne before daylight."

The 458th's first mission in support of the desperately awaited opening of the Western Front went without incident. Hansen remembered that everyone on the base seemed to step with extra purpose. "We had been waiting for that day for a very long time," he said. "And every one of us was anxious to do everything we could for the men down on the beaches."

Just as the airmen were ready to do whatever it took to make certain the invasion was a success, so were their commanders. Because the day had started so early and because many of the crews flew multiple missions, the men were given amphetamine tablets. "It was the only time during the war that we were offered drugs," recalled Hansen. He and his crew briefed for their second mission at three that same afternoon: "I had a different copilot for the afternoon sortie. The normal practice was for the pilot to preflight the inside of the aircraft, and for the copilot to preflight the outside. Well, I thought that's what happened. I finished with the inside and asked if he was ready, and he said 'sure,' but somewhere along the way, something got crossed."

When it came their turn for takeoff, Hansen and his copilot started their aircraft down the runway. "As we started rolling pretty fast, it became apparent that the airspeed indicator wasn't working," he recounted. Hansen had a couple of options. He could try to abort the takeoff, but stopping their B-24, fully loaded with bombs and fuel, was a risky proposition. It was quite likely that the big plane would run off the end of the runway, and there was no guarantee that it would not break up and subsequently catch fire and explode. It would not have been the first time, by far, that such a thing had happened.

Hansen's second option was to take the aircraft flying without the air speed indicator. Without the instrument, he would have to fly the plane by power settings, feel, and secondary instruments. If he made a mistake, if he misjudged the aircraft's speed on the slow side, the bomber would stall and spin. The crash would be spectacular.

"I decided to take the aircraft flying," Hansen said. "It was D-Day, and the mission was important." Hansen hauled the aircraft airborne and carried extra power to make sure that it stayed flying. "Once I got into formation, I knew that I could fly using the other aircraft as a reference; so long as I stayed with them I wouldn't get too slow and stall."

In the meantime, the crew discovered that a protective cover was still on the aircraft's pitot tube. It had not been removed during the preflight prior to the mission; it was this cover that prevented the air speed indicator from operating. "The flight engineer went to work to get it removed," Hansen recalled. "He updated me as he worked with a long screwdriver to try to slide it clear." Ultimately, the flight engineer punched a hole through the side of the aircraft and removed the cover. Hansen was subsequently able to finish the mission with no problems.

This incident emphasizes the fact that fighting the war was not only about strategy and doctrine, but also about managing details. And when those details were not managed well, it was important to have the flexibility and skill to overcome that mismanagement. In this case, flexibility and skill were apparent. However, there were times that they were not exercised, and the results were disastrous, as evidenced by the high accident rate that characterized USAAF operations out of England.

All the planning, all the energy, all the men and machines that had been thrown into the mighty fight over Europe on the Allied side had produced the desired effects. Indeed, the thousands of aviators that had been killed in those contested skies had not died in vain. Rather, the absence of any real counterblow from the Luftwaffe on D-Day, the fact that more soldiers and sailors were not killed that morning, was proof that the lives of the fallen airmen had been redeemed many times over.

But the Luftwaffe was not yet dead. Rather, the lack of any real response from the Luftwaffe was caused almost entirely by failure on the part of the German leadership. To be sure, the Germans knew an invasion was coming as preparations during the previous several months were made at a furious pace. Luftwaffe planners had drafted elaborate plans to move aircraft on very short notice from deep within Germany to bases across all of northern and central France, where they were to join units already operating there. Once the aircraft were refueled and rearmed, the crews would execute large coordinated strikes against the invasion forces. It was the possibility of just this sort of response that made the Allied leadership so fearful.

Although it made little difference in the long run, Hitler was the chief reason why there was no Luftwaffe response early on. Just as he was loathe to commit his panzers against what he feared was a ruse, he likewise was reluctant to unleash his airmen. No doubt some credit should go to the architects of the Allied deception plans. At any rate, the Luftwaffe finally started moving late on the morning of the invasion and continued its staging operations at a halting pace over the next several days. It developed into a disaster for a variety of reasons. Many of the bases that had originally been part of the plan were so beaten up by the Allied air forces that they were abandoned in favor of ad hoc airfields quickly carved out of farmland or forest. In the confusion, much of the support equipment, fuel, and ammunition was lost or never trans-ferred—or attacked and destroyed by Allied aircraft while en route.

When the movement finally got underway, the Luftwaffe's mainte-nance men and other ground-support personnel were also delayed or lost or shot up in transit. Many of them never made it to their intended desti-nations. Intermediate airfields intended to service the aircraft en route to their destination bases were overwhelmed by swarms of hurrying Ger-man fighters, and in some instances, they were depleted of fuel and other materiel. Aircraft were often shot down by marauding Allied fight-ers before they ever got to their destinations. Some Luftwaffe pilots were unable to find their intended bases, and many of them simply set their aircraft down in whatever clearing they could find and walked away. Still others, piloted by neophyte crews, were wrecked along the way or upon landing.

It developed then that once the initial push to get aircraft from Germany into France was over on June 9, what was actually in place was a tattered and worn version of the force that was intended. Instead of 1,000 aircraft or more, there were only about 300 ready for combat operations.[4] Discovered by Allied aircraft, the hastily deployed force was picked apart on the ground and in the air before any sort of grand coordinated attack could be executed.

Typical of this picking apart was an encounter described by 1st Lt. George Bostwick, a P-47 pilot with the 56th Fighter Group. On June 7, he was orbiting with his flight leader over the German airfield at Grandvilliers, just east of the invasion beaches. They were bounced by three FW-190s. "We turned into them and broke into a large cumulus cloud," he recorded in his combat report.[5] "Breaking out . . . I found myself directly astern an Me-109, about five hundred yards ahead of me." Somehow, Bostwick had traded three FW-190s on his tail for one Me-109 on his nose.

The German fighter went into a gentle righthand turn. Bostwick closed to 400 yards and began to fire, whereupon the Me-109 went into a tighter turn and began to emit black smoke. "He then pulled straight up as if to execute a loop," Bostwick recalled. "I followed him through this maneuver, firing short bursts, but not effectively. As we reached a vertical position however, I got in a good long burst."

The Me-109 disappeared into a cloud layer just as Bostwick's aircraft, short of air speed, stalled. Bostwick regained control of his P-47 just as the enemy fighter fell out of the cloud inverted and enveloped in fire. It smashed to the ground just beyond the Grandvilliers airfield boundary.

Any fleeting chance that the Luftwaffe might have had of chewing up the landings on the beachheads quickly disappeared. Exacerbating everything was the problem of command and control; the Luftwaffe's situation during the first few days following the Allied landings was one of absolute disorder and confusion. Orders could not be sent to units because the units frequently could not be found. Or if a unit's commander was located, there was no guarantee that he had a unit to command; it was frequently scattered across a handful of other small airfields or lying wrecked in the countryside.

Gradually, the situation stabilized enough for the Luftwaffe flyers to get into action in a somewhat coordinated fashion. Despite the fact they were so badly outnumbered and increasingly ill-trained, they did score some successes. Adi Glunz, an FW-190 pilot with JG 26, downed three P-47s in a very short time on June 10, 1944. The next day, JG 26's 4th Staffel, an FW-190 unit, was caught up in a whirling dogfight with P-38s from the 55th Fighter Group. Gerd Wiegand bagged one Lightning before being shot down himself. He recorded that half a dozen of the American fighters circled his parachute until he hit the ground with a smashed thigh. He was out of flying for good, which probably saved his life.[6]

More typical, though, was what happened to *Unteroffizier* Heinz Gehrke, also of JG 26. His unit had gotten caught up in a whirling melee with American fighters, but he had squirted out of the fight unharmed and managed to land at an outlying field for fuel and ammunition. Airborne once more, he ran afoul of a dozen P-47s from the 78th Fighter Group which had heretofore been tearing up ground targets. It was as if he were a lamb that had stumbled across a pack of wild dogs. He turned and ran:

> I turned east and flew balls-out at minimum altitude. They came after me, ignoring the fact that I was flying only two to three meters above the ground, pulling up for each hedgerow and tree. With beautiful precision the Thunderbolts made one attack after another. As I pulled up to miss a power line, my crate cracked open. My engine was hit, and began to smoke heavily. I climbed out. My chute opened, and I found myself sitting stupefied on the ground.

Gehrke was rescued by German troops and was back in the cockpit within two weeks.[7]

It is important to understand that most American bomber crews were not blasted out of the sky. And most crews did not have men shot dead or blown apart at their positions. And most crews suffered no lasting injuries because of their wartime service. Had it been otherwise, the Luftwaffe would have won.

Indeed, most men, although their ships may have been taken under terrific fire, survived their combat tours and made it back to the United States. Once home, they completed their military careers in one capacity or another, usually without being ordered back overseas. And following the war, most of them returned to the civilian world and went on with their lives.

Art Hodges of the 491st Bomb Group (H), was one of these men. He was a B-24 pilot who flew his aircraft, *Rage in Heaven*, into the group's airbase at Metfield, England, on June 2, 1944. Most of the group had arrived from the United States a couple of weeks earlier, but Hodges and his crew had been stuck at Belém in Brazil with engine problems. That they had missed the indoctrinations and pre-combat preparations that their comrades had undergone meant little as Hodges and his crew took part in the group's second mission two days later, on June 4, 1944. D-Day was coming, and Allied commanders believed that every sortie made a difference.

Hodges and his crew flew virtually every mission that followed during the next couple of months. "I left a good job at home," Hodges said, "and I had a wife I was anxious to get back to."[8] For those reasons, he wanted to finish his combat tour as quickly as possible and return to the States. "I made the point with my crew that the sooner we finished, the sooner we got to go home. And I laid out the obvious logic that we couldn't finish if we didn't fly. Well, they didn't all see it exactly like I did, but in the end it worked out for everyone."

Hodges made sure that the group's schedulers knew that he and the crew of *Rage in Heaven* were always available. The schedulers took advantage of that fact. "We flew a lot," Hodges admitted. "We went to Munich two days in a row. That was kind of tough." Still, his bomber never sustained major combat damage. "We saw a lot of flak on a lot of missions," he stated. "And some fighters, too. And one time we lost an engine. But other than that, we made it through okay. No one was ever wounded and our plane held together pretty well. Of course, that's the way we wanted it—nobody ever wanted a 'dramatic' mission."

Ultimately, Hodges's reasoning played out as he hoped. Although fate could have knocked his ship from the sky on any one of the thirty missions he flew with his crew, it never did. "I'd been lucky all my life," he remembered. In fact, if the time that *Rage in Heaven*'s crew took to complete their tour—thirty missions in seventy days—was not a record for that time in the war, it must have been close. After arriving in England in early June 1944, Hodges was on a ship headed back to the States in early September.

So, in mid-1944, newly trained Luftwaffe pilots were pitched into the fight where they stayed until they were killed or too badly wounded to fly. On the other hand, the Americans were able to send comprehensively trained bomber crews to England, use them for three months, then send them home. This was a telling indicator of how the air war was playing out.

CHAPTER 16

Fighter-on-Fighter Combat

Contrary to popular perception, protracted engagements that pitted one pilot against another were not the norm for fighter-on-fighter combat during World War II. In reality, most of the fighters that were shot down by other fighters were ambushed—that is, their pilots often were not aware they were under attack until very late or, in some cases, until bullets or cannon shells started slamming into their aircraft. Indeed, once the firing started, the fight was usually over quite quickly. Easy kills against unaware targets were typical.

The encounter of September 15, 1944, described by Lt. Walter Pitts, a P-47 pilot with the 56th Fighter Group, provides a good example from both the offensive and defensive perspectives:

We were letting down through a break in the clouds near Lochem when a squadron of 15 plus FW-190s crossed under us on the deck headed west. I cut my throttle and eased behind one, while Col. Schilling singled out one abreast of me. I fired about half my ammunition at this one before he started smoking. As he started to smoke, his engine quit and I overran him as he nosed down. I banked up and saw him crash and burn. The pilot did not get out. When I turned to look for another e/a [enemy aircraft], an FW-190 was shooting at me.[1]

Ultimately, as other P-47s pitched into the fight, Pitts was able to turn the tables on his attacker and shoot him down.

It was not that there were not engagements that started on more even terms. There were. But those fights took, in air combat terms, a very long time to reach a culmination point. This was because, armchair experts aside, the performance specifications of most of the frontline fighters in Europe were markedly similar. For instance, the top speeds of mid-model versions of the P-38, P-47, and P-51 at 20,000 feet were 407 miles per hour, 406 miles per hour, and 420 miles per hour, respectively. In comparison, the top speeds of the Me-109G and the FW-190A at the same altitude were 389 and 401 miles per hour.

When the P-51 is thrown out of the mix, the difference between the slowest type and the fastest was less than 20 miles per hour. This difference was even less significant in real combat conditions when such factors as individual engine performance, fuel load, fuel quality, aircraft finish, airframe trim, and even ammunition load are considered. For instance, a bent, dirty P-47 with a worn engine and a full load of fuel and ammunition might be easily outpaced by a clean Me-109 in good trim with a recently overhauled engine and half loads of ammunition and fuel. Of course, the factors could be applied in opposite fashion resulting in an even larger difference than the hard specifications suggest.

Although there were disparities in top speeds, turn rates, and roll rates, the differences were not always so great that a pilot could turn them to immediate advantage. It could take minutes to get into position for anything better than a fleeting deflection shot. And during those minutes, there were many things that could happen to upset the calculus of a one-versus-one air combat. Most likely was the entry of another aircraft—or more—into the fight. Individual fighters did not usually come together in a vacuum; rather, air combat happened when opposing formations clashed and blew apart as pilots chased each other up and down and across the sky. That a fight between a pair of aircraft might be joined by one or more others was a distinct possibility. A pilot gaining an advantage against an adversary could find himself on the defensive almost immediately when his one-versus-one engagement turned into a one-versus-two-or-more match.

This discussion is underscored in dramatic fashion by the experience of Lt. Preston B. Hardy, a P-51 pilot from the 4th Fighter Group.

On August 18, 1944, his squadron was on a low-level mission to strafe targets of opportunity in the vicinity of Beauvais, France. They were jumped from behind by a formation of more than a dozen Me-109s. Hardy broke hard left into the enemy fighters:

> I selected one and shot at about 40 degrees [deflection angle off the Me-109's tail], getting strikes on [the] engine and cockpit area. I believe I hit the pilot because the 109 rolled over, went in and exploded. I saw a chute, another kite explode, and then another chute. While turning with a Hun on my tail, another 109 made a head-on attack at me, almost ending in a collision. The 109 on my tail disappeared (I later learned that my wingman shot him off as he passed by). I kept turning and climbing and trying to select a Hun but every time I started for one, he'd have 1 or 2 other[s] to protect him. I finally bounced one at 7,000 feet, but before I got in range astern, he broke left and I shot a 40-degree deflection shot, seeing strikes on [the] right wing-tip. Looking back, I found 3 Me-109s on my tail. After 5 turns in Luftberry [sic], they broke off and I bounced one. Before I could fire I was bounced by 5 Me-109s. After getting rid of these I came home.[2]

Aside from the fact that it was difficult to get into a good firing position in the middle of a free-wheeling melee, other factors came into play. For instance, the sky over Europe was seldom clear of clouds. Pilots on the verge of getting shot out of the sky often dove into the wet, shadowy safety of stratus layers or into the blinding white cushions of billowing cumuli where, although they ran the miniscule risk of running into like-minded flyers, they were usually able to shake their pursuers and reset the game.

Given that the first-line fighters among the belligerents were so closely matched, the chief discriminator in aerial combat was pilot skill and experience. It made no difference that one aircraft was twenty or thirty or forty miles per hour faster than another if the inexperienced pilot flying it insisted on staying balled up in a close-quarters fight against a better-turning aircraft, instead of using his aircraft's higher speed to his advantage. Likewise, if he lost sight of his opponent, it did not matter a bit if a young tyro was flying an aircraft that was superior in every respect because he could not fight what he could not see. On the other hand, he could certainly get shot down by an enemy he did not see.

The 325th Fighter Group, flying out of Lesina, Italy, drove these points home to its newcomers. Barrie Davis remembered, "We had a P-40 that we used to train newly arrived pilots. They'd show up and think that our P-51s were the hottest planes in the sky. And of course the P-51 was very good. But we'd send them up in a P-51 against one of our old hands in the P-40. It didn't take them very long to learn that a mediocre aircraft well flown was much better than a great airplane poorly flown."[3]

Flying was only part of the equation that produced aerial victories. The last part was the killing—that is, actually bringing weapons to bear. There were plenty of skilled pilots who were poor shots, and their records reflected that fact. Others among them compensated by simply flying so close to their quarry that it was difficult to miss when they finally opened fire.

The greatest scorer in the history of aerial warfare compensated for his sharpshooting shortcomings in this manner. German ace Erich Hartmann was credited with 352 kills, most of them against the Soviets, while flying the Me-109. Aside from advocating close-in gunnery, Hartmann eschewed traditional dog fighting as unproductive and dangerous. It took too long to score, and it was too easy to get jumped by an unseen enemy. Rather, he favored quick hit-and-run tactics. He ripped into formations, closed to pointblank range, and scored a quick kill or two before dashing for home or setting up for another attack on his own terms.

My only tactic was to wait until I had the chance to attack the enemy and then close in at high speed. I opened fire only when the whole windshield was *black* with the enemy. Wait! Wait!— until the enemy covers your windshield. Then not a single shot goes wild. The farther you get away from the enemy, the less impact and penetration your projectiles have. With the tactic I have described, the enemy aircraft absorbs the full force of your armament at minimum range, and it doesn't matter what your angle is to him and whether or not you are in a turn or any other maneuver. When all your guns hit him like this, he *goes down!*[4]

Hartmann's tactics, as well as his successes, make a point. His achievements did not depend on the type of aircraft he flew. Although the various models of the Me-109 with which he fought were excellent fighters, he could have done as well flying, for instance, the FW-190 or the P-47. In fact, because many of his aerial victories were scored below 15,000 feet, he likely could have done very well in the oft-maligned P-39.

One difference in equipment that was very telling was the K-14 lead computing gyro gunsight that started to appear in American fighters in 1944. The new device, essentially a British design, took much of the art and science of deflection shooting out of the hands of the pilot and presented it to him in the form of a moving reticle. Basically, the pilot maneuvered to put the reticle over an enemy aircraft before firing his guns. Properly used, the gunsight was extremely effective, even earning the nickname of "ace maker." An excerpt from Lt. H. W. Brown's encounter report of September 11, 1944, reads like a paid advertisement. The 355th Fighter Group pilot scored three quick victories at the controls of his P-51 and declared: "The K-14 sight is a pilot's dream. The accuracy in deflection shooting is unbelievable."

When making performance comparisons between two aircraft, the tendency is to review raw specifications and jump to conclusions about how those aircraft would fare if matched against each other. The truth is that during World War II, there were too many variables in fighter-versus-fighter combat to declare with certitude that one aircraft was better than another in close-in combat. For example, at most altitudes, the P-47 was not as maneuverable as the FW-190. Nevertheless, a P-47 pilot did not need to "saddle up" on an adversary to pound it with gunfire. If he were a skilled deflection shooter—admittedly, a difficult talent to master—it took only a short burst from the big fighter's eight .50-caliber machine guns to mince an adversary. If an engagement took place at altitude, the P-47 always had the option of diving away. No model of the FW-190 or the Me-109 could catch the powerful American fighter in a dive.

Nor could they escape the P-47 in a dive. Dick Hewitt of the 78th Fighter Group was engaged with an FW-190 when it rolled over hard and pulled earthward. He remarked to himself that there was no way the FW-190 could outrun his aircraft in a dive but that the German was welcome to try. He subsequently followed the enemy fighter down and bagged it. This engagement, among many others, underscored the fact that once a German flier was locked into a fight with the P-47, he had better kill it or be ready to die.[5]

But killing the massive American fighter was not easy, and the amount of damage it could absorb was renowned. A now-legendary incident that illustrated the type's toughness occurred on June 26, 1943. Robert S. Johnson was a P-47 pilot with the 56th Fighter Group and was part of a formation that was bounced by nearly twenty FW-190s. Johnson's ship was clobbered by 20-millimeter cannon shells. The engine was hit, the hydraulics and oxygen were shot away, and rounds riddled the fuselage and smashed into the armor plating surrounding Johnson's seat. A hazy fog of hydraulic fluid and oxygen filled the cockpit, ignited, and scorched him.

The fire quickly went out, but Johnson nearly lost control of his aircraft. Hypoxic and terrified, he tried to get out of his ship, but the canopy jammed and refused to slide back. He attempted to scrabble through the canopy where the Plexiglas was shot away, but he was not able to squeeze through the small opening with his parachute. Finally, as the aircraft descended to a more oxygen-rich altitude, Johnson regained his wits and realized that he might be able to nurse his ship back to England. He pointed the wreck westward and girded himself for the ride back to base, hoping that he could make the trip unmolested.

He was not so fortunate. He caught sight of a beautifully painted FW-190 arcing up to his altitude. Its pilot pulled alongside and looked the P-47 over before dropping back into a firing position. Johnson hunkered down behind his armor plate as the German pilot savaged the hulking American fighter with more than 200 7.92-millimeter machine-gun rounds during three separate firing runs. The cacophony of the bullets striking not only the aircraft's wings and fuselage, but also the armor against which Johnson was pressing his back, was mind-numbing.

Although the aircraft was sieved by the German's gunfire, it nevertheless stubbornly droned toward England, seemingly impervious to the hurt it had sustained. The FW-190 pilot, exasperated and out of ammunition, finally pulled abreast of the P-47, saluted, and went home. Ultimately, Johnson nursed his aircraft back to the 56th's base at Manston.

In the end, despite this terrifying episode at the beginning of his combat career, he was credited with twenty-seven aerial victories in ninety-one missions.

Like the P-47, other fighter types had strengths and weaknesses. As long as both its Allison engines were in top form, the P-38 was a fast craft. But those engines could be problematic, especially in the cold and wet conditions that characterized northern Europe. In the event that one or both of the engines behaved badly, the P-38 became little more than a big slow target with a pilot aboard. However, in a slow-speed knife fight, because its engines were counter-rotating, the P-38 was quite poised and stable, whereas single-engine fighters became difficult to control because of engine torque. The P-38's guns—four .50-caliber machine guns and a 20-millimeter cannon—were concentrated in the nose and were easier to aim. And when those guns found their mark, they tore it to bits.

On the German side, the FW-190 and Me-109 were both fairly maneuverable and carried good enough armament depending on the variant, of which there were many of both types. Although neither were the fastest aircraft in the sky, both were quick enough when compared to their adversaries. Visibility from the Me-109 was not as good as some of the other aircraft. In fact, William Heller, a B-17 pilot with the 303rd Bomb Group (H), observed that attacking Me-109s "always seemed to skid one way and then the other; I always supposed that it helped them see to their rear." Another shortcoming of both the Me-109 and FW-190 was that neither fighter had very long range. Even though both types operated over their own territory for much of the war, their pilots often had to break off engagements because of fuel concerns.

The capabilities of the different aircraft, Allied and German, were so similar that as they evolved, they repeatedly leapfrogged each other in terms of raw performance. Generally, improvements were made only in relatively small increments, but over several years, the cumulative changes were significant. The Me-109K that finished the war shared virtually no components with the Me-109E that fought the Battle of Britain less than five years earlier. The modifications the type had undergone made it a heavier but vastly more powerful aircraft than its predecessor.

Over a shorter time span, the American types also evolved. The P-47 in particular adopted a paddle-bladed propeller that greatly increased its rate of climb. Its range was also enhanced by a variety of modifications, and a new bubble canopy improved the pilot's visibility. Likewise, later models of the P-51 also adopted the bubble canopy and carried six rather than four .50-caliber machine guns. And those six guns, with a better installation, were less prone to jam than the four guns of the earlier models. The early P-38 was a fast aircraft, but its maneuverability was uninspiring. Yet when later variants were equipped with maneuvering flaps, its pilots could turn and fight with either of the primary German fighters.

Aircraft designs and improvements notwithstanding, success rested more with the pilot than any other factor. The earmarks of a good fighter pilot were not just flying skills and good gunnery. Success in air combat was more complex than that. One of the most important attributes was good eyesight. A pilot who could spot enemy aircraft at long ranges could position himself and the rest of his formation for an undetected attack—the most successful tactic of all. Perhaps even more important, good eyesight, in combination with a keen scan in all directions, kept the successful pilot and his comrades from being caught unawares.

Likewise, patience was a virtue in the air war over Europe. A pilot who regularly flung himself pell-mell into enemy aircraft formations without first assessing their composition and disposition, as well as his own situation, was likely to get into trouble sooner or later. Fortune did indeed favor the bold, but only to a point. There were not many impetuously aggressive high-scorers in the fight above Western Europe.

A certain degree of physical conditioning was also a requirement. As nimble and light as the aircraft looked, the controls on all the fighters of the day were heavy, especially in a high-speed, hard-turning engagement. A protracted fight lasting several minutes could literally wear a pilot out; it did not matter if an aircraft was capable of a given degree of performance if the pilot did not have the strength to make it deliver.

Ottomar Kruse was an FW-190 pilot with JG 26. His flight bounced a formation of about a dozen P-47s near Aachen on September 16, 1944. The attack went badly, and a wild dogfight began. "Tracers first from one, then from another side. Again and again I was able to slip away. After a short time, my arms and shoulders ached from the constant sharp turns. I had taken several hits. One hole in the canopy, where a shell had gone past my neck."[6] Kruse was ultimately shot down and captured. Whether he would have been bagged if he had not been tired is arguable, but his recollection of the fatigue caused by the hard, turning fight is telling.

As important in a good fighter pilot as any other attribute was situational awareness, which came with experience and maturity. This was the ability of a pilot to not only complete the task at hand, but to also be alert to what was going on outside the sphere of his own immediate fight. A good fighter pilot watched for enemy aircraft that might surprise him from any quarter and, if he was very good, kept an eye on his wingman or flight lead, ready to give assistance if they were in trouble or about to get into it. The successful pilot also paid attention to his own airplane. He had a good idea of how much ammunition he had expended and how his engine was performing, and if he was smart, he kept an especially keen watch on his fuel. More than one pilot found himself in a fight only to realize he did not have enough gas to get home.

Of course, the savvy fighter pilot knew not only his own aircraft's capabilities, but also his opponent's. He fought in a way that considered the overall situation and then optimized his own mount's strengths while exploiting the weaknesses of his adversary's aircraft. For instance, an experienced Me-109 pilot in early 1944 was smart not to trap himself in a turning fight with a larger number of P-47s at high altitude. A more intelligent option was a high-speed slashing attack on the edges of the formation, followed by a quick escape. On the other hand, at low altitude, where his aircraft enjoyed a turning advantage and where the P-47 could not dive away, that same Me-109 pilot might have more margin to "mix it up" so long as he did not get too slow or get boxed in by a greater number of P-47s.

Against the P-51, that same Me-109 pilot might consider that although the P-51 was faster and perhaps a bit more maneuverable, the differences were not so great that they could not be overcome by pilot skill. This seemed to be the case on May 12, 1944, when Lt. Col. John C. Meyer of the 352nd Fighter Group was on a bomber-escort mission near Frankfurt. His unit chased away several formations of enemy aircraft. During these pursuits, Meyer closed on a single Me-109 and sent it down in flames. Its pilot bailed out, and the aircraft crashed into a German airdrome. Meyer put his situation to good use and subsequently set afire one of the several He-177s parked at the airfield. He was, in turn, jumped by another Me-109:

As I pulled up, I observed a Me-109 on my tail at 250 yards, firing. He was painted robin egg blue on bottom and sides and either black or dark brown on top. In about a turn and a half, I was on his tail, then he dropped some flaps, and I was unable to get sufficient deflection. Unlike other Huns who in similar situations have broken for the deck and set themselves up, this Jerry continued his tight turn and seemed very willing to continue the fight. I tried dropping 10 degrees, then 20 degrees, of flaps, and although this helped momentarily to decrease the radius of turn, my airspeed dropped off so much that I think nothing was gained by this. At this time, I was receiving ground fire from the field directly below, this combat taking place at about 3,000 feet. Just then, another 109 joined the fight, climbing above then dropping down behind me and, as he lost ground, climbing back up and attacking as I completed the next orbit. I then broke for the deck flying as low as possible and headed south into the sun using valleys and hills for evasion. The Huns followed me for a while but always out of range.[7]

This engagement is instructive for several reasons. First, it showed that there were German pilots capable of taking on the P-51 in a one-versus-one engagement. Second, Meyer was an experienced pilot flying what was arguably the best fighter in the world at that time. At that point in the war, he already had several aerial victories and would eventually be credited with twenty-four. That he was effectively dueled by what was obviously a skilled Me-109 pilot shows how comparable the aircraft were in a close-in dogfight at that altitude. Third, it shows how a one-versus-one combat could be influenced by external factors—in this instance, the second Me-109 and the ground fire from the airfield. Finally, it demonstrates Meyer's situational awareness and maturity; he recognized that the fight was no longer developing to his advantage, and he used his aircraft's superior speed to change the nature of the fight from a hard-turning combat to a tail chase, from which he made a good escape.

Dogfighting was not a skill easily or cheaply acquired, and it was not an expertise exclusive to either side. Barrie Davis of the 325th Fighter Group, based out of Lesina, Italy, flew both P-47s and P-51s and learned this axiom firsthand. "A couple of times when I was directly astern of an enemy plane and just about ready to blast him, the guy cut his throttle, dropped his flaps, and seemed to stand still in the air. At full throttle, I reacted too slowly and flew out in front of him, quickly switching roles from pursuer to pursued. It was not fun."[8]

Yet Davis was the embodiment of the successful fighter pilot; having survived dangerous situations, regardless of whether it was by luck or by skill, he *learned*. "After two tough experiences with that situation," he recalled, "I learned to anticipate. During a mission on August 22, 1944, while escorting bombers attacking the Odertal Oil Refinery in Germany, I shot down an FW-190, then heard the bombers calling for help over Lake Balaton. I saw six Me-109s making passes at B-17 and B-24 stragglers. I was chasing an Me-109, when it seemed to come to a sudden halt but, having seen this before, I was pretty much prepared. I chopped my throttle and dropped my flaps, but still coasted up directly underneath him."

"I had to look nearly straight up to keep sight of him," Davis continued, "and was so close that I could see where oil streaks reached from his engine down the belly of the plane. I could literally count the rivets in his fuselage." Only barely above stalling speed and hanging from their propellers, Davis and the German staggered through the sky in an ad hoc formation. "Then the other pilot, unable to see me directly below, wagged his wings looking for me—first one direction, then the other—and dropped off in a shallow dive to the right."

It was what Davis had been waiting for—an opportunity to bring his guns to bear. "I tacked in behind him and began firing. Strangely, I could see no hits even at that very close range. Then I saw the tracer rounds go over his wings and converge in front of him. At that time we were putting the tracers in the ammunition belts about fifty rounds from the end so that we'd know when were about out of bullets."

In this instance, the tracers cued Davis that his gunfire was bracketing the enemy fighter rather than hitting it. "So, I kicked a little rudder and my bullets swung over and hammered his fuselage and engine; the pilot bailed out. We were so close that he came over the right wing of my plane, and I could see the hobnails in his boots as I passed him by." The German pilot was lucky that he missed Davis's propeller and wing. Assuming he survived his parachute jump, he may have learned lessons from his encounter with Davis and subsequently used those lessons against Davis and his comrades.

Pilots and aircraft aside, luck played a major role in the fighting over Europe. "It's better to be lucky than good" was a maxim repeated over and over again, only half in jest. Few successful combat flyers discounted the role that chance played in their success. Examples of fate's inventiveness abound. Not far from Ploesti, Romania, on June 28, 1944, Arthur Fiedler of the 325th Fighter Group was separated from the rest of his squadron and found himself in a scrap. He fired on an Me-109 and noticed a few strikes as he tightened his turn to maintain the advantage. It was then that all the guns of his P-51 jammed. Fiedler only barely managed to keep from flying out in front of the enemy fighter, where he would have become an easy kill. Instead, he found himself flying close formation on the enemy pilot's wing. For a surreal moment, the two pilots sat in their respective cockpits, staring at each other. Fiedler's options were not very good. He had no weapons. And if he tried to turn away and escape, there was a good chance the German would shoot him down. Fiedler was flummoxed and started to reach for the handgun he had strapped beneath his arm. Incredibly, the enemy pilot jettisoned his canopy and bailed out.

Admittedly, this is a bizarre example of how luck could come into play. The more obvious, numerous, and mundane cases were mechanical or engine problems. It did not matter how good or experienced a pilot was when those sorts of gremlins struck. For instance, if his engine failed, he was nothing more than a passenger in a not-very-good glider. The experience of Lt. Steve Pisanos was a case in point. Pisanos, a Greek immigrant, left the United States to serve with the RAF in 1941 and was eventually commissioned into the USAAF during 1942. His experience included operations in the Spitfire, the P-47, and the P-51. None of it did him any good on March 5, 1944. On that day, his engine failed over northern France. Pisanos might as well have been a brand-new pilot on his first mission—his experience was not going to repair that engine in flight. He belly-landed his aircraft south of Le Havre and was subsequently out of the fight through no fault or shortcoming of his own.

Just as the bomber crews hated the big antiaircraft guns because there was nothing they could do about them, the fighter pilots—to an admittedly lesser extent—also rolled the dice when it came to high-altitude flak. Henry Hughey, a ball-turret gunner with the 487th Bomb Group (H), recalled: "I was keeping my eye on a group of Mustangs flying escort when one of them just disappeared in a fireball from a direct flak hit. That poor guy literally never knew what hit him."

Providence notwithstanding, winning the skies over Europe could not happen without well-trained pilots in good machines flying good tactics wherever and whenever they were needed. The nation that could field such a force would win the war.

James Kunkle's last combat mission highlighted the many considerations that played into fighter combat over Europe during World War II. He was one of the very few airmen who worked on the production line of the aircraft he flew in combat operations: "During the summer of 1941, I was a college freshman working at North American on the NA-73, the predecessor to the P-51. I made 35 cents an hour. Later that year and into 1942, I worked at Lockheed on the P-38."[9] Kunkle, already a pilot, was biding his time until he could get into the service. "When they finally changed the minimum age and the requirements for college, I went down to the recruiting station with everyone else in the world and signed up. I was afraid the war was going to end before they called me to training."

But the war did not end, and Kunkle arrived in England during May of 1944 as a newly minted P-38 pilot. The unit he would eventually join was the 370th Fighter Group at Andover. The group had arrived in theater during February as part of the Ninth Air Force's rapid buildup in preparation for operations on the continent. Despite the rush to get units into the fight, the 370th had only just started flying combat operations in May. "The group was originally trained as a P-47 outfit," Kunkle recalled, "and was just completing the transition to the P-38. It hadn't been an easy changeover because most of the guys had never flown a multi-engine aircraft before. The P-38 was a great airplane, but with two engines and their turbo superchargers and such, it kept you pretty busy. It wasn't necessarily an easy airplane to learn."

Kunkle's observations were consistent with those outlined in a USAAF performance trial dating from 1943. In that report, the authors noted that the aircraft handled well but that it would take longer to learn than other types: "The subject aircraft is easy to fly. However, a longer period of time will be required for a pilot to become familiar with the operations and maximum performances of the aircraft than is required for a normal single engine fighter."[10] Nevertheless, the 370th completed its transition to the P-38 and was ready in time to support the D-Day landings in June. It was well-blooded by the time Kunkle joined the unit in July following his administrative processing and indoctrination to flying operations in Europe.

Most of the 370th's missions were in support of the army as it battled to break out of Normandy and subsequently fought through northern France. "We were the first group to carry napalm; the P-38 was pretty well suited for that," said Kunkle. "We could carry two of the 165-gallon tanks on a pair of hard points below the center section." Napalm canisters were not purpose-built, aerodynamically optimized weapons, but rather were fashioned from external fuel tanks. As such, the only way to deliver them with any degree of accuracy was to drop them from low altitude, very close to the intended target. But the effects were devastating: the napalm exploded in a sticky, fiery, oxygen-sucking blast that terrified the German soldiers whom it did not maim or kill.

Aside from napalm, the group also flew dive-bombing missions with pairs of 500- or 1,000-pound bombs. "We even carried the 2,000-pound bombs when we could get them," remembered Kunkle. The group also strafed and provided escort for the Ninth's medium bombers. These missions were all in keeping with the tactical nature of the unit's mandate.

Nevertheless, the Luftwaffe did not discriminate against the 370th just because their mission was more tactical than strategic. "We quite often came into contact with German aircraft," Kunkle recalled. "The pattern with the German formations was almost always the same. Their radar controllers always knew where we were and we rarely knew where they were. Almost without fail, the first time we became aware they were in the area was when they showed up behind and above us. I used to joke that it would have been more practical if they had installed the pilot's seat facing to the rear."

Still, the 370th comported itself fairly well, despite the fact that it so often started those air-to-air engagements at a disadvantage. "The P-38 was pretty good in a fight," remembered Kunkle. "That was especially true of the later models we were flying that had been built with a lot of improvements." One of those improvements was the installation of maneuvering flaps. Kunkle recounted using the flaps: "They were set up so that you could reach up without really looking and slap the handle down with your right hand. This would give you half flaps which really helped tighten your turn. They weren't supposed to be deployed above 250 miles per hour, but I used them whenever I thought I needed them." With these flaps, the P-38 could turn on at least equal terms with the German fighters.

"Aileron boost was another great improvement," Kunkle said. "With the boost, the P-38 could roll just about as well as anything else whereas that was not the case beforehand. And the fact that we had counter-rotating engines meant that we didn't have to deal with torque at slow speed like the single-engine fighters did."

Kunkle's last air combat took place on September 16, 1944. "It was a group effort. One squadron was dive bombing while another was strafing. My squadron, the 401st, was assigned as top cover." Kunkle was flying in the tail-end position of the trailing flight. It was a dangerous spot, the most vulnerable to attack from the rear. Aircrews derisively called it Purple Heart Corner. "We'd learned it was a good idea to put someone with some experience back there. It helped keep us from being surprised." On that particular day, Kunkle was that "someone."

The group began its attack from about 9,000 feet just south of Aachen near the German border with Belgium when Kunkle spotted the enemy fighters: "I looked to our rear and caught sight of two groups of German fighters as they rounded a formation of cumulus clouds. One group was back at our seven o'clock position and the other was on the opposite side at our five o'clock."

Kunkle called out the enemy aircraft over the radio and broke into a hard lefthand turn. "I made a head-on firing pass through the formation that had been to my left." His attack was successful, and a single FW-190 went down. Despite that initial success, Kunkle found himself alone. His radio call had gone unheard, and the two enemy formations—numbering in excess of fifteen aircraft—belonged entirely to him.

The enemy felt likewise. For whatever reason, all of the German fighters, a mixed bag of Me-109s and FW-190s, turned to engage Kunkle rather than chase down the rest of the 370th. It did not take them long to score: "As I was finishing my head-on pass through the first group, someone from the second group shot up my right side and put rounds into my instrument panel and the center nacelle behind my cockpit. Those rounds set the hydraulic tank on fire."

The fight quickly turned into a rat race as Kunkle turned and wheeled and yo-yoed up and down with the enemy aircraft. "Of course I had targets everywhere," Kunkle recalled. On the other hand, there were enemy aircraft at every turn, all jockeying to get him in their sights. "I ended up behind an FW-190 that literally filled my windscreen—I felt like my gun barrels were bracketing his rudder."

As Kunkle blasted the German aircraft, he simultaneously fell prey to one of his target's comrades. "I saw white flashes on my left wing as the main and reserve fuel tanks on that side were hit. Almost simultaneously the left cold air vent in my cockpit turned into a blow torch." Fuel from the stricken tanks had leaked into the vent piping and ignited. An instant later, Kunkle's aircraft blew itself apart.

"I don't remember the aircraft exploding," said Kunkle, "or even how I got out of it. When I regained consciousness I was falling through a cloud." Kunkle fell through the gray moistness for only a few seconds before coming out the bottom. "I was on my back looking up at the sky. I turned myself over so that I was falling facedown. At the time, I thought I was over enemy-held territory, so I waited until I got close to the ground before I pulled the ripcord. I didn't want to hang so long in my parachute that the Germans would have time to get to me."

Kunkle's parachute blossomed just as it should have. "I wanted to be able to get out of my chute as quickly as possible so I undid the strap that ran across my chest while I was still coming down. Then I pulled my .45 from its holster underneath my left arm, but I didn't realize my hands were burned and it fell away to the ground."

In fact, Kunkle had third-degree burns on his hands, face, and neck, and although he did not realize it, he had sustained cracked vertebrae as well. Quite likely, he was also suffering from shock. "I came down toward a courtyard behind a red brick house. There was a tree right in the middle of the courtyard, and it caught my parachute. I came to a stop only about six inches above the ground." Kunkle could not have planned a softer landing.

"Everything after that was kind of fuzzy," he continued. "I lost track of time, but somehow I let myself out of my parachute. And I found my pistol again although I have no recollection of doing so." Kunkle made his way out to a nearby road where he spotted a group of soldiers in a ditch. "I thought they might be Germans, but their helmets had nets on them, and I was pretty sure our guys had nets on their helmets. As I got close and they came toward me, I threw my hands up and tossed my .45 over my shoulder—I didn't want to get into a shooting match with them."

The soldiers were part of the U.S. Army's 1st Infantry Division. They took care of the wounded and badly shaken Kunkle as best they could. His gutsy one-sided fight against the German fighters had been observed by the soldiers in the area almost like a ball game. Ultimately, Kunkle was evacuated from the battlefield and back to England, where he spent an extended period recuperating from his injuries. For his actions—engaging the two groups of enemy fighters while hopelessly outnumbered—he was awarded the Distinguished Service Cross, second only to the Medal of Honor.

Aachen was still open for business two days later on September 18, when Howard Dentz, a P-47 pilot with the 365th Fighter Group, was on an armed reconnaissance mission. The precepts of success in fighter combat, especially good situational awareness, still applied. "We were reconnoitering somewhere around Aachen," he recalled, "and FW-190s were reported in the area which was covered with scattered clouds and poor visibility. I was flying top cover, and somebody called out 'bandits' and 'break' and started screaming over the RT [radio transmitter]. I couldn't see anything. I had lost sight of my squadron leader who was in broken clouds about 4,000 feet below me, so I came down and when I broke out of the clouds I spotted him in a shallow turn to the left. Why shallow, I'll never know, because his wingman was right beside him, and right on his wingman's tail was an FW-190. I don't think the squadron leader knew he was there."

"The 190 was pulling lead," Dentz said, "and hitting the wingman right in the cockpit. He was surprised and never had a chance. The German pilot saw me coming and rolled away and down. I cranked in a hard left turn after him, pulled enough lead, and fired at about 300 yards. I just fired a short burst right into his cockpit and saw him slump over. By then, we were down to about 8,000 feet, so I followed him to make sure, then I pulled up and watched him strike the ground and blow up."[11]

This frame from a gun-camera sequence shows how close-fought aerial combat could be. Note the FW-190 in the lower-left corner: it is only several feet away from the pursuing fighter. USAAF

An Me-109G taxiing. Note the pilot's restricted visibility as well as the various bumps, bulges, and other protuberances scabbed onto the airframe as it was developed to keep pace with Allied fighters. BUNDESARCHIV, BILD 1011-674-7774-27 /

LEFT: A B-26 an instant after being struck by heavy flak. USAAF

RIGHT: Expendable external fuel tanks such as this resin-impregnated, pressed-paper 108-gallon variant were critical to the USAAF's ability to provide fighter escort to its bombers deep into Germany. USAAF

William C. Heller (standing, far right) led his crew to Schweinfurt on "Black Thursday." He credited the crew's teamwork with the successful completion of their combat tour. USAAF

The ubiquitous 88-millimeter flak gun. By 1944, there were approximately 10,000 of these weapons arrayed against the Allied air forces. BUNDESARCHIV,

It was only by luck that the pilot of this Me-262 narrowly escaped being shot down by Joe Shea of the 357th Fighter Group. USAAF VIA SHEA

For the most part, USAAF fighters were shipped overseas partially assembled and then rebuilt at depots. USAAF

Gun-camera film sometimes produced ambiguous results. In this instance, that was definitely not the case. USAAF

Frederick W. Castle receives an Oak Leaf Cluster to his Distinguished Flying Cross award on December 4, 1944. He perished aboard a B-17 twenty days later and was posthumously awarded the Medal of Honor. USAAF

James Kunkle of the 370th Fighter Group was shot down after engaging two separate formations of Luftwaffe fighters on his own—an action for which he received the Distinguished Service Cross. JAMES KUNKLE

The top turret and gunner of this North Africa–based B-24 were blown apart. JOHN BLUNDELL

Strafing attacks on Luftwaffe airfields were exceedingly dangerous not only because of enemy fire. Consider the altitude of the aircraft from which this gun-camera film was taken. USAAF

Spaatz listens with interest to intelligence reports provided by Allied officers at a base somewhere in North Africa during 1943. USAAF

The United States gave nearly 2.5 million young men to the USAAF. USAAF

Lt. Gen. Ira C. Eaker presents the Distinguished Service Cross to S/Sgt. James
L. Frazier Jr. at Widewing, England, December 1943. USAAF

Lt. Gen. Ira C. Eaker, Italy, April 1944. USAAF

A Fifteenth Air Force B-24 over Hungary, September 1944. USAAF

The B-24 could carry a heavier load of bombs faster and farther than the B-17, but it was not as rugged and could not fly as high. USAAF

All the support equipment, bases, fighter escorts, aircrews, and bombers—virtually everything in the strategic air forces—existed only to put bombs on target. Here, Fifteenth Air Force bombs fall on a Wiener Neustadt Me-109 factory in Austria. USAAF

Howard Dentz (center) scored three aerial victories while flying P-47s with the 365th Fighter Group. DENTZ

Howard Dentz's P-47 was destroyed on the ground at Metz-Frescaty airfield in France during the *Bodenplatte* attack of January 1, 1945. DENTZ

It did not matter how artsy a photographer might get: the P-47 was a difficult aircraft to make pretty. USAAF

A view into the B-17 ball turret. USAAF

Ground crews move to quickly refuel a P-51 after it is parked. USAAF

An early FW-190A. Not as numerous as the Me-109, the type still saw considerable combat against USAAF forces. BUNDESARCHIV, BILD

1011-361-2193-25 / DOELFS / CC-BY-SA

An FW-190 pilot prepares to jump clear of his aircraft. USAAF

As the war developed, the USAAF received more replacement aircraft much faster than Germany could shoot them down. USAAF

The P-51 was the longest-ranged of the Allied fighters. USAAF

Maurice Duvic saved the life of his crew's bombardier. DUVIC

Ken Barmore went from raw civilian to B-24 pilot in less than a year. He was shot down over Ploesti on May 5, 1944, only fifteen months after leaving his parents' house. BARMORE

Ready-to-fly aircraft did not just "happen." Many men put in many hours to make the aircraft ready to take on the Luftwaffe. USAAF

Brig. Gen. Uzal Ent and Col. Keith K. Compton after leading the TIDALWAVE mission against Ploesti on August 1, 1943. Approximately 500 men were killed or taken prisoner. USAAF

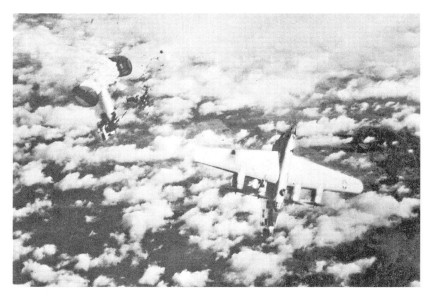

Each time a heavy bomber was lost, so too were ten well-trained men with loved ones half a world away. USAAF

P-39s were assembled at the depot at Burtonwood, England, before being passed on to operational units in North Africa and the Mediterranean. USAAF

This FW-190A was photographed in January 1945. Used less widely than the Me-109, the FW-190 nevertheless outperformed it in many respects. USAAF

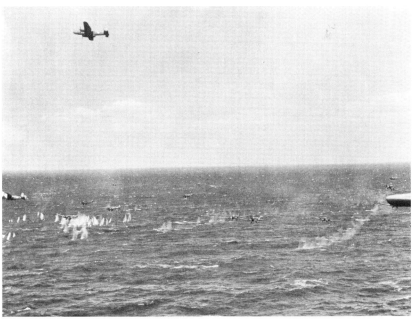

A rare photo of actual air combat. Note the Ju-52 transports taking fire low over the water. Although the date is listed simply as April 1943, this is likely the same engagement during which Jack Walker, a P-38 pilot with the 82nd Fighter Group, downed a Ju-52 on April 5, 1943. USAAF

Had the jet-powered Me-262 been made operational as early as possible, the air war over Europe would have developed differently. USAAF

His American captors give this young Luftwaffe pilot the opportunity to survey the wreckage that was his fighter. He was shot down on January 1, 1945, during *Bodenplatte*. USAAF

Prince Gustaf Adolf of Sweden, Hermann Göring, and King Gustaf V of Sweden in Berlin, February 1939. UNKNOWN VIA FORUM FOR LIVING HISTORY

Flamboyant, hard-drinking Ernst Udet, here with an Albatross D.III circa 1917, was Germany's second-highest-scoring ace during the First World War. As a high-ranking Luftwaffe officer, he was unable to satisfy Göring and Hitler and committed suicide in 1941. UNKNOWN

This FW-190A from JG 4 took part in *Bodenplatte* on January 1, 1945, and crash-landed at the 404th Fighter Group's base at St. Trond. There it was painted red, and U.S. insignia were applied, although it never flew again. USAAF

This Me-109 was downed during *Bodenplatte* on January 1, 1945, near Halstroff, France. The tiny windscreen is evidence of how limited the visibility was from the cockpit of this iconic fighter. USAAF

Gun-camera footage captured a P-47 in the act of downing a German fighter.
USAAF

This Me-109G was one of many captured examples that were exploited by the Allies to better familiarize their airmen with its capabilities. USAAF

Arnold understood the importance of support personnel to his war-making efforts. Here he chats with a Twelfth Air Force crew chief. USAAF

An ordnance man directs the positioning of a bomb body prior to it being fitted with a fuze and fins and loaded on the wing of a P-51. USAAF

Adolf Galland, a Luftwaffe ace and eventually commander of its fighters, on an inspection tour in southern Italy, 1943. Intelligent, outspoken, and aggressive, he often clashed with the Nazi leadership. Here he is wearing the Knight's Cross with Oak Leaves, Swords, and Diamonds. BUNDESARCHIV, BILD 101I-468-1421-35 / KETELHOHN / CC-BY-SA

CHAPTER 17

The Men Who Made
It Possible

B ehind every success that pilots and aircrews like Dentz achieved, there were men working in the background that played major supporting roles. Just as the aircraft the USAAF operated would have been worthless without pilots, so would they have been useless without the mechanics, logisticians, administrators, and other support personnel who made them flyable and kept them that way. The fact was that aircrew made up only a small portion of the men in the USAAF—only about 15 percent were pilots and crews. Although the nonflyers were not subject to the terrors of air combat, neither did they experience the recognition and respect that came with it.

Still, theirs was an exhausting existence spent making repairs to aircraft in the wet and the cold, or huddled over a poorly lit desk in a dank hut, or toiling away at any one of hundreds of other difficult and unheralded tasks that were nonetheless necessary to keep the air war going. In fact, most of them trained or worked anonymously in the United States. At no time during the war did the percentage of the USAAF's personnel strength deployed outside the United States exceed 50 percent.[1]

William Lundy of the 44th Bomb Group (H), a B-24 unit based at Shipdham, remembered the English winter of 1942–43 as especially miserable for the mechanics:

So much of the time it was bare-handed work in freezing weather, and one could only continue as long as he could feel the wrench in his hand. Then someone else must take over while you somehow managed to work some feeling back into your frozen digits. There were no structures or buildings with heat close by, no line shacks, nothing—no place with a fire in which to warm up. . . . My remedy was to don my gloves and run up and down the taxiway, slapping my hands together—literally beating the circulation back into my fingers.[2]

The mechanics kept up this type of work in the cold and rain and mud until the war was over. There was no combat tour length for them; they were simply there for the duration. Aircrews aside, when Arnold sent his men to Europe, he did not plan to send them back Stateside until the fighting was done.

A classic example was S/Sgt. Virgil Embry of the 86th Bombardment Group (Dive), a mechanic who shipped out from New York City on April 29, 1943. He did not arrive back in the States until September 28, 1945. Still, during his service overseas, he experienced and saw more than he would have had he stayed in his home state of Kansas.[3] Just a sampling of his diary entries vividly recount his experiences in Tunis, Sicily, Italy, Corsica, France, and Germany:

September 14, 1943: . . . left Barcelona [Tunis] by air transports, headed for some place in Italy. We flew all the way only about twenty-five feet off the water with plenty of our planes overhead for escort . . . the most beautiful sight I had ever seen. Upon arriving at our new field in Italy the Germans were shelling it, so we had to return to Barcelona.

* * *

December 23, 1943: Saw Humphrey Bogart and his wife in person. They put on one of the best shows I have seen overseas.

* * *

January 18, 1944: An A-20 bomber crashed last night, just missing our barracks.

* * *

January 23, 1944: Another A-20 cracked up last night near our barracks.

* * *

February 19, 1944: Major Holmes was killed today when his plane didn't come out of a dive. He was one of the nicest officers I ever met . . .

* * *

February 27, 1944: Taffy, our mascot, had six pups this morning. Doesn't seem like it was very long ago that she was only a pup, back in Africa.

* * *

March 11, 1944: A pilot landed an A-36 on our runway today with a load of bombs, and forgot to lower his landing gear. The plane was blown to pieces.

* * *

March 22, 1944: Krell, Hurt and I went up on Mt. Vesuvius early this morning. She was really erupting and throwing fire and smoke over a thousand feet above the mountain top.

* * *

April 24, 1944: The Germans flew low in formation over our field and dropped flares, lighting it up so that you could read a newspaper anywhere on it. They dropped their bombs all around the field, but did no damage to us.

* * *

May 20, 1944: We lost four airplanes [A-36s] today. That is the most we have ever lost in one day.

* * *

June 14, 1944: I went into Rome today for a little while. The town is very beautiful and clean, and the people were very friendly.

* * *

July 21, 1944: One of [our] pilots came back from a mission with his bombs, and when he got over the field, for some reason he dropped them right on the runway.

* * *

August 10, 1944: Joe Louis gave us a little show tonight. One of the boys from our ack-ack crews got in the ring with him. He came out with a few teeth loose and a bloody nose. Joe was very nice . . .

* * *

December 6, 1944: Jim got hit in the neck this morning when a gun in one of our planes went off accidentally.

* * *

January 11, 1945: I got the sad news that Dad had passed away . . .

* * *

February 18, 1945: While I was pre-flighting our little Cub this morning it got away from me and crashed into a P-47.

* * *

March 22, 1945: One of our men got his arm cut off when an airplane ran into him.

If their tour of duty had no defined end, neither did the workdays for many of them, especially the mechanics. If an airplane needed repair, the ground crew worked until it was fixed. If it took all day and all night to get a job done for the following day's mission, then that was the way it was. Nonetheless, when especially perplexing or troublesome problems arose, the men pitched in to help each other. Joseph Deshay of the 357th Fighter Group remembered: "Our squadron mechanics were such that we all pooled our thoughts and efforts to 'keep 'em flying.'"[4]

Ground crews understood their role in the fight against the Luftwaffe and often sought every advantage for their pilots and crews. Willard Bierly of the 357th recalled maintaining the guns of the P-51: "A good armorer sent home for nickels that were the same diameter and a lot harder than the fiber discs in the buffer that dampened the rearward thrust of the [machine gun's] bolt. The grand idea was to increase the gun's rate of fire, and that was accomplished because there was a minimum of dampening effect with a harder disc. It was soon realized that although this practice did increase the rate of fire, it was hard on the guns and resulted in malfunctions."

He also recollected the excitement when the group's aircraft returned to base: "When the pilots returned the first thing we watched for was the end of the gun barrels. If the reddish-brown patch [covering the gun barrels] was still evident we knew the guns had not been fired, but if the muzzles had a dirty, dark gray appearance we could expect a story and hope for an opportunity for the crew chief to paint another swastika on the side of the Mustang. That was the name of the game."

Then there were the losses. Merle Olmsted of the 357th Fighter group recounted his own experiences: "Of course, when a crew lost an aircraft and pilot, it was a depressing time but we seldom knew, except in a general way, what had happened. My crew lost two pilots. One of these, Lt. Otto Jenkins, a double ace, bellied in behind Allied lines and returned, only to die five months later in a fiery crash on home base. The other, not our regular pilot, lost his life when [serial number] 44-14245 crashed not far from base in what was probably a weather related incident."

As did all his peers, Howard Dentz, a P-47 pilot with the 365th Fighter Group, heaped praise on the men who serviced and maintained his aircraft:

The way it worked was that when you got to a unit and started flying, you flew anyone's airplane—whatever was available. After you got a little experience and other guys got shot down, you got your own airplane and could put your name on it and whatever. Well, a pilot named Maraga got shot down, and I inherited his ground crew. Arthur Beck was the crew chief's name—a hell of a great guy. Another champ was Bill Meyers, the armorer. But I didn't have a personal airplane until we were flying out of Normandy. One day, Major General Pete Quesada brought in an old war-weary razorback [P-47C or early P-47D]. The Eighth Air Force had gotten new bubble-canopied P-47s and we got their old aircraft. Anyway he brought this thing in and it was trailing black and white smoke. It was a mess. It could barely take off and was so slow it couldn't stay in formation. Of course, it was assigned to me. My crew chief, Beck, was pissed off. I asked for a new engine but was told no. They were keeping the new engines for the brass. So I told Beck to do what he could; change the plugs, whatever."

The next morning, I went out to the flight line and Beck was standing there with bags under his eyes. The whole crew looked tired. He told me he had worked all night and changed the plugs and he wanted me to go try it out. Well, the damned airplane leapt off the ground. The engine was marvelous, I couldn't believe it. I got back and told him that I believed that he did a lot more than just change the plugs. He said that he may have changed a magneto or two, as well.

In actuality they had broken into an engine crate and exchanged the old engine for a brand new one. Well, of course they got found out and were threatened with a court martial. A maintenance ground officer came out and leaned pretty hard on me. I guess I got a little carried away. I told him to lay off my crew or I was going to blow his damned head off. Eventually engineering left my guys alone because my commanding officer intervened.

As it turned out, I ended up with the fastest airplane in the squadron. My mother had sent me seven cans of Simonize wax. We waxed the hell out of that airplane. It was olive drab with a light blue underside. My commanding officer came down to fly it and asked if I wouldn't mind trading airplanes. I told him hell no!

Although his Ninth Air Force unit, the 363rd Fighter Group, was constantly on the move, Robert Macdonald remembers that the often primitive conditions rarely kept the ground crews from completing their work. "Out of 81 combat missions, I had to abort only once. The aircraft had low oil pressure. My crew chief was so disappointed that he cried. It was a matter of pride."

He recalls a lighter side of the crew that maintained his aircraft: "They were a superb bunch. I never even did a walk-around on my aircraft before I went flying—I just climbed in and took off. The only thing I ever had to worry about was whether or not they had gotten drunk the night before and had used up all of the aircraft's oxygen to sober up." He had an arrangement with his mechanics that was typical in his unit. "We used to get liquor rations that were supposed to be allotted out in individual shots after each mission. We never did that. We just took the whole bottle—the pilots kept the scotch and the crew chiefs got the gin."

The photos are ubiquitous in the context of the bombing campaigns over Europe. They show great clusters of high-explosive bombs falling from the bellies of B-17s and B-24s. But virtually no one gives a second thought to those bombs and to the tremendous effort it took to get them over enemy territory.

First, of course, they had to be manufactured; the United States produced them in quantities that, before the war, might have seemed preposterous. After their production, the bombs were transported via road or rail to ports where they were subsequently loaded onto ships and sent overseas. Once they arrived at their destinations, assuming they were brought safely through the German submarine gauntlets, they were unloaded and transported to various dumps and depots and eventually distributed to airbases where they were loaded into the big bombers.

Each step of the manufacturing and transportation process involved numerous details, and simply building the infrastructure—the containers and lifts and hoists and dollies and cranes—and getting it all into place was an enormous task. Likewise, quickly training people to operate it safely and efficiently was also a huge imperative. It was left to the workers at the next-to-last stop of the bomb-delivery chain to get the big brutes prepared for their missions and into the aircraft. The most common of the high-explosive bombs used by the heavy bombardment groups were 500- and 1,000-pound variants, which were heavy and awkward to handle. Primitive conditions in often nasty weather made working with them even more problematic.

Before the bombs could be loaded, their fins and fuzes had to be attached, and they had to be moved to the aircraft hardstands. There, lifts of different sorts were used to shackle them into place inside the bomb bays. Poorly documented are the crushed hands, limbs, and even bodies that were the price of getting bombs ready for killing the enemy.

Aside from their bulk and balkiness, the bombs were also dangerous for the obvious reason that they were stuffed with high-explosive material. And while not necessarily prone to unintended detonation, accidents did occur. Some of them were catastrophic. Art Hodges recalled the massive explosions that wracked the bomb dump at the 491st Bomb Group's base at Metfield on July 15, 1944. "They rattled everything so hard that buildings were flattened and men were literally knocked to the ground. Glass windows were broken miles from base. But at the time, we had no idea what had happened."

What had happened was that hundreds of tons of bombs exploded. The huge blast was followed by a colossal smoke plume that filled the sky. The panicked residents of nearby Metfield and Bungay could do little but wonder at the explosions, while military personnel on the base scrambled to help the wounded and control the effects of the blast. The first explosions were followed by a second set. Keith E. Randall of the 491st Bomb Group (H) recorded them both:

> Explosion. At approximately 7:30 P.M. on the evening of July 15, 1944 a section of the Metfield bomb dump went up. The first one, I was in the game room, as it went off the whole place seemed to shake. The concussion was great and the ears hurt for a while. Almost 20 minutes later the second and worst of all went off. I was in the hall of the aero club at the time, and the concussion almost knocked me off my feet. . . . They were unloading 1000 pounders at the time. Seven men were said to be killed.[5]

Remarkably, only five personnel were killed, and an equal number of B-24s were destroyed while another six were badly damaged. Art Hodges remembered that the effects on the remaining aircraft were much more extensive than what was officially recorded. "The shock wave from the explosion literally bent aircraft and damaged internal structures and components." This sort of damage wasn't immediately apparent, but it manifested itself when the crews checked out their aircraft. "We spent several days test flying airplanes," Hodges recounted. "My ship was never the same; it wouldn't trim correctly and I always had to fly in a slight list in order to get fuel to transfer properly out of the wing." Although he wrote repeated maintenance gripes against it, *Rage in Heaven* flew the rest of its life slightly off kilter.

The explosions at the bomb dump were considered so unsettling that the event merited a visit from the top brass. Doolittle and his staff toured the site two days later on July 17. A team was formed to investigate the cause and make recommendations. The cause of the blast was never determined for certain, however. It was speculated that a commonly used shortcut for getting bombs unloaded from a truck was the cause. This makeshift procedure entailed making sure that the bombs were loose in the truck bed, then putting the truck in reverse and getting it moving. The final step was for the driver to jump on the brakes and let the bombs fly out of the truck bed and onto the ground. It was an expedient but unsafe scheme, and it was likely that one bomb struck another sharply enough to trigger the deadly detonations. In the end, the explosions were marked off as an accident rather than the result of any sort of enemy action.

The bombs were needed to destroy the people and places that supported the Luftwaffe and the rest of the German military. They were the tool by which the goals were achieved; every bomber and fighter base, every bomber and support facility, every bomber and fighter crew existed so that bombs could be delivered against Germany. Just as the bombs were worthless without the aircraft, likewise the aircraft were useless without the bombs.

Although the aircrews suffered the most from flak, it also made the lives of the maintenance crews difficult. Walter Baker of the 387th Bomb Group (H) out of Lavenham, Suffolk, remembered a mission to Frankfurt, where the target was a jet engine factory. "The crew chief," Baker recounted, "came up to us and said, 'You fellas make sure you bring this bird back in good shape—I've got a 48-hour pass coming up.'"

The crew brought the ship back in nothing resembling "good shape." Baker recounted: "Man that flak was thick! We could smell it— we could smell the cordite. We got back on the ground and they counted more than a hundred holes in our plane. I don't suppose that crew chief got his pass." Remarkably, no one aboard the aircraft was wounded.

Baker praised the mechanics. "They were good—we never aborted once for a mechanical problem. And they worked hard. There were a couple of times when we got back from a mission and they started work almost before the propellers stopped turning. And they stayed there through the night and were still there when we showed up the next morning to fly another mission; they really were a dedicated bunch."

CHAPTER 18

FRANTIC

The notion of shuttle missions—launching bombers from one location and recovering them at another—had been discussed since
early in the war. The concept had merit since shuttle bombing, depending
on geography, presented the opportunity to hit targets that might otherwise be out of range. For instance, targets in eastern Germany and
Poland were difficult to hit from England and Italy. The Germans realized this and moved to concentrate important manufacturing plants in
those areas. On the other hand, if American bombers could fly out of
bases located not only in England and Italy, but also in Soviet-held territory, they could hit every inch of Nazi-controlled Europe.

At an operational and tactical level the concept also had advantages.
During typical missions, it was difficult and dangerous to get the big
bomber formations turned around and headed for home after the target
had been hit. Likewise, it was treacherous to pass back through the hornet's nest of defenses that had been stirred up on the inbound leg of the
mission; flak defenses were alert, and German fighter pilots often had
time to land, refuel, rearm, and then hit the bombers a second time as
they headed back to base. Shuttle bombing removed this option. Moreover, if the Luftwaffe was compelled to guard against bomber attacks
coming from multiple directions, its defensive lines would be thinned
even more than they already were.

The British tested the shuttle model on the night of June 20, 1943, when they sent sixty Lancasters against Friedrichshafen, Germany, and recovered them in Algeria. They subsequently departed their Algerian base and returned to England on the night of June 23, hitting the Italian port of La Spezia en route. The USAAF tried the concept during the epic Schweinfurt-Regensburg mission of August 17, 1943. In an effort to confuse and scatter the German defenses, the plan had 146 bombers attacking aircraft factories in Regensburg before landing at bases in North Africa. Simultaneously, 230 bombers were to fly a separate route against the ball-bearing works at Schweinfurt before returning to England.

In a weather-related miscue that had nothing to do with the shuttle aspects of the mission, the timing was botched when the Schweinfurt formation was not ordered to take off until too late. Consequently, the separation between the two forces was great enough that the German fighters were able to hit the Regensburg raiders and then land, refuel, and rearm in time to take off and attack the Schweinfurt group. Although bombing results were excellent, the Eighth lost sixty B-17s. To that date, it had been the worst American one-day loss by far. The Regensburg group was so badly shot up that it did not leave North Africa for England—as a much smaller formation until August 24. It hit the Bordeaux-Merignac airdrome in France en route.

The British and American shuttle raids were not particularly instructive, and no great benefits were realized, although, admittedly, it was difficult to reach definite conclusions after only two missions. Interest in the concept continued, particularly where the Soviet Union was concerned. Adherents of the idea believed that bases behind Soviet lines offered not only military advantages, but political benefits as well. A comprehensive series of shuttle missions would demonstrate unity between the United States and Stalin's socialist state. If it proved to be successful, American leaders hoped that Stalin would provide bases in Siberia from which the United States could strike Japan.

Arnold was an advocate of the idea and received permission to approach the Soviets late in 1943. Eisenhower, Spaatz, Eaker, and Doolittle also got involved at various levels; certainly, targets could be hit that would advance the goals of Pointblank, and in the process, there was a good chance that more German pilots would be shot down.

The Soviets were initially cool to the notion, but following intensive lobbying and after Arnold dangled the possibility of several hundred B-24s for the Red Air Force through Lend-Lease, Stalin gave his approval on February 2, 1944. From that point, planning and preparations moved apace to prepare three bases in Ukraine for American bombers and fighter escorts. The airfields were located at Poltava, Mirgorod, and Piryatin, and the operation was given the code name FRANTIC.

The chief disadvantage of shuttle bombing was that it required essentially twice the maintenance, supply, and logistical footprint as traditional single-base operations. Not only were additional airfields required, but so was a duplicate set of just about everything, including maintenance and support personnel, fuel and bomb depots, support equipment, and billeting, to name just a portion. And aside from the men and materiel, making it all work required exquisitely detailed planning and preparation, as well as the transport to get everything into place.

The effort also required cooperation. In this case, it required close coordination with the paranoiac Soviet government, an inflexible machine that was, at its very best, pedantically inefficient. American planners ran into difficulties at every turn, especially where getting materiel and personnel into Ukraine was concerned. The two sides were constantly at odds over what and whom the Americans could bring into the Soviet Union, as well as when, where, and how they could do it. In some instances, the rigid rules and regulations were adhered to, while in other cases the Americans simply bullied their Soviet counterparts until they got what they wanted.

However, the Soviets were not pushovers. Their general attitude was one of perverse obstinacy marked by brief episodes of keen enthusiasm. Divining the attitude and demeanor of their hosts was an ongoing pastime for the Americans. Moreover, Soviet military culture was an inflexible one in which retribution for disobedience and failure was harsh and swift. There is no doubt that this was a chief consideration when the Soviets dealt with their characteristically impatient American allies. Whereas the Americans might want quick action on a particular issue, the Soviets typically failed to act until receiving guidance from their superiors.

Despite the squabbling, equipment did pour into the Soviet Union, mostly via Iran and the northern port of Murmansk. Red Army laborers, many of them women, worked with vigor to get the airfields ready in time. A separate American command, USSTAF East, was created, with 1,200 personnel, and moved into Ukraine to run the American side of the operation. Simultaneously, the two sides negotiated the operational aspects, although the Americans chafed at the Soviet insistence on oversight of every facet.

For instance, the Soviets tried to drive the selection of targets, initially suggesting raids that could have easily been executed from Fifteenth Air Force bases in Italy. Moreover, they were extremely reluctant to share intelligence and demanded to review American plans at least a day in advance, ostensibly to coordinate with their air defense units. Additionally, whether by design, perversity, or simple paucity of resources, the communications links between the three bases were so rudimentary and unreliable that the Americans resorted to courier planes to maintain contact.

On an individual basis, relations were much warmer. Although the Soviets maintained a dim view toward American fraternization with their women, there were social engagements and other activities that encouraged harmony at the working level. The Soviets did not restrict American movement in the towns around the airfields, and they permitted their guests to bring in and share whatever reading material they chose. On the other hand, they resented the small black-market economy that inevitably sprang up on and around the bases, where American candy, cigarettes, and clothing went for a premium.

For their part, Soviet personnel on the bases were often accused of petty theft. And Soviet guards sometimes shot dogs that the Americans had adopted; this cruelty almost had individual American troops up in arms. Still, considering the dramatic differences in culture, relations at the working level were generally harmonious. Paul Winkleman was an assistant crew chief with the 303rd who recalled his experiences with his Soviet counterparts:

> To each crew chief, three or four Russian helpers were provided. Some were boys of 15 or 16 who had received aircraft maintenance training. Others were veterans who were recovering from battle wounds. Many of these men had fought in the bloody vicious battles with the Germans there on the Eastern

Front in the previous two years where life expectancy was very short. . . . We found their soldiers to be fun loving and humorous. Nearly all of them had lost some or all of their family from war causes in the past three years. One of my crew, Peter, an infantryman from the Vladivostok area of Siberia, had been wounded seven times, once in the throat so he could speak barely above a whisper.[1]

Winkleman was one of only a handful of enlisted maintenance men from his unit who made the trip; this was typical. The American units brought only the absolute minimum number of mechanics with them not only because the Soviets insisted on it, but also because it was difficult to get them to the Ukraine. For the short periods the Americans were there, they found they could operate with skeleton crews as long as the Soviets provided labor for menial tasks such as lifting bombs and fueling aircraft.

Still, that did not mean that there were no problems. Ted Conlin of the 357th Fighter Group remembered one incident that highlighted these sorts of difficulties: "On August 8, 1944, we had finished our operations and were set to go back to England via Italy. After we got airborne and out a little way from the field, my engine started backfiring and misbehaving."[2] Uncomfortable with the notion of a poorly performing engine taking him across enemy territory all the way to Italy, Conlin turned back. After parking his aircraft and describing the problem, Conlin's crew chief learned that his Russian counterpart had fueled the P-51 with 80-octane fuel rather than the 100-octane it was designed to use. Conlin's was one of several aircraft that had been serviced with the wrong fuel type. "The Russian crew chief's officer came over to see what was going on," Conlin recounted. "And when he learned what had happened, he pulled out his pistol to shoot the Russian crew chief—he was furious! He absolutely would have killed him too, if I hadn't stepped in to stop him. And really, the only reason he paid attention to me was because I outranked him. Otherwise, that poor crew chief would have been a dead man."

Getting the American mechanics to Ukraine by any means other than air transport was impractical, so they were transported aboard the same bombers that were flying the raids. Don Allen was a P-51 crew chief for the 4th Fighter Group and volunteered for what was described to him as a very special mission. He was stunned when he learned that he was going to Ukraine. He was even more astonished when he learned he was going there, with his tools, as a B-17 waist gunner. He remembered, "My 'gunnery training' consisted of test firing my .50-caliber machine gun high over the North Sea."[3]

Eventually, the three bases were ready for operations. Veteran flying units were chosen for the first raid, and all personnel were given extensive training not only on the operational aspects of the effort, but the cultural facets as well. For one, they were ordered not to engage their hosts in political discussions. The American leadership was anxious to ensure that everything went as well as possible; too much time, effort, and political capital had been expended for it to go otherwise.

The first phase of the effort, FRANTIC I, was personally led on June 2, 1944, by Gen. Ira Eaker, now commander of the Mediterranean Army Air Forces. The 128 Fifteenth Air Force B-17s, escorted by 64 P-51s, departed their Italian bases and savaged the railroad marshaling yards at Debrecen, Hungary, with 250 tons of bombs. The only loss was a single B-17, which exploded in midair for unknown reasons. The bombers landed at Poltava and Mirgorod to much fanfare, while the P-51s recovered at the fighter base at Piryatin. FRANTIC was underway.

Not much happened during the next couple of days as the weather was particularly poor. Boredom became an issue, although an intelligence report from the 325th Fighter Group recorded: "On the evening of 3 June, a dance was held in the village for the pilots. It was a somewhat stiff affair, but enjoyable. Some of the girls were quite good, but none of them was allowed to become too familiar with the Americans."

On the morning of June 6, 1944, at the very same time that Allied troops were dying on the Normandy beachheads, 104 B-17s and 42 P-51s took off from the Ukrainian airfields to hit the Romanian airbase at Galati, about twenty miles from the Black Sea. Barrie Davis of the 325th Fighter Group was airborne that day as part of a three-ship flight of P-51s led by his friend, Wayne Lowry. Bob Bass piloted the third aircraft.

There was a melee when enemy fighters rose to meet the Americans, but none of Lowry's flight scored during the fracas. It had been one of those confounding fights when the sky was full of aircraft one moment and empty the next. With the action over, Davis rejoined

Lowry, and the two flew line abreast northeast toward Piryatin, their base in Ukraine. Bass had gotten separated.

Soon after they set course, Lowry looked over his right shoulder and spotted a third aircraft, presumably flown by Bass, climbing toward Davis from behind. It was not until the other aircraft opened fire on Davis that Lowry realized it was an Me-109. He immediately broke toward the enemy aircraft to force it off Davis's tail.

The Me-109 pilot was an excellent shot. His first round blasted Davis's canopy away and knocked the twenty-year-old pilot out. Davis remembered nothing of the incident until he regained consciousness: "I was cold. My canopy had been blown off, the temperature at 20,000 feet was well below zero, and the moisture on my boots from walking through the dew that morning was frozen."[4]

While Davis, stunned and confused, worked to recover his wits, Lowry chased the Me-109 away. The enemy pilot was Ion Dobran, a veteran Romanian pilot who had already downed a number of Soviet aircraft since 1941. This was his first encounter with the Americans. After a running battle, Lowry scored some hits and forced the Romanian fighter down. Unhurt, Dobran put his aircraft into a field, undid his harness, climbed clear of his aircraft, and ran. He was terrified that the American would shoot him on the ground. Lowry had no interest in doing any such thing and turned back to the northeast, hoping to catch up with Davis.

In the meantime, Davis flew nearly 300 miles back toward Piryatin in his stricken P-51. "Aside from the fact that the canopy had been shot away and the right wing was pretty well shredded, my Mustang flew very well," Davis commented. Lowry was nowhere in sight, but neither was the enemy fighter that had mutilated his aircraft.

Davis made it safely out of Romania and descended his topless Mustang across the Ukrainian countryside before safely touching down at Piryatin. He remembered that "the ground crews gave me some funny looks when I landed." Those looks were more than justified. The damage he found when the propeller finally ticked to a stop was sobering. "He not only had mutilated my right wing and blown off my canopy," remembered Davis, "but he also hit all four propeller blades and shot off half the tail. And when the crew chief took the inspection plate off the top of the fuselage fuel tank—right behind the cockpit—he found an unexploded 20-millimeter cannon shell."

On that day, Davis was living proof that luck often played a bigger role than skill in the vicious air combat over Europe. Still, he had not gotten away unscathed. "The flight surgeon and his assistant spent an hour picking metal and plastic out of my face, head, shoulders, and legs. They wrapped me in gauze but that started coming loose by evening; I looked like something out of the mummy movies and just ended up tearing it all off."

Without a flyable aircraft, Davis became one of the myriad logistical details that were part of the unique operation. When FRANTIC I closed on June 11, 1944, he had no aircraft to fly; his P-51 had been written off as irreparable, and it was decided that he would ride back to Italy aboard one of the B-17s. He did not like the idea at all: "I had seen too many of them blow up, burn, and crash when the Luftwaffe attacked. I also didn't have any of the insulated clothing that the bomber crews wore. I figured that even if the Germans didn't get me I'd freeze to death."

Still, he had no other choice and was loaded aboard a Red Air Force C-47 for the trip from the fighter base at Piryatin to where the bombers were based at Poltava. "I got concerned when the left engine started running rough," he recalled. "And I got even more concerned when the pilots put the plane down on a small, unimproved airstrip and climbed out with a tool kit, pulled off the engine cowling and started working on it. If an American pilot had done that, no one would have gotten back on the aircraft."

The Soviet aircrew's repairs were good, and Davis was safely delivered to Poltava, fed, and put into a tent with a bomber crew. He spent a restless night, worried about the next day's trip. As a fighter pilot, his fate was in his own hands, but aboard a bomber, he was little more than a piece of baggage.

His savior came in the early morning in the form of an enlisted man. One of the P-51 pilots back at Piryatin had taken ill, and a pilot was needed for his aircraft. Davis dashed out of the tent almost before he was dressed. A bumpy truck ride and three hours later, he was back at the fighter base. "I never learned who the sick pilot was," he remembered, "but I should have found and thanked him!"

FRANTIC I ended when the Fifteenth Air Force units returned to Italy on June 11, 1944. Along the way, they hit the Romanian airbase at Focsani with no losses. FRANTIC II kicked off a week later on June 21, 1944. By that time, Spaatz's oil plan was well underway, and on that date, 114 of Doolittle's Eighth Air Force B-17s, escorted by 70 P-51s, hit oil targets around Ruhland before heading southeast and landing at the Ukrainian bases. Ominously, they were followed by a German He-177.

The unwelcome German aircraft had not gone unnoticed. At Mirgorod, Col. Joseph Moller, part of the American leadership there, had seen the aircraft fly past and requested permission from the Soviet base commander to send P-51s after the intruder. The commander refused; he did not want to lose face by letting the Americans defend themselves. When Moller pressed him further and asked how he planned to defend the base, he remembered that the Soviet officer "just shrugged. Their flak was terrible. They couldn't hit a barn door with it." The exchange degenerated into an argument during which Moller pointed out that the Americans were trying to be good allies. The commander caught him off guard when he responded, "You are our enemies."[5]

At the Poltava base, a group of American pilots took matters into their own hands. Associated Press correspondent Eddy Gilmore was spending time with some of the flyers when the He-177 arrived overhead. Its distinct sound drew an immediate reaction:

They looked at the plane high overhead. Then they looked at one another for an instant and began running for their planes. As they took off, leaving me standing in a dust storm, I saw the high-flying plane was already heading away to the west. I had been associated with the war long enough to suspect that this was a German reconnaissance ship.[6]

The Luftwaffe pilot eluded his American pursuers and landed safely at Minsk. The photographs the He-177 brought back, together with a mission map to Poltava recovered from a downed P-51 that same day, were compelling.[7] Once they understood what they had found, the German commanders wasted little time in readying a special force of Ju-88s and He-111s for a night strike against the Ukrainian bases. Within a few short hours, the hastily organized force, estimated at more than 150 aircraft, took off and headed southeast to hit the ill-protected American aircraft.

At the Ukrainian bases, there was little that the Americans could do other than hope that the Germans would have scant interest in what they discovered or would be unable to mount an attack. Otherwise, in the event that the Germans did strike, they had no good option other than to trust the Soviet defenses. After a brief discussion with a companion and following several vodka and grapefruit cocktails, Gilmore recalled, "Neither of us worried particularly about it, and it certainly was with light heart that I went to bed that night."

The German aircrews were probably not flying with "light heart" as they cruised toward the Ukrainian bases. Rather, their attitude as they readied for the attack was almost certainly one of grim determination. They carried a total of 110 tons of bombs and antipersonnel mines.

Gilmore was awakened by the crude Soviet air-raid alert, the clanging of metal on metal, but decided against heading for the shelters. He remarked to a companion that he had never taken cover during the London blitz and saw "no point in doing it down here." He became a bit more apprehensive when the engine roar from the German raiders grew louder. When bombs started to fall close by, he finally decided that staying alive was preferable to bravado and made his way with false nonchalance from his tent to some nearby slit trenches. When the bombs hit closer, he dropped all pretenses and hurriedly took cover:

> The bombs were pouring down now. The earth trembled. There was a tremendous explosion and a blast of warm air curled around my face down there in my hide-out. I couldn't resist turning my head and looking up at the sky. It was full of "chandeliers," those lights that the German bombers dumped out of their planes to illuminate their targets. They lit up the heavens and made the Poltava shuttle-bombing base almost as light as daylight. I peeped out of the trench. Whole acres seemed to be ablaze. The frightening whistle of a bomb cut through the night. I dropped to my stomach in the dirt again.

Bombs and antipersonnel mines fell for nearly two hours. The attackers were so emboldened that they dropped low enough to strafe. Through it all, the Soviet antiaircraft defenses were utterly inadequate; not a single German aircraft was downed. The scene the next morning was one of utter ruin. Aircraft still burned, as did the fuel dump, where nearly half a million gallons of aviation gasoline were incinerated.[8] At least forty-three B-17s were destroyed, as well as more than a dozen P-51s. Another twenty-six B-17s were heavily damaged but deemed repairable. Casualties included two dead Americans. The Luftwaffe had never before struck American airmen on the ground with such devastating effect.

Cleaning up the mess was a substantial undertaking. The aircraft required triage; sorting the salvageable from the ruined took considerable effort even before repairs could be commenced. And the base had to be cleared of the mines the Germans had dropped. The Soviet method for performing this particular task stunned the Americans. Eddy Gilmore recalled: "Several short explosions were followed by twenty or thirty people wailing and crying at once. . . . The wailing finally stopped. We couldn't make out what it was all about, but a few minutes later, one of the American officers told us that the Soviet officers had marched a group of their soldiers out onto the airfield and they'd walked into whole nests of butterfly bombs."

Anger swelled on both sides following the raid; there was obvious American antagonism toward the Soviets for their failure to protect the airfield, and among the lower-ranking Americans, there was resentment that their leadership had left them so vulnerable. For their part, the Soviets were upset that the Americans now demanded to be allowed to protect themselves. In the meantime, everything flyable was moved to outlying bases. Consequently, a German raid the following night destroyed no aircraft although fuel and bomb depots were hit hard again. Perhaps the biggest effect of the second strike was a further increase in tension between the Soviets and the Americans.

Spaatz kept a broad perspective; he knew that the aircraft losses could be replaced soon enough and did not want American grumblings to undo what had taken months to put together. He ordered U.S. personnel to desist from comments or observations critical of the Soviets. For his part, Eaker probably was not surprised by the attack or its success; he had noted the inadequacies of the Soviet defenses earlier that month and had been anxious to get his men and aircraft back to Italy.

Like Spaatz, Eaker wanted to ensure that the operation continued and even suggested it be expanded. To his mind, it certainly served the

Combined Bomber Offensive's greater goal of destroying the Luftwaffe: "We all want to destroy the German Air Force—where better than in Russia where the German has indicated his willingness to fight?"[9]

FRANTIC II ended on June 26, when the Eighth Air Force units departed the Ukrainian bases for Italy, hitting an oil plant at Drohobycz, Poland, along the way. They returned to England on July 5, after bombing a railroad marshaling yard at Beziers, France, en route.

The next phase, FRANTIC III, did not commence until almost a month after the Eighth had left the Ukrainian bases. It differed from the first two phases as it was comprised only of fighters. Specifically, on July 22, 1944, the Fifteenth Air Force sent seventy-six P-38s from the 14th and 82nd Fighter Groups and fifty-eight P-51s from the 31st Fighter Group to the Ukraine via Romania. En route, they struck the airfields at Buzau and Zilistea, destroying forty-one aircraft on the ground and twenty in the air.

On July 25, a mixed force of P-38s and P-51s left Ukraine to hit the Germans at their airfield at Mielec, Poland. There, fifteen aircraft were destroyed, three of them in the air. The return trip was marked by a wild turkey shoot when the ravaging Americans lucked across a massive formation of forty-four Ju-87 Stukas. In the free-for-all, twenty-seven of the obsolete German dive bombers were shot down.

The excitement was not over. The 82nd's mission diary recorded: "Brief exchange of fire between P-38s and 2 [Red Air Force] Yaks which made pass at -38s near front line upon return. No damage. P-38s easily outturned Russian fighters. 8–10 Russian P-39s flew [through] formation almost immediately afterwards."[10] FRANTIC III ended the following day when the Americans passed back through Romania to Italy, destroying twenty more Axis aircraft along the way.

FRANTIC IV was a reprise of the earlier fighter-only FRANTIC III. August 4 saw the return of P-38s from the 82nd Fighter Group, along with P-51s from the 52nd Fighter Group. The en route target was the airfield at Foscani and was requested by the Soviets as the Red Army was readying for its Jassy-Kishinev offensive into Romania later that month. It was on this mission that one of the most unique incidents of the war took place.

At Foscani, the American fighters tore into the airfield and surrounding targets, including several locomotives. Capt. Richard Willsie, a P-38 pilot with the 82nd Fighter Group, exploded a Ju-52 in the landing pattern. Still, flak and fighter defenses were heavy, and the 82nd's commander, Col. William Litton, was shot down. At nearly the same time, Willsie's right engine was shot out. "As I feathered the propeller, I spotted a 109 coming in on my right. I turned into the dead engine and came around on him."[11] Willsie took a desperation shot at the overshooting fighter as he simultaneously wrestled with his broken bird.

Willsie's aircraft, which was now streaming coolant from its other engine, caught the attention of Flight Off. Dick Andrews. He knew his comrade would not be able to stay aloft for much longer. "I pulled over, flying his left wing, and said, 'Pick a good field and I'll come down and get you.'" Andrews asked for cover as Willsie set up for an emergency landing. "One of the other pilots yelled, 'Don't be a damned fool!' I had been called worse, so I went ahead."

Willsie put his aircraft down in a field amidst heavy ground fire, emptying his guns at targets of opportunity as he did so. Above him, several of the P-38s fired down on the enemy troops. Meanwhile, Andrews made one abortive pass before completing another circuit and setting his aircraft down nearby.

Willsie scrambled out of his aircraft while at the same time Lt. Nick Pate downed an Me-109 that was getting into position to shoot up the two American pilots. As Willsie closed on Andrews at a full sprint, Andrews climbed out of his aircraft and heaved his parachute overboard to make more room. "I was thinking so fast, I almost didn't realize that bullets were flying around until one grazed the canopy just beside me."

Breathless, Willsie leapt onto the wing of the twin-boomed fighter while Andrews climbed back into the cockpit and flattened himself as best he could. As Willsie was much more experienced, Andrews insisted that he pilot them out of the field. There was no time for discussion, and the panting Willsie saddled himself atop Andrews; they both thrashed and struggled to get their limbs inside the aircraft.

The canopy only barely closed, and Willsie was scarcely able to move the control yoke. Nevertheless, he pushed the throttles forward then eased off them again as the nose wheel started to bury itself in the dirt. Meanwhile, Romanian troops worked their way closer. Willsie finally got the big fighter moving and rolled in as much nose-up trim as he could while the aircraft slowly accelerated. All the while, both pilots watched with widening eyes as a line of trees at the end of the field grew steadily larger. Willsie recalled: "I kept it on the ground as long as I could. I barely had flying speed when I yanked it off"

More than two hours and a vicious thunderstorm later, Willsie and Andrews touched down at Poltava. Tree branches were pulled from the aircraft's undercarriage. The following day, when the public relations officer asked the two men to shoehorn themselves back into the aircraft's cockpit for a photo opportunity, they were unable to do so. Andrews remembered: "Try as we might, we couldn't remember what we had done." The motivation of bullets zipping overhead was not to be underestimated.

For his actions that day, the commander of the Fifteenth, Nathan Twining, personally awarded Andrews the Silver Star and promoted him to second lieutenant.

Frantic continued, but only at a desultory pace, and as the summer wore on, the operation became less relevant. The Red Army achieved success after success as it drove toward Germany. Consequently, the justification for the American missions, especially as the front moved farther away from their Ukrainian bases, became less apparent. Indeed, the front was several hundred miles away even at the time of FRANTIC III.

At the same time, morale began to sag among some of the Americans associated with the scheme. This was particularly so when it became obvious that FRANTIC was not going to reach the size or permanency originally intended. Too, the Soviet high command hardened its views on fraternization and grew more and more dissatisfied with the American influence on the communities surrounding the airbases. Women seen with American men were beaten. Perhaps encouraged by their leadership, fights between Soviet troops and American men became more common. In fact, it was still early in the FRANTIC operation when, on July 15, USAAF personnel were restricted to their living or working areas at night and allowed away from the bases during the day only in groups of two or more.[12]

FRANTIC V was an abbreviated effort conducted by the Eighth from August 6 through August 8. On the sixth, the force hit the Focke-Wulf plant at Rahmel Poland, while the synthetic oil production plant at Trzebinia, Poland, was hit the following day. Having been in Ukraine less than two full days, the Americans left and hit airfields in Romania before recovering at Fifteenth Air Force bases in Italy.

FRANTIC VI was once again executed by the Eighth. Escorted by sixty-four P-51s, seventy-five B-17s hit Chemnitz en route to the Ukraine on September 11. The last Frantic bombing mission took place two days later when the Eighth Air Force units departed for Italy hitting targets in Hungary along their route. It was a whimpering finish for an effort that had been planned for a grander scale of operations.

Actually, there was one more iteration of FRANTIC. The Polish Home Army initiated a nationwide rebellion against the German occupation on August 1, 1944. Fighting in Warsaw took center stage as Russian troops reached the edge of the city. The German reaction was astonishingly brutal, and troops there began killing Poles indiscriminately at the rate of thousands each day; the insurrection's leaders cried out for help. The Red Army units refused and maintained their positions.

The British and Americans were nearly apoplectic at the Soviet inaction and resolved to help by dropping supplies to the Polish fighters. The British flew several missions from Italy at great loss, while the Americans pleaded with the Soviets to allow them to fly aid missions using the Ukrainian bases. The Russians refused permission until mid-September. On September 18, the Eighth sent three bomb groups over Warsaw, where they dropped tons of carefully prepared material before continuing on to the Ukrainian bases. Of nearly 1,300 supply containers dropped, fewer than 300 landed in Polish hands. The Germans captured the remainder. The mission was a disaster.

When it was all said and done, FRANTIC produced nothing that compelled the war to end any earlier than it would have if the operation had never taken place. From June 2 until the last bombing mission on September 13, 1944, eighteen FRANTIC raids were flown. Although in many instances, good bombing results were achieved and a fair number of enemy aircraft destroyed, it is questionable that the effects were worth the resources expended. Predictably, the Soviets never gave access to the Siberian bases from which the United States hoped to attack Japan.

The overall consensus on the American side was largely consistent with what Doolittle later wrote: "Operation FRANTIC was not a success as far as I'm concerned. While the concept made sense, there was an almost complete lack of cooperation from the Soviets who didn't seem to believe in strategic bombing or realize how they could benefit from what we were trying to do."[13] Likewise, the Germans were unimpressed by FRANTIC. The threat of American strategic-bombing sorties originating from the east did not induce them to reorganize the Luftwaffe's fighter defenses to any great extent, and on the whole, they viewed the effort as a political stunt.

If nothing else, FRANTIC gave American leaders some sense of what they would encounter in future dealings with the Soviets.

CHAPTER 19

Mishaps, Miscues, and Near Things

Human error has been the chief cause of accidents since man started flying, and it has never taken a break during wartime. That truth applied especially during World War II, when a massive number of humans were operating a massive amount of equipment in situations that provided massive opportunities to commit errors.

Walter Baker remembered one incident that nearly killed the crews of two B-17s of the 487th Bomb Group (H), based out of Lavenham, Suffolk: "We were essentially finished with the mission. We were formed up and descending back over England not far from the field, when the camera ship, which was flying in the position in front of us, broke formation and made an early turn to get on the ground first."

It was the practice at that time for each group to fly at least one camera-equipped aircraft on each mission. The camera captured images of the target immediately before the bombs were released and then continued taking photographs as the bombs hit the ground. Because the effects of a raid could make a difference to plans for the following day, higher headquarters was always eager to learn the results of a mission as quickly as possible. Consequently, the camera ships were usually the first to land so that the film could be downloaded and processed.

"Anyway," Baker continued, "for whatever reason—it wasn't normal procedure—the pilots of the plane behind us decided they needed to fill the hole in the formation left by the camera bird. I was supposed to be strapped in at my table, but I was standing up at the time, peeling off my Mae West and all my flying gear. I wanted to save a few minutes so I could get out of the plane quicker when we landed. All of a sudden, there was a big crashing noise, and our pilots started maneuvering violently. I found myself doing mid-air gymnastics in that little radio compartment with all my gear floating around me." Unknown to him, the pilots of the trailing ship had badly bungled the position swap and had lifted the rear of their aircraft directly into the outboard right engine of Baker's aircraft. "We sawed their rudder right off. Luckily, everyone was able to get safely on the ground although I'm sure it must have been interesting for that other crew. I stayed strapped in after that day."

Robert Hansen witnessed a more deadly variant of the same story. He was a B-24 pilot with the 458th Bomb Group (H), based out of Horsham St. Faith in Norwich. On May 23, 1944, he and his crew were scheduled for a short raid to the Luftwaffe airdrome at Bourges, France, as part of the USAAF's campaign to keep the Germans grounded during the coming invasion. "For whatever reason," Hansen recalled, "my copilot, Bill Fuqua, was scheduled to fly with another crew. But we were assigned another copilot and got started and taxied out okay."

Once airborne, Hansen and his substitute copilot eased their plane, *Sky Room*, into the group's formation. Hansen expertly worked the bomber's controls with a continuous series of corrections and counter-corrections as he concentrated on maintaining his position within the group. That concentration was destroyed when the 458th's formation came together at right angles with a formation of B-17s from the 351st Bomb Group (H). The two formations detonated into a wildly maneuvering jumble of mismatched bombers.

Caught by surprise, Hansen reacted instinctively and wrestled his big bomber clear of the other aircraft. "I can well remember how my windshield was filled with B-17s," he recalled. "To this day, I don't know how we missed colliding with them, but somehow we did." Then, just as suddenly as the two groups had merged, they separated. Falling to the ground were two aircraft, a B-17 and a B-24. Three parachutes blossomed from the B-17 while none issued from the B-24. The radios were quiet as the rattled crews brought their ships back into their respective formations. There was nothing that could be said that would save the men aboard the stricken aircraft, and the mission still had to be flown.

Hansen and the rest of his crew learned only after they returned that their regular copilot, William Fuqua, had been aboard the B-24 destroyed in the midair collision. "We had no idea why he was assigned to a different crew that day. And we never really asked—it wouldn't have made any difference." When Hansen and his crew were given the opportunity to attend Fuqua's funeral two days later, they declined. Instead, they pledged to fly the mission scheduled for that day in honor of their fallen comrade.

It was only four days later, on May 27, while once more forming for a mission, that the 458th lost another aircraft to a midair collision. These mishaps illustrate the fact that simply getting the bomber streams formed and ready for action was a very dangerous business in itself.

Hansen recalled how Fuqua's death reverberated back home. "Bill's wife and mine had met each other in Topeka right before we left for overseas. When she received the telegram stating that Bill had been KIA, she called my wife." Hansen's wife was understandably distraught; if one person of a bomber crew had been killed, it followed that the rest of the crew must have met a similar fate. She had no way of knowing that Fuqua was lost while flying with a different crew. "So that really worried her," Hansen said, "until she got a letter from me."

When Hansen returned to the States, he visited Fuqua's parents in Trenton, New Jersey. "They had convinced themselves that he was probably still alive someplace in Germany, even though the notification said KIA." Fuqua's parents were just two of many thousands of mothers and fathers who had to reconcile themselves to the horror of a son lost in the fight over Europe.

The P-51's resemblance to the Me-109 caused its pilots considerable distress throughout much of the war. Especially early on, it seemed that the Mustang pilots had trouble getting close to anything American without getting shot at. The experience of Fred Crawford of the 52nd Fighter Group on June 16, 1944 is instructive.[1] On that day, the group was escorting bombers against the ball-bearing factories at Bratislava, Czechoslovakia.

Near the target, the bombers were hit by Me-109s, and the 52nd jettisoned its external fuel tanks and prepared to fall on the enemy fighters. Not eager to tangle with the P-51s, the Me-109s dived away as the Americans pressed their attack. Crawford recalled: "We pushed throttles to the wire as we dove. During one of my visual sweeps of the cockpit, I read the airspeed indicator at over 550 miles per hour."

Crawford and his flight lead closed on a pair of Me-109s as all four of them leveled off just above the ground. He remembered, "[S]uddenly, I saw over on the left a bunch of twin-tailed P-38s strafing some kind of a ground target. The two 109s whipped right past them followed by us." The P-38s were from the 1st Fighter Group, and Crawford kept an eye on them, wary that they might mistake him and his flight lead for the enemy. "Sure enough, they broke off their target and took out after us. This might get dangerous, I thought, until we could be sure they recognized us, so I called a break left."

Crawford made a series of aggressive, climbing turns and lost sight of his wingman. Then, "[o]ut of my peripheral vision, I caught an image of a P-38 just below and behind me coming up from the right." The "friendly" fighter blew holes all through Crawford's P-51 and set it afire. He had no choice but to jump. He jettisoned the canopy from his burning aircraft and leapt out of the cockpit, but he was dragged down the side of his aircraft before falling free—he had forgotten to disconnect his oxygen and radio connections.

Clear of the wreck that the P-38 had made of his aircraft, Crawford waited some time before pulling the ripcord to his parachute. He wanted to be certain he was well clear of the pilot who had shot him down. Despite the P-38 pilot's best efforts to kill him, Crawford survived to be captured and made a prisoner of war.

The mortality rate was highest amongst the most inexperienced pilots. This axiom applied to all of the air forces, Axis and Allied alike. Not only were the new arrivals more vulnerable to enemy action, but they had a difficult time simply keeping abreast of the fast-paced nature of combat operations regardless of whether the enemy ever showed.

Weather, accidents, and poor navigation, among other factors, took a significant toll on aircrew new to combat.

Frank Mertely signed up as an aviation cadet on August 7, 1942, and flew his first combat mission as a P-51 pilot with the 325th Fighter Group out of Lesina, Italy, exactly two years later on August 7, 1944. He was still green three days after that on August 10, when the 325th was assigned escort duties for a raid that sent 604 bombers against five different refineries at Ploesti.

Leading the group that day was Herky Green, a leading ace with seventeen aerial victories at that time and a veteran of the fighting in the Mediterranean since January 1943. Mertely was assigned to fly on Green's wing. "I was tasked to monitor the bomber channel."[3] By listening to the radio transmissions from the bombers, the fighter units could better time their rendezvous or determine which bomber groups might be under attack and where.

The downside to Mertely's assignment was that he could monitor only one radio channel at a time. Accordingly, when Green dragged his flight into a line of clouds, Mertely was ignorant of the fact that the squadron had been attacked. Compounding that ignorance was that Green slipped away from him in the murk. "I lost sight of him," Mertely said. "So I switched over to the squadron frequency and learned that we were being jumped from behind, which of course generated a lot of chatter."

Although Mertely knew that his squadron mates were relatively nearby, he was not able to find them, nor could he see any enemy fighters: the sky could swallow a great many airplanes very quickly. "I called Herky to ask his location," Mertely recalled, "and all he could tell me was that he was over by a cloud. Well, I looked around, and there were about a million clouds."

Novice that he was, Mertely still did not lose his head. He could have raced off in any number of directions, but as time passed, the odds of catching sight of his comrades grew increasingly small. Nevertheless, there was a greater concern: the longer he stayed over enemy-held territory, the greater the chances of being bounced. He did the smart thing. "I decided to head for home, and I let Herky know my intentions." Mertely put his Mustang in a climb and turned to a heading that he hoped would take him back toward Lesina. Still, as inexperienced as he was, he could not help feeling vulnerable so far from his base and completely alone.

"At some point in my climb, I saw some specks, so I turned toward them," Mertely remembered. "Not knowing whether they were friendly or not, I turned my gun switch on. As I closed, I saw they were P-51s with candy-striped tails [31st Fighter Group], but I didn't know if they were going to the target or home." The wayward young pilot joined on the trailing aircraft and tried to make radio contact. As it developed, no one in the other group was particularly interested in the stray pilot. "I got no response, so I left. It was at about this time that I realized that my directional gyro wasn't working. All that remained to me was my remote compass which was inherently inaccurate, so I used the sun as a guide. I knew that it was about noon so I turned to put it off my left shoulder."

The sky was busy that day, and Mertely knew no strangers: "I kept going and saw more specks ahead that turned out to be B-24s. I was careful to approach them slowly from one side rather than from the rear." As inexperienced as he was, Mertely knew better than to approach the bombers—with their anxious gunners—from behind. If he were misidentified, his P-51 would not be the first mistakenly shot down by friendly bomber crews. "I was able to make radio contact and asked them what their heading was so that I could reset my directional gyro. They obliged and asked me if I wanted to go home with them." The bombers were happy to have the fighter pilot accompany them not only because it cost them nothing, but because he would be one more arrow in their defensive quiver if they were attacked by enemy aircraft.

By now, Mertely was feeling more confident: "I thanked them but they were going too slow, so I pressed on by myself." Still, he was not exactly sure of his position. "I switched to the emergency radio channel and heard aircraft calling for headings from Big Fence, the homing station." Mertely followed suit. "After a few calls, they got a good fix on me and gave me a steer to Lesina."

Not long afterward, Mertely was safely home. This, his third combat sortie, was unremarkable because, despite his inexperience, he made it so. Rather than panicking when he became separated from his comrades, he kept his composure and found his way home despite navigational difficulties. The mission provided him with a host of lessons that he put to good use until the war ended almost nine months later.

Every pilot quickly learns that forgetting even the smallest details can have very grave consequences. And what can be dangerous in peacetime can be absolutely deadly in combat. This fact was not lost on Arthur Fiedler, a P-51 pilot with the 325th Fighter Group. "I was flying on Herky Green's wing," he said, remembering a bomber-escort mission to Vienna on August 23, 1944. "We hadn't met up with the bombers yet when someone called out a gaggle of Me-109s low in front of us, and headed away. Well, Herky had the fastest reactions in the world; before any of us could react, he called out, 'Drop tanks,' released his own, and pushed over into a steep dive."

Fiedler mashed down on the button atop his control stick to shed his P-51's wing tanks and chased after Green. "We nosed straight over. The blood pushed straight into my head—I hated negative g's." Rather than a blackout—which is caused when blood is drained from the head during positive-g flight—negative g's force blood from the body into the head, and the result, called a redout, is very uncomfortable.

Green led Fiedler and the rest of the squadron down after the German fighters. "I can distinctly remember taking a moment to look around while we were in the dive," Fiedler said, "and thinking, 'Holy Christ, I've never seen sixteen aircraft going straight down like this.'" The Mustangs fell like stones, and it was only when they were just out of range that the Me-109 pilots spotted them. "They went immediately into a dive as well. But it was too late—we had too much speed on them. Herky and I were chasing a flight of three Me-109s, and I lined up behind the one on the right. As we closed the range, I put my gunsight on top of his tail. And then it was like someone threw a white sheet over my windscreen." Fiedler had forgotten to activate his windshield deicer, and when the aircraft, cold-soaked at high altitude, dove into the warmer, moister air, a thick sheet of white ice instantly blanketed the inside of his windscreen. Rapidly and blindly closing on the enemy fighters and surrounded by his own squadron, Fiedler knew he had no business pressing his attack.

"I was worried that I'd fly out in front of one of the Germans so I yanked back hard on the control stick and zoomed up to about 25,000 feet." Above the fight, Fiedler activated his windshield de-icer and scratched at the canopy with his fingernails while he searched for something better to clear the ice. "I pulled out a big hunting knife and started scraping." He worked at the ice with a great deal of enthusiasm; arcing around an aerial battle, blind and alone, was a good way to die.

"As I was scraping, my attention was caught by a flash of reflected light low and to my left. I watched it for a few seconds, trying to figure out what it was. A flash like that could have been light reflected from a canopy or from one of our bare-metal P-51s." Search as he might, Fiedler could not make out what had made the reflection. "So there I was, scraping away and looking down at this flash and trying to also look around and make sure I didn't get shot down. Then, all of a sudden, tracers started going down my left side." Fiedler dropped his knife and hauled the aircraft over into a hard, righthand descending turn. "We had been told that both the Me-109 and the FW-190 had a hard time following us in high speed turns to the right."

Looking over his shoulder and past the tail of his aircraft, Fiedler spotted half a dozen Me-109s chasing after him. "I was pulling almost as hard as I could. The aircraft bucked and rocked as I pulled it into heavy buffet, right to the edge of a high-speed stall. I actually had to push the stick forward a couple of times just to keep from losing control."

Although it was unlikely that the enemy fighters could have bagged him in the middle of a high-speed stall, they would almost certainly knock him down as soon as he recovered control at a slower speed and lower altitude. Fiedler continued: "The aircraft was shaking so much I couldn't tell if my tail was getting shot off, or if the buffet was that violent. I was too scared to roll out of the turn because if I actually was getting shot in the tail those bullets would walk right up the fuselage and into the cockpit—and me! As it was, after about 360 degrees of turn, I finally rolled my wings level and looked behind me to find that the Me-109s were gone. I don't know if they were running out of fuel, or if someone had chased them away or if I was more trouble than I was worth. Regardless, they had given up the chase and despite all the shuddering I had felt in the turn there were no holes in my aircraft."

Fiedler survived the mission and made his way back to the 325th's base at Lesina. He had missed a good fight during which his leader, Herky Green, had bagged his eighteenth confirmed victory to become— at that time—the leading American ace in the Mediterranean theater. Fiedler never again forgot to use his windshield de-icer.

Young men have always committed reckless and irresponsible acts, which sometimes come at a cost. That was certainly true during World War II. Barrie Davis of the 325th Fighter Group recalled an unnecessary—and embarrassing—episode:

> Among some of us at our base at Lesina [Italy] there was a running competition to see who could get all three wheels on the ground in the least amount of time after pitching up in the landing circuit. If a person came in at about 250 mph and pitched up very steeply, then hauled the stick back into his lap in a very tight, steep, short final approach, it was possible to get on the ground in about 90 seconds. Well, I consistently made it in about a minute and held the unofficial record.
>
> On one particular day, I made a perfect pitch-up, looked down through the top of my canopy at the tower as I turned on final, and came over the end of the runway perfectly. And then the wind stopped blowing and my plane stopped flying. It slammed down on the runway in a nice three-point attitude but hit so hard that the landing gear nearly broke through the top of the wing. The tower called over the radio: "Mayfair 24, you've set a new record of 57 seconds!" Yes, I responded, and it cost an airplane.
>
> It was totally stupid!

Davis also related a story that underscored the fact that indecision at the controls of an aircraft could be deadly. The 325th Fighter Group was returning to its base in Italy from a mission to the Bucharest area and was over a range of mountains in Yugoslavia when the engine on one pilot's aircraft simply stopped. Davis remembered: "We were at about

18,000 feet, and as he descended in a glide, guys were calling out all sorts of advice for him to get his engine restarted. Nothing worked. After a time, he was getting too close to the mountains."

Davis joined several others as they called for the pilot of the failed aircraft to bail out. "Finally, we saw his canopy fly off and watched him stand up in the cockpit. But he just stood there!" Calls for the pilot to jump rang in Davis's earphones as he and his comrades watched the lifeless P-51 glide barely above the peaks.

Davis recounted what happened next: "He pulled his ripcord while he stood there on his seat. The parachute canopy spilled out of his pack and into the slipstream and then got tangled over the rudder before pulling the poor guy out. Both the plane and the pilot smashed into the side of a mountain." One more transmission punctuated the horrible scene: "That damned fool!"

Another incident that Davis recalled highlighted the maxim that people can be their own worst enemies. It occurred during a return trip from a mission to the Ploesti area during 1944: "My flight usually had enough fuel to remain with straggling bombers and we were happy to do so. On this particular day, we were escorting a crippled B-24 home when, evidently with his transmitter on, the copilot commented to the pilot that the town ahead appeared to have some antiaircraft batteries. The pilot agreed. Well, they continued on the exact same course—right over the town!" There were several flak bursts all around the Liberator. One of the antiaircraft rounds found its mark and the big bomber went down, mortally hit.

The P-51 was a powerful machine and could quickly get its pilots into trouble. Joe Shea remembered his first flight with the 357th Fighter Group based at Leiston. "I had a ton of P-40 time before I got to England," he remembered. "I was a really experienced pilot. But when I pushed the throttle forward for the first time on the P-51, the plane took off at a 30-degree angle to the left and just kept going." The torque of the Mustang's Packard Merlin had caught Shea by surprise.

The field was wet, and Shea was wary about pulling the throttle back. "I was sure the mud would have sucked the landing gear in, and I would have ended up tipping over on the nose; I just kept on the power until I was able to horse the thing airborne." After wrestling his aircraft away from the ground, Shea had just enough airspeed to stay aloft, but not enough to turn away from the airfield's control tower. "I just cleared it," he said. "But I ended up taking the windsock off the top. When I got back, I was still really mad that no one had told me about the torque on the P-51. I was furious. In the end, no one ever said a word about me almost crashing into the tower."

Joe Black of the 357th fighter group was one of the well-prepared replacement pilots who were arriving in England during the latter part of the war. Despite his excellent training, he was particularly anxious during his first few sorties—typical of virtually every aviator who has flown combat.[4]

"It was February 1, 1945, and we escorted a group of B-17s to Wesel, where they were supposed to hit one of the bridges going over the Rhine," Black remembered. "It was actually pretty boring as there wasn't much going on. And the bombers missed the bridge." Following the ineffective raid, the group turned their escort duties over to another batch of fighters and began hunting for targets of opportunity. Black was flying on the wing of Leonard "Kit" Carson, a leading ace. "Carson spotted a lumber yard that was serviced by a railroad spur," said Black. "He briefed us very carefully. We were supposed to make a low, fast pass and drop our wing tanks on the yard. The tanks would split open and spill fuel all over the place. Then we were going to make a second pass firing our guns. The idea was that our tracer rounds would set the fuel on fire and all that lumber would go up in a huge inferno. Well, I was so nervous that I fired my guns on the first pass and dropped my wing tanks on the second!"

Factories in the United States churned out nearly 300,000 aircraft during World War II. Most of the men and women in those factories had never worked in an industrial setting. The finished aircraft that those workers pushed out of the massive assembly lines were immediately shipped or flown to operational units based at far-flung points all over the world. There, at the tail end of incredibly long logistics chains, they were maintained in the field by an army of mechanics, mostly in their teens and twenties. They were young men from a widely disparate set of backgrounds who only a year or two earlier might have had difficulty distinguishing a condenser from a spark plug or a fuel filter.

When the miracle of American aircraft production, distribution, and maintenance during the war is considered, it is not surprising that things sometimes did not go perfectly. Bob "Punchy" Powell of the 352nd Fighter Group was flying a P-51 out of the group's airfield at Bodney, England, when things did not go as they should have. "I had just gotten airborne," he recalled, "and was climbing through about 300 feet when the airplane just burst into flames."

This was not a simple engine malfunction with a bit of smoke and fire out the exhaust stacks. Rather, the front of Powell's Mustang was engulfed in a fire that reached all the way back over his cockpit. He recounted that "[o]ur procedures for an emergency just after takeoff were to simply put it on the ground straight ahead because you normally wouldn't have enough altitude and airspeed to do any sort of maneuvering. The problem in this instance was that I had a tree line directly in front of me."

Powell managed to see well enough through the flames to make a quick turn away from the trees and drop his still-burning aircraft into a freshly tilled field. "God was with me that day," he recalled. "I landed perpendicular to the rows and the freshly turned dirt kicked up and over the nose of the aircraft and momentarily squelched the fire."

Almost before the aircraft skidded to a halt, Powell released his belt and shoulder straps, jerked his oxygen and radio connections loose and reached up to slide the canopy back. "It was stuck. I couldn't get it open so I tried the emergency release and it still wouldn't let go." Fighting panic, he shifted his body lower in the tiny cockpit and kicked the canopy off. "I was up and out of there about as quick as you can think about it."

He was only about thirty yards away, with the last of his comrades roaring over his head, en route for the day's mission, when his aircraft exploded. "The whole midsection, right where I had been sitting, blew up," he said. "I turned and kept running through a small section of woods and out the other side. I came out almost directly in front of my squadron's pilot lounge."

Powell rushed inside the Nissen hut, where he found the squadron's intelligence officer, Capt. David Lee, on the telephone. "It looks like Punchy's gone in," Powell heard him say. "There's a lot of fire; I think he's done for." "The hell I am!" Powell shouted. Lee looked up and saw the panting pilot standing—more or less intact—in front of him. "He seemed pretty surprised—and happy—to see me there," Powell recalled.

The two of them climbed into a jeep and drove to the crash site. Emergency vehicles were already on the scene, as was the unit's medical officer. "I was feeling pretty cocky by that point," Powell said. "We pulled up, and I got out of the jeep and walked over to where guys were trying to put the fire out. They were also looking for my body. I shouted to Doc Lemon, our flight surgeon, 'Hey, Doc! Who was it?' He looked right at me and said, 'It was Punchy! Punchy's gone!' Then he took another look, and it really threw him for a loop. He was obviously confused. 'Hey,' he said. 'Hey, that's you!'" Lemon was clearly relieved to find that Powell was unhurt.

"We never did find out for sure what had happened," Powell remembered. "We figured that a fuel line had probably vibrated loose and spewed fuel all over the hot manifold and that's almost certainly what caused the fire, but we never knew for sure."

Weather was an indiscriminate and universal enemy to all aircrew of every type and nation. It was hated—and could be deadly. Robert Powell recalled one particular episode when the 352nd Fighter Group's P-51s took off into heavy clouds: "We got airborne and straight away tucked into formation on our flight lead, Lt. Col. John Meyer because we were almost immediately into the clouds—and they were thick!" Powell remembered that the squadron punched into the weather at only 700 feet. "We were supposed to come out of it at 8,000 feet, but we didn't. We passed through 8,000 feet, then 10,000 feet and were still in it as we climbed through 15,000 feet."

Extended formation flying in thick clouds was intense, mind-numbing work. Even in good weather, formation flying required precise and minute movements of throttle and stick, a neverending series of coordinated corrections and countercorrections. But in the shadowy gray gloom of heavy clouds, the pilot had to strain to maintain contact with his flight leader, the only visual reference he had. Thus impaired, he fought a continuous battle with vertigo. His mind and body told him he was in a steep turn when he was actually straight and level. Or they tricked him into believing that he was in a catastrophic vertical dive when he was in fact flying a gentle climbing turn. All of these very compelling psycho-physiological cues had to be ignored, and his training and flight leader had to be trusted.

Each pilot was under the added pressure of knowing that all around him were more than a dozen other pilots who were wrestling with the same vertigo demons. If only one of them fell out of position, it could spell disaster. The chances of a midair collision were considerable, and the prospect of a Packard Merlin-powered propeller smashing into the cockpit was terrifying.

"[W]e were passing through about 20,000 feet and were still stuck in heavy clouds," Powell continued. "I was so tense and working so hard to stay in position that to this day I can feel the cold sweat running underneath my clothing from my armpit and down my left side—and the P-51's cockpit was not that warm! Finally, someone came up and broke radio silence—that was forbidden. Anyway, he said, 'I'd eat a sack of shit to get out of this stuff!' And only an instant later someone else answered, 'You can start right now, brother, because my pants are full of it!' When we reached 27,000 feet, still in the overcast, we got a call that the mission had been scrubbed and we were to return to base. Lieutenant Colonel Meyer directed the squadron leaders to return on their own, and we dropped down under the overcast and headed for home via the North Sea. It had been a difficult and fruitless mission."

Indeed, weather claimed lives in ways that could only be guessed at when aircraft failed to return from encounters with clouds or storms or fog. Barrie Davis was nearly killed when he lost control of his fighter several times in a single incident while flying in heavy clouds. "It was one of my earlier missions," he recalled. "I was flying a P-47 as a wingman. Clouds built up as we crossed the Adriatic on our way toward our rendezvous point."

The weather grew increasingly thick as the squadron continued northeast. Pilots tightly tucked their aircraft together in an effort to maintain the formation's integrity. It was not enough, and the individual four-ship flights within the squadron soon lost sight of each other. "As visibility decreased," Davis recalled, "my flight leader began flying slower and slower. I kept my eyes glued to his wing because if I became separated from him there was a good chance that I'd run into someone else."

Davis recalled that at the edge of stall, his flight leader turned into him, essentially making it impossible for him to stay in formation. "My airplane fell into a spin, and the gyros tumbled on my main attitude indicator. I had no choice but to try and recover using only my airspeed indicator and the needle and ball!" It was a nearly impossible task. The lag in the airspeed indicator and the "needle" (turn indicator) was such that it was very difficult to keep from over-controlling the aircraft. "I fought the spin," Davis said, "and watched the altimeter, and then hoped for the best. I was able to stop the spin and pull the Thunderbolt out of its dive but then I probably pulled it into a vertical climb because it stalled and spun again!"

Davis fought his aircraft inside an icy, gray shroud. There was not a single visual cue to tell him whether he was upright or upside down, turning or level, climbing or diving. All he had were simple backup instruments and his training. "There followed another spin," he recounted. "Six times, this happened, and I was ready to give up, with a sharp admonition to my P-47 to go ahead and tear itself apart if that's what it wanted. Eventually, I regained my senses and was able to recover control of the airplane. I set a course as quickly as I could after the gyros settled."

Davis was rattled. It took him thirty minutes of slow climbing on a northerly heading for him to realize that he was headed deeper into German-held territory rather than home. "A 180-degree turn, still in the soup, set me on my course back to Lesina. Finally, at 19,000 feet, I broke out of the clouds. By the time I reached Lesina the weather was clear and the guys on the ground had no clue as to what my problems had been."

That Davis had been able to recover his fighter from multiple spins at progressively lower altitudes while in the clouds was remarkable. It is absolutely certain that there were plenty of other pilots who, when they encountered the same conditions, did not.

In fact, Luftwaffe pilots received very spotty instrument flight training. For the most part, it was only the bomber and transport pilots and the night fighter crews who received anything more than a cursory exposure to flying in poor weather. When American raids came during foul weather, it was not unusual for German fighter pilots to perish because of the weather instead of enemy fire.

CHAPTER 20

Jets, Rockets, and Tante Ju

The Luftwaffe experimented zealously and continuously with advanced aircraft designs. This was due in part to the fact that Germany's leaders realized that the nation's industrial base could never compete with the Allies in terms of aircraft production. Consequently, the Luftwaffe looked to various technologies to surmount the overwhelming masses of fighters and bombers that it knew the Allies would bring to bear.

The most promising of those technologies was the jet engine. Unhampered by the physical limitations imposed by the propeller and mercifully less complex than the internal combustion engine with its pistons, heavy engine blocks, and myriad other mechanical components, jet propulsion promised aircraft speeds well beyond what the best American and British fighters could manage. Still, it was an immature concept that required significant investment and study. Accordingly, Germany poured considerable resources and talent into the development of a reliable, operationally relevant jet engine.

Simultaneously, Germany's aircraft designers eagerly embraced the idea of producing new machines that could take advantage of the jet engine's power. Even before the war, the latest reciprocating engines were evolving into excessively complicated and often problematic powerplants. Consequently, the prospect of putting together new designs free of the limitations that traditional aircraft engines imposed was exciting and new.

Between the engine developers and aircraft designers, the engine men had the most challenging task. Jet-engine technology was very new. Not only did designs have to be put to paper, built, prototyped, and tested, but a brand-new manufacturing base and support network had to be assembled from nothing. Especially challenging was the problem of finding, producing, and distributing materials that could withstand the punishing heat at the heart of jet propulsion.

On the other hand, the discipline of aircraft design was already decades old. Although the jet engine was revolutionary, designing aircraft that could take advantage of it was not exceedingly difficult. This was borne out by the fact that factory-fresh jet aircraft were ready long before there were engines to power them.

Among these new aircraft was the Ar-234, designed and produced by Arado. Intended as a bomber, it had a top speed approaching 500 miles per hour and an operational altitude of 30,000 feet. Outwardly, its design was fairly unremarkable, with one Junkers Jumo 004 engine slung beneath each straight, high-mounted wing. It was characterized by tall, tricycle landing gear and a fuel-filled, tubular fuselage. It was fully aerobatic, and despite its size—nearly eleven tons—had a crew of only one.

The Ar-234 first flew during September 1943. It was an event that set off alarm bells among American and British military leaders; at that point, they had no fighters with a realistic chance of intercepting it. Significant numbers of operational Ar-234s could cause real problems.

Ted Conlin, a P-51 pilot with the 357th Fighter Group, knew nothing of this on May 21, 1944: "I had flown my first mission only about a week earlier. On this particular day, we were flying a fighter sweep somewhere near Hanover; the weather was kind of sad, and we really hadn't found anything of interest." At that time, the Luftwaffe did not make a regular practice of chasing after Allied fighters; rather, the Germans preserved their resources to intercept the bombers. "Anyway," Conlin continued, "we were flying over a complete undercast when the sky around us erupted with flak. We got caught in a barrage, a flak trap."

Conlin recalled that the 357th, desperate to get clear of the murderous explosions, "scattered like a bunch of geese. It was really unnerving to get ambushed like that. You're flying along, and not much is happening, and then all of a sudden, the entire sky erupts." Conlin lost sight of his flight lead during the mad scramble to get away from the flak. Deep inside Germany and more than 400 miles from his base at Leiston, he knew that it was dangerous to be alone. "I spotted two other P-51s and latched onto them." He did not know it at the time, but his new best friends were Harry Ankeny and Rodney Starkey, also of the 357th. Ankeny was leading, with Starkey on his right wing. Conlin joined the other two pilots on Ankeny's left wing.

Conlin recounted how the ad hoc formation did not immediately turn for home but rather stooged about for a bit. "We flew north for a while and the weather started to clear." The three P-51s reached Germany's northern coast near Wismar on the very west end of the Baltic Sea, less than fifty miles south of Denmark. "We caught sight of an airfield right on the coast," Conlin remembered. "It was stuck out on a tiny little peninsula." The airfield they had spotted was Tarnewitz, a Luftwaffe test station. Tarnewitz was a noted weapons test center where technicians specialized in the installation of new armament arrangements on all manner of aircraft. It was not a large base, but it was at the cutting edge of various aircraft developments.

Ankeny, at the head of the three-plane formation, likely had no idea what Tarnewitz was or what sort of work the Germans did there. That it was an enemy airfield was all the excuse he needed to shoot it up. "We gave it a good look," Conlin said, "and let down in a big, easy turn about ten miles to the southeast. While I was looking it over, the other two guys kind of ran away out in front of me. It was then that I realized that I was only running at about 45 inches of manifold pressure, whereas I'm pretty sure they were running all out at more than 60!"

Conlin hurriedly put the power to his P-51's engine and raced to catch up with Ankeny and Starkey. "We were coming in at about a hundred feet or so. I noticed some light antiaircraft fire as we got close, and had just about caught up with the other two guys as we reached the airfield." Only a few feet above the ground, in a line-abreast formation on a northwesterly heading, the three pilots were constrained to take whatever targets were directly in front of their aircraft. "I can remember," stated Conlin, "that I was aligned along a taxiway that ran into a big, concrete apron at the center of the field. And I could see the other two guys shooting—they shot up two Me-110s."

Conlin did not fire his guns until the last minute. "There was a hangar at the far end of the field, and it looked like there were personnel on the ground getting ready to tow a big twin-engine aircraft out of it. I only had time for a couple of short bursts, but I put about 80 rounds of API—armor-piercing incendiary—right into it." Barely clearing the top of the hangar, Conlin rolled the Mustang into a hard righthand turn and pulled for the coast, less than a mile away. "As I banked into the turn, right on the deck, I spotted a big antiaircraft gun, an '88.' The crew was scrambling to get the barrel cranked down and turned around after me."

Seconds later, Conlin was racing northbound, just feet above the Baltic, hurrying to get clear of the guns at Tarnewitz. It was not long before the German defenders made him aware that as fast as he was going, he was not as speedy as a cannon round. "A big geyser erupted right in front of me. And then another. They had finally gotten that big gun turned around. I started maneuvering like mad while they continued shooting at me. I was hunched over in the cockpit; in my mind I could just imagine one of those big shells crashing through the tail of my aircraft and into the back of my seat, crushing my body up against the engine firewall."

The Germans did not shoot Conlin down. He converted his airspeed to altitude and zoomed up past 8,000 feet in a wide lefthand turn as he rejoined Ankeny and Starkey. They set a course for Leiston on the Anglican coast, but almost immediately, they were caught up in another vicious flak trap. "It was pretty bad, but we managed to hang together as we cleared it," Conlin recounted. "And along the way, we picked up a straggler, another P-51, from the 354th Fighter Group." They all ultimately made it safely back to England.

Conlin parked his aircraft and debriefed his sortie. "Later," he remembered, "I was at the bar, and the intelligence guys called over and had me come back; they sure were excited. They had reviewed my gun camera film and realized that the aircraft I had shot up in the hangar was one of the new jets, an Ar-234. It was really kind of a big deal because we didn't know much about it at the time."

Ultimately, Germany was not able to capitalize on the promise of the Ar-234. It finally went operational several months after Conlin's mission, but in numbers too few to influence the war. In the field, it proved to be fast and effective and reliable enough for regularly scheduled operations, but the challenges associated with fielding such a new technology, in combination with the shortages and disruptions caused by the unrelenting bombing campaigns, meant that the Ar-234 would never be more than a high-performance bit player.

"I was just sitting there with my arms folded," remembered Howard Wilson, a B-24 pilot with the 461st Bomb Group (H), based out of Cerignola, Italy.[1] It was August 22, 1944, and Wilson was on an indoctrination flight, his second mission, as the guest of another crew.

> We were hitting the railroad yards north of Vienna, Austria. All along the way we were shadowed by Me-110s which tracked our airspeed and altitude, and radioed the information back to the flak batteries. Every so often the P-51s dived down and chased them off, but after a few minutes a new one would show up. We were close to the target area when all of a sudden six enemy aircraft dove down from behind and then came up from under and attacked the box of bombers in front of us. It was unbelievable how fast they were moving. I remember guys were shouting into the radio and intercom, "Jesus Christ, what was that?"
>
> The intelligence officers really gave us a hard time when we got back. They showed me flash cards, and I picked out the Me-262. They told me, "Lieutenant, you couldn't have seen these aircraft because they aren't operational!"

Regardless of what Wilson had or had not seen, it was at about this time that the Germans began to field the Me-262 jet fighter. The aircraft had a top speed of more than 100 miles per hour faster than the best Allied piston-driven aircraft, but they were virtually unknown to rank-and-file American flyers.

Based on a prewar design, the Me-262, aside from the fact that it was jet-propelled, was a radical aircraft. The wing-mounted engines drove the aircraft's designers to sweep the wings moderately to the rear owing to center-of-gravity considerations. This was a happy accident as the mild wing sweep yielded aerodynamic benefits. Nevertheless, the project suffered a painful and protracted development because of technical and political difficulties. Its engines proved to be particularly problematic. Not only was the science of turbojet propulsion new, but the materials required were not particularly well understood, much less readily developed and available. The first Me-262 flight that was entirely jet-propelled (and did not include a back-up piston engine installed in the nose) took place on July 18, 1942, with Jumo 004 engines.

Aside from difficulties with engines, the Me-262 had to compete with other projects for resources and engineering. Its near-term potential was not recognized, and it was not given a high level of priority. Still, development continued, albeit at a sorely fractured pace. Galland flew a more developed example on May 22, 1943, out of Lechfeld near Augsburg. This was long before the Eighth Air Force had grown into the giant it would become—months prior to the first ominous raids on Regensburg and Schweinfurt. He was keenly enthusiastic and recognized immediately that the type, if appropriately armed, would be deadly against the American bomber formations and invulnerable to any fighter escorts the Americans might be able to field in the near term. "On landing, I was more impressed and enthusiastic than I had ever been before. . . . This was not a step forward; this was a leap!"[2]

Yet Galland's enthusiasm did not translate into immediate orders for production of the Me-262. Göring shared Galland's keenness for the new fighter, but Hitler was not persuaded. Exercising maddening obstinacy, Hitler believed that the jet acolytes were overpromising and that the Me-262 would be yet another project that would fail to bear fruit. Accordingly, he did not give it priority over other projects.

However, as the months passed and the design began to prove itself, its potential began to impress Hitler. By then, in late 1943, the RAF and the USAAF had incinerated Hamburg; other cities were also taking a beating. The American daylight raids, although they had stopped penetrating deeply into Germany, were seen as especially dangerous. Hitler was desperate for revenge against the Allies and rightly pointed out that the Me-262 as a bomber would be difficult to intercept.

On the other hand, he failed to appreciate the fact that Germany could never build enough of the type for it to make a difference as a bomber. Nevertheless, he still ordered that it be built to drop bombs.

How much Hitler's meddling overlapped with the type's technical difficulties is unknown, and consequently, it is difficult to assess how much
earlier the Me-262 would have been fielded were it not for him. Technical difficulties aside, American air raids during this period also slowed
down the development and production of the new design.

All the same, the Me-262 started flying operations in the summer of
1944, even before it was fully out of development. The aircraft had star-
tling performance, with a top speed of more than 550 miles per hour and
an operational altitude exceeding 35,000 feet. As a fighter variant, it was
equipped with four 30-millimeter cannon that proved to be devastat-
ingly effective against the bombers. Even deadlier—when they
worked—were the 5.5-centimeter rockets it sometimes carried.

Still, the aircraft had its faults. The biggest problem, as it had
always been, was the engines, which were notoriously unreliable and
averaged only several flights before failing. Moreover, they had to be
handled with great care: the throttles could be advanced only in very
small increments; otherwise, there was a risk that the engines would
flame out. Aerodynamically, the aircraft was superb in straight-line
flight but was a poor-turning dogfighter—in part because the engines
generated such low thrust. Consequently, the Germans tended to execute
slashing, high-speed attacks against the bombers and generally avoided
fighters unless surprise could be achieved. Howard Dentz, a P-47 pilot
with the 365th Fighter Group, recalled an encounter with a group of
Me-262s: "They made a pass at us, but didn't fire and dove away. We
had water injection which gave us almost 2,500 horsepower and could
go like a scalded cat. But they just sort of sniffed at us and decided to
leave before we caught them short of fuel."

However, the Luftwaffe jets did not always get away. John Brown,
a P-51 pilot with the 55th Fighter Group, described how he downed one
of the new fighters on April 10, 1945, when a flight of six Me-262s hit
the bombers that the 55th was escorting. He chased after one of the jets
that had started a wide lefthand circle: "He tried to rack it [his turn] in a
little more. At about 400 yards, I opened fire with a 30-degree deflection
shot. I saw strikes and pieces fly off the jet. . . . At about 350 yards, I
opened fire from dead astern, seeing many strikes. I started to pull out
and at 7,000 feet whipped around in a tight turn and saw this jet hit the
ground and explode."[3]

In fact, it was easiest for Allied pilots to score against the Me-262 when it was taking off and landing; it was particularly vulnerable during these stages of flight since its jet propulsion offered no real advantages at slow speeds. That was the case on March 21, 1945, when Robert Anderson, a P-51 pilot with the 78th Fighter Group, bounced a flight of Me-262s just taking off:

> The last one to take off made a large circle to the left and I cut him off. Just about the time I got into range, he went over the a/d [airdrome]. They chucked everything in the book up at us and I was hit several times by flak at this point. I took a short burst, getting a few hits, when one filament of my sight burned out. The Me-262 got out of range, but I kept after him. He made another turn apparently trying to lead me over the a/d again. I cut him off in this turn, got a good long burst, and observed several hits in the cockpit and left side of the fuselage. We were about 50 feet at the time. The plane went into the ground and exploded.[4]

Nonetheless, these encounters were not the norm: the Me-262s were generally able to stay clear of Allied fighters when they chose to. As Galland and his followers had believed, they were effective against the bombers. JG 7 managed to launch thirty-seven of the jets against the American bomber formations on March 18, 1945. They brought down twelve bombers and a single fighter for the loss of only three of their own. That level of success was something the Luftwaffe had not enjoyed for a very long time.

But it was too little too late. The advanced new fighter was never built in enough numbers to make a difference. What it could have done for the Luftwaffe had it had been fielded a year or even six months earlier remains an open-ended argument.

The case for the Me-163 Komet is less compelling. If the Me-262 was advanced, the Me-163 was even more so. Essentially a small rocket-powered glider with a detachable trolley for takeoff and a landing skid instead of conventional landing gear, the Me-163 made its first flight on September 1, 1941. The airspeeds reached during subsequent flights were astonishing. A month after its first flight, on October 2, 1941, the type exceeded 620 miles per hour—a record for manned flight at the time. It could climb through 35,000 feet in less than three minutes.

All that performance came at a cost. It carried only enough fuel for just more than seven minutes of powered flight. This meant that the Me-163 bases had to be situated along anticipated bomber routes, almost like flak guns. Once launched, the little fighters had time for only a couple of passes at the bombers. Equipped with two 30-millimeter cannon with a slow rate of fire and traveling nearly three times as fast as the bombers, it was actually quite difficult for an Me-163 pilot to kill a bomber, and once the craft was out of fuel, the pilot had to glide back to base at the mercy of Allied fighters.

The Me-163's extremely caustic and volatile fuel, designated C-Stoff, was made up of hydrazine hydrate and methanol. Inside the engine, it was oxidized by T-Stoff, an unstable type of peroxide. Separately and together, they made the aircraft a nightmare to operate. C-Stoff ate through everything, including the skin of the men who serviced and flew it—special clothing had to be worn—and fuel fittings were constantly leaking. Fully fueled aircraft often exploded for no apparent reason. Ultimately, although the Me-163 started operations in the late spring of 1944 and continued flying sporadically until nearly the end of the war, the unfortunate men who flew the tiny rocket plane were credited with only about a dozen aerial victories. It proved to be a huge waste of engineering talent and materiel.

Howard Dentz, a P-47 pilot with the 365th Fighter Group, was among the first to encounter the Me-163:

> We had just bombed a railroad yard near Julich and were circling around at about 14,000 feet just looking for trouble when I tangled with an Me-163. I think it was my most hair-raising experience. I saw the thing and wasn't sure what it was. There was a vertical trail in the sky that seemed to just stop abruptly. I wondered what the hell it was and kept looking and looking where the trail ended. And then I saw this fly-speck growing larger and larger and larger, and I thought to myself that this has got to be one of those Komets we had been briefed about. Sure enough, that's what it was.

I dove away to pick up speed and to keep it in sight. Then I turned back and we came at each other head-on, then he went under me. He hit his rocket again and I pulled up to watch him. I remember thinking that it was a little bit amusing because he wasn't going to hit me and I obviously wasn't going to hit him. He didn't make another pass but instead he pulled way up again and gained altitude, then shut his rocket off and I lost sight of him. Later, I learned that they [the German pilots] didn't think it was worth a damn for attacking other fighters. Because of the high speed, about 600 miles per hour, they couldn't set up properly for an attack.

There has been a recent tendency to glorify and romanticize the men who won World War II. In many cases, they have been stripped of character flaws and vices and even personalities. Although it is well-intentioned, this practice of whitewashing does that generation a disservice.

The truth is that their character was similar to that of the men who preceded and succeeded them. A humorous story that Barrie Davis of the 325th Fighter Group cited drives this point home.[5] It occurred during the shuttle-bombing operations to Ukraine: "A very beautiful Russian girl worked on the chow line. Prior to the 325th's arrival, the American engineers from the Eighth Air Force took delight in greeting the young girl each morning with, 'Say, do you want to fuck?' Well, she thought this was an American greeting and started using it herself. Ultimately, an American officer who was fluent in Russian translated the phrase for the girl." Davis recounted that the horrified young woman "was so embarrassed that she went into hiding. But by the time we arrived, she had been found by her Russian superiors and put back to work on the chow line."

However, the story did not end there. "One of our crew chiefs went down the chow line and realized he was missing a fork. Having no idea of what had happened previously, he innocently told the girl, 'Hey, I wanna fork.' Naturally enough, she misunderstood the request and thought the guy was just another smartass American. She slugged him so hard he hit the ground."

Another episode that took place at Lake Lesina, where the 325th was based, further underscores the point. Davis related that female companionship in the area was "practically nil." He remembered how "[o]ne of our GIs set an Italian whore up in business by Lake Lesina in a military tent with a cot, blankets, and a couple of chairs. It wasn't long before business was thriving. In fact, our young entrepreneur felt compelled to 'borrow' a 2½-ton truck in order to provide transportation for customers to and from the squadron area." Davis remembered that "when the group headquarters learned of this enterprise, the GI was arrested and a court martial was convened. A smart young lieutenant was assigned as his defense attorney. He was convicted of only one crime, the 'misuse of government property, to wit: a tent, blankets, two chairs, and a truck.'"

Dick Brennan of the 367th Fighter Group, a P-38 outfit, recalled a room party among some of the pilots while the unit was based at Juvincourt in France. The only two musical instruments at hand, an accordion and a bass fiddle, were played with vigor: "About fifty well-stewed guys in a four-man room with good music, but LOUD." Following a fire-extinguisher fight, a new arrival came into the room naked except for his shoes. He "turned back the lid on the red hot stove and used it for a urinal." Brennan noted that the resultant vapors cleared the impossibly crowded room almost immediately.[6] It was hardly a Norman Rockwell moment.

The misbehavior was not all shenanigans and harmless tomfoolery. The World War II generation, like every one before or since, had a dark side. Clayton Gross was at Camp Kilmer in 1943 en route to England and acedom with the 354th Fighter Group. He was out late one night when he and his friend heard a woman screaming in the barracks area: "Several more times the scream rent the air as we double-timed around the corner. In a dim light from a distant bulb, I could see a fatigued-uniformed soldier on his knees over the screamer. Both Red and I shouted as we saw the circumstances and the attacker jumped up and took off. On the ground was a very hysterical WAC, her blouse torn open and her skirt and other clothes in disarray.[7]

The Germans had been in Greece at varying levels of strength since 1941. But aside from its strategic geography, Greece offered little of value to the Nazi state. It was riven by numerous political and guerilla factions that fought amongst themselves as much as anyone else. Still, the Germans maintained bases there, and the Fifteenth occasionally took them under attack.

Arthur Fiedler of the 325th Fighter Group, based in Lesina, Italy, remembered:

> Herky Green, our previous group commander, had been bumped up to higher headquarters, and my plane was getting an engine change, so I was assigned to fly his. His crew chief, Sergeant Brown, was really particular about that plane. He got right into my face when I was strapping in. "Lieutenant," he warned, "best you bring this bird back in one piece!"
>
> That day, September 6, 1944, was the only day I flew a mission to Greece. Our squadron put up sixteen aircraft to escort a force of B-24s against the airdrome at Kalamaki, just south of Athens. I was leading a flight of four on the right rear side of the squadron box formation we were flying. My wingman was in position on my left side and the other two-ship element was flying to my right. The commanding officer led the flight of four directly in front of me and the other two flights of four made up the left side of the box.

The mission had been uneventful. The weather developed to be better than expected, and the rendezvous with the bombers went without incident. In fact, expectations were that the entire mission would be fairly routine. The Luftwaffe had been scarce in southern Europe since Ploesti had fallen the previous month, and Athens was not surrounded with the same sorts of flak defenses as tougher targets like Munich or Vienna. The bombers were flying at only about 14,000 feet. "They did this," Fiedler recalled, "whenever they didn't expect a lot of flak or fighters. It was much more comfortable for them to fly at lower altitudes where it wasn't so cold and where the bombers performed better."

The eastbound raid reached a point about fifteen miles west of Athens when Fiedler got his first indication of impending action: "In front of me I saw the tail of the CO's aircraft wagging back and forth as if his wing tanks were stuck and he was trying to shake them off. And then, as I looked through him, in the distance, I could see a pair of Ju-52s very low over the water." The Ju-52 was a lumbering three-engine transport with fixed landing gear that dated from the early 1930s. Nicknamed "Tante Ju" ("Aunt Ju") by its crews, it was sturdy and easy to fly and maintain, yet hopelessly outclassed by later machines. Nonetheless, it remained the backbone of the Luftwaffe's transport force.

The Ju-52s approached the east-west runway at Megara from the east over the Aegean. The base had been active for most of the war and had been variously used by the Greeks, the British, the Italians, and the Germans. Under Axis control since 1941, when the British had been ejected from Greece, the dusty airfield was an occasional target for Allied bombers.

Fiedler did not care about any of that. "I was excited. German aircraft were getting hard to find at that point in the war." Without waiting for any signal or command, Fiedler reflexively released the two seventy-five-gallon fuel tanks that hung from his wings, pushed the nose of his fighter down, and pointed toward the two transports. "I was quite pleased with myself—I was going to beat the entire squadron to those two enemy planes."

Accelerating fast in his steep dive, Fiedler was sure that the two Ju-52s belonged to him. "I thought that I was so smart; I believed that I'd gotten the drop on everyone else. But it didn't turn out that way at all." He took an instant to throw a quick look up at the squadron mates he had just left behind. "There were three other holes in the formation where the other flight leaders had pulled the same trick. I was competing with three other guys—we were all gunning for the same aircraft!"

Fiedler's airspeed in a seventy-degree dive quickly increased past 400 miles per hour. His heading was taking him toward a head-on pass with the two transports. "I realized that there was no way that I was going to be able to come out of my dive and set up in time to make a good head-on pass against those guys. But at the same time I wanted to make sure I beat the other flight leads to the punch."

The P-51 flattened out of its dive as Fiedler hauled back on the control stick and banked left so that he could create enough turning room to make a righthand turn behind the second of the two silvery Ju-52s. It was trailing the first by about 250 yards. "I stayed as fast as I could for as long as I could," Fiedler recalled, "then reversed my turn to the right, chopped the power and slowed to 410 knots and dropped ten degrees of flaps." The flaps added lift to Fiedler's wing and allowed him to tighten his turn. The g forces pushed him down into his seat as he strained to maintain his focus. "It worked," Fiedler said. "I was able to outturn the other guys—they ended up overshooting behind me." Fiedler finished his turn and rolled back to level flight just above the water and about 150 yards behind the trailing enemy aircraft. "I opened fire and didn't really see any hits except on the left main landing gear and the left wing root. Then, all of a sudden, the aircraft exploded and nosed straight down." There likely were no survivors as the Ju-52 hit the beach hard, just at the waterline, and continued to burn.

There was almost no time for Fiedler to set up his attack on the remaining transport, which at that point was just touching down on the runway. Fiedler's Mustang closed on it fast. "I immediately lined up on the other airplane," he said. "It touched down, then bounced high in the air then came back down and bounced again. I fired and hit the runway just behind his port engine. Then I hit his left wing and engine and he exploded." The transport churned up a huge cloud of dust as it careened off the right side of the runway at a forty-five-degree angle. Flashing past, Fiedler saw that it had tipped over on it nose, smoking.

"Then," Fiedler remembered, "another P-51 flew over the top of me so close that it rocked my airplane—I thought we'd had a mid-air." He pulled the Mustang hard into a near-vertical climb to get away from the ground and make certain that he had enough altitude in case he needed to bail out. "But the plane was flying okay and flak was bursting all around me, so I stuffed the nose back down and got right back on the deck—and by that I mean about five or ten feet above the ground."

To the south of Megara, there was a ridge, and Fiedler slid quickly over to the other side, away from the enemy guns and east toward Athens and Kalamaki. "In the distance, I could see enemy aircraft kicking up dust as they came into Kalamaki. I think they were hurrying to get on the ground and away from us. By the time I got within range, the only aircraft that hadn't pulled into a revetment was a lone Ju-88. He was taxiing so fast that I think he may have crunched the aircraft trying to get parked. Anyway, I climbed up to about fifteen feet, let my nose drop slightly and settled the pipper of my gunsight right on his canopy." Six streams of lead converged from the .50-caliber machine guns and tore into the German twin-engine bomber. Fiedler noted with satisfaction how the glass nose of the enemy aircraft disintegrated into a sparkling cloud of crystalline powder.

Fiedler recalled:

> I was really moving—and low. I bent the plane hard over in a left-hand turn and saw this guy running across the airfield toward some sort of gun emplacement. He looked up at me and realized that he wasn't going to make it. I continued my turn around and pointed right at him. Then, I saw him pick something off the ground and heave it up at me; whatever it was went tumbling over my left wing missing my prop by only a couple of feet.
>
> Well that made me mad! So I whipped into a right-hand turn so I could get back around and shoot him. Suddenly, the ground right in front of me erupted in a huge explosion. I felt my right wing lift up and heard a rattle like someone had thrown a bunch of marbles against the plane.

Fiedler instantly lost interest in his belligerent, rock-hurling friend. Shaken by the explosion and uncertain of what had caused it—perhaps antiaircraft fire or a bomb from the raid—he raced for the perimeter of the field and safety. "The aircraft was flying fine," he recalled, "so I ended up joining with some of the other guys and getting back home without any trouble."

Back at Lesina, Fiedler pitched his aircraft into the landing circuit and did two victory rolls for the brace of Ju-52s he had killed. "Sergeant Brown," he recollected, "was so excited he could hardly stand it. He told me: 'Lieutenant, you can fly this bird any old time you want!'"

But there were problems when Fiedler went to debrief the intelligence officer. "I told him about the first Ju-52 I'd shot down, and when I started to debrief him on the second, John Simpson interrupted and said, 'Hey, you didn't shoot that second one down, I did.'" 1st Lt. John Simpson was flying the P-51 that had nearly run into Fiedler. "I couldn't believe it," Fiedler said. "I hadn't seen any hits from his aircraft, and I had been much closer. So we got into a back-and-forth over who shot who and about who almost ran into whom. In the end though, we couldn't agree, so we had to wait until the gun camera film was developed. Well, the aperture of the cameras was set according to what the weather, or light conditions, were supposed to be in the target area. It was forecast to be cloudy but it turned out to be sunny and the film was overexposed and showed nothing."

There was no conclusive way to settle the dispute. "Normally when that happened," Fiedler said, "we either flipped a coin or cut a deck of cards—there were no partial credits in the 325th. It was all or nothing." Simpson approached Fiedler. "He was just about ready to rotate home," Fiedler remembered. "He told me that he was out of opportunities to score any more aerial victories, whereas I was going to be around for another six months. Anyway, he asked me if I'd let him have that second kill. I thought about it a little bit, and in the end, I agreed."

While the fighting raged overseas and the fate of the Luftwaffe seemed more and more to be a foregone conclusion, the USAAF kept up the pace of its aircrew training back in the States. The training program was a huge machine whose weakness—if it had one—was its uncompromising nature. A large number of washouts felt they had been ejected by the system for the smallest deficiencies. On the other hand, the training establishment was not designed to commit scarce resources to save pilot candidates in ones and twos. Rather, it was more efficient to keep turning the crank and use the men who came out the end of the chute.

Still, exceptions were made. "I wrecked a B-17 once," recalled Samuel W. Smith, who eventually made it to the 303rd Bomb Group at Molesworth.[8] "I had a really sharp crew, and we were going through the last phase of combat crew training at Sioux City, Iowa. Anyway, we were about fifteen flights ahead of everyone else in our class." Toward the end of a training mission, Smith bluffed the tower into giving him permission to allow his copilot to make some practice landings. This was normally not allowed without an instructor aboard the aircraft.

"So I gave my copilot the controls and threw my feet up while he made a really nice approach. I started messing with some switches and then watched as he came in for a perfect touchdown." Smith almost swallowed his heart when the B-17 settled through its normal landing attitude and came down belly-first onto the runway. The screech of metal on pavement was ear splitting. "I looked out and saw the propellers hitting the pavement and curling themselves around the engine cowlings as we skidded down the runway."

The bomber ground to a halt. Smith considered the implications of what he had just done and sat nearly paralyzed in his seat. "I tried to think of some reason that I could use to explain my way out of what had happened. But there was no doubt what had happened—I had screwed up in a big way. Tom Zenick, our flight engineer, took a look at the switches. He said, 'Shit, Smitty, you raised the gear.'"

"I came out of the airplane," Smith continued, "and the base CO, who was a colonel, drove up with a captain. I saluted smartly while the colonel shouted at me, asking what had happened. Before I could answer, he yelled at the captain to get up in the cockpit and check the switches. I told him there was no need, but he ordered the captain up there anyway."

The colonel calmed down enough to order Smith to explain himself. "I just told him what happened. I told him that I had made all the decisions—the wrong decisions—and that the entire incident was my fault. Nothing had failed with the aircraft and my crew hadn't done anything wrong; it was all me."

The air corps' decision validated the axiom that "honesty is the best policy." "They held a board a couple of days later," Smith remembered. "That colonel—the one who had been so agitated—actually spoke up on my behalf because I had been forthright and honest. Anyway, they spoke with my crew to see if they would fly with me again. And they reviewed my record. In the end, they decided that if I could pass a check ride, they'd let me stay with the program."

A few days later, Smith was scheduled for his check ride. "They put me with Major Iron Pants," he said. "This guy had a horrible reputation as the meanest, toughest instructor ever. Well, I had one of those days where I couldn't have done anything wrong if I had flown with my eyes closed. He told me that it was one of the best check rides he'd ever given."

Smith ultimately took a B-17 and a crew to England, where they successfully flew twenty-four combat missions. He brought back everyone he took over—unhurt.

CHAPTER 21

More Fighters and G's

Descriptions of fighter operations during World War II often leave out details when in actuality quite a bit of planning went into each mission. Barrie Davis described what was normal for the 325th Fighter Group, based out of Lesina, Italy. "Usually, we knew the day prior to a mission that we would be expected to fly. It was left to the flight leaders as much as possible to decide who the other three pilots in their flight would be. And if the squadron commander wasn't going to lead his unit for some reason, he or the S-3, the operations officer, designated who would take his place. It was up to the planning staff at group headquarters to decide which squadron would lead and what the order of takeoff would be."[1]

If it were determined that a maximum effort was required for a particularly important or tough mission, Davis remembered that every available aircraft would be scheduled. Subsequently, a squadron would fly up to six flights of four aircraft each rather than the typical four flights of four. Early on, it was sometimes difficult to scrape enough healthy pilots together to man every aircraft. However, as the war progressed and replacements became more numerous, pilot shortages were less of a problem.

Davis continued: "We learned of the mission, the target, and our assignments when we reported for the briefing in the morning. The briefings were conducted in a small building near our group headquarters.

There was a large wall map that demarcated our operational area which stretched from where we were based in Italy, west to southern France, north to Switzerland, across southern Germany and into Poland, east to include Czechoslovakia, Yugoslavia, Hungary and Romania, and over to Greece and everything around and in between. Before each briefing the map was covered with a curtain. When all the pilots were seated, the curtain was raised and a red line delineated our mission route. As the curtain was pulled up, if the line ran far north, deep into German territory, the moans from the pilots would get pretty loud."

Unlike the bomber crews, the fighter pilots did not take much time to assemble their formations once they got airborne. Moreover, their aircraft were much faster, so they could afford to take off later and still reach a rendezvous point at the designated time. Consequently, Davis noted that "[w]e could sleep much later in the morning, and usually had time for a good, if early, breakfast before reporting for the briefing."

After receiving the briefing for a given day's mission, there was usually enough time to sort out particulars among the various flight leaders before the pilots collected their flying gear and headed to their aircraft for a quick preflight and engine start. Davis remembered one task that was particularly important especially in the context of missions that could last six hours or more: "The last activity prior to take-off was a visit to the toilet. Our squadron, the 317th, had a six-holer on the flight line, of which we were quite proud. The other squadrons only had four-holers."

Davis also recounted that there "were varying degrees of eagerness among the pilots to fly missions. Some guys had real go-getter attitudes whereas others tended more toward reluctant. Our group commander, Col. Chester Sluder, was really enthusiastic. It bothered him that he was often in the wrong place at the wrong time and missed some of the fights we got into. Consequently he gave standing orders that he was to be notified whenever bogies or bandits were spotted. He really wanted to be in on the kills."

Davis described one mission during which Sluder had a new pilot on his wing. The group got caught up in a freewheeling battle with a large gaggle of Me-109s. Sluder managed to get behind one of the enemy aircraft and double-checked the area around him before closing for the kill. He was stunned to find that his wingman was no longer covering his tail. Rather, an Me-109 pilot had obligingly taken on that task.

As the German opened fire, Davis recalled that, "Colonel Sluder broke hard away and managed to escape his assailant but lost the sure victory he was about to blast out of the sky. When we returned to Lesina and were in debriefing, the colonel queried the young lieutenant: 'Where were you?!?' The young man responded, 'Colonel, I saw we were outnumbered so badly that we didn't have a chance, so I went home!' Sluder was so taken aback that he didn't say a word."

Most fighter pilots were young, usually in their early twenties. Davis and Arthur Fiedler, both aces, were twenty years old when promoted to captain. It was a young man's air war. "Colonel Sluder was thirty-one years old," Davis commented, "and we thought he was too old to fly combat."

Davis, a six-victory ace, described his own attitude: "As for me, I can't say that I looked forward to every mission, but I was willing to take any assignment. The one I refused was after I had seventy missions and was given orders to return to the States. While spending a couple of days waiting for transportation to Naples, there wasn't much for me to do so I attended a briefing for a mission to France." After the pilots went out to their aircraft, Davis was approached by his squadron commander. One of the pilots had taken sick, and a replacement was needed. "He grinned at me and asked, 'Dave, do you want to go?' I started to say yes, but then I thought better of it. I was dressed for travel; my flying gear was packed away, I had low quarter shoes on, no warm underwear, nothing that would have been any good if I had gone down. So I declined. Still, I regret refusing that mission to this day."

Whereas the Eighth Air Force's sphere of operations included western and northern Europe, it could not penetrate deep to the east or south. Those areas belonged to the Fifteenth. By the end of August 1944, the Italy-based Fifteenth had destroyed the oil complexes in Romania, and as summer turned to fall, it continued to hit targets across a wide arc from west to east and north into much of Germany. Its operations encompassed Hungary, which had for some time been a reluctant partner with Germany. The Nazi state relied heavily on raw materials, especially oil, from Hungary.

"We were out on a strafing mission just north of Budapest," remembered Arthur Fiedler of the 325th Fighter Group. "But we really didn't have any business being up there—the weather was atrocious." Nevertheless, Fiedler's squadron, the 317th, found a hole in the clouds and snaked down below the lowest of the ragged layers until all four flights of four aircraft each were strung in a long westbound line along the Danube. According to Fiedler, "The group was supposed to look for things to strafe from Budapest to Vienna. Our squadron was assigned the section from Budapest west to Gyor, about seventy miles away."

The date was October 12, 1944. The Germans were hard-pressed everywhere. Whereas Hungary had been securely under Axis control only a few months earlier, the Soviets had recently swept through Romania and were now pressing hard toward Budapest. Aside from German or Hungarian aircraft, it was possible that the squadron might also encounter Red Air Force machines.

"The four flights were following each other in trail, about a couple of hundred yards apart, right where the river made an east-west turn just north of the city," Fiedler said. "I was leading the third flight and conditions were awful. The clouds were down almost to the ground in places and only went up to about 900 feet at the very best." With barely half a mile of visibility, the pilots strained into the gloom and looked for anything that might merit getting shot at. "We were also very wary of running into high tension wires. Then, out of the corner of my eye, I caught just a glimpse of something at about nine o'clock; it was a big airplane." The mystery aircraft quickly disappeared behind a shroud of ragged clouds, and Fiedler wondered at what he had seen. "At first, I thought that it was a B-17, but that didn't make any sense as there was no reason for a B-17 to have been down there that low with us."

Fiedler gently lifted the nose of his aircraft, dipped the left wing, and slipped over the top of the two-ship element on his left side. "I really didn't want to alert the entire squadron," he said. "If it turned out to be anything, I wanted it to myself." For several seconds, it seemed that Fiedler's disappearing act would succeed. "But my wingman called and asked where I was going. I just kind of shrugged him off and told him that I thought I might have seen something."

It turned out that he had indeed seen something. "I caught sight of it again," Fiedler said. "It was an He-111!" Still, he was cautious. "We had been told that the Russians operated a twin-engine bomber that looked something like an He-111, so I didn't want to start shooting it up right away. I had to make certain that it was an enemy aircraft."

As Fiedler closed the distance to the other aircraft, he noted its unusual camouflage. "It wasn't like anything I'd ever seen. The aircraft was silver, but it was painted with black wavy lines, like sine curves. They were stacked on top of each other and ran across the fuselage at an angle. It was the strangest paint scheme I'd ever seen." He was confused about the nature of the other aircraft. "I was certain it was an He-111—it had that distinctive notch cut out of the bottom of its rudder. But it didn't have any markings. Nothing. I kept getting closer, and closer; I figured I'd see if I could get close enough to see if it had any writing on it at all, Cyrillic or German."

Fiedler finally closed into a parade formation just off the right rear of the aircraft and low. "If I'd pulled my nose up just a little bit I would have cut his right horizontal stabilizer off." Still, there was nothing on the aircraft that marked its nationality. "And then the gunner in the top turret spun around, lowered his guns, and started shooting at me!"

Fiedler had already started to bring his guns to bear as soon as the turret started moving. The sharp sound of bullets striking his aircraft only increased his agitation. Markings or not, he now had a very good indication the other aircraft was not friendly. Fiedler returned fire with his P-51's six .50-caliber guns. "The turret just disappeared from the rounds I put into it. Then I shot away his cockpit and his left engine before putting more bullets into the fuselage and right engine. He nosed over and went right down into the ground."

Fiedler noted almost immediately that the enemy gunner had shot out his pitot system. He had no reliable means of determining his air speed, which was dangerous enough in fine weather, but potentially disastrous in instrument flying conditions. "With no air speed or rate-of-climb indicator, I was in no condition to continue the strafing mission. I immediately established a climb setting on my engine and used my artificial horizon to set an angle that would give me a safe, yet high rate of climb so that I could get above the clouds as quickly as possible. As soon as I did, I set course for home!"

Fiedler hoped that he would find someone to join so that they could pace him on the approach to landing. Without an air speed indicator, he might get too slow and stall. Low to the ground, he might not recover before crashing. "There wasn't anyone else airborne when I got back so I called the tower, told them I was going to land uphill, and proceeded to do so. It turned out to be one of the best landings I ever made. However I didn't realize that the He-111 gunner had also shot my hydraulic system out. Even though the flap handle was down, I had no flaps."

Without the extra drag that the flaps would have normally provided, the Mustang rolled at a faster than normal clip. "As I approached the end of the runway, I applied the brakes only to find I didn't have any! I yelled at the tower to stop the trucks that were crossing the end of the runway only to have them reply that they had no radio contact with them."

Fiedler was still making about sixty miles per hour as he approached the end of the runway.

> I realized that all I could do was make a ground loop, and I spun the airplane off the left side of the runway. I was still in the cockpit when a lieutenant colonel jumped up on my wing from out of nowhere and screamed at me, "What the hell do you think you're doing?" I explained that I had been shot up by a bomber. He then asked if I had shot the bomber down, to which I responded in the affirmative. He patted me on the shoulder, shouted, "Good work!" and disappeared.
>
> "I visited with my ground crew for a little bit and then went off to debriefing. I described the entire engagement with the He-111. Then, incredibly, my wingman stepped up and explained that he was the one who had shot it down. I was stunned. I couldn't believe what he said.

A sharp exchange followed during which Fiedler's wingman kept up his insistence that it was he who had downed the enemy aircraft. "Well, we had the gun film developed," Fiedler recounted, "and sure enough, my camera showed that I had shot that airplane down from very close range." His wingman's gun film confirmed that Fiedler had indeed bagged the enemy aircraft. Fiedler's aircraft could be seen maneuvering about the He-111 as he gunned it into the ground. But incredibly, through the entire sequence, the wingman was firing his guns toward both Fiedler and the other aircraft.

"He had been shooting from much too far away—about 1,000 yards. He couldn't have hit anything from that range. Of course, I got credit for the kill. And I made sure that wingman never flew in my flight again."

Aerial victories and the credit for them were a serious subject for most of the USAAF's fighter pilots. Many of them saw them as tangible metrics of their contribution to the war effort and a validation not only of the nation's investment in their training, but of their personal skills. Of course, there was also a certain panache and glamor associated with being an ace, an unofficial status granted for downing five or more enemy aircraft in aerial combat. Herman Schonenberg was a P-51 pilot with the 55th Fighter Group. He recalled an incident that underscores how important—almost to a ridiculous degree—credit for an aerial victory was to some of his comrades.[2]

On the day of his second mission, August 27, 1944, the 55th was part of the escort for a bombing raid to Berlin. Once freed from its escort duties, his flight started a descent to hunt for targets of opportunity. Schonenberg recalled:

We were headed south when we encountered several airplanes. My flight leader and I attacked a twin-engine Do-217 that was towing a big glider. When we started our attack, the Germans released the tow rope. Evidently the glider was loaded with a lot of people because they were shooting at us from inside as we made our firing passes. That was very disconcerting. The Do-217 went down into an open field, skidded a considerable length, and fired up. The glider was completely destroyed. I don't know what they were loaded with but both aircraft burned pretty badly when hit.

My flight leader was given credit for the Do-217 although I also got some pretty good hits on it. It was his last mission, and we both lucked out. He got his only victory, and I inherited his aircraft and crew. I also remember—it was a funny thing— some of the other guys almost got into a fistfight back in the ready room over who shot the glider down. Eventually two pilots were given one-half credit each.

Indeed the entire notion of crediting aerial victories or kills and tallying up individual scores has been the subject of intense debate since World War I. Nearly every book about fighter combat has one version or another of "The List": a tally of the highest-scoring aces and the number of aerial victories with which they were credited. At the top of the Luftwaffe roster is Erich Hartmann with 352 kills. The highest American scorer in Europe was Francis Gabreski with credit for 28 aerial victories. Johnnie Johnson led the RAF with 38 confirmed kills.

But Erich Hartmann did not score 352 aerial victories. Neither did Francis Gabreski score 28 or Johnnie Johnson 38. It is almost certain that few of the credited scores of any of the highest-scoring aces are an exact reflection of the number of aircraft they actually shot down. Their scores were likely lower. There were real challenges associated with crediting, without error, a definite number of downed enemy aircraft to an individual pilot.

The biggest issue was the very dynamic nature of aerial combat. When aircraft were hurtling through the air at hundreds of miles per hour trying to kill each other in three dimensions, there was no single pilot who could keep track of it all. Fear, adrenaline, and the basic task of tending to business in one's own aircraft, not to mention watching a wingman or a flight lead—and actually accomplishing the mission—all tended to warp reality. It would be odd indeed if there was no confusion about what happened.

Gun camera film, while helpful, was not the end-all in the confirmation of kills. It could provide indisputable proof of a victory; after all, if the film clearly showed an enemy pilot bailing out or a wing falling off or the aircraft exploding into pieces, there was no doubt that the aircraft was destroyed. However, a puff of smoke or a flash of flame were indications that required subjective interpretation. There was more than one argument between a pilot and a debriefing officer about whether the damage to an enemy aircraft recorded by a gun camera indicated a killing blow.

Moreover, not every fighter was equipped with a gun camera, or if a fighter had one, it frequently did not work. The images were often of very poor quality. Vibrations from the guns could make the recorded images extremely sketchy and difficult to evaluate. Sometimes there was no film. Primitive conditions in some locations were not conducive to the type of handling demanded by sensitive film and optical equipment. One pilot remembered his experience with watching gun-camera film: "There was one ace who would get so close to the enemy aircraft that the whole screen would be filled with just a *part* of the plane he was shooting down. There was no question about his kills. Then there were guys . . . well they'd put in a claim for something, and all you could see was a dark speck or something, all blurry, on the movie screen."

There were other shortcomings associated with crediting kills solely on the basis of gun-camera footage. There were aircraft that had already been mortally hit yet were hit and claimed again by another eager adversary. Gun films for the most part were not of sufficient quality to show if an aircraft had already been damaged. Then there was the other side of the issue. No doubt there were aircraft that were mortally hit but not obviously so. They went down and were never credited to anyone as victories.

In the absence of definitive film footage, most units required confirmation of a kill by another witness. In some cases, this was easy enough, as the wingmen or other members of the same unit were nearby and the action was isolated. But in big, wheeling melees that encompassed many units and aircraft, this could be difficult. With flaming wrecks everywhere, enemy and friendly, it might not be difficult to convince oneself that he saw the kill his buddy claimed.

That mistakes and vagaries were sometimes the norm is borne out by the records. Widely written about are the inflated claims of both sides during the Battle of Britain and the subsequent fighting over the English Channel. Records show that both German and British pilots made claims two, three, and sometimes four times higher than the actual number of aircraft downed. Similarly, USAAF claims of enemy aircraft downed during bombing missions into Germany were often hugely at odds with German records of losses.

The whole issue of disparate claims did not exist, for the most part, because the pilots were chasing glory or medals. As mentioned earlier, it was very difficult to keep track of what was going on during aerial combat. If a pilot put bullets into an enemy aircraft and caused it to start smoking, he probably did not follow it to the ground to watch it explode, particularly if the enemy's wingman was pulling for a shot on him. In his own mind, it was probably easy to believe that the enemy aircraft was damaged so badly that it went down. Afterward, during debriefing, if he could find someone to corroborate a mortally wounded aircraft in that same area and at that same time, he may have been awarded the kill, whether it was valid or not.

The process of awarding aerial victories varied greatly from service to service and also depended on the location and timeframe. The USAAF in Europe, late in the war, was particularly stringent. "I don't remember anything that didn't seem right," remembered one pilot. Confirmation practices also varied by nation. Although careful postwar research has done much to clear some of the confusion, ultimately, the true tallies of most of the high scorers are simply unknowable. If nothing else, their officially credited victories serve as a relative measure of their skills.

Pilots experience g forces—accelerations of gravity—as they maneuver their aircraft. A person at rest is subject to a single g. A pilot making a gentle turn experiences just more than one g, whereas a pilot aggressively flying a modern fighter with an exceptional thrust-to-weight ratio might regularly sustain six or more g's with periods of up to nine g's or even more. A common misperception is that World War II pilots regularly endured these sorts of bone crushing g's as they turned and twisted and tumbled in the skies over Europe. The reality was somewhat different.

Fighters of the period were not powerful enough to maintain high air speeds in hard turns, a prerequisite for sustained high g's. Although it is true that at high air speeds, a World War II pilot could pull back on his control stick aggressively enough to lose consciousness or even cause the aircraft to come apart, none of the aircraft could maintain enough airspeed to generate those sorts of g's more than momentarily. The reason was that the drag created by an aggressive turn caused the aircraft to lose air speed, and the engines were not powerful enough to overcome this drag. The harder a pilot turned, the quicker his airspeed decayed, and because high g's generally required high air speeds, the g's became progressively lower.

Consequently, a close-quarters dogfight was generally not a high-g affair. Physics precluded it. The same is true even in modern air combat. For instance, depending on the situation, an air-to-air engagement can be so hard-turning that it degenerates into a slow-speed groveling match in which neither aircraft is capable of pulling more than a couple of g's.

Still, it would not be true to say that a World War II dogfight was not hard work. With the body under g's, the heart has to work much harder to pump blood to the brain, and even a load of three or four g's could quickly wear a pilot down. Beyond about four g's, most pilots begin to feel some discomfort, experience some degradation in alertness and lose visual acuity, particularly in the peripheral field of view. As g's increase past about six, the probability of blackout is great.

Barrie Davis, an ace who flew P-47s and P-51s with the 325th Fighter Group out of Italy, recalled his experiences with the phenomenon of high g's: "The only plane I flew with a g-meter was the AT-6 we used for instrument training. Several times we used it to determine who could take the most g's. We found that we would gray out at about four g's and black out when the g-forces exceeded five. We had no g-suits and fought the effects of g's by yelling and tensing our abdominal muscles."

Davis also remembered his experience with g's during combat. On July 2, 1944, the 325th, equipped with P-51s, was assigned to protect a formation of Fifteenth Air Force B-24s on a mission against the Bákos Locomotive Depot in Budapest, Hungary. Davis was one of the squadron's flight leaders that day. "One pilot from my flight aborted, leaving three of us to continue. South of Budapest, I saw three vapor trails several thousand feet above us. I called out the bogies [unknown aircraft] and took my wingmen in a climbing turn to the east and into the sun."

The three Mustangs closed the distance to the other aircraft, which turned out to be Me-109s. Davis, in a lefthand turn, fired on the lead aircraft from its low, ten o'clock position. At the same time, the German fighters turned toward him and his flight. "Coolant streamed from the enemy plane, and he attempted to escape by diving straight down. I followed, firing, but scored no hits. Both aircraft were at full throttle in a vertical dive, approaching their air speed limitations. The German fighter began to come apart. "At 18,000 feet, pieces began to rip loose from the Me-109. First, part of the engine cowling came loose, then the right wingtip and parts of the right horizontal stabilizer. I was indicating more than 510 miles per hour, still diving straight down."

Davis's air speed was beyond prescribed safe limits for his aircraft, yet the Mustang held together. The German pilot's mount was beyond saving. Davis continued: "At 15,000 feet, the enemy pilot jettisoned his canopy and bailed out. His parachute deployed immediately, but the silk ripped loose from the shroud lines and the poor guy plummeted to the earth." Davis took an instant to register how the ripped parachute twisted lazily and uselessly toward the earth.

The enemy pilot was falling to his death. Davis would join him if he did not get his own aircraft out of its screaming dive. Doing so required him to pull back on the control stick with enough strength to keep him from hurtling into the ground, but not so much as to tear his aircraft apart or render himself unconscious. "I started a pull-out, and the centrifugal force [g-loading] blacked me out." Davis was out cold. Nonetheless, the action he had taken to get out of the dive worked, and the Mustang slowed down as it nosed skyward. "I regained consciousness gradually, looked out, and found myself in a climbing turn."

As he collected his wits, Davis noticed light-caliber shell bursts in front of him at about 18,000 feet. "At first I thought it was ack-ack, but that didn't make sense because the smaller shells would have never made it to that altitude. That's when I looked to my rear and found an Me-109 lobbing shells at me!" Fortunately for Davis, the enemy pilot's gunnery was off the mark.

Davis turned hard into the Me-109 in an effort to force the enemy pilot to overshoot. "After a short but spirited fight, I began firing at him from 250 yards and closed the range down to 50 yards." Like the earlier pilot, this one also tried to escape by pulling over into a steep dive. Davis followed. "At 13,000 feet, the Me-109 exploded, and it seemed like the lights went out. Oil from the explosion completely coated my windshield and canopy, leaving me completely in the dark—I could see nothing outside." Davis turned his aircraft for home, struggling to see well enough to navigate. "When I got back to Lesina, I cracked the canopy and, still unable to see ahead, made a fair landing by looking out the side."

Safely back on the ground, Davis taxied back to his parking area. "Earlier, we had experienced trouble with oil leaking from the propeller, and my crew chief, John Mooney, climbed up on the wing and apologized thinking that the oil was from the propeller. He was relieved when I told him, 'Don't worry, Sarge, that's German oil!'"

This episode not only offers an excellent example of how g forces could affect a pilot in combat, but it also highlights the sturdiness and outstanding flying qualities of the Mustang. Davis reflected on both: "I have no idea how long I was blacked out. It was my good fortune to have been flying a superb airplane that could withstand the terrific g forces. From the time I started my pull-out until I regained my senses with the plane gaining altitude at 18,000 feet, the plane was flying itself."

Howard Dentz, a Thunderbolt pilot with the 365th Fighter Group, offered anecdotal evidence that the P-47 was one of the sturdiest fighters ever built where g-forces were concerned. "A P-51 lost his wing right in front of me," Dentz recalled. "We were both chasing the same Me-109. The 109 pulled it in real tight, and when the P-51 tried to follow it, his wing flew off, and he fireballed." Continuing after the German aircraft, Dentz started disintegrating it with his eight .50-caliber machine guns before it disappeared in the clouds.

He offered more evidence in favor of the P-47: "Our engineers estimated that one of our pilots pulled over eleven g's—and with no g-suit. He was horribly messed up and lost a piece of his colon. About four inches of it—it just turned inside out. He bled terribly but fortunately didn't faint and was able to get it back on the ground. He had had an FW-190 on his tail and needed a high-g turn to shake it. You could bend that P-47 but you couldn't break it."

Aerial combat during World War II was also exhausting because the control forces were so heavy. On the other hand, because the pilot often strained as he worked the controls, his muscles tensed and made it more difficult for the g's to drain the blood from his head. This tensing or straining is a technique that has long been taught in order to increase aircrew resistance to heavy g's.

The forebear of the modern g-suit was introduced toward the end of the war. Most pilots never had an opportunity to wear it since it arrived so late. Like modern g-suits, it was similar to a snug pair of chaps or trousers with a hose that connected to a fitting in the cockpit. As the aircraft sensed g's, pressurized air was pumped into the suit. This caused air bladders inside the suit to inflate and squeeze the pilot's lower abdomen and legs so that the blood stayed in the upper body and head. The g-suit increased a pilot's tolerance by approximately a single g.

CHAPTER 22

The Big Blow That Wasn't

As the summer of 1944 went on, Spaatz and his USSTAF were fully mature. He had the bombers to do the bombing that had to be done, and those bombers had the ability to go virtually anywhere he cared to send them. Eisenhower had relinquished direct control of the Eighth and Fifteenth so that the strategic campaign could be pursued with more vigor. Importantly, although it would occasionally show signs of resurgence, the Luftwaffe was largely beaten. Furthermore, Arnold's frenetic interference was easing. Essentially, there was little concern about whether the Eighth and Fifteenth would be able to achieve their objectives; the main debate was about how to use them in the most efficient manner. The situation had changed dramatically in Spaatz's favor during the two years since he had come to Europe.

By the fall of 1944, *General der Jagdflieger* Adolf Galland had been in charge of the Luftwaffe's fighter forces for nearly three years. During that time, he had seen those forces frittered away in one failed campaign after another. Virtually always outnumbered, his units had been forcibly ejected from North Africa and the Mediterranean not only by superior numbers of aircraft, but by superior numbers of good aircraft flown by competent pilots.

In the East, Galland's pilots were also outnumbered. And if the skill and initiative of the average Soviet pilot were not quite up to those of his own flyers, it was much better than it had been only a year or two earlier, and it was steadily improving. Worse, the Red Air Force, no matter how badly the Luftwaffe handled it, kept growing. The fight in the East was a giant, seeping hurt for which the Luftwaffe could find no cure.

But the great destroyer of Galland's men and machines was the daylight bombing campaign over Germany that the Americans mounted almost daily from their bases in England and Italy. Practically no one in the Luftwaffe survived any length of time against the seemingly innumerable aircraft the Americans piloted with such skill. Inexperienced Luftwaffe fighter pilots were sent against the great bomber streams only to be overwhelmed by the better-trained and much more numerous American escorts. Simply getting into position to fire on a bomber was a challenge, and actually knocking one of the big aircraft down before getting bagged by the protective fighters was an enormous accomplishment. It was dangerous work, and an assignment to Luftflotte Reich, the organization charged with protecting Germany from the American bombers, was tantamount to a death sentence.

The situation was just as bad over the battlefields of France. Following the Normandy invasion, Galland had been forced to throw his reserves above the hard-pressed German Army only to see the men and machines serve as little more than target practice for the American and British pilots. To be fair, his men still knocked down enemy aircraft, but not enough. Occasional tactical successes were of little consequence in the grander scheme.

The Luftwaffe's political and military situation was a desperate one. Its flak and fighter defenses were unable to protect Germany's war industry and had scant impact on the battlefield, at least in the West. At the same time, it consumed enormous resources and labor. It was true that it had a wealth of aircraft the likes of which it had never enjoyed before. In fact, under Albert Speer's direction, fighter production had increased through the summer and peaked at more than 3,700 aircraft during September. But it was also true that those aircraft were disappearing at the hands of barely qualified pilots. The Luftwaffe was a moribund fighting organization that increasingly was little more than an ill-trained flying mob. Hitler himself, in a furious frenzy over the impotence of the Luftwaffe's fighters against the Allied air raids, told Galland that he would disband the fighter arm.[1]

Desperate for a plan that might produce results, Galland latched onto the one idea he believed might have an impact on the USAAF bomber streams. He would try to out-American the Americans. No longer would he—at the direction of his superiors—fling disparate groups of aircraft at the massive formations only to have them shot down piecemeal. Rather, just as the Eighth and Fifteenth Air Forces were crushing Germany day-by-day with immense masses of aircraft, he would hold back his fighters from the bloody gristmill in the West until he had an enormous reserve of men and machines. Then, on a clear day when his neophyte pilots could see to take off and land, he would hammer the bomber streams with a single stroke made up of an enormous swarm of fighters.

For *Der Grosse Schlag* ("The Great Blow"), Galland began to set aside fighters and pilots. His goal was to build a force of more than 3,000 aircraft so that at a minimum, he could strike the bombers with more than 2,000 fighters as they approached their targets and then mount another several hundred more sorties as the bombers retraced their routes back to their bases. Galland hoped in this single engagement to shoot down 400 or 500 heavy bombers and was prepared to accept losses of a like number of his own aircraft and approximately 150 pilots. "This," he wrote, "was going to be the largest and most decisive air battle of the war."

But even Galland could not resist the temptation to commit his aircraft before he had the great force readied; on November 2, 1944, he was guilty of the same sort of squandering that he disparaged in his leaders. On that date, the Eighth put nearly 1,200 heavy bombers over central Germany against various oil targets. Even though the weather was marginal, Galland sent nearly 500 fighters after them. Of that number, only about 300 made contact with the bombers.

The greenness of the Luftwaffe pilots was apparent to the American escorts. Capt. Glenn Webb was a P-51 pilot with the 20th Fighter Group who, with his wingman, had followed a two-plane group of Me-109s through the clouds as they dived away southwest of Merseberg: "Shortly we passed over a grass landing field and got some light flak.

I spotted a 109 50 feet below flying 180 [degrees] to me on my right, 300 yards away. I broke to the right and got on his tail 800 yards behind. I closed a bit when he made a snap turn to right and crashed into the ground."[2]

Donald Penny, a P-51 pilot with the 339th Fighter Group, had an encounter that was also indicative of the poor quality of the German pilots at that time: "I and my flight dove to attach [sic], one of the ME 109's broke up, and the other broke down; I followed the one that broke up. The pilot bailed out immediately with out [sic] my having to fire at him."[3]

The day was a disaster for the Germans. The bombers obliterated their targets while the Luftwaffe lost 120 aircraft and 70 pilots. The Eighth lost 40 bombers, only 26 of them to fighters. It had cost the Luftwaffe nearly 5 fighters to bring down each heavy bomber. This was hardly the effect that Galland was hoping for. If the exchange ratio held, it would cost him not 400 fighters to destroy 500 bombers, but more than 2,000 fighters and well more than a 1,000 pilots. Although a larger force would, at some point, overwhelm the escorting fighters, he still had nothing close to the numbers of men and aircraft required to achieve the results he wanted. Hitler was unimpressed, calling the results "thoroughly unsatisfactory."[4]

Nevertheless, the German high command refused to execute the "Big Day" concept as it was designed and continued to test it in poor weather with half-measures of aircraft that were well less than the numbers originally intended. There were three additional large—but not large enough—actions launched on November 21, 26, and 30. The results were no more encouraging. If the definition of stupidity was repeatedly making the same mistake with the expectation of a different outcome, then these ill-considered actions were clear indicators of the dismal state of the Luftwaffe's leadership.

The clashes did show that there were still a few pilots in the Luftwaffe who were able to give good accounts of themselves. Allen Rosenblum was a P-47 pilot with the 78th Fighter Group who encountered a group of Me-109s near Hannover on November 21. He turned to give chase with the rest of his flight:

My right wing tank would not release but, after pulling manual release and side-slipping my plane, it released. I had meanwhile lost my element leader. . . . I looked to the right and saw a gaggle of P-47's chasing three bandits. I took out after them and when a rat-race ensued I was caught in the middle of it. One Me-109 broke across my nose, so I took out after him. We fought for ten minutes. I fired several bursts and finally saw strikes on his canopy and wings. He started into a spin . . . and spun into the ground and exploded.[5]

This particular fight was notable for a couple of reasons. First, in a sky full of aircraft, Rosenblum and his opponent were unmolested during what was a very long fight. Second, the length of the fight highlights the point that the top-line fighters of both sides were fairly equally matched. In the end, though, the American pilot prevailed, and the Luftwaffe lost another from what had become a very small pool of skilled pilots.

"The Big Day" died before it was ever executed. Hitler was unmoved by Galland's enthusiasm for the concept and underwhelmed at the results his pilots had delivered during November. Consequently, he ordered the bulk of the fighter units to prepare to support offensive operations in the West. The Luftwaffe, tottering but upright, was about to be misused once more.

In the meantime, operations continued over the near-static front in the West. Howard Dentz of the 365th Fighter Group scored his second aerial victory on December 8, 1944, while on an armed-reconnaissance mission:

There was a squadron of us, and I was flying in White Flight as the top-cover leader. We were between cloud layers at about 14,000 feet and the visibility was poor—very hazy. Enemy fighters had been reported in the area although none of us could see them.

I looked left, then I looked right and to our rear, and there were four Me-109s sitting on our asses in a perfect formation to match ours. At that instant it struck me how the Germans were so overconfident—they liked to show off. This guy had obviously set up each one of his pilots to shoot down one of us. But they were still a little bit too high, and were back on the throttles to keep from overrunning us.

I don't know what made me do it, because I'd never done it before. I chopped back the throttle and those big propeller blades went into fine pitch. The airplane lost about fifty miles an hour just like that. In an instant all four 109s were right in front of me. These guys were really sharp, because they all started to roll to dive out of the way. I fired and cut the tail off of the leader as he rolled and started to go down. He bailed out.

I banked around, and my element leader was peeling off to go after the other three but he lost them in the clouds. So I came back and photographed this German in the parachute. We had a two-way switch; camera, and guns with camera. So I turned off the guns and came around and took his picture, and scared the shit out of him I'm sure. But I wanted to confirm my kill in case my wingman had missed it.

But not all of the pilots of the 365th were so gallant. "We had a West Point graduate leading the squadron on a day when we had been out strafing railroads and shoving bombs into tunnels," Dentz recalled. "He spotted an old Me-109, the kind that still had braces under the tail [Me-109E]. He dove down on this guy who obviously got quite shaken when he saw thirty-six P-47s coming at him. The German just rolled over and bailed out. When he hit the ground our flight leader came back around and strafed and killed him. I never quite forgave him for that. I was very full of the idea of chivalry and that is absolutely the way that most of us felt."

The aircraft that Galland had been husbanding for his massive blow were taken from him in order to support Gerd von Rundstedt's Ardennes offensive, more commonly known as the Battle of the Bulge. The operation commenced during the early-morning hours of December 16, 1944; weather was so poor that the Luftwaffe's fighters could offer little support. On the other hand, the much more numerous Allied aircraft were not able to fly either. Nevertheless, when the weather cleared, the German aircraft were sent out to support ground operations. As they had been during the summer over France, they were brutally savaged during the next couple of weeks. Austrian flak officer Karl Laun recalled the performance of the supporting Luftwaffe fighters at the commencement of the operation: "Instead of the advertised 1,000 planes, approximately 50 Messerschmitt and Focke Wulfs arrive, who are evidently, very reluctant to enter into dogfights. One can easily sense it from down here; how they wriggle and turn to get out of the *Jabos'* [U.S. fighters] field of vision."[6]

CHAPTER 23

The General Falls

Henry Hughey distinctly remembered the morning of December 24, 1944: "It was a clear and beautiful day." Hughey was a B-17 ball-turret gunner with the 487th Bomb Group (H), based out of Lavenham, Suffolk. From high above the North Sea as the group climbed to altitude, he had watched the morning dawn crystal clear. That day's mission would prove to be a brutal one. The 487th was scheduled to be at the head of the biggest bombing mission in history. More than 2,000 heavy bombers were scheduled to hit Luftwaffe airfields, German Army targets, and lines of communication in order to provide relief for hard-pressed U.S. ground units. The Ardennes offensive—Hitler's desperate lunge back toward the Atlantic—was nearing a culmination point.

Brig. Gen. Frederick W. Castle, the assistant commander of the 4th Combat Bomb Wing of the 3rd Air Division, was aboard the lead aircraft of the 487th. The bragging rights for heading the USAAF's most massive bombardment effort of the war would belong to him. The mission was expected to be an unusually tough one, and he had himself written into the schedule in place of the original pilot. Huey recalled his reaction upon learning that the general would be at the front of the formation: "Castle had a reputation for taking the tough ones, so we were all a bit anxious."

Indeed, the thirty-six-year-old Castle had been a major player within the Eighth Air Force since early in the war. When Eaker, still in the

United States, chose his initial staff of six officers, Castle was among them. He was known as a level-headed, hard-working, and ambitious warhorse. After doing more than his fair share of staff work, he asked for and received command of a heavy bomb group, the 94th. Although somewhat aloof, he was respected by his men, and he performed well enough to get promoted out of the assignment he had worked so hard to get.

This particular mission—officially, it was Mission Number 760—was Castle's thirtieth. The group was on schedule when Castle, sitting in the copilot's seat of *Treble Four*, pointed the formation east. Sharing the cockpit with Castle, at the pilot's position, was Capt. Robert Harriman. Winds along the way put the stream of big bombers about seventeen minutes behind schedule as it neared the third checkpoint over Belgium at 26,000 feet. The group's fighter escort, delayed by patchy fog at its own base, failed to make the rendezvous.

Hughey's ship, piloted by Richmond Young, was also at the vanguard of the massive string of bombers; it was flying in the number-three position on *Treble Four*'s left wing. Folded into the glass bubble of his gun turret, Hughey watched the white-checked landscape below him rotate as he scanned for enemy fighters. "I always kept that thing spinning. I had to—I didn't have eyes in the back of my head."

Harriman and Castle aboard *Treble Four* got into trouble early. The number-one engine had been streaming oil for a while and finally began to lose power. Heavily loaded as the ship was, it was difficult for the two pilots to stay at the head of the bomber stream. It was then that the formation came under attack, which Hughey described:

> I saw an Me-109 go down the right side of our aircraft from front-to-rear. I called out, "There goes a 109 . . . and another . . . and another!" Three fighters passed close by us—they had attacked from twelve o'clock high. From that point we started getting hit pretty hard.
>
> I remember swinging around and looking up toward the nose and seeing the number three engine on Castle's aircraft smoking. And then, the landing gear came down! Now that made me mad. It really did. That was the signal to surrender. You don't find that in any of the reports. But I was right there. I had as perfect a

view as could be, and I know that landing gear came down. I later heard that he might have been trying to signal that he was passing the lead to his deputy because his radio was shot out. Anyway, the landing gear came back up almost immediately.

Actually, there were others whose recollections aligned with Hughey's. Robert W. Brown was a pilot farther back in the formation. He later wrote:

In seconds, I saw fire streaming from the general's B-17 number-three engine and right wing root. Flames reached its horizontal stabilizer and burned the fabric off the right elevator. The left wingman's bomber [Hughey's ship] was also smoking, but it didn't show any fire as it turned slowly to the left and disappeared from my view. Then I saw the general turn his Fort down and to the left, and the Fort to his right also turned away from its position, leaving a slim trail of smoke. I don't recall seeing it again. I watched as the Fort's landing gear was lowered—an accepted indication that you were out of the fight.[1]

Unable to maintain speed with at least two engines failed, Harriman and Castle slid *Treble Four* to the left and out of the formation. The German fighter attacks continued. The 487th's low squadron, the 836th, was hammered particularly hard: six of its thirteen aircraft were brought down despite the furious fire its gunners put out.

Hughey was busy too. "There were Me-109s and FW-190s all over the place. An FW-190 came in from level at about four o'clock and started hammering away at us. He put cannon fire into an aircraft further right in the formation and blew a tremendous hole in the tail section right in front of the guns. I knew the gunner—his name was Keith Cole—and I thought to myself, well, Cole's gone. I saw him afterward, though; he only had two little pieces of shrapnel in his fanny!"

Hughey opened fire with his twin .50-caliber machine guns. A double trail of half-inch slugs arced out from his turret and down into the nose of the rapidly closing fighter. "I hit him in the engine. I saw smoke, then fire. I put in a claim for that one." Hughey did not have time to watch the FW-190 hit the ground; the fighting was too intense.

It had gone from intense to hopeless for Harriman, Castle, and the rest of the crew aboard *Treble Four*. Their crippled ship attracted more Me-109s, and they rapidly lost altitude as the German fighters took turns shooting them up. The tail gunner and the radio navigator were wounded, and the bomber began to burn. It was apparent that the ship was beyond saving, and the order to bail out was given.

The men scrambled to get out. Four of the crew quickly obeyed those orders. The bombardier, Paul Biri, was about to jump when Harriman appeared and asked him to wait. Harriman could not find his parachute; if he could not locate it soon, he wanted to jump together with Biri.[2] If Harriman did find his chute, he did not use it. He never got out of the bomber. As it descended through 12,000 feet, the right wing outboard of the number-four engine exploded and fell away. The aircraft went into a violent spin to the right, and Biri was thrown clear. *Treble Four* continued to come apart as it fell toward the earth. Biri opened his parachute and made it to the ground, where he injured his ankle upon landing.

He was luckier than another member of his crew. Claude Rowe, an officer tail gunner, was likely the first one out. Blood discovered in the tail section at the crash site indicated that he was probably wounded before he jumped. In any event, he was killed by a German pilot as he descended in his parachute. A French schoolboy recounted what he saw that day when he, his classmates, his parents, and a group of American soldiers watched a handful of parachutes float down from the spiraling wreck of *Treble Four*:

> Over our heads an abominable action took place. A German Focke-Wulf 190 fighter made a long circle, and returned to fire upon one of the parachutes descending towards us. We distinctly saw the poor fellow being jarred around by machinegun fire that was hitting him; his parachute was also being hit, and it began to descend more rapidly towards the countryside of Seny. In the schoolhouse, there were cries of horror and rage.[3]

Claude Rowe's body was recovered. An official investigation noted that he had parachuted and that he had apparently been killed by enemy fire.

The radio operator, Lawrence Swain, was also killed in the jump from the bomber. His parachute caught fire as he fell away from the wreck. Unable to hold air, the parachute fluttered rather than achieving a full blossom. Swain plummeted to his death. Harriman and Castle were also killed. Their remains were found in the wreck and on the ground surrounding it, as well as in the nearby trees. A single dog tag, Castle's, was also found among the debris. Six of *Treble Four*'s crew of ten survived.

Hughey had seen Harriman and Castle's B-17 catch fire and spiral earthward, but he was too far removed to have any idea what was happening to the ship and crew. He was also busy fighting the surprisingly numerous and ferocious force of enemy fighters. Rescue finally came in the form of P-51s. They engaged the Germans with an incredible fierceness, and the relief for the 487th was almost immediate. The group made its run to the target virtually unmolested.

"The target was the airfield at Babelhausen," Hughey remembered. "We really hit it good—right on the mark. It was like a Hollywood film. We saw the bombs marching right down the runways. The hangars and other buildings just disintegrated into splinters."

In due course, Castle was awarded the Medal of Honor for his leadership of Mission Number 760 and for his performance aboard *Treble Four*. His citation read:

> He was air commander and leader of more than 2,000 heavy bombers in a strike against German airfields on 24 December 1944. En route to the target, the failure of 1 engine forced him to relinquish his place at the head of the formation. In order not to endanger friendly troops on the ground below, he refused to jettison his bombs to gain speed maneuverability. His lagging, unescorted aircraft became the target of numerous enemy fighters which ripped the left wing with cannon shells, set the oxygen system afire, and wounded 2 members of the crew. Repeated attacks started fires in 2 engines, leaving the Flying Fortress in imminent danger of exploding. Realizing the hopelessness of the

situation, the bail-out order was given. Without regard for his personal safety he gallantly remained alone at the controls to afford all other crewmembers an opportunity to escape. Still another attack exploded gasoline tanks in the right wing, and the bomber plunged earthward, carrying Gen. Castle to his death. His intrepidity and willing sacrifice of his life to save members of the crew were in keeping with the highest traditions of the military service.

The award of the nation's highest military honor to Castle is somewhat problematic. He was an officer and leader of the highest caliber. He was respected by superiors, peers, and subordinates alike and had been given command of the 94th Bomb Group (H) in June 1943 for the express purpose of improving the performance of the struggling unit. The results of his leadership were dramatic, and the 94th became a stalwart among Eaker's steadily growing stable of bomb groups. Indeed, Castle himself was awarded the Silver Star for his leadership of the mission against the Focke Wulfe plant at Oschersleben on July 28, 1943. His career's meteoric rise saw him promoted from captain in 1942 to brigadier general by 1944. Castle was a brave, capable man, and his credentials were impeccable.

Those credentials and his unquestionably valuable service since before the Eighth ever got to England were probably the chief reasons he received the Medal of Honor. Although what Castle did was undoubtedly brave and honorable, it is difficult to say that his performance was more courageous than that of at least dozens, if not hundreds, of other pilots who were killed over Europe and who did not receive the Medal of Honor.

The citation tried too hard to justify Castle's worthiness for the award. For instance, it stated, "In order not to endanger friendly troops on the ground below, he refused to jettison his bombs to gain speed maneuverability." First, if it tried, the best B-17 crew in the world would have had difficulty finding and hitting a specific group of troops on the ground from that altitude. Second, the bombs could have been salvoed unarmed. They would not have exploded; the only way they could have hurt someone is if they had literally landed on top of them.

Second, the citation declared, "His lagging, unescorted aircraft became the target of numerous enemy fighters which ripped the left wing with cannon shells, set the oxygen system afire, and wounded 2 members of the crew. Repeated attacks started fires in 2 engines, leaving the Flying Fortress in imminent danger of exploding." The truth was that virtually every ship that was shot down during the war had sustained incredible damage. Aircraft did not fall from the sky because they were flyable. The *Treble Four* was in no way unique.

Finally, the citation said, "Without regard for his personal safety, he gallantly remained alone at the controls to afford all other crewmembers an opportunity to escape." In truth, Castle bravely did what he was supposed to do—and what many other pilots had done. He held the aircraft stable until his crew had an opportunity to escape. It is very doubtful that he planned on flying until he was dead. When the aircraft went out of control, it was at 12,000 feet. Had it not fallen into a spin, he would have had ample opportunity to jump clear and no doubt would have. In other words, it is likely at the time that he was planning his own escape once the crew was out of the ship.

These facts were not lost on other aircrews who suggested that if the originally scheduled pilot been at the controls, he likely would not have received the Medal of Honor for doing the same thing.

The valor of the bomber crews in their fight against the Luftwaffe has been thoroughly treated in hundreds of books. The reason it has been recorded so comprehensively was because it was so truly extraordinary. Men fighting brutal, life-and-death battles miles above the earth fires the imagination and elicits great marvel and admiration. Still, it must be considered that the men who fought so fiercely did so because they had to. If they did not fight, they died. And sometimes, despite their courage and bravery, they still fell. But in the end, once engaged in battle, they fought because they had nothing to lose.

But there was no fighting the German flak batteries. Against the wicked barrages of exploding shells, there was nothing the bomber crews could do; their guns were useless to stop the flak. It was this sense of helplessness that bothered the crews the most. The simple truth was that surviving the antiaircraft guns was a numbers game. It did not matter how skilled the crews were. Fate did not care about skill.

It could be argued, then, that the greater courage was exercised by the men not while they were airborne, but rather when they made the decision to climb aboard their aircraft before each and every sortie. This was especially true given the fact that every one of them was a volunteer. They could, at any time, have simply decided that the odds were too badly stacked against them and that they wanted no more of the deadly aerial combat that was necessary to defeat Nazi Germany.

There was likely not a single airman that did not consider the implications of quitting. That very few of them asked to be relieved of their flying duties is remarkable, especially considering the high loss rates that were sustained during 1943 and the first half of 1944. "But we had a sense of commitment," remembered Robert Hansen, a B-24 pilot with the 458th Bomb Group (H). "We were all volunteers, and we knew very well what we were there for. So the number of men who asked to be taken off of their combat crew was not very large."

Nevertheless, it happened. The reality of seeing their comrades shot out of the sky diminished the motivations that got the crewmen into bombers in the first place. No longer were the recruiting posters so compelling, nor was the higher rank, the better pay, or the glamor of air combat. Fierce battles were waged not only in the skies over Europe, but also in the consciences of the men who manned the bombers. Moral imperative, obligation, pride, and sense of duty were pitched against fear and the primal urge to survive.

"When a crewman decided that he didn't want to fly anymore," recalled Hansen, "he had to talk to his chain of command, and was given opportunities to change his mind, but no one was ever forced to fly against their will." The nose-turret gunner on Hansen's crew asked to be reassigned off of flight duty shortly after they started flying combat operations. "He only flew a few missions with us and during those sorties we had to rescue him a couple of different times. More than once, he inadvertently let his oxygen system freeze up, and he lost consciousness. The navigator or bombardier had to go into his compartment to revive him. It wasn't only dangerous for them to be up and moving around, but it also distracted them from the mission."

Generally, men removed from flight status were reassigned to some other duty on the same airfield. There was a huge need for armorers, clerks, and other types of nonflying personnel. Hansen recalled: "They normally weren't bothered or given a hard time because of their decisions." Indeed, there were probably many among those still flying who empathized since they had battled the very same demons.

The USAAF actually recognized the need to rest its aircrews and had the luxury of being able to do so. It set up a group of what it called "rest camps" or "rest homes." These were generally estates or large private homes set up in bucolic locations far removed from the hubbub of the daily machinations of the air war. At these quiet places, which were operated by the Red Cross, the men were free to do as they liked with no demands whatsoever made on their time or energy. They might play board games, hike, bike, play tennis, ride horses, or go boating. If they chose, they could simply sleep or read through their entire stay. The food was typically excellent and available whenever it was wanted.

Crews of all types and ranks were sent to rest and recuperate. And the benefits were recognized. An Eighth Air Force representative declared: "Very definitely, I can say that rest homes are saving lives— and badly needed airmen—by returning them to combat as more efficient flyers. There isn't any word to describe the varying states of mind of combat flyers when they are just plain tired."[4]

Herman Schonenberg, a P-51 pilot with the 55th Fighter Group, was representative of the sorts of men who were sent to what the aircrews themselves commonly called the "Flak Farm." He candidly recalled his experience: "Somewhere in the middle of my tour I kind of flaked out a little bit. I did dumb things like taking off and forgetting to pick up my landing gear. I'd call my lead and tell him to slow down, that there was something wrong because I couldn't catch up. Or I'd leave my takeoff flaps down and so on. When you got to that point, you knew something was wrong. I remember telling the doc that I thought that I had better quit. He checked me out and told me that I was like a lot of other guys and just needed a rest. So they sent me to a flak home in southern England." After a couple of weeks recuperating, Schonenberg returned to his unit, where he spent some time instructing new arrivals before returning to combat once again.

Like their bomber-crew counterparts, the fighter pilots had joined the U.S. Army Air Forces at least partially out of a sense of duty. However, once they were trained and in their operational units, they were driven by a more complex mix of motivations. They were compelled to fly by obligation, camaraderie, competition, pride and no small measure of fear.

The fear that most often drove them was the fear of ridicule or failure. No one wanted to be thought of as weak, unwilling, or unable, especially in front of his comrades. Robert "Punchy" Powell of the 352nd Fighter Group remembered how that fear drove him to do something that he would rather not have: "It was snowing like I'd never seen it snow there before. It was obvious to everyone that there was no way that we were going to go flying; the mission was a sure bet to be scrubbed." Nevertheless, the unit went through the motions, and the briefing was conducted as normal although more attention was paid out the snow-spattered windows than to what was being said at the front of the room. "Even after the mission had been briefed," Powell said, "it was clear that there was no way we were going to fly—the snow was coming down that hard. In fact, I can remember saying that there was no way that anyone in the world could *make* me go flying in that miserable weather."

It was only when the group was ordered to man their aircraft that Powell started to become anxious. "Even after we started our engines and taxied to the edge of the field, I was certain that we wouldn't go. In fact, I swore to myself that I *wouldn't* go." But he did. "When my flight leader gave the signal, we all pushed our throttles forward and took off in that stuff. I figured if they were going to do it, then I was too. There was no way I was going to chicken out in front of those guys."

There is little doubt that almost everyone else in the flight was driven into the sky by the same sorts of thoughts. They were not going to fail in front of Powell and the rest of the unit. According to Powell, "We all went. Our pride was stronger than our fear."

CHAPTER 24

Bodenplatte

Prior to the Ardennes offensive, Luftwaffe leaders crafted a plan intended to paralyze, at least for a brief period, the Allied tactical air forces operating in the West. Grounding those air elements during the first few crucial days of the campaign would give it a better chance of success. Since killing the American and British aircraft in the air had proved to be a nearly impossible task for the hard-pressed Luftwaffe, the German planners hoped to catch them on the ground, where they could be more easily destroyed.

The plan, developed by *Generalleutnant* Dietrich Peltz and his staff, called for an early-morning strike by 1,500 or more fighters against sixteen USAAF and RAF airbases on the continent. Considering the broken force that the Luftwaffe was at the time and taking into account the fact that the German high command insisted that it be used regardless, the scheme, dubbed *Bodenplatte*, had potential. For one, it accounted for the poor training level that was typical of most of the German pilots and did not call for them to perform at a level beyond reasonable expectations. Indeed, instead of bombarding the pilots with exhortations or threats or political palaver, the Luftwaffe leadership provided realistic and practical planning.

For instance, because the navigation skills of the fighter pilots were so poor, twin-engine bombers were assigned as pathfinders from the fighter bases to the targets. Moreover, the routes were to be marked by

flares and other devices. Each pilot was also given a set of carefully prepared charts customized for his unit's particular target. Finally, the
novice airmen could expect to catch the Allied aircraft on the ground.
This was a particular blessing as blasting aircraft parked on the ground
was much easier than shooting them out of the sky, particularly when
they were manned by much better trained pilots.

The strike was originally intended to coincide with the opening of
the Ardennes offensive on December 16, 1944. Foul weather precluded
the attack, and most of the German flyers familiar with the plan assumed
that it had been overcome by events. Accordingly, most of them were
surprised when orders came through on December 31, 1944, directing
the execution of *Bodenplatte* on the following day, January 1, 1945.
Although it is often speculated that the date was chosen in an attempt to
catch the Allied flyers in a post-celebratory funk, the reality is that it
coincided with Wehrmacht ground operations.

Utmost secrecy was directed, and every German fighter pilot available, from the highest-ranking staff pilot down to the greenest new-
comer, was scheduled to fly the mission. All of them were cautioned
against drinking and ordered to bed early. In the meantime, the belea-
guered ground crews worked furiously through the freezing night to
ensure that the maximum number of aircraft were available.

On the same day that the orders were received, December 31, 1944,
Howard Dentz, a P-47 pilot with the 365th Fighter Group, caught up
with a formation of aircraft that quite likely was being staged for the
next day's mission:

> I was flying a razorback with a damned needle-nosed prop and
> my wingman was flying a paddle-blade prop with a bubble
> canopy. We were just stooging around near Trier, Germany,
> looking for trouble at about 16,000 feet when along came what
> must have been a brand new group of about fifty FW-190s.
> They flew in perfect formation about 6,000 feet over the top of
> us. I was scared.
>
> The leader detached and started a maneuver I'd never seen. It
> was kind of a powered tail slide, perfectly controlled. As I
> turned to keep sight of him I tried to figure out what the heck he
> was going to do. Then I realized that he meant to come down

into the middle of our turn, pop his throttle and try to shoot us both down. Another cocky German stunt, I thought.

But he made a mistake. He got into a position where I was able to rack it in, pull my nose up, and fire. I hit him right in the cockpit. He spun over the top and then went down and crashed and burned. The rest of the Germans just flew off. I tried to climb, to get close enough to shoot, but they were too damned high and we were getting low on fuel. With more fuel, with another pair of Jugs [P-47s] with paddle-blade props, we could have gotten more of them. I'm sure that they must have been young untrained pilots, otherwise they would have dived and been all over us.

Final orders for the attack were disseminated that night, New Year's Eve. The plan called for a coordinated strike to hit all the target airfields at 0920. The different *Jagdgruppen* staffs busied themselves with final planning, calculating backward from the target time to determine when the crews should be awakened. Allowances had to be made for getting the crews up, feeding them, transporting them to the airfield, briefing them, getting them to their aircraft, starting those aircraft, preparing them for takeoff, and getting them airborne and to their targets.

Early on January 1, 1945, the German pilots were wakened in the dark, hurriedly fed, and given their briefings. As much as Peltz and his staff had allowed for the shortcomings of the attacking crews, they had still produced a fairly complex scheme. Recognizing this, many of the *Jagdgruppen* leaders finished their briefings that morning with variations of this bit of advice: "If you don't know what you're doing, just follow me."

Nevertheless, despite the plan's complexity, most of the German pilots were excited by the mission. *Feldwebel* Oscar Boesch, an FW-190 pilot with Sturmstaffel 1, JG 3, recalled:

I was surprised at how calm I felt and was somewhat refreshed knowing that is was now our turn to attack Allied aircraft. . . . At last I thought, some payback, and our day of revenge. . . . We were always outnumbered as we took our daily beatings. . . . Every day we endured attacks by Mustangs, Spitfires, Lightnings,

Thunderbolts and Typhoons. They shot up everything they saw; even a man on a bicycle was not safe on the streets! As I strapped myself into the 190, I believed that this important mission would bring a much-needed reprieve from Allied superiority on the Western Front.[1]

Luftwaffe crew chiefs broke the shivering stillness of the frigid dawn with the coughing growl of aircraft engines. The pilots, breath steaming against the strengthening light, climbed into their cockpits, strapped themselves in, and made final preparations for the attack. At their pre-calculated times, they taxied out of their parking spots, rolled out to their runways, advanced their throttles, and roared into the sky. *Bodenplatte* was underway as nearly 1,000 German aircraft headed for their targets.

As many of the most experienced German flyers feared, the plan unraveled almost immediately. The formations stayed as low as they dared, anxious not to tip off their presence to Allied radar operators. It was difficult to navigate so close to the ground, especially since a frozen mist shrouded much of the landscape. Consequently, many of the formations, despite their twin-engine pathfinders, became lost. Some of the planned route markers, flares and smoke pots, were never laid, and some of those that did get placed were missed. As it developed, eleven of the thirty-four formations—nearly a third of the attacking force—never found their targets.

Moreover, some formations got airborne late while others broke up as pilots lost sight of each other in the early-morning haze. Most tragic of all was the fact that German antiaircraft gunners had not been briefed on the operation. Accordingly, unaccustomed to seeing their own aircraft in such large formations, some gunners mistook them for Allied aircraft and shot down many of them. In fact, German losses to their own antiaircraft fire made up a significant part of the total losses, perhaps a quarter or more. And, as might be expected, some of the groups were hit by early-morning Allied patrols.

This was the case at Y-29, the airfield at Asch, Belgium. There, eight P-47s of the 366th Fighter Group had just taken off for ground-attack missions in support of the U.S. Army's counterblows against the staggering German offensive. On the ground at Y-29 were twelve P-51s of the 487th Fighter Squadron, led by Lt. Col. John C. Meyer. The 487th was part of the 352nd Fighter Group, on loan from the Eighth Air Force in England to the Ninth. There was confusion about their actual assignment, and Meyer had yet to receive permission to take off. Just a few miles away, unbeknownst to the Americans, a mixed force of Me-109s and FW-190s from three different units of JG 11 adjusted their formations and made ready to attack Asch and the nearby RAF base at Ophoven.

When the pilots of the 366th spotted the German fighters, part of them were already in their strafing runs at Ophoven. Lt. Melvin Paisley called out the enemy aircraft: "Two o'clock low, coming in on the deck!"[2] The P-47 pilots immediately shucked their bombs and drop tanks, then hurled themselves at the enemy formations. There began the wildest melee of the day.

Paisley used his underwing five-inch rockets to good effect when he fired two of them at an Me-109 before bagging it with a third. That he was able to use the air-to-ground rockets so effectively against an aerial target was remarkable. He stayed aggressively engaged with the attacking Germans and knocked down two more fighters that morning. Five other P-47 pilots of the 366th also scored that day.

Meyer, at the head of his Mustangs at Asch, no longer cared about getting permission to take off. He gunned the throttle of his P-51 and tore down the runway as German fighters picked out various targets at the airfield. As soon as his aircraft broke ground, Meyer lined up on an incoming FW-190. He recorded the event in his encounter report: "I attacked one, getting a two second burst at 300 yards, 30-degree deflection, getting good hits on the fuselage and wing roots. The E/A [enemy aircraft] half-rolled, crashing into the ground."[3] Behind him, the rest of Meyer's pilots hurried their aircraft into the sky while Meyer's victim skidded to a halt in a furiously burning fireball.

Lt. Sanford Moats got airborne and spotted about fifteen FW-190s on the deck and closing on Ophoven. A few thousand feet higher, he noted a like number of Me-109s flying cover. Two of the FW-190s turned hard after Moats's wingman, Lt. Dean Huston. The two Mustangs turned hard left into them, and a circling engagement followed. Closing on one of the German fighters, Moats checked over his left shoulder and called for Dean to break harder to the left as the other

FW-190 was closing for a shot. "I then fired a short burst at 300 yds and 30 degrees deflection at the 190 ahead of me, observing strikes in the cockpit area and left wing root. He burst into flame and I saw him crash and explode as I continued the turn."[4]

Moats turned back over the field, where dozens of aircraft, German and American, were engaged in a frenzied fight amongst a flurry of anti-aircraft fire. He attacked an FW-190 that was in a strafing run for his next target:

> I fired a short burst at 200 yards and 20 degrees deflection, observing a concentration of strikes on both wing roots. Both wings folded up over the canopy of the E/A [enemy aircraft] and he dropped straight in. The pilot did not get out. I continued my left turn and rolled out slightly above and behind another 190 which broke left. I fired a short burst and observed strikes on the left side of the fuselage, canopy and left wing root. He burst into flames, the canopy came off, and he crashed. The pilot did not get out.

Moats knocked down two more FW-190s that morning and got shot up by the base's antiaircraft guns for his trouble.

Moats's squadron mate, Capt. Henry Stewart, got off to a much slower start. After giving chase to a single Me-109, he pulled off because of intense ground fire. He then tangled with a second Me-109 "but could not get into a firing position."[5] Giving up on that target, Stewart "followed another 109 up through the clouds at about 150 miles per hour but could not close and almost spun out." He tried again with a fourth Me-109: "I fired but did not observe any strikes."

His luck remained flat. He turned back toward the field and gave chase to a fifth Me-109. If nothing else, Stewart was persistent. "I closed on him and pulled the trigger, nothing happened. My knee had shut my switches off." Stewart got his guns working again and scored a few strikes before a squadron mate obligingly stepped in and knocked the German down in flames.

Stewart caught sight of two P-51s chasing down another Me-109. When the fleeing German twisted away from his two pursuers, Stewart's luck finally changed: "I cut my throttle and slid in behind him at about

100 yds and 100 feet off the deck. I fired and observed many strikes. The 109 went straight in and exploded." A short time later, on a roll, Stewart sent two more Me-109s down in flames.

On the ground at Y-29, the ground crews were being treated to what one of them called, "The Greatest Show on Earth." Arthur Snyder was a P-51 crew chief and had just finished servicing an aircraft when the attack began:

> We were waiting for the pilots to come out to the planes for takeoff for a short mission over the front when we noticed puffs of black smoke up ahead and then the air raid sirens went off, so we thought it best to get away from the planes as that is what the Jerries would go for. However I only got about 10–15 feet from my plane . . . when we saw the Jerries coming in over the woods right at us. The fellow next to me flattened out and I started to do likewise but then I quickly realized that if the Lord wanted me I was ready.[6]

Evidently, it was not Snyder's time. He dropped to his knees and ducked as rounds struck and exploded an aircraft next to him. A German shell casing dropped near where he was kneeling. He picked it up—it was still warm—and pocketed it. With the rest of the men on the base, he watched the 352nd's pilots tear the Germans apart.

The 352nd's performance that morning was one of the most remarkable of the war. From a standing start, while under attack, its P-51s scrambled from the icy runway and downed twenty-three Luftwaffe pilots without sustaining a single loss. Indeed, of the twelve P-51 pilots that got airborne, eleven of them scored.

At the same time that the fracas at Asch was being fought, the Luftwaffe was hammering the Metz-Frescaty airfield in France, about 150 miles to the southeast. Howard Dentz, a P-47 pilot with the 365th Fighter Group, remembered that morning well:

> When they came over, we recognized the characteristic sound of the German engines and the big fat props they had on their Me-109s. We all jumped out of bed. We had rifles that we had collected from the battlefield; I had a German Mauser that I had

carved down to a sporting stock. We ran out in snow up to our knees in nothing but our skivvy drawers. So there we were shooting at 109s with rifles. In retrospect, it was really hilarious.

We got hit bad. The same German unit [JG 53] that had been based there before us flew in with Me-109s and wiped out our entire squadron on the ground. My airplane was burned up. It had a full load of gas and three 500-pound bombs loaded on it. My assistant crew chief, Victor Morales, was in the airplane when bullets went through the cockpit and into the fuel tank. He didn't get hit but a fire started which he bravely tried to put out with his hat! He ended up getting burned a bit before he got out of the plane.

Seven of the attacking aircraft were shot down by the Maxon M45 .50-caliber antiaircraft machine guns that were guarding our airfield. Out of the seven German aircraft shot down, all of the pilots, but one—he bailed out—were killed.

Dentz recalled the surviving German, *Oberfeldwebel* Stefan Kohl:

He was a handsome son-of-a-bitch. He was tall and had a marvelous fur-lined jacket and gorgeous boots. Exactly what you would expect a German fighter pilot to look like. He was arrogant too, and spoke impeccable English. They brought him over to us while our airplanes were still burning, and he said, "Well, fellas, how do you like that?"

As it turned out, he was interned at our base for a time and was actually an interesting guy to have around. He bragged a great deal about the "superiority" of the Luftwaffe, and we encouraged him to talk, getting a lot of valuable information from him. Well, two weeks later, after every single aircraft had been replaced, we took him out to the flight line and said, "Well, buddy, how do you like that?" He said, "Ah yes, that is why we are losing the war. Every time we shoot you down, you just bring in replacements. You have an unlimited supply of planes and pilots and bombs and ammunition and gasoline and such."

To varying degrees, scenes like those at Asch and Metz were repeated at thirteen other Allied airfields that morning. Estimates of the number of RAF and USAAF aircraft destroyed run from 300 to 400 with very few casualties. On the other hand, German aircraft losses ran just under 300. The final tally of Luftwaffe pilots killed or taken prisoner was 213.

The common practice among air historians is to denigrate the planners of *Bodenplatte* and label the operation as a foolish waste of men and resources. There is some merit to the argument since the Luftwaffe did lose experienced leaders at the tactical level. Certainly, it was the largest single-day loss of aircraft and pilots for the Germans during the entire war.

On the other hand, it should be acknowledged that the aircraft and pilots would have certainly been lost anyway. They would have been squandered over the battlefields in the West or knocked out of the sky in the fight against the strategic bombers. They certainly would not have destroyed as many aircraft as they did during *Bodenplatte*. In fact, if the planned force of 1,500 fighters had been available, if a third of the force had not gotten lost, and if the attack had been executed according to plan, the results could have been spectacular. Ultimately, Peltz took a reasonable gamble that did not pay off as he hoped. Regardless, by the time of *Bodenplatte* the Luftwaffe was already hopelessly broken. After the operation, it was only more so.

Following *Bodenplatte*, Göring's recriminations against his fighter pilots forced a culmination point. Unable to bear his inane browbeatings any longer, the fighter hierarchy confronted him in January 1945. During a meeting coordinated by Galland—by this time, he was persona non grata to Göring—other fighter pilot leaders, including Johannes Steinhoff and Hannes Trautloft and led by Günther Lützow, told the *Reichsmarschall* that it would be best for all if he were to step down as the head of the Luftwaffe.

Predictably, Göring disagreed and threatened to have Lützow shot and Steinhoff court-martialed. Galland was relieved as head of fighters and replaced by Gordon Gollob, a Nazi toady of the first order. Ironically, it was Hitler who protected the dissidents. Although they were removed from their postings, they remained unharmed. Morale among Germany's flyers sank even lower.

The Luftwaffe was clearly staggering to stay alive, even though it still fielded some experienced pilots. By and large, most of those seasoned pilots were not old hands who had been in service for years, although some were still flying after chalking up hundreds of missions; rather, they were relatively new pilots who had accumulated tremendous experience in a very short time.

Indeed, the Luftwaffe flyers got airborne virtually every day, sometimes multiple times a day—as long as fuel was available. Those who were not killed early in their careers became very experienced very quickly. Whereas many of the much more numerous American pilots considered themselves lucky to even spot an enemy aircraft so late in the war, their German counterparts found themselves literally fighting for their lives during the majority of their sorties. Consequently, new German pilots took away fresh lessons virtually every time they got airborne—that is, if they lived.

This stands in marked contrast to the experiences of many Americans who never even had the opportunity to engage in aerial combat. According to one, "I saw a couple of German planes in the distance once or twice, but I was never in a position to do any shooting." Essentially, a German pilot might have had as much aerial combat experience after two or three sorties as an American pilot would have had after fifty.

By that time in the war, the American fighter groups had virtually all the pilots they could use. The men they introduced to combat were well-trained and prepared and had 300 or more flight hours. They were coached and led by men who had experience in combat and had the time and resources to carefully mentor newly arrived novices. On the other hand, new German pilots were showing up at frontline units with roughly 100 flying hours. They were usually shot down very quickly.

Joe Black, a P-51 pilot with the 357th Fighter Group at Leiston, started his combat flying career at just this time. Having arrived in England during December 1944, he finished his in-theater indoctrinations within a few weeks and flew his first combat sortie in early January 1945. He remembered an encounter with a particularly savvy Me-109 pilot: "I was flying on Chuck Weaver's wing."[7] Weaver had joined the unit the previous year and already had several kills to his credit. "Anyway, we were on our own as a flight of four at about 15,000 feet looking for targets of opportunity. And we spotted a flight of four Me-109s coming at us from the opposite direction well below us, probably at about six or seven thousand feet."

Weaver wasted little time and rolled the flight over into a split-S as the enemy fighters passed under the P-51s. According to Black, "They saw us before we got into range. They broke up into two flights. One pair of Me-109s went to the left and the other went to the right. Chuck and I chased after the left-hand pair and they ducked down into a deck of clouds."

Weaver and Black dove through the undercast and trolled around underneath it looking for the German fighters. "Sure enough," Black said, "out popped one of these guys and he took some shots at us." Before the two Americans could swing around and bring their guns to bear, the German pilot climbed back into the clouds. "We played this game of cat-and-mouse for a while with this guy. He'd pop out and we'd take shots at him or he'd take shots at us. He put a couple of holes into the back of my airplane, and I think he put some into Chuck's plane too."

This went on for a while. In the grand scheme of things, it was not a fight that was going to decide anything at all, even in a tactical sense. Rather, it was a risky and lethal contest—almost a game—between determined and competent opponents. "Finally," Black said, "Chuck started getting really frustrated with this guy. He told me to get behind him and just far enough in the clouds that I could barely see him. He was going to act as bait for this guy. When the German tried to get his guns on Weaver, I was supposed to pop out and shoot him down."

The plan almost worked. "Sure enough, this Me-109 showed up again and I was able to get off a good, two-second burst. I'm not sure if I hit him hard or not, but he immediately climbed up into the clouds again and was gone. We never saw him after that and ended up going home empty-handed. That one left us shaking our heads for a while; that guy was smart—and good!"

German manufacturing began to come completely undone in early 1945. The oil plan had virtually grounded the Luftwaffe and stalled the Wehrmacht's armor, and the effects of the transportation plan had started to pile up. The rail and road networks were critically damaged and exceedingly dangerous for the Germans to travel. Consequently, the concept of dispersed production nodes—forced by the American air attacks on Germany's great factories—fell in on itself. With the transportation infrastructure in a shambles, it was not only difficult to get raw materials to the scattered workshops, but it was equally hard to collect the goods they produced.

In short, the USSTAF was running short of traditional targets. At the same time, a number of other factors converged to compel Spaatz to reconsider a plan that had been shelved during the summer of 1944. THUNDERCLAP was designed as an all-out bombing raid directed against the city of Berlin. Although transportation and government targets were identified, it was primarily intended as a terror attack. High-level planners hoped that the raid would be so crushing that it would cause Germany to give up. The Third Reich's major cities were burned out, the British and Americans were pressing the western borders, and the Soviets were closing rapidly from the east.

But whereas Spaatz endorsed the idea, Doolittle hated it. To his mind, the American campaign had been a clean fight up to that point, and he saw no need to sully the record with blatant terror bombing when the war was so near an end. Spaatz outranked him. More than 1,000 B-17s were sent against Berlin on February 3, 1945, while a separate force of more than 400 B-24s hit targets around Magdeburg. The Germans did not give up and took out twenty-five bombers.

Maj. Gen. Haywood Hansell was an architect of AWPD-1, AWPD-42, and the plan for the Combined Bomber Offensive, as well as a combatant commander in the Eighth Air Force and the Pacific. He noted the Allied tendency toward area targets during this period:

When command of the air was so completely established that the RAF Bomber Command was free to roam the air over Germany in daylight, there was every reason to expect that Bomber Command would take up at long last the selective destruction of industrial targets which it had been forced to abandon early in the war. . . . Instead, Bomber Command, after a few sporadic attacks against selected targets, reverted to area urban bombing in an effort to give a last body blow to the wavering morale of the German State.

Where the U.S. was concerned, Hansell noted that Spaatz's strategic air forces "did not conform completely to the new direction. But in the spirit of 'cooperation,' they did attack selected targets in proximity to the urban targets of Bomber Command, and by doing so diluted the intensity with which they pursued the American interpretation of the Combined Bomber Offensive." In other words, Spaatz "piled on" against quasi–area targets in a show of solidarity with the British.

CHAPTER 25

Deadly to the End

Although the Luftwaffe was very nearly dead, the killing in the skies never really abated even during the last few months of the war. Walter Baker of the 487th Bomb Group (H) had been in England less than a month at the start of March 1945. He was a B-17 radioman just getting used to his base at Lavenham, Suffolk, and had gotten only a couple of missions under his belt, but he was already starting to get a good handle on his job. He remembered that "[u]nless something went wrong, there really wasn't a lot for the radioman to do." The bomber pilots controlled their own four-channel VHF set for communications between aircraft and to talk with the airbase's control tower. On the other hand, the radioman, from his compartment just ahead of the bomb bay, operated long-range radio sets using Morse code to tap out status or strike reports. But that was only required if he was aboard a lead or command aircraft.

If things really went wrong and his ship was mortally hit the radioman was tasked to send distress signals. This was particularly important if it appeared the aircraft would be ditching into the English Channel or North Sea. Passing a good position report for air-sea rescue upped the crew's chances of survival considerably.

The radio operator in the B-17 was also responsible for a single .50-caliber machine gun mounted on the fuselage above and behind him. It was intended to provide a field of fire to cover the upper-rear quarter of the aircraft. "We were also trained as waist gunners," Baker recalled. "But at that time in the war there were enough waist gunners to go around and they would volunteer to go on missions so that they could get their quota and go home. So, for a lot of missions, I didn't have much to do but watch."

The target for the 487th on March 1, 1945, was the railroad marshaling complex at Ulm. From his little table on the left side of the fuselage, Baker leaned over and peered out the window to his right; part of his duties called for him to watch for enemy fighters or other dangers. Through the black puffs that marked the flak explosions and beyond the far edge of the bomber stream, he caught sight of a silver B-17. It was obvious to him that the ship had fallen out of one of the formations farther ahead. Something was wrong: it was losing altitude as the bomber elements behind it—Baker's among them—overtook it.

Then, seemingly out of nowhere, like a shark out of the murk, a mottled-gray Me-109 appeared behind the stricken bomber. "He was some distance behind the B-17," recounted Baker, "but then he flew in closer. I saw smoke come from him and then he dove away." It was possible that the smoke was from the enemy fighter's guns, or perhaps it came from the engine as the German pilot added power to dive away. There was even a chance that the bomber's gunners had damaged it with their machine guns. Regardless, the B-17 was doomed. "It went out of control and then into a spin. The right wing came off before it hit the ground. No one got out."

Baker turned and looked out the window to his left. "There was another B-17 level with us about a half mile away and flying perpendicular to the formation, straight at us, in a gentle right-hand turn." He kept his eyes glued to the other aircraft and watched as only a few of its ten-man crew jumped clear. "And then it exploded. It was just a bright flash. There were no pieces; there was nothing except the engines falling away."

The bomber stream continued grinding eastward. Within seconds, there was nothing but a fading smudge in the sky to mark where the ill-fated bomber had met its fiery end.

Germany's largest cities had been bombed to ruins by early March 1945. Nevertheless, the rubble was in pieces that were too big for the Allied air commanders, and the aerial wrecking ball that was the USSTAF continued its operations at a furious pace. The target for the B-17s of the 487th Bomb Group (H) on March 2, 1945, was Dresden.

"We were formed up and crossing the coast near Helgoland," said ball-turret gunner Henry Hughey, "when the flight was bracketed by a salvo of eight bursts of flak. We had drifted off course and into one of the German flak corridors. Still, it didn't look like anyone had gotten hit." But it no longer looked that way during the run from the initial point to the target. "The number four engine started losing oil pressure and we had to feather it. Then number two started losing oil pressure and we had to feather that one too." The pilot, Richard Young, knew that the aircraft would not make the return trip to England.

"Once we dropped our bombs, instead of making the turn for home with the rest of the group, we took up a heading for Poland," Hughey said. The failing ship had a much better chance of making the Soviet lines in Poland than it did crossing back across Germany to Allied-held territory. It was when the B-17 was settled on a course toward Warsaw that the number-one engine failed. "We were coming down pretty good, and it was snowing like hell. We couldn't see much of anything, and it wouldn't have mattered anyway—we didn't have any maps for Poland. Finally, we caught sight of a railroad, and our navigator, Bruce Bavender, shouted for the pilot to just follow it because 'every railroad went somewhere.'"

A short fighter strip presented itself through the shadowy whiteness, and Young and his copilot, Lawrence Bross, just barely skimmed over a four-lane highway and tried to drop the big bomber onto the short field. "Fortunately, they realized there was no way they were going to get it down," Hughey recounted, "and they added power, cleared the boundary and then just plopped it into a big clearing on the far side of the field. We got down and out of the airplane okay, and then the Russians came and got us. Things worked out really well for us especially since one of our crewmembers, John Welko, spoke both Russian and Polish—his father was Russian and his mother was Polish!"

Hughey and the rest of the crew were in for a surprise when they came to recover equipment from the aircraft the following day. "The

Russians had discovered that we had landed in a minefield. They would-n't let us go out to the airplane until they cleared it. They built little berms around the mines to focus the blast upward then exploded them right where they were buried."

Ultimately, Hughey and the rest of the crew were shuttled south out of Europe through Poltava, down into North Africa, into Italy, and then back to England. There, with only a few weeks left before the end of the war, they went back to flying missions. According to Hughey, "our air-craft was fitted with new engines by the Russians. They flew it for quite a while after that."

That Germany would lose the war was apparent to all the belliger-ents by early 1945. The biggest uncertainty was how long the Nazis would continue to fight. Despite the fact that their cause was lost, many Germans continued to fight hard. Herman Schonenberg, a P-51 pilot with the 55th Fighter Group, learned that reality firsthand on March 18, 1945: "We were scouting around the Frankfurt area, just north of, but within sight of the city itself when we spotted a formation of about six German aircraft made up of Me-109s and long-nosed FW-190s [FW-190D] at about 12,000 feet." Schonenberg and his flight flung them-selves at the German fighters. "During this fight the German 88-millimeter flak batteries were peppering away—firing into the fight—the whole time. They didn't seem to care who they might hit."

"I was on top-cover for a while and finally got into the melee when an FW-190 came up and attacked us. The way he was flying it seemed that he was a better pilot than most of us. It was a very tight fight and I remember seeing another FW-190—his engine consumed by fire—go whizzing by and crash into a barn. All of a sudden I had the FW-190 I was fighting in my sights. I hadn't expended more than a total of thirty rounds out of all six guns when I hit it in the wing root section—I was about three-quarters inverted at the time. The pilot bailed out. I came very close to him and could see that he was a big man. I remember that he was waving his pistol—shooting at me!"

The crews reporting for combat duty overseas at the beginning of 1945 were considerably better trained and prepared than their predecessors had been even a year earlier. A primary reason was that many of the kinks and difficulties associated with getting the massive training machine working had been mitigated. But even more important was that the training was being informed by experience brought back by veterans who knew what worked and what was important.

"Our crew was young and sharp, and we had shown up pretty well trained," remembered Samuel W. Smith, a B-17 pilot with the 303rd Bomb Group (H). "We flew our first mission on February 24th, 1945. We did fairly well, and after a few more missions, I was pulled aside and asked if I wanted to take the crew through special training so that we could fly in the deputy squadron leader position."

The offer had advantages and disadvantages. If Smith accepted the offer, his crew would have to fly only thirty missions rather than the standard thirty-five. The downside was that the aircraft flying in the lead positions were especially targeted by the German fighters. The thought was that a formation without its leader would be less effective. "There was a little bit of grumbling among the crew," said Smith, "but I agreed that we'd do it."

Smith and his crew flew a practice mission on March 20, 1945. "We were flying with a 'Mickey' operator so that he could get some practice bombing with the radar. It was important to our upgrade training because the lead and deputy lead aircraft were the only ones that carried radar equipment." Soon after parking their aircraft, Smith was asked if he would be willing to fly a mission that day. "Hell, I figured it had to be a milk run up to the front lines. We wouldn't be taking off until early afternoon, and we almost always planned to get back before dark, so it couldn't have been a tough one by my way of thinking." Smith briefly considered the idea and subsequently agreed to sign on for the mission. "In the briefing, they pulled back the curtain covering the mission's target routing and the room erupted in groans. The target was an oil refinery in Hamburg; it produced large quantities of aviation gasoline. I thought to myself that my crew was going to kill me. We'd had a pretty rough one to Hamburg a week or so earlier."

The initial portion of the mission was uneventful. The route took the bombers out over the North Sea, past Helgoland, between Denmark and

Sweden, and down into Germany. "The flak was pretty heavy once we got over the continent," said Smith, "and it stayed with us all the way through the initial point and to the target. Once we dropped our bombs and started for home, the flak stopped and it got really quiet. And then the jets came. I saw a bomber on my right side sort of stagger and fall about a hundred feet, and then it just exploded. And I never even saw the jet that shot it down."

The 303rd's mission report recounted the attacks: "A force of 15 to 20 ME-262 German fighters attacked the 303rd BG (H) Forts for about 30 minutes as they came off the bomb run and started home. The enemy fighters pressed their attacks as close as 50 feet, sometimes zooming right through the formation. Most aircraft attacked on the tail level, although a few hit on the nose and from the sides."

According to Smith, "Things were really popping. I saw aircraft getting hit everywhere I looked. I got a call over the intercom from our tail gunner, Jens Jensen. He said 'I've got an Me-262 coming in from low, six o'clock!' I told him to get on it and keep on it. At the same time I told our ball turret gunner, Mike Kucab, to spin around to lend Jens a hand. As a pilot, that was an unnerving feeling to have things going on back there that you couldn't see."

It was only a few seconds later that the crew felt the aircraft, *My Darling*, vibrate as Jensen and Kucab opened fire on the German jet. "Then," recollected Smith, "Mike came up on the intercom and said, 'Goddam Jens, you got the sonofabitch.'" The crew reported that the Me-262 exploded, broke into two pieces, and fell toward the earth.

The enemy attacks continued despite the fact that the bomber stream was escorted by P-51s. "The Me-262s were just too fast for the P-51s," said Smith. And they did nothing to deter the next enemy aircraft to target *My Darling*. "I looked forward and saw a jet coming straight at us. He was dead-level and coming in with zero deflection; we were going to be the easiest shot in the world."

Smith called over the intercom for Tom Zenick, the engineer, to get the top-turret guns onto the enemy fighter. At the same time, the navigator, Russel Knudsen, opened fire with the twin .50-caliber machine guns in the chin turret. Again, the ship reverberated from the recoil of the .50-caliber guns. But the Me-262 continued straight at *My Darling*. "I couldn't sit there and let him shoot us down," Smith recalled. "I pulled the throttles back, and pushed the nose over. I could see his tracers curving over the top of us as we dropped down. Then, he flashed directly underneath us. In that split second I could see the pilot turn around in his cockpit to look up at us as he passed."

Although their plane was punched through with about a dozen substantial holes, Smith and the rest of the crew brought it safely out over the water and back to Molesworth. Nevertheless, the potent weapon that was the Me-262 had made an indelible impression. In substantial numbers, it was a fighter that could have seriously challenged Allied air supremacy only a year earlier.

"Once we got back and safely down on the ground," Smith said, "the crew gathered around. They looked at me and said, 'Sam, the next time you want to take us along on one of your milk runs, you can forget it!'"

Valid targets in Germany were being quickly ground into nonexistence, but the American bombing effort reached a crescendo during March 1945 when raids were launched on all but a handful of days and a record 100,000 tons of bombs were dropped. That number was nearly equaled the following month when 95,000 tons were delivered. In contrast, the tonnage for October 1943, the same month of the Black Thursday raid on Schweinfurt, was a mere 9,000 tons. Although that early raid had startled the Germans out of their lethargy with respect to the daylight-bombing campaign, the bombing figures from 1945 clearly showed their failure to deal with it.

The problem with the American fighters being so ubiquitous over Germany was that it was easy for the Germans to set up ambushes. Joe Black of the 357th recalled a mission on March 24 in the Ruhr Valley: "We were supposed to stop anything that was moving. If it was moving, we were supposed to shoot it up." The Allies had crossed the Rhine into Germany earlier that month and were pressing eastward. Stopping the movement of German men and materiel would make those operations faster and less dangerous.

"We spotted a junction where a road, a railroad and a canal all came together," recounted Black. "There were boxcars lined up in the marshalling yard, and barges on the canal, and I could see traffic on the road—a staff car and a truck." The squadron arced around in a wide turn to set up for the attack then pushed over into a dive. "We were about halfway down when the sides of those boxcars dropped down. They were filled with guns—20- and 40-millimeter cannon. I could literally see the rounds coming up at us. And the barges were shooting at us too! And then, black and white puffs started bursting all through and around our formation—I was scared to death." Black opened fire on the staff car, leveled off very low above the ground and just kept going. "I got right down on the deck—about twelve feet—and made that airplane fly as low and as fast as I could. I covered about eight miles before I finally pulled the stick back and zoomed up to about 14,000 feet. And I was all alone!" It took a few minutes before Black, still recovering from the near thing that the bushwhacking had been, found another P-51, and made his way home, rattled but unharmed.

By early 1945, the urgency to get men immediately into the cockpit and into the shooting war was not nearly as great as it had been a year before. The great training factories back in the States were still cranking out enormous numbers of well-trained pilots, and the ones who were doing the fighting were living longer, in large part because they were better trained.

"The 357th Fighter Group did a smart thing with us new guys when we showed up," Joe Shea recalled. He had arrived at the 357th's base in Leiston on January 15, 1945. Rather than throwing them immediately into combat, the group put the new arrivals through a short but comprehensive training course they called Clobber College. Heading it up at the time was Leonard "Kit" Carson, a leading ace who ultimately finished the war with 18.5 victories. Carson drove home lessons in the air with particular emphasis on instrument flying and defensive maneuvering. He also held his young pilots accountable in the classroom. "He had us study a map of Europe, including all the major cities and waterways," said Shea. "And then from those cities, we had to memorize headings, distances, and the fuel required to get back to our base. And then, before they'd let us fly in combat, we'd have to draw it all out by memory. It was one of the most useful things they could have done and it came in handy a number of times."

Much of what Shea and his peers was taught was useful because the war stayed deadly to the end. Shea recalled one of his most harrowing experiences:

It was late in the war and we had just come off a target some- where in Germany when someone called out, "Break, break!" But they didn't give a direction for us to turn or tell us what was going on, or anything. Well, everyone started turning in a hun- dred different directions and someone accidentally got on the trigger and shot down the guy in front of him. It killed him. Within hours, orders came down from above that we were to disarm our guns once we had cleared the target area and were headed home.

A couple of days later we had a mission in the Brunswick area near Berlin. Upon leaving the target area, I did as instructed and turned off my gun switch. As we were still far inside Germany, we kept up a constant scan, looking for enemy aircraft. As my scan moved up toward our front I observed a small cloud forming right in front of us, about a thousand yards away. I knew instantly that a German had me in his sights. The cloud was being caused by explosive cannon shells. I immedi- ately checked behind me, and sure enough, there was an Me-262 blazing away at me and closing very fast.

Two things were absolutely clear to me. First, he was missing me. Second, with the rate of closure he had, he needed to start slowing down immediately or he would end up flying right in front of me. I didn't turn at all because I didn't know if he was missing me high, low, or to either side. If I turned I might fly into his fire.

It was a smart move. Just one of the enemy jet's 30-millimeter can- non rounds could have knocked Shea's P-51 out of the sky.

Just as Shea predicted, the German pilot realized that he was closing too fast. "He started fish-tailing," Shea said, "trying to slow down. But he wasn't able to hack it. He ended up just barely faster than me, and his right wing passed over my left as he flew right in front of me." The Mustang pilot held his fire. "I didn't want to start shooting right away because I was afraid he'd blow up right in front of me and then I'd end up in my chute." Exercising extraordinary patience, Shea waited until the German pilot was more than 100 yards away before centering the enemy fighter in his gunsight and pulling the trigger. "Nothing happened." It was then that Shea realized that his guns were not armed. As ordered, he had secured them as the flight had turned west for home. "Well, I was so excited that when I realized what the problem was, I dove for the gun switch which was down low between my legs. But as I went down, I smacked my head so hard on the gunsight that I went unconscious—I was out cold!"

Shea was out for only a few seconds. "As I came out of my stupor, I could hear this noise: 'Tickety-tink-tick-tinkety-tick-tick-tick.' I didn't know what it was." When Shea recovered his wits, he found himself only a few feet below his flight lead's aircraft. The other pilot was firing rounds at the fast retreating German, and his shell casings were making staccato music as they fell onto Shea's aircraft and bounced off of his wings and canopy. "My flight lead may have knocked a piece or two off of that guy," Shea remembered, "but we didn't get him. I lost some sleep over that one for a little while." Indeed, a snapshot taken by his gun camera clearly shows the German jet sitting less than 200 yards in front of him—a perfect target.

Nazi Germany was in a shambles by April 1945. The Luftwaffe as a coherent fighting force was finished. It fought in scattered actions as best it could. Johannes Steinhoff was flying Me-262s by now, not because it would make any difference, but rather because he saw it as his duty. Still, he recognized the futility:

We were like dayflies who had come to the end of their day, where the dream dissolves into nothingness. Why did we still fly? Whom were we doing it for? I had no idea, for example, what the general [Galland] thought when he was not flying, or when he sat in his chair in the ops room, staring straight ahead of him with a cigar in the corner of his mouth. A lot of drinking went on every evening.[1]

By mid-April, the Eighth and Fifteenth were flying tactical missions in support of army movements. No strategic targets remained. The Eighth flew its last bombing mission of the war on April 25, while the Fifteenth flew its final raid the following day.

For all intents and purposes, the Luftwaffe was dead.

CONCLUSION

The Allies had done it. Only a short time earlier, it had seemed that Europe would be forever under the pitiless thrall of Nazi Germany. Instead, England kept the Germans off its island, and the Soviets trapped the German armies in a bear hug from which they would never escape. Both nations gave the Americans just barely enough time to pull off the organizational, industrial, and strategic miracle that was the USAAF, the greatest air force that ever was. That air force killed the Luftwaffe and made it possible for the Allies together to destroy Nazi Germany.

Of course, the world was changed forever. In just a very few years airpower was transformed from an adjunct capability to a dominant—perhaps *the* dominant—war-making instrument. It was unlike anything the world had ever known; its global reach, its speed, and its destructive power offered capabilities that no army or navy could ever rival. As such, it became, and remains, a diplomatic tool as much as a military one.

The mission and size of the USAAF morphed during and after the war such in such a way that it broke away from the Army and became a separate service in 1947. The U.S. Air Force, the USAF, was the world's premier air force when it was formed only two years after World War II; many decades and conflicts later, it remains so. Arnold, Spaatz, Eaker, and Doolittle were all advocates of a separate service and helped it through considerable birthing pains. Spaatz, in fact, took over from Arnold following Arnold's retirement in 1946 and became the Air Force's first chief of staff in 1947. He held the post only long enough for the fledgling service to get its legs under itself and retired less than a year later. After additional decades of public and private service, he passed away in 1974 at age eighty-three.

Arnold's health continued to deteriorate following the war. In retirement, he wrote his memoirs, *Global Mission*, and was honored in 1949 with a promotion to General of the Air Force, the only person to date ever to hold the rank. Accordingly, he was and is the only person ever to have held five-star rank in two separate services. He died in 1950 at sixty-three.

Eaker retired on the eve of the Air Force's birth in 1947 as a major general and was subsequently promoted to lieutenant general on the Air Force's retired list in 1948. He stayed active as a business executive and devoted considerable energy to national security affairs. He also wrote a regular column that was syndicated to more than 180 newspapers. Congress passed special legislation awarding him four-star rank, which he received in 1985; this was in addition to a special gold star award for his military service and his work in national security. He passed away in 1987 at ninety-one years of age.

Doolittle reverted to reserve status as a lieutenant general until retiring in 1959. Like Eaker, he stayed very involved in business, aviation, and national security affairs and, also like Eaker, was awarded a fourth star in retirement in 1985. He died in 1993 at age ninety-six.

Most of the more than two million men who served in the USAAF went home and returned to civilian life. War seldom births good things, but good things did come to many of the men after their service. First, the training they received and their exposure to other people and places—and to military discipline—was a benefit that the vast majority would never have experienced had it not been for their time in uniform. Second, the passage by Congress of the G.I. Bill (Servicemen's Readjustment Act of 1944) provided for the college or vocational education of returning veterans, as well as unemployment insurance, loans, and a host of other benefits. The men enthusiastically embraced those opportunities and produced, within just a few years, a workforce that was educated and productive beyond anything ever seen not only in the nation, but in the world. As much as anything else, it was the G.I. Bill that contributed to the primacy of the United States following World War II.

On the German side, Göring was tried at Nuremberg, found guilty, and sentenced to hang. He committed suicide before he was executed. Göring deserved to be executed whereas most Luftwaffe officers did not. Indeed, the Western Allies did not treat their former foes as badly as they might have. Galland, like many ranking Luftwaffe officers, was thoroughly debriefed by the British and Americans before being released in 1947. Following his captivity, he traveled to Argentina as a military and aviation consultant, and after returning to Germany in the

1950s, he went into private business. In the years after the war, he made friends with many of his former enemies and was a colorful and popular figure in aviation circles for the rest of his life. He died at age eighty-three in 1996.

At the end of the war, Johannes Steinhoff was horrifically burned in a takeoff accident while flying Me-262s. He survived but was so badly injured that there was little prospect of him living outside the hospital. Although he still bore dreadful scars, years of reconstructive surgery and his own personal fortitude restored his health to a point where he was able to accept a leading role in the construction of the postwar Luftwaffe. He eventually rose to the rank of full general and chief of staff of the Luftwaffe from 1966 to 1970. He died in 1994 at age eighty.

Nearly 34,000 Americans died in the air war against Germany. What they might have accomplished had they lived is unknowable. What would have happened had they and their surviving comrades not been willing to make the ultimate sacrifice is.

AFTERWORD

"Once the war ended on May 8, 1945, we flew two or three missions with planeloads of maintenance men and intelligence officers and other support personnel," remembered Samuel W. Smith, a B-17 pilot with the 303rd Bomb Group. "It was a good way to show them how, even though they had been hundreds of miles away, they had contributed to winning the war. It was sometime in May when my crew and I were detached from the 303rd and sent to Valley Wales in Scotland. They detached us from the Eighth Air Force and assigned us to the Air Transport Command. We were supposed to move aircraft from the United Kingdom back to the States."

In fact, it was still May when Smith's crew was assigned to take an aircraft back to the States that had only recently arrived—it had just fifty-seven hours of flight time. They would be part of a mixed train of about sixty-five B-17s and B-24s that would also be carrying people, tools, and other equipment.

Smith remembered that he was chatting with his copilot, Arthur "Shawnie" Shanafelt, the night before their departure when an old friend brought two other officers by his bunk to visit:

> They were a pair of skin-and-bones, tired-looking captains that had been shot down and subsequently spent the rest of the war as POWs. They kind of put the hard press on for me to take them back to the States the next day. Of course, I would have had to break about every regulation in the book to do that, but these guys were captains and I was just a lieutenant. Plus, there was the fact that these fellas had had a pretty rough go of it. Still, I was pretty non-committal about the entire idea.

Smith did not give much more thought to the two former prisoners of war until the next morning when he got out to his aircraft, ready to make the long trip back to the United States. "And there," he said, "were these two guys huddled under the aircraft with their musette bags, all ready to go; they had spent the night there so as to be sure not to get left behind. Ah hell, I thought to myself. By the book, I should have just told those guys to get out of there."

Smith could not or would not abandon the pair of brothers-in-arms. "I had a little conference with Shawnie. I told him that if these guys had been any of my friends, I'd tell them to climb aboard without thinking about it for a minute. And I figured that these guys were somebody's friends. Well, Shawnie felt the same way."

Still, there were issues and complications that had to be considered. For one, there were not enough parachutes aboard the aircraft in the event that something went wrong. Smith talked with his two new friends: "I told them that if something happened, and we had to jump from the aircraft, my crew got the parachutes. They readily agreed. I reminded them that it'd be cold as hell—we were going via Iceland—but that we'd share cold-weather gear as much as we could. They were fine with that too." With the terms set, Smith told the two men that he would take them along. "They just leapt for joy. They danced and ran all around that airplane, they were so happy! I felt about two inches tall that after everything they'd been through, I had to be so hard-nosed. And yet they were euphoric."

Smith briefed the rest of the crew, who were more than ready to adopt the stowaways. "I told them that we'd take care of these guys but that we didn't want to know their names or anything about them. We didn't want to get them or ourselves in trouble later. The less we knew about them, the better it'd be for all of us. And if we got caught, our story would be that we didn't know they were aboard the aircraft until we were already airborne."

The string of aircraft taxied out, and aside from some radio problems, Smith's crew and his stowaways took off and made it to Reykjavik with no real trouble. The crews stayed in Iceland for only a few hours, during which time Smith bought a couple of meals and had them smuggled out to the former prisoners. "During the brief for our next leg, the lieutenant colonel in charge quite pointedly said that if any of us had any unmanifested passengers, we were to report to him immediately. Somehow, word had gotten out about us because he kept looking directly at me. Still, I wasn't going to give those guys up." Smith reflected on the situation more than sixty years after the fact: "In hindsight, perhaps they just wanted to get the names of our stowaways because if anything had happened to us, no one would have ever known who they were."

The next leg to Goose Bay, a night flight, was a bit more dicey than the first leg had been. "We ran into some heavy ice along the way and got cleared to a different altitude by one of the picket ships that were posted along our route. From that point, we were able to shed the ice pretty well." The strung-out stream of aircraft arrived the morning after leaving Iceland. After a delay of about four hours and a mess-hall meal during which a sergeant on the base staff uncovered but did not report their ruse, they were on the final leg of their journey. "We raced a thunderstorm and a B-24 into Bradley Field in Connecticut."

Smith's ship was the first to arrive, and his was one of the first crews to pass through the area since the Nazis had surrendered.

The whole base had turned out in force and in style. The band was there and so was the mayor. And they had a bunch of the prettiest WAACs [Women's Auxiliary Army Corps] I'd ever seen to act as our escorts. As soon as we got the engines shut down, I quickly took care of some cockpit duties then got ready to climb down to meet the entourage. Before I did, our stowaways came up and passed their thanks and said they were going to stay out of our way.

Once I got out of the aircraft, I looked over my shoulder and caught sight of the two skinny captains. They had their little musette bags, pretty much all they owned in the world, and were already over the airfield fence and walking across a grain field and out of our lives. I never found out who they were or whatever happened to them. Now I'd give my eye teeth to find out.

Samuel W. Smith had captained his bomber and crew through twenty-four missions over Europe. He had been qualified as a squadron leader and fought flak and fighters, including the hot new German jets, through fiercely contested skies. He had watched as friends died in fiery explosions miles above the earth. When he finally made it back to Texas to marry his hometown sweetheart in August 1945, he had to get signed permission from his parents: he was only twenty years old. It would be several more months until he would be able to vote and buy a beer.

NOTES

CHAPTER 1: BUILDING OF AN AIR FORCE

1. Henry H. Arnold, *Global Mission* (New York: Harper and Brothers, 1949), 165.
2. John W. Huston, ed. *American Air Power Comes of Age: General Henry H. "Hap" Arnold's World War II Diaries*, vol. 1 (Maxwell Air Force Base: Air University Press, 2002), 69.
3. Arnold, *Global Mission*, 178.
4. Huston, *American Air Power*, 9.
5. "Transport: Sleek, Fast and Luckless," *Time*, 20 February 1939.
6. Huston, *American Air Power*, 102.
7. Richard G. Davis, *Carl A. Spaatz and the Air War in Europe* (Washington D.C.: Center for Air Force History, 1992), 56.
8. Huston, *American Air Power*, 106.
9. John Gutman, SPAD XII/XIII, Aces of WWI (Oxford: Oxford Publishing, 2002) 77.
10. Davis, *Carl A. Spaatz*, 40.
11. Ibid., 56.
12. Ibid., 51.
13. Ibid., 52.
14. Finish Virtual Pilots Association. "Günther Rall." www.virtualpilots.fi/hist/WW2 History-GuntherRallEnglish.html, accessed 6 March 2010.
15. Howard Mingos, *The Aircraft Yearbook for 1946* (New York: Lanciar Publishers, Inc., 1946), 474.

CHAPTER 2: THE NAZIS AND EAKER

1. Haywood S. Hansell, Jr., *The Air Plan That Defeated Hitler* (Atlanta: Higgins McArthur/Longino & Porter, Inc., 1972), 69.
2. HistoryNet.com, Interview with World War II Luftwaffe Eagle Johannes Steinhoff, www.historynet.com/interview-with-world-war-ii-luftwaffe-eagle-johannes-steinhoff .htm/3, accessed 14 March 2010.
3. Ewan Butler, *Marshall without Glory* (London: Hodder & Stoughton, 1951), 84–87.
4. Gen. James H. Doolittle and Carroll V. Glines, *I Could Never Be So Lucky Again* (New York: Bantam Books, 1992), 192–93.
5. Arnold, *Global Mission*, 276–90.
6. James Parton, *Air Force Spoken Here: General Ira Eaker & the Command of the Air* (Bethesda: Adler & Adler Publishers Inc., 1986), 17.
7. Parton, *Air Force Spoken Here*, 24.
8. Ibid., 32.
9. Ibid., 127.

CHAPTER 3: SPAATZ AND EAKER GO TO ENGLAND

1. Davis, *Carl A. Spaatz*, 71.
2. Ibid., 75.
3. Parton, *Air Force Spoken Here*, 137.
4. Davis, *Carl A. Spaatz*, 80.
5. Personal interview with Harold R. Popeney, 30 May 1998. All subsequent quotes by or references to Popeney are derived from this interview.
6. Davis, *Carl A. Spaatz*, 83.
7. Ibid., 85.
8. Parton, *Air Force Spoken Here*, 87.
9. Arnold, *Global Mission*, 296.

CHAPTER 4: FIRST MISSION AND THE MOVE TO NORTH AFRICA

1. Memorandum for the President from War Department, Office of the Chief of Staff, April 1942, Subject: Basis for preparation of attached outlined plan for Invasion of Western Europe.
2. Davis, *Carl A. Spaatz*, 85.
3. Arnold, *Global Mission*, 320.
4. Ibid., 321.
5. Parton, *Air Force Spoken Here*, 170.
6. Telephone interview with Arthur Hodges, 6 October 2009. All subsequent quotes by or references to Hodges are derived from this interview.
7. Parton, *Air Force Spoken Here*, 175.
8. Davis, *Carl A. Spaatz*, 177.
9. Adolf Galland, *The First and the Last: The Rise and Fall of the Luftwaffe—1939–45 by Germany's Commander of Fighter Forces* (New York: Ballantine Books, 1967), 118.
10. Galland, *The First and the Last*, 134.
11. Personal interview with John Walker, 14 July 1998. All subsequent quotes by or references to Walker are derived from this interview.
12. Dan Rathbun, www.portlyautey.com/Rathbun.htm, accessed 8 March 2010. All subsequent quotes by and references to Rathbun are derived from this source.
13. Eric Hammel, *Air War Europa: America's Air War against Germany in Europe and North Africa, 1942–1945* (Pacifica, CA: Pacifica Press, 1994), 76.

CHAPTER 5: CASABLANCA AND FIGHTERS IN NORTH AFRICA

1. Davis, *Carl A. Spaatz*, 103.
2. Ibid., 158.
3. Parton, *Air Force Spoken Here*, 189.
4. Davis, *Carl A. Spaatz*, 159.
5. Parton, *Air Force Spoken Here*, 193.
6. Galland, *The First and the Last*, 124.
7. Parton, *Air Force Spoken Here*, 287.
8. Davis, *Carl A. Spaatz*, 161.
9. Parton, *Air Force Spoken Here*, 220.
10. Ibid., 222.

11. Ninth Air Force, *Desert Campaign: The Story of the Ninth U.S. Army Air Force in Support of the British in Africa* (Ninth Air Force, 1943), 44–45.
12. Telephone interview with Hugh Dow, 1 November 2009. All subsequent quotes by or references to Dow are derived from this interview.
13. Galland, *The First and the Last*, 145.
14. Telephone interview with Maurice Duvic, 20 November 2009. All subsequent quotes by or references to Duvic are derived from this interview.

CHAPTER 6: ROMANCE, SUBMARINES, AND SICILY
1. Maurice Paulk diary.
2. Louise Smedley-Hampson, *A Wartime Romance: S/Sgt Joseph "Zip" Zsampar (11019777) and Pauline "Bobby" Roberts from September 1942 to 14 May 1943*, N.d. All subsequent quotes by or references to Zsampar and Roberts are derived from this source.
3. Norman C. Kiefer, *The Green Nosed Flying Eight Balls: A History of the 506th Bomb Squadron* (Belleville, MI: 506th History Publications, N.d.), 28.
4. AAG Historical Office Headquarters (AAFRH-18), *The Early Operations of the Eighth Air Force and the Origins of the Combined Bomber Offensive* (Maxwell Air Force Base, AL: Air University Press, 1946), 99.
5. Kiefer, *Green Nosed Flying Eight Balls*, 67.
6. Will Lundy, *44th Bomb Group Roll of Honor and Casualties* (Marshfield, MA: Green Harbor Publications, 1987) 63. All subsequent quotes by or references to the Paul Reed crew are derived from this source.
7. Hansell, *Air Plan That Defeated Hitler*, 137.
8. Telephone interview with Walter Baker, 3 October 2009. All subsequent quotes by or references to Baker are derived from this interview.
9. Davis, *Carl A. Spaatz*, 244.
10. Glenn Stell, written recollection of the mission of 7 July 1943. San Diego Aerospace Museum. All subsequent quotes by or references to Stell are derived from this source.
11. Parton, *Air Force Spoken Here*, 272.
12. Ibid., 276.
13. Johannes Steinhoff, *Messerschmitts over Sicily* (Baltimore: The Nautical & Aviation Publishing Company of America, 1987), 41.

CHAPTER 7: TIDALWAVE
1. Assistant Chief of Air Staff, Intelligence, Historical Division, *The Ploesti Mission of 1 August 1943, AAFRH-3* (Maxwell Air Force Base, AL: USAAF, 1944), 40.
2. Jay A. Stout, *Fortress Ploesti: The Campaign to Destroy Hitler's Oil* (Havertown, PA: Casemate, 2003), 33.
3. Stout, *Fortress Ploesti*, 34.
4. Telephone interview with Ernest Poulson, 15 November, 2009. All subsequent quotes by or references to Poulson are derived from this interview.
5. Assistant Chief of Air Staff, Intelligence, Historical Division, *The Ploesti Mission*, 168.
6. Ibid., 100.

CHAPTER 8: THE GUNNERS

1. Telephone interview with Henry Hughey, 3 October 2009. All subsequent quotes by or references to Hughey are derived from this source.
2. Donald Caldwell, *JG 26: Top Guns of the Luftwaffe* (New York: Ballantine Books, 1991), 223.
3. John Weal, *Focke-Wulf Fw 190 Aces of the Western Front* (London: Osprey Publishing, 1996), 49.
4. Carey W. Mavor, *World War II Stories: In Their Own Words.* "Heroes: The Army Air Corps." carol_fus.tripod.com/army_ac_hero_cwmavor.html, accessed 7 March 2010.
5. Telephone interview with Robert Powell, 4 October 2009. All subsequent quotes by or references to Powell are derived from this source.

CHAPTER 9: BLACK THURSDAY AND LONG-RANGE FIGHTERS

1. Major-General Kehrl, report on the firestorm in Hamburg in August, 1943.
2. Galland, *The First and the Last*, 162.
3. Ibid., 164.
4. Telephone interview with William Heller, 28 November 2009. All subsequent quotes by or references to Heller are derived from this source.
5. William Hess, *B-17 Flying Fortress: Combat and Development History of the Flying Fortress* (St. Paul, MN: Motorbook International, 1994), 65–67.
6. Parton, *Air Force Spoken Here*, 315–18.
7. Ibid., 130.
8. Ibid., 318.
9. Ibid., 328.
10. Davis, *Carl A. Spaatz*, 260.
11. Ibid., 262.
12. Huston, *American Air Power*, 55.
13. Parton, *Air Force Spoken Here*, 268.
14. Telephone interview with Arthur Fiedler, 14 November 2009.
15. Encounter report, 4th Fighter Group, Allen Bunte, 29 March 1944.
16. HistoryNet.com, Interview with World War II Luftwaffe Eagle Johannes Steinhoff, www.historynet.com/interview-with-world-war-ii-luftwaffe-eagle-johannes-steinhoff.htm/4, accessed 14 March 2010.

CHAPTER 10: DOOLITTLE, PHASED ESCORT, AND FREEDOM FOR THE FIGHTERS

1. Parton, *Air Force Spoken Here*, 336.
2. Ibid., 338.
3. Doolittle and Glines, *I Could Never Be So Lucky Again*, 347.
4. Ibid., 350.
5. Ibid., 350.
6. Ibid., 347.
7. Chuck Widener, "A Gunner's Tale," *Airman* (February 2004): 34–39. All subsequent quotes by or references to Sweatt are derived from this source.
8. Caldwell, *JG 26*, 200.
9. Doolittle and Glines, *I Could Never Be So Lucky Again*, 352.

CHAPTER 11: BIG WEEK, INTERNS, AND FLAK

1. The 457th Bomb Group Association, "The Mission: An Account as Recorded by Archie Bower, Pilot on Aircraft s/n 42-97457," 1 March 2010, www.457thbomb group.org/New/Recollections/Cooke/mission1.html and www.457thbombgroup .org/New/Recollections/Cooke/mission.html#Schneider. All subsequent quotations and references to the mission flown by the Archie Bower crew on February 25, 1944, are derived from these sources.

2. Galland, *The First and the Last*, 205.

3. Air Ministry of the United Kingdom, *The Rise and Fall of the German Air Force (1933 to 1945)* (Richmond, England: The National Archives, 2008), 307.

4. Encounter Report, 357th Fighter Group, Capt. Glendon Davis, 6 March 1944.

5. Davis, *Carl A. Spaatz*, 415.

6. Ibid., 379.

7. Ibid.

8. Ibid., 446.

9. Ibid., 448.

10. Green Harbor Publications, "The 44th Bomb Group Roll of Honor," 1 March, 2010. www.greenharbor.com/ROHPDF/ROHMay44.pdf. All subsequent quotations and references to the mission flown by the Frank Tomer crew on May 25, 1944, are derived from this source.

11. 100th Bomb Group (Heavy)—the Bloody Hundredth, "1st Lt. Samuel L. Barrick," 1 March 2010. www.100thbg.org/mainpages/crews/crews1/barrick.htm. All subsequent quotations and references to the incidents associated with the mission flown by the Samuel Barrick crew on March 16, 1944, are derived from these sources.

12. United States Strategic Bombing Survey.

13. Telephone interview with Joe Black, 18 October 2009. All subsequent quotes by or references to Black are derived from this source.

14. Joseph M. Dell, *World War II Combat Experience of Joseph M. Dell, P-47 Pilot with the 86th Fighter-Bomber Group, 527th Squadron* (N.p: n.p., n.d.).

15. Vannevar Bush, *Pieces of the Action* (New York: William Morrow and Company, Inc. 1970), 106–12.

CHAPTER 12: PILOT TRAINING

1. Larry Forester, *Fly for Your Life: The Glorious Story of England's Greatest Air Ace, Robert Stanford Tuck, and His Deadly Spitfire* (New York: Bantam Books, 1981), 287.

2. Ken Barmore's wartime diary, notes, and recollections of his World War II service, self-published, 2009. All subsequent quotes by or references to Barmore in this chapter are derived from this source.

3. Mingos, *Aircraft Yearbook for 1946*, 460.

4. Ibid., 81.

5. United States Strategic Bombing Survey.

6. Charles A. Watry, *Washout! The Aviation Cadet Story* (Carlsbad, CA: California Aero Press, 1983), foreword.

7. Caldwell, *JG 26*, 259.

8. United States Strategic Bombing Survey.

9. Great Britain, Air Ministry, The Rise and Fall of the German Air Force (London, 1948), 316.
10. Encounter report, 364th Fighter Group, James Fowle, 23 December 1944.

CHAPTER 13: GROUND ATTACK AND BOMBER BAILOUTS
1. Parton, *Air Force Spoken Here*, 383.
2. Wartime recollections of John Blair Watson. All subsequent quotes by or references to Watson are derived from this source.
3. Telephone interview with William Harvey, 4 October 2009. All subsequent quotes by or references to Harvey are derived from this source.
4. Telephone interview with Foster Heath, 24 October 2009. All subsequent quotes by or references to Heath are derived from this source.
5. Northwest Historical Association, "Anonymous by Request," nwha.org/news_ 1Q2003/news_page10.html, accessed 17 January 2010.

CHAPTER 14: THE OIL PLAN
1. Telephone interview with Ken Barmore, February 12, 2010. All subsequent quotes by or references to Barmore are derived from this source.
2. Galland, *The First and the Last*, 208.
3. Richard G. Davis, *Bombing the European Axis Powers: A Historical Digest of the Combined Bomber Offensive, 1939–1945* (Maxwell Air Force Base, AL: Air University Press, 2006), 453.

CHAPTER 15: D-DAY
1. Caldwell, *JG 26*, 225.
2. Galland, *The First and the Last*, 215.
3. Telephone interview with Robert Hansen, 21 November 2009. All subsequent quotes by or references to Hansen are derived from this interview.
4. Caldwell, *JG 26*, 231.
5. Encounter report, 56th Fighter Group, George Bostwick, 7 June 1944.
6. Caldwell, *JG 26*, 234.
7. Ibid., 237.
8. Telephone interview with Arthur Hodges, 6 October 2009. All subsequent quotes by or references to Hodges are derived from this interview.

CHAPTER 16: FIGHTER-ON-FIGHTER COMBAT
1. Encounter report, 56th Fighter Group, Walter Pitts, 15 September 1944.
2. Encounter report, 4th Fighter Group, Preston Hardy, 18 August 1944.
3. E-mail from Barrie Davis to author, 5 October 2009.
4. Raymond F. Toliver and Trevor J. Constable, *Fighter Aces of the Luftwaffe* (Atglen, PA: Schiffer Publishing, Ltd., 1996), 125.
5. Richard Hewitt, *Target of Opportunity: Tales and Contrails of the Second World War* (Lawrence, KS: R. A. Hewitt, 2000) 102.
6. Caldwell, *JG 26*, 273.
7. Encounter report, 352nd Fighter Group, John Meyer, 12 May 1944.
8. E-mail from Barrie Davis to author, 1 October 2009.
9. Telephone interview with James Kunkle, 29 November 2009. All subsequent quotes by or references to Kunkle are derived from this interview.

10. Army Air Forces Proving Ground Command, *Tactical Suitability of the P-38F Type Airplane* (Florida: USAAF, 1943).
11. Personal interview with Howard Dentz, 4 February 1998. All subsequent quotes by or references to Dentz are derived from this source.

CHAPTER 17: THE MEN WHO MADE IT POSSIBLE
1. Mingos, *Aircraft Yearbook for 1946*, 477–78.
2. William Lundy, *History of the 67 Bombardment Squadron, 44th Bomb Group, The Flying Eight Balls* (Self-published, 1982), 48.
3. Diary of S/Sgt Virgil R. Embry, 27 April 1943 to 7 October 1945.
4. Desay, Bierly, Olmsted, *A View from the Flight Line*, www.cebudanderson.com/viewfromtheline.htm, accessed 7 March 2010.
5. Keith E. Randall diary.

CHAPTER 18: FRANTIC
1. Hell's Angels, 303rd Bomb Group (H), Unusual Stories, www.303rdbg.com/unusual-3.html, accessed 16 January 2010.
2. Telephone interview with Ted Conlin, 5 October 2009. All subsequent quotes by or references to Conlin are derived from this e-mail.
3. *Don Allen: His shuttle bombing mission story or, What a nose artist does in his spare time*, www.fourthfightergroup.com/resource/allenshuttle.html, accessed 19 January 2010.
4. E-mail from Barrie Davis to author, 17 January 2010. All subsequent quotes by or references to Davis in this chapter are derived from this e-mail.
5. Turner Publishing, *390th Bomb Group: 50th Anniversary Commemorative History* (Nashville, TN: Turner Publishing, 1985), 17.
6. Eddy Gilmore, *Me and My Russian Wife* (New York: Doubleday & Company, Inc. 1954), 209–16.
7. Donald Caldwell and Richard Muller, *The Luftwaffe over Germany: Defense of the Reich* (London, England: Greenhill Books/Lionel Leventhal Ltd., 2007), 211.
8. Parton, *Air Force Spoken Here*, 405.
9. Ibid., 407.
10. Headquarters, 82nd Fighter Group, 25 July 1944, Mission No. 737, Narrative Report.
11. Thomas Cleaver, "Piggy Back in a P-38," *Flight Journal* (August 2008).
12. Parton, *Air Force Spoken Here*, 409.
13. Doolittle and Glines, *I Could Never Be So Lucky Again*, 381.

CHAPTER 19: MISHAPS, MISCUES, AND NEAR THINGS
1. George Crawford, *Three Crawford Brothers: The World War II Memoirs of Three Pilots* (Bloomington, IN: AuthorHouse, 2008), 415.
2. E-mail from Barrie Davis, 10 October 2009. All subsequent quotes by or references to Davis in this chapter are derived from this e-mail.
3. E-mail from Frank Mertely, 3 November 2009. All subsequent quotes by or references to Mertely are derived from this e-mail.
4. Telephone interview with Joe Black, 18 October 2009. All subsequent quotes by or references to Black are derived from this interview.

CHAPTER 20: JETS, ROCKETS, AND TANTE JU

1. Interview with Howard Wilson, April 14, 1998. All subsequent quotes by or references to Wilson are derived from this interview.
2. Galland, *The First and the Last*, 255.
3. Encounter report, 55th Fighter Group, John Brown, 10 April, 1945.
4. Encounter report, 78th Fighter Group, Robert Anderson, 21 March, 1945.
5. E-mail from Barrie Davis to author, 1 October 2009. All subsequent quotes by or references to Davis in this chapter are derived from this e-mail.
6. Richard Gross, *"The Dynamite Gang": The 367th Fighter Group in World War II* (Fallbrook, CA: Aero Publishers, Inc. 1983), 15.
7. Clayton Gross, *Live Bait: World War II Memoirs of an Undefeated Fighter Ace* (Portland, OR: Inkwater Press, 2006).
8. Telephone interview with Samuel W. Smith, 30 October 2009. All subsequent quotes by or references to Smith are derived from this interview.

CHAPTER 21: MORE FIGHTERS AND G'S

1. E-mail from Barrie Davis, 1 October 2009. All subsequent quotes by or references to Davis in this chapter are derived from this e-mail.
2. Telephone interview with Herman Schonenberg, 23 July 1998. All subsequent quotes by or references to Schonenberg are derived from this interview.

CHAPTER 22: THE BIG BLOW THAT WASN'T

1. Galland, *The First and the Last*, 229.
2. Encounter report, 20th Fighter Group, Glenn Webb, 2 November 1944.
3. Encounter report, 339th Fighter Group, Donald E. Penny, 2 November 1944.
4. Danny S. Parker, *To Win the Winter Sky: Air War Over the Ardennes, 1944–1945.* (London, England: Greenhill Books/Lionel Leventhal Ltd., 1994), 95.
5. Encounter report, 78th Fighter Group, Allen Rosenblum, 21 November 1944.
6. Parker, *To Win the Winter Sky*, 173.

CHAPTER 23: THE GENERAL FALLS

1. *The Euro Group Gazette*, Issue 171 (23 October 2002), "The Battle of the Bulge in the Words of Robert W. Brown," www.euro-downloads.com/gazette/G171.htm, accessed 13 March 2010.
2. Brig. Gen. N. B. Harbold, *Report of Investigation (Death of Brig. Gen. Frederick W. Castle)*, Headquarters 3D Air Division, U.S. Army, 16 January 1945.
3. Thad J. Russell, C.R.I.B.A., *The Fallen B-17G of Brigadier General Frederick Castle in the region of Fraiture, Belgium*, www.criba.be/index.php?option=com_content&view=article&id=13:the-fallen-b-17-g-of-brigadier-general-frederick-castle-in-the-region-of-fraiture-belgium&catid=3:us-air-force&Itemid=8, accessed 22 October 2009.
4. Edward Castens, *The 446th Revisited* (Dorset, England:446th Bombardment Group Association,1995), 107.

CHAPTER 24: BODENPLATTE

1. James P. Busha, "Operation Bodenplatte," *Flight Journal* (February 2005).
2. Jerry Scutts, *P-47 Thunderbolt Aces of the Ninth and Fifteenth Air Forces* (Oxford, England: Osprey Publishing, Ltd., 1999), 77.

3. Encounter report, 352nd Fighter Group, John Meyer, 1 January 1945.
4. Encounter report, 352nd Fighter Group, Sanford Moats, 1 January 1945.
5. Encounter report, 352nd Fighter Group, Henry Stewart, 1 January 1945.
6. Letter from Arthur Snyder to author, 10 December 2004.
7. Telephone interview with Joe Black, 18 October 2009. All subsequent quotes by or references to Black are derived from this interview.

CHAPTER 25: DEADLY TO THE END
1. Johannes Steinhoff, *The Final Hours: The Luftwaffe Plot against Göring* (Dulles, VA: Potomac Books, Inc., 2005), 163.

BIBLIOGRAPHY

BOOKS

390th Bomb Group. *50th Anniversary Commemorative History*. Nashville, TN: Turner Publishing, 1985.

AAG Historical Office Headquarters (AAFRH-18). *The Early Operations of the Eighth Air Force and the Origins of the Combined Bomber Offensive*. Maxwell Air Force Base, AL: Air University Press, 1946.

Air Ministry (A.C.A.S. [I]). *The Rise and Fall of the German Air Force (1933 to 1945)*. Richmond, England: The National Archives, 2008.

Baker, David. *Adolf Galland: The Authorized Biography*. London, England: Windrow & Greene Ltd., 1996.

Batchelor, John, and Bryan Cooper. *Fighter: A History of Fighter Aircraft*. New York: Charles Scribner's Sons, 1973.

Baumbach, Werner. *The Life and Death of the Luftwaffe*. Costa Mesa, CA: The Noontide Press, 1991.

Bekker, Cajus. *The Luftwaffe Diaries: The German Air Force in World War II*. Edited and translated by Frank Ziegler. New York: Da Capo Press, 1994.

Bishop, Chris, ed. *The Encyclopedia of Weapons of World War II: The Comprehensive Guide to over 1,500 weapons systems, including tanks, small arms, warplanes, artillery, ships and submarines*. New York: Barnes & Noble Books, 1998.

Brulle, Robert V. *Angels Zero: P-47 Close Air Support in Europe*. Washington, D.C.: Smithsonian Institute Press, 2000.

Bush, Vannevar. *Pieces of Action*. New York: William Morrow and Company, Inc., 1971.

Butler, Ewan. *Marshall without Glory*. London, England: Hodder & Stoughton, 1951.

Caldwell, Donald. *JG 26: Top Guns of the Luftwaffe*. New York: Ballantine Books, 1991.

―――, and Richard Muller. *The Luftwaffe over Germany: Defense of the Reich*. London, England: Greenhill Books/Lionel Leventhal Ltd., 2007.

Comer, John. *Combat Crew: A True Story of Flying and Fighting in World War II*. New York: Pocket Books, Simon & Schuster, Inc., 1988.

Conte, Ralph. *Attack Bombers, We Need You! A History of the 416th Bomb Group*. Nashville, TN: JM Press, 2001.

Crawford, George. *Three Crawford Brothers: The World War II Memoirs of Three Pilots*. Bloomington, IN : AuthorHouse, 2008.

Davis, Richard G. *Carl A. Spaatz and the Air War in Europe*. Washington, D.C.: Smithsonian Institute Press, 2006.

―――. *Bombing the European Axis Powers: A Historical Digest of the Combined Bomber Offensive, 1939–1945*. Maxwell Air Force Base, AL: Air University Press, 2006.

Doolittle, Gen. James H. "Jimmy," and Carroll V. Glines. *I Could Never Be So Lucky Again*. New York: Bantam Books, 1992.

Dugan, James, and Carroll Stewart. *Ploesti: The Great Ground-Air Battle of 1 August 1943*. New York: Random House, 1962.

Forrester, Larry. *Fly for Your Life: The Glorious Story of England's Greatest Air Ace, Robert Stanford Tuck, and His Deadly Spitfire*. New York: Bantam Books, 1981.

Galland, Adolf. *The First and the Last: The Rise and Fall of the Luftwaffe 1939–45 by Germany's Commander of Fighter Forces*. New York: Ballantine Books, 1967.

Gilmore, Eddy. *Me and My Russian Wife*. New York: Doubleday & Company, Inc. 1954.

Girbig, Werner, and Helmut Lipfert. *The War Diary of Hauptmann Helmut Lipfert: JG 52 on the Russian Front, 1943–1945*. Translated by David Johnston. Atglen, PA: Schiffer Publishing Ltd., 1993.

Goebel, Robert J. *Mustang Ace: Memoirs of a P-51 Fighter Pilot*. Pacifica, CA: Pacifica Press, 1991.

Griehl, Manfred. *Luftwaffe over America: The Secret Plans to Bomb the United States in World War II*. Translated by Geoffrey Brooks. New York: Fall River Press/Lionel Leventhal Ltd., 2004.

Gross, Clayton Kelly. *Live Bait: WWII Memoirs of an Undefeated Fighter Ace*. Portland, OR: Inkwater Press, 2006.

Gross, Richard. *"The Dynamite Gang": The 367th Fighter Group in World War II*. Fallbrook, CA: Aero Publishers, Inc., 1983.

Gutman, John. *SPAD XII/XIII, Aces of WWI*. Oxford, England: Oxford Publishing, 2002.

Halley, James J. *The Role of the Fighter in Air Warfare*. Edited by Charles W. Cain. New York: Ziff-Davis Flying Books, 1978.

Hammel, Eric. *Aces against Germany: The American Aces Speak 2*. Novato, CA: Presidio Press, 1993.

———. *Aces at War: The American Aces Speak 4*. Pacifica, CA: Pacifica Press, 1997.

———. *The Road to Big Week: The Struggle for Daylight Air Supremacy over Western Europe, July 1942–February 1944*. Pacifica, CA: Pacifica Military History, 2009.

———. *Air War Europa: America's Air War against Germany in Europe and North Africa, 1942–1945*. Pacifica, CA: Pacifica Press, 1994.

Hancock, W. K., and M. M. Growing. *History of the Second World War: British War Economy*. U.K. Civil Series. London, England: H. M. Stationary Office, 1949.

Hansell, Haywood S., Jr. *The Air Plan That Defeated Hitler*. Atlanta: Higgins McArthur/Longino & Porter, Inc., 1972.

Hewitt, R. A. *Target of Opportunity: Tales & Contrails of the Second World War*. Lawrence, KS: N.p., 2005.

Huston, John W., ed. *American Air Power Comes of Age: General Henry H. "Hap" Arnold's World War II Diaries*. Maxwell Air Force Base, AL: Air University Press, 2002.

Johnsen, Frederick A. *B-24 Liberator: Rugged But Right*. Walter J. Boyne Military Aircraft Series, vol. 3. New York: McGraw-Hill, 1999.

Keegan, John, ed. *The Rand McNally Encyclopedia of World War II*. Greenwich: Bison Books Corp., 1986.

Kiefer, Norman C. *The Green Nosed Flying Eight Balls: A History of the 506th Bomb Squadron*. Self-published., N.d.

Kreipe, Werner, and Rudolf Koester. *Technical Training within the German Luftwaffe.* Edited by Karl Gundelach. Maxwell Air Force Base, AL: Air Force Historical Research Agency, 1955.

Lundy, William. *History of the 67 Bombardment Squadron, 44th Bomb Group, The Flying Eight Balls.* Self published, 1982.

Maddox, Joey. *Bleeding Sky: The Story of Captain Fletcher E. Adams and the 357th Fighter Group.* N.p.: n.p., 2009.

McCarty, Lyle. *Coffee Tower: A History of the 459th Bombardment Group in World War II.* Paducah, KY: Turner Publishing Company, 1997.

McNab, Chris. *Order of Battle: German Luftwaffe in WW II.* London, England: Amber Books, Ltd., 2009.

Mets, David R. *Master of Airpower: General Carl A. Spaatz.* Novato, CA: Presidio Press, 1988.

Mingos, Howard. *The Aircraft Yearbook for 1946.* New York: Lanciar Publishers, Inc., 1946.

———. *The Aircraft Yearbook for 1942.* New York: Aeronautical Chamber of Commerce of American, Inc., 1942.

Parker, Danny S. *To Win the Winter Sky: Air War over the Ardennes, 1944–1945.* London, England: Greenhill Books/Lionel Leventhal Ltd., 1994.

Pitt, Barrie, ed. *The Military History of World War II.* New York: The Military Press/Crown Publishers, 1986.

Schneider, Sammy, ed. *Missions by the Numbers, 485th Bomb Group (H): An Account of the 187 Missions Flown by the 485th Bomb Group over Europe.* N.p.; n.p., n.d.

Scutts, Jerry. *P-47 Thunderbolt Aces of the Ninth and Fifteenth Air Forces.* Oxford, England: Osprey Publishing, Ltd., 1999.

Speer, Albert. *Spandau: The Secret Diaries.* Translated by Richard and Clara Winston. New York: MacMillan Publishing Co., Inc., 1976.

Spick, Mike. *Aces of the Reich: The Making of a Luftwaffe Fighter-Pilot.* London, England: Greenhill Books/Lionel Leventhal Ltd., 2006.

Stedman, Robert F. *Jagdflieger: Luftwaffe Fighter Pilot 1939–45.* Oxford, England: Osprey Publishing, 2008.

Steinhoff, Johannes. *The Final Hours: The Luftwaffe Plot against Goring.* Washington, D.C.: Potomac Books, Inc., 2005.

———. *Messerschmitts over Sicily.* Baltimore, MD: The Nautical & Aviation Publishing Company of America, 1987.

Stout, Jay A. *Fortress Ploesti: The Campaign to Destroy Hitler's Oil.* Havertown, PA: Casemate, 2003.

Suchenwirth, Richard. *Historical Turning Points in the German Air Force War Effort.* USAF Historical Studies, No. 189. Maxwell Air Force Base, AL: USAF Historical Division, Research Studies Institute, Air University, 1959.

Toliver, Raymond F., and Trevor J. Constable. *Fighter Aces of the Luftwaffe.* Atglen, PA: Schiffer Publishing, Ltd., 1996.

Tyler, Leslie J. *Wild Blue Yonder: An Adventure of Hitler's Hostages.* Grawn, MI: Crystal Publishing, 1992.

Watry, Charles A. *Washout! The Aviation Cadet Story.* Carlsbad, CA: California Aero Press, 1983.

Weal, John. *Focke-Wulf Fw 190 Aces of the Western Front.* Edited by Tony Holmes. Osprey Aircraft of the Aces 9. London, England: Osprey Publishing, 1996.

Wood, Tony, and Bill Gunston. *Hitler's Luftwaffe: A Pictorial History and Technical Encyclopedia of Hitler's Air Power in World War II.* London, England: Salamander Books, Ltd., 1978.

———. *Bf 109E/G/K Aces of the Western Front.* Edited by Tony Holmes. Osprey Aircraft of the Aces 29. London, England: Osprey Publishing, 1999.

DIARIES

Dell, Joseph, M. *World War II Combat Experience of Joseph M. Dell, P-47 Pilot with the 86th Fighter-Bomber Group, 527th Squadron.* N.p: n.p., n.d.

Randall, Keith E. *845th Bomb Squadron, 491st Bomb Group-USA Army Air Force.* N.p.: n.p., n.d.

GOVERNMENT MEMORANDUMS AND REPORTS

Army Air Forces Proving Ground Command. *Tactical Suitability of the P-38F Type Airplane.* Florida: Eglin Field, 1943.

Assistant Chief of Air Staff, Intelligence, Historical Division. *The Ploesti Mission of 1 August 1943, AAFRH-3.* Maxwell Air Force Base, 1944.

United States Strategic Bombing Survey (European War). *The Defeat of the German Air Force.* 1945.

United States War Department, Office of the Chief of Staff, George Marshall to President Franklin D. Roosevelt. *Basis for Preparation of Attached Outline Plan for Invasion of Western Europe.* April 1942.

INTERNET REFERENCES

"Transport: Sleek, Fast and Luckless." *Time* magazine. February 20, 1939. www.time.com/time/magazine/article/0,9171,760764,00.html

Centre de Recherches et d'Informations sur la Bataille des Ardennes (C.R.I.B.A). "The Fallen B-17 G of Brigadier General Frederick Castle in the region of Fraiture, Belgium," trans. Thad J. Russell. (30 January, 2001). www.criba.be/index.php?option= com_content&view=article&id=13:the- fallen-b-17-g-of-brigadier-general-frederick-castle-in-the-region-of-fraiture-belgium&catid=3:us-air-force&Itemid=8

The Euro Group Gazette, Issue 171, October 23, 2002. www.euro-downloads.com /gazette/G171.htm

Finnish Virtual Pilots Association. "Günther Rall." www.virtualpilots.fi/hist/WW2 History-GuntherRallEnglish.html

Green Harbor Publications. "The 44th Bomb Group Roll of Honor" May to June, 1943. www.greenharbor.com/ROHPDF/ROHMJ43.pdf

———. "The 44th Bomb Group Roll of Honor" May 1944. www.greenharbor.com/ ROHPDF/ROHMay44.pdf

Hells Angels: 303rd Bomb Group (H). "My Most Unusual 303rd Experience," page 3.www.303rdbg.com/unusual-3.html

82nd Fighter Group: *Adorimini*—Up and at 'em. July 25, 1944. www.82ndfighter group.com/82mr440725.htm

100th Bomb Group (Heavy) The Bloody Hundredth. "1st Lt. Samuel L. Barrick." www.100thbg.org/mainpages/crews/crews1/barrick.htm

4th Fighter Group: Official Site of the 4th FG, AAF, WWII. "Don Allen: His shuttle bombing mission story, or what a nose artist does in his spare time." www.fourthfighter group.com/resource/allenshuttle.html

The 457th Bomb Group Association. "The Mission: An Account as Recorded by Archie Bower, pilot on aircraft s/n 42-97457." www.457thbombgroup.org/New/ Recollections/Cooke/mission1.html

Northwest Historical Association. "WWII Veteran Interviews." nwha.org/news_1Q2003 /news_page10.html

The Clarence E. "Bud" Anderson Website. www.cebundanerson.com/viewfrom theline.htm_16_feb_10

U.S. Naval Air Station, Port Lyautey, Morocco: Remembrances of a Great Duty Station. "Photographs (1942) and Narrative from Dan Rathbun WW2 Collection." www.portlyautey.com/Rathbun.htm

World War II Stories: In Their Own Words. "Heroes: The Army Air Corps." carol_fus.tripod.com/army_ac_hero_cwmavor.html

PERIODICALS

Busha, James P. "Operation Bodenplatte." *Flight Journal.* February 2005.

Cleaver, Thomas M. "Piggy Back in a P-38." *Flight Journal.* August 2008.

Prescott Evening Courier. 11 February 1939, page 1.

ACKNOWLEDGMENTS

Some men relax by working wood, or fishing, or golfing, or shouting at small children. I write. And I'm blessed to have a family that gives me the time and support to do so. Thank you, Monica, Kristen, and Katherine. I additionally have a pair of colleagues, Dr. James Perry and Dr. John Stillion, who gave a considerable amount of their time to review the manuscript. Their kind attention provided insights I hadn't considered and saved me from several small embarrassments. I'm additionally thankful that my agent, E. J. McCarthy, and Stackpole's history editor, Chris Evans, had the savvy to recognize that this work was not just "another Nazi book," but rather was something that really has never been done before. And I'm thankful to the wonderful writer Eric Hammel, who helped me start my own career.

Many veterans were gracious with their time. Their firsthand accounts are the jewels around which this effort is organized; it would not be what it is without their help. Further, I must give a hearty tip of my hat to technology, in particular the internet (regardless of who invented it). Used properly, it is a tool that can enrich and speed the writing of a book in a way that would otherwise be impossible.

Finally, I especially want to acknowledge those men, named and unnamed, who won the war. Had they not, our lives would not be, or at the very least, they would be much less varied, rich, and free.

INDEX